Keter

Keter

THE CROWN OF GOD
IN EARLY JEWISH MYSTICISM

Arthur Green

PRINCETON UNIVERSITY PRESS
PRINCETON, NEW JERSEY

Published by Princeton University Press, 41 William Street,
Princeton, New Jersey 08540
In the United Kingdom: Princeton University Press, Chichester, West Sussex

Library of Congress Cataloging-in-Publication Data

Green, Arthur, 1941–
Keter : the crown of God in early Jewish mysticism / Arthur Green.
p. cm.
Includes bibliographical references and index.
ISBN 0-691-04372-8 (alk. paper)
1. Crown of God in rabbinical literature. 2. Mysticism—Judaism—History.
3. Cabala. I. Title.
BM496.9.C76G74 1997 97-3727
296.3'112—dc21 r97

This book has been composed in Times Roman

Princeton University Press books are printed on acid-free paper and meet the guidelines for permanence and durability of the Committee on Production Guidelines for Book Longevity of the Council on Library Resources

Printed in the United States of America

10 9 8 7 6 5 4 3 2 1

לקריינדל

v. 12:4

Contents

Preface ix

Abbreviations xiii

CHAPTER ONE
Ancient Israel: Crowns Above and Below 3

CHAPTER TWO
Coronation and *Qedushah* 12

CHAPTER THREE
The Heavenly Coronation: Primary Texts 20

CHAPTER FOUR
God's Crown and Israel's Prayer 33

CHAPTER FIVE
The Name on the Crown 42

CHAPTER SIX
Crowns, *Tefillin*, and Magic Seals 49

CHAPTER SEVEN
The Angels Crowned 58

CHAPTER EIGHT
Israel Crowned at Sinai 69

CHAPTER NINE
Coronation and Marriage 78

CHAPTER TEN
Medieval Reconsiderations 88

CHAPTER ELEVEN
The Hymn of Glory 106

CHAPTER TWELVE
The Way to Kabbalah 121

CHAPTER THIRTEEN
Sefer ha-Bahir 134

CHAPTER FOURTEEN
The Early Kabbalah 151

Preface

THE RECOVERY OF ANCIENT MYTH and the creations of the religious imagination through the ages comprise one of the more interesting and constant intellectual preoccupations of our time. The humanistic task of exploring myths of various eras and civilizations has proceeded for more than a century and a half, since romantic and nationalist thought in Europe of the early nineteenth century pushed aside the Enlightenment rejection of myth and began to seek in it an ancient truth or wisdom. Myth, it was concluded, had the power to address the human mind on some more profound level than the language of ordinary discourse, and thus it might save moderns from the alienation and rootlessness they had come to feel with the decline of traditional society and literal belief in the old religious traditions. This turn to the wisdom of the mythic past (along with that of the mysterious East) has been renewed in the postwar era and has become a dominant feature of intellectual and spiritual life in the late twentieth century. The fascination with myth and its study in both historical and anthropological contexts has been an ongoing project, transcending the important changes in both philosophical outlook and research methodology that have characterized the entire post-Enlightenment period, sometimes itself playing a key role in the development of those new trends.

The composing of a *mythologia judaica*, a sensible accounting of the myths, symbols, and religious imagery that moved the hearts of faithful Jews in the world of late antiquity, however else they might have defined themselves, is a significant part of this project. The reason is not only the intrinsic interest that latter-day Jewish scholars and readers might have in their ancestors' inner world, but also Jewry's key role in the preservation and transformation of the archaic mythic legacies of the Near East and their transmission into all the Western faith-languages of later history. As we move beyond the onetime scholarly assumption that the Bible knew myth only to refute it, or as we come to soften the overly sharp distinctions scholars once made between sacred myth and sacred history, we come to understand that Hebrew Scripture itself is among the most important sources for the recovery of this ancient human legacy. In the postbiblical world as well, Jews and the various competing versions of Judaism were important repositories for the mythic imagination: sometimes figures from the archaic prebiblical world reappeared with new vigor in the apocalyptic and pseudepigraphic works of the last pre-Christian centuries, at other times new motifs, including some borrowed from the surrounding cultures of the Hellenistic world. In many cases it was the presence of a mythic theme in Judaism that allowed for its incorporation, however transformed, also into Christianity, thence to be diffused throughout the cultures of Europe and beyond.

The present study of God's crown attempts a small contribution to this effort. It seeks to isolate this motif from its context in the literary sources of ancient Judaism in order to highlight its range of meanings and its place in the imaginative universe of those who invoked it in prayer, wrote of it in homilies, or conceived it as a symbol. It seeks to show that this range of meanings is best illustrated by a synchronic reading of literary texts written by Jews—and some others close to them—in the late antique world, a reading that transcends the conventionalized boundaries between "Jewish" and "Christian" sources in the earliest centuries of the Common Era, as well as between the "rabbinic" and "merkavah" literatures of a somewhat later period. The imagination does not usually adhere to such boundaries, and myths have a way of creeping across all the lines drawn by cautious theologians in order to rein them in.

The latter chapters (10–14) of this work turn our attention to somewhat later historical developments. There I am interested in seeing the relationship between the ancient myth of the angels crowning God and the emergence of *keter*, or "crown," as a key symbol of the Kabbalistic universe in the Middle Ages. The process that leads up to the emergence of *Sefer ha-Bahir*, the proto-Kabbalistic midrash in which this symbol is first clearly evidenced, there becomes my primary concern. In a broader sense, this process may also be seen as the transformation of a symbol as it moves from the realm of living myth to that of the language of mystical symbolism, a process highly characteristic of the growth of Kabbalah as a whole, but seen perhaps most clearly in this vivid example. The drama that lies at the very center of Kabbalah is one of ascent: the rising of the "last" or "lowest" of the ten divine manifestations, and along with it the entire cosmos, to unite with the very highest. I hope to trace the origin of this key motif in the crown mysticism of a much earlier age, thus showing also the way in which discrete stages in the history of Jewish mystical speculation and experience are linked with one another.

A few words need be added here about the somewhat unusual methodology of this study, which is at once a phenomenological, historical, and literary undertaking. In treating a symbol in a discrete way, seeing it as a living entity that is continuous in its range of meanings across the lines usually drawn between religious groups and historical eras, I am certainly partaking of the phenomenological method now widely accepted in Religious Studies. The crown is seen here as a religious symbol in the full sense of that term. It is not reducible to political power, ecclesiastical authority, or anything else. It is invoked as a sign of the elusive divine reality that human religious language is ever seeking to grasp by means of such symbolic expression. As we shall see, in this context the crown essentially symbolizes the attempt of humans to bestow their gift or blessing on their God.

But this work is also fundamentally about historical development. Medieval Jews had their own way of rereading the earlier legacy they had received and recasting it in new theological and philosophical language. While myths and symbols indeed persist, it will be abundantly clear to the reader that I by no means claim that everything to be found in tenth- or twelfth-century understandings of the crown was already present in the first or second century, when the motif is first seen. Even though we are working here with texts that are difficult to date, with concepts that elude clear definition or discoverable origin, and with esoteric traditions that are highly tradition-bound, this work deals with two distinct periods: the rabbinic-gaonic, primarily in the Near East, and the early medieval, primarily in Western Europe.

Both the historical and the phenomenological aspects of this study depend at every turn on close readings of literary sources, the only witness we have to the spiritual and intellectual life of an aniconic religious tradition of antiquity. The most important of these texts, here translated by the author, are found in Hebrew at the back of this volume, for the convenience of the scholar who wants to see them in the original language, on which so much of interpretation turns. The writers of these sources were themselves exegetes, used to close and subtle readings of the sources they revered. This habit of mind is amply reflected in their own writing, a fact this study regularly seeks to take into account. To say it all just a bit differently, the author believes that the people, its myths, and its literary/exegetical oeuvre are all living entities, growing and developing over the course of time. This study of the crown seeks to reveal to the reader the life animating all of these.

The idea for this book originated in a series of lectures I delivered at the University of California at Berkeley in 1991, sponsored by the Bay Area Jewish Studies Colloquium. I did much of the writing during a sabbatical semester in Jerusalem. I am grateful to the Reconstructionist Rabbinical College for that opportunity. I am also grateful to the staff of the Gershom Scholem Library at the Jewish National and University Library for the use of their wonderful collection.

Several scholars in Jerusalem read the manuscript during my visit there; I am especially grateful to Rachel Elior, Moshe Idel, and Yehuda Liebes for their advice. My American colleagues Michael Fishbane and Elliot Wolfson also offered some helpful suggestions. Responsibility of course remains entirely my own. Heartfelt thanks also to Michael and Ariel Elior for their help and patience in printing the manuscript, as well as to Michael Rindner and Susie Tanchel, my assistants at Brandeis during the final stages of preparation.

Abbreviations

AJS Review	*Association for Jewish Studies Review*
Am.	Amos
ARW	*Archiv für Religionswissenschaft*
attr.	attributed to
b.	*bavli* (=Babylonian Talmud)
b.h.	biblical Hebrew
Cant.	Canticles (=Song of Songs)
I, II Chron.	Chronicles
Cor.	Corinthians
Dan.	Daniel
Dan, *ʿIyyunim*	Joseph Dan. *Studies in Ashkenazi-Hasidic Literature.* Ramat Gan: Massada, 1975.
Dan, *Torat ha-Sod*	Joseph Dan. *The Esoteric Theology of Ashkenazi Hasidism.* Jerusalem: Bialik Institute, 1968.
De Princ.	*De Principiis* (Origen)
Deut.	Deuteronomy
Eccles.	Ecclesiastes (=Kohelet)
EJM	*Early Jewish Mysticism.* Jerusalem: Jerusalem Studies in Jewish Thought, 1987.
Ex.	Exodus
Ezek.	Ezekiel
Farber, *Concept*	*The Concept of the Merkabah in Thirteenth Century Jewish Esotericism—Sod ha-Egoz and Its Development.* Doctoral Dissertation. Jerusalem: Hebrew University, 1986.
Gen.	Genesis
Ginzberg, *Legends*	Louis Ginzberg, *Legends of the Jews.* 7 vols. Philadelphia: Jewish Publication Society, 1909–38.
Gruenwald, *Apocalyptic*	Itamar Gruenwald. *Apocalyptic and Merkavah Mysticism.* Leiden: E. J. Brill, 1980.
h.	Hebrew
Hab.	Habakkuk
Halperin, *Faces*	David Halperin. *The Faces of the Chariot.* Tübingen: J.C.B. Mohr, 1988.

Heb.	Hebrews
HUCA	*Hebrew Union Collge Annual*
Idel, *Kabbalah*	Moshe Idel. *Kabbalah: New Perspectives.* New Haven: Yale University Press, 1988.
Is.	Isaiah
JAAR	*Journal of the American Academy of Religion*
JBL	*Journal of Biblical Literature*
Jer.	Jeremiah
JJS	*Journal of Jewish Studies*
Josh.	Joshua
JQR	*Jewish Quarterly Review*
JSJT	*Jerusalem Studies in Jewish Thought*
JSOT	*Journal for the Study of the Old Testament*
JSQ	*Jewish Studies Quarterly*
JTSA	Jewish Theological Seminary of America
Jud.	Judges
Lam.	Lamentations
Lev.	Leviticus
M.	Mishnah
Matt.	Matthew
MGWJ	*Monatsschrift für die Geschichte und Wissenschaft des Judentums*
Mic.	Micah
Neh.	Nehemiah
NT	New Testament
Num.	Numbers
PAAJR	*Proceedings of the American Academy for Jewish Research*
Pes.	*Pesaḥim*
Pesiqta DRK	*Pesiqta de-Rav Kahana.* Ed. B. Mandelbaum. New York: Jewish Theological Seminary, 1987.
Prov.	Proverbs
Ps.	Psalms
R.	Rabbi
REJ	*Revue des Etudes Juives*
R.H.	*Rosh Ha-Shanah*
I, II Sam.	Samuel
Schaefer, *Synopse*	Peter Schaefer. *Synopse zur Hekhalot-Literatur.* Tübingen: J.C.B. Mohr, 1981.
Scholem, *Jewish Gnosticism*	Gershom Scholem. *Jewish Gnosticism, Merkabah Mysticism, and Talmudic*

	Tradition. New York: Jewish Theological Seminary, 1960.
Scholem, *Origins*	Gershom Scholem. *Origins of the Kabbalah*. Philadelphia: Jewish Publication Society, 1987.
supp.	supplement
s.v.	*sub verbo*
WCJS	*World Congress of Jewish Studies*
Wolfson, *Demut Yaʿaqov*	Elliot Wolfson. "*Demut Yaʿaqov Ḥaquqah be-Kisseʾ ha-Kavod.*" In *Massuʾot: Studies in Kabbalistic Literature and Jewish Philosophy in Memory of Prof. Ephraim Gottlieb*. Jerusalem: Bialik Institute, 1994, pp. 131–85.
Wolfson, *Feet*	Elliot Wolfson. "Images of God's Feet: Some Observations on the Divine Body in Judaism." In *People of the Body*. Ed. H. Eilberg-Schwartz. Albany: SUNY, 1992, pp. 143–81.
Wolfson, *Speculum*	Elliot Wolfson. *Through a Speculum That Shines: Vision and Imagination in Medieval Jewish Mysticism*. Princeton: Princeton University Press, 1994.
y.	*yerushalmi* (=Jerusalem Talmud)
Zech.	Zechariah

Keter

CHAPTER ONE

Ancient Israel: Crowns Above and Below

מלכותא דארעא כעין מלכותא דירקיעא

say the rabbis (b. *Berakhot* 58a); "Earthly kingdoms are like the kingdom of heaven." The modern scholar of religion would certainly prefer to say it the other way around: "The kingdom of heaven is depicted in the image of the earthly kingdom." Religious societies of the most varied sorts, existing at great temporal and geographical distance from one another, portray the realms of their deities or sacred beings awash with trappings familiar from the domain of this-worldly kingship. Various forms of correspondence between the cosmic or primal kingship of the gods and that of the temporal sovereign are usually noted by such societies, human kingship said to be in imitation of the divine. While such associations are both ancient and widespread, their origins are now being traced by historians of ancient religion. One such scholar, who sees Mesopotamian links between gods and kings arising some twenty-three centuries before the Common Era, writes of that Sargonic age, as it is called: "If, then, the monarch was to be deified, it was presumably essential that, at the least, the "real" gods be treated like monarchs. . . . The new ideology of the deified king, in other words, implied an assimilation of god and king that worked both ways—the king became more like a god, but at the same time the gods bcame more like kings and, inevitably, like human beings altogether."[1]

Often a direct link between the two kingdoms is also provided by ancient myths and rituals, either in the descent of the gods into the person of the earthly ruler or in the ascent of the earthly king, or his mythic ancestor, to the heavens. This link becomes the source of legitimation for the earthly ruler's authority, joining the domain of the sacred with the powers of the earthly realm.[2]

[1] W. Hallo, "Text, Statues and the Cult of the Divine King," in *Congress Volume* (*Vetus Testamentum* Supplements #40; Leiden: E. J. Brill, 1988), p. 59f.

[2] Sacral kingship is a major theme in writings on the history of religion. Though much of its "historical" basis has been whittled away, A. M. Hocart, *Kings and Councillors* (Cairo: Egyptian University, 1936) is still a worthwhile classic treatment. A summary of onetime anthropological views is found in Frazer and Gaster, *The New Golden Bough* (New York: New American Library, 1959), #70, 73–75. See also the writings of T. H. Gaster mentioned in the following notes. An important collection of essays is *The Sacral Kingship* (Leiden: E. J. Brill, 1959). On the ancient Near East in particular, see S. Pallis, *The Babylonian Akitu Festival* (Copenhagen: Bianco Lunos, 1926); I. Engnell, *Studies in Divine Kingship in the Ancient Near East* (Uppsala: Almquist & Wiksells, 1943); E. O. James, *Myth and Ritual in the Ancient Near East* (London: Thames and

The religion of ancient Israel represents both a continuation and a break with regard to this widespread pattern. The kingship of God is a central theme of the Hebrew Bible, and kingship is probably the most widespread single metaphor used to describe the relationship of God, His creation, and His people. But by now the specific analogy of earthly to heavenly kingship has to a large extent been lost. God is indeed King, and that means that certain trappings of earthly royalty—a throne, for example—will be attributed to Him. Particularly emphasized in the Bible are God's kingly rule in connection with both the origins of the universe—God reigns as triumphant Creator—and its final state, when God is enthroned once again in redeeming glory. But the earthly king of Israel does not seem to exist as a human embodiment of divine rule or glory. On the contrary, we will recall that early biblical sources reflect great ambivalence about monarchy altogether and question whether it is the proper form of rule for Israel. It is with more than a little reluctance that God's prophet designates a king "to be ruler over My people Israel" (I Sam. 9:16).[3]

Biblical scholarship has struggled long and hard to come to this realization, which even today is not universally accepted. The notion of sacral kingship in ancient Israel, one that tied biblical religion more closely to both real and imagined myths of its ancient Near Eastern context, has not wholly been abandoned. Some of the most extensive scholarly discussion of sacral kingship, enthronement of the deity, and correspondence between earthly kingship and that of heaven has been occasioned by the biblical text, and particularly by the Psalter.[4]

Hudson, 1958), esp. "The Sacral Kingship," pp. 80–112; G. Buccellati, "The Enthronement of the King and the Capital City" in *Studies Presented to A. L. Oppenheim* (Chicago: Oriental Institute, 1964); G. Widengren, *The Ascension of the Apostle and the Heavenly Book* (Uppsala: Lundequist, 1950); idem, *The King and the Tree of Life in Ancient Near Eastern Religion* (Uppsala: Lundequist, 1951); H. Frankfort, *Kingship and the Gods* (Chicago: University of Chicago, 1978); W. Hallo, "Cult, Statue and Divine Image: A Preliminary Study," in *Scripture in Context II*, ed. Hallo et al. (Winona Lake, IN: Eisenbrauns, 1983), pp. 1–17; idem, "Texts, Statues, and the Cult of the Divine King" (above, n. 1), pp. 54–66.

[3] Note the frequent repetition of *ʿami* (my people) throughout these earliest kingship narratives. Cf. I Sam. 15:30; II Sam. 3:18, 5:2, 7:7, 7:8, 7:ll. These verses want to leave no doubt as to whose people Israel really are.

[4] A great deal has been written on kingship and coronation in ancient Israel and its roots in Canaanite and Mesopotamian religion. As indicated, much of the earlier scholarship on this matter has been largely discredited and is interesting only for a history of scholarship itself. This discussion centered around certain Psalms and their alleged relation to the coronation rites. The association of coronation and the ancient New Year festival is also much discussed. This is not the place for a full bibliography on the subject, particularly as many such bibliographies are readily available. The key figure in this discussion was Sigmund Mowinckel; controversy was often focused on reactions to his *Psalmenstudien* (1921). The best recent survey and evaluation of this material is by M. Z. Brettler, *God Is King: Understanding an Israelite Metaphor* (JSOT Supplement Series #76; Sheffield: JSOT, 1989). See the bibliography there. What may be called the more recent rounds of discussion on sacred kingship in ancient Israel begin with G. Von Rad,

It is still widely held that the major motifs of divine kingship in the Bible are somehow related to the Canaanite setting against whose backdrop the religion of Israel took its early shape. A particular object of dispute has been the New Year festival, which in Mesopotamia—and possibly in Canaan—represented an annual renewal of the chief god's victory over his enemies or the forces of chaos. This victory was celebrated in a rite of enthronement, where the king was seated amid various trappings of glory and authority, ensuring the stability of both earthly and heavenly kingdoms for yet another year. That enthronement ceremony was typically preceded by a *hieros gamos* or sacred marriage rite, in which the cosmic union of heaven and earth, male and female, god and goddess was reenacted by the king.[5]

Israel's proclamations of divine kingship, combined with surviving textual echoes of suppressed tales of the great premundane battles, make it clear that similar motifs were well known among the Hebrews, whose most ancient myths certainly paralleled those of the surrounding cultures.[6] But the royal/sacral New Year festival as such seems not to have existed in Israel, or at least there is no clear evidence that points to it. If there is anything that arouses suspicion in this regard, it is the total absence of a so-designated New Year feast in the Pentateuchal festival lists, indicating a possible attempt to suppress a pre-Israelite survival that was seen as unattractive by the editors of those texts. Neither was there a royal enthronement ceremony at the New Year in ancient Israel nor, of course, could there have been a *hieros gamos* in the proper sense. YHWH has no consort, and the cult of Israel had no place for such erotic rites.[7]

"Das judäische Königsritual," in *Theologische Literaturzeitung* 62 (1947): 211–16; N. H. Snaith, *The Jewish New Year Festival: Its Origin and Development* (London, SPCK, 1947); R. de Vaux, *Ancient Israel* (New York: McGraw-Hill, 1961): 102–7; idem, *The Bible and the Ancient Near East* (Garden City, NY: Doubleday, 1971), pp. 152–66; A. R. Johnson, *Sacred Kingship in Ancient Israel* (Cardiff: University of Wales Press, 1967); M. Buber, *Kingship of God* (New York: Harper and Row, 1967); T. H. Gaster, *Myth, Legend, and Custom in the Old Testament* (Gloucester, MA: Peter Smith, 1981), pp. 773–81; Geo Widengren, *Sakrales Königtum in Alten Testament* (Stuttgart: W. Kohlhammer, 1955); Z. Ben Barak, "The Coronation Ceremonies of Joash and Nebopolassar in Comparison," in *History of the Jewish People and the Land of Israel* (Haifa) 5 (1980): 43–56. Both Brettler and Ben Barak offer careful treatments of earthly kingship/coronation in ancient Israel.

[5] On sacred marriage and its relation to coronation and the New Year festival, see Hocart, *Kings and Councillors*; T. H. Gaster, *Thespis* (New York: Anchor, 1961), pp. 63ff., 94ff., as well as his other works cited above; H. Gottlieb, "Myth in the Psalms," in *Myth in the Old Testament*, ed. B. Otzen et al. (London: SCM, 1980), pp. 62–93. These are the "believers."

[6] On these parallel myths see most recently J. Day, *God's Conflict with the Dragon and the Sea: Echoes of a Canaanite Myth in the Old Testament* (Cambridge: Cambridge University, 1985). Here too a great deal has been written, but it is beyond the scope of our direct interest here.

[7] M. Wheatley, The Hieros Gamos in the Ancient Near East and in Israel (Doctoral Dissertation, University of Iowa, 1966; and see bibliography there) is a thorough denial of the presence of *hieros gamos* in either Canaanite or Israelite religion, including a denial of any cultic background to the Song of Songs. While important as a corrective to the loose scholarly claims of the preced-

But old mythic motifs do not disappear. Revolutions, as we have known so well in our century, do not succeed overnight in creating a "new man." The old myths may go underground for a while, protecting themselves from the excesses of revolutionary zeal, but they will reappear, perhaps in new form, for another generation. Though the body of myth was transposed somewhat awkwardly to the setting of a monotheistic faith, its power was not lost on the Israelites, who continued both to tell and to reshape the ancient tales. Sacral kingship did not die out in Israel, but it was limited to the heavens (at least for the duration of premessianic time), giving birth to the postbiblical esoteric literature that will concern us in much of this study. Whatever human needs and dreams are fulfilled in the rite, image, or metaphor of sacred marriage did not disappear from the subconscious minds of Israelites simply because they had become monotheists. The celebration of God's victory at creation—the original *Sitz im Leben* of divine kingship in the Bible—came increasingly to be linked liturgically and hermeneutically with celebration of His victory over Pharoah and the election of Israel as His earthly beloved. In a process that took many centuries, lasting well into the postbiblical period, this linkage took the place of *hieros gamos* in the myth structure of ancient Israelite and later Jewish faith. We trace some of the later history of this motif in the course of the following pages.[8]

Even with regard to the New Year, it is not at all the case that ancient mythic associations were permanently suppressed, particularly if we take postbiblical Judaism into account. In the neo-Babylonian literature, a portion of the New Year rite involved the "tablets of destiny" that were in the possession of the gods. These tablets, on which the fate of all mortals was inscribed, were rewritten or adjusted on this day, when lots were cast in heaven to determine humans' fate. The earthly celebrant of the festival was said to have been privileged to see and read these tablets. Thus he gained supernal knowledge concerning his subjects, becoming empowered over them and blessed in his earthly realm. Attention has been called by various scholars[9] to the remarkable parallel between this tradition and a central motif of the rabbinic New Year celebration. "Three books are opened on the New Year," says the Talmud, "one of the completely wicked, one of the completely righteous, and one of those in between. The righteous are inscribed immediately for life, the wicked for death. Those in between are left hanging until the Day of Atone-

---

ing generations, he is often only stating the obvious (that there is no actual enactment of a sacred marriage rite in Israel), and he has little eye for more subtle shifts or restatements of myth.

[8] Tikva Frymer-Kensky has touched on some of the issues in her *In the Wake of the Goddess* (New York: Free Press, 1992).

[9] The tablets of the gods are renewed each year. Marduk is said to cast lots, according to which these "tablets of destiny" are reset. The passing on of these heavenly tablets is a part of the annual coronation rite. Cf. G. Widengren, *The Ascension of the Apostle and the Heavenly Book* (Uppsala: Lundequist, 1950), p. 7ff., including discussion of the presence of this motif in Enoch.

ment. If they merit, they are inscribed for life; if not, for death."[10] The various supplications to "inscribe us in the book of life," well known in connection with this season, are of great antiquity and are adjacent to this mythic theme.

The collections of *piyyuṭim*, or Hebrew liturgical poetry, beginning as early as the fourth or fifth century and continuing into the early Middle Ages, include some thousands of hymns composed for this day. They are meant to adorn and embellish (sometimes in dazzling wonder, and often in alphabetical acrostics triple or quadruple, backward or forward!) the glorious kingship of God. These poems typically include references to the angels, the heavenly throne, the eternity of divine rule, God's awesome judgment, and (though somewhat less frequently) the offering of a crown to God. A classic example of this last motif is found in the conclusion of *We-Yeʾetayu*,[11] an exceptionally lovely composition in blank verse written by an anonymous poet in seventh-century Ereṣ Israel:

> Mountains will break forth in singing,
> Islands in joyous exultation.
> They will accept the rule of Your kingdom
> And exalt You in mighty chorus.
> Those far off will come and hear,
> Bringing you a kingly crown.

Our main concern here will be the role played by this motif of divine coronation, not in the New Year celebration, but in the daily liturgy of the synagogue and in the Jewish esoteric literature of late antiquity and the early Middle Ages. Before this discussion, however, a brief backward glance at the role played by coronation in the biblical (earthly) kingship traditions is required. Although the religion of biblical Israel had undergone a tremendous series of transformations by the earliest period we discuss here, the canonical status of the biblical text dictated that terms, images, and particular verses—sometimes taken entirely out of their original context—remained formative for later Judaism, in this area as indeed in nearly all others.

[10] Attention called partly by Widengren, *The Ascension of the Apostle*, 27f., 38; Gaster, *Festivals of the Jewish Year* (New York: William Sloane, 1955), 113f. N. H. Snaith's total denials of such connection (*The Jewish New Year Festival*, pp. 65ff., 205f.) are unconvincing to me, as they are to Gaster. The passage quoted is from b. *R. H.* 16b There are many survivals of Babylonian materials into later Jewish sources, including both apocalyptic and midrashic literature. Among these note the Enoch materials mentioned in the preceding note, probably a way-station to the emergence of the "books of the living and the dead" motif in the Rosh Ha-Shanah liturgy, as well as 3 Enoch (*Sefer Hekhalot*; included in Schaefer, *Synopse* #28) where a pair of supreme angels known as *Shofariel* YHWH *memit* and *Shofariel* YHWH *meḥayeh* are presented as keepers of the divine lists! It may be an indication of the decline of this myth, however, that in that text even Meṭaṭron, who is reporting to "Rabbi Ishmael" the merkavah voyager, does not claim to have looked into those lists but only to have seen the angels themselves.

[11] In the standard High Holy Day prayerbooks, Rosh Hashanah *Mussaf* service. In the critical edition of *Maḥzor le-Yamim Noraʾim*, ed. D. Goldschmidt (Jerusalem: Koren, 1970), pp. 227–28.

The chief method of inaugurating kings in ancient Israel was anointing with oil, rather than coronation.[12] This tradition goes back to the earliest memories of kingship in Israel (Jud. 9:15; I Sam. 9:16) and is related to the consecration of priests by anointing. Nevertheless, crowns were associated with kings and served even as symbols of royalty. Saul was said to wear a *nezer* that was snatched from his head and brought, along with the band from off his arm, to David at Ziklag (II Sam. 1:10). When young Joash is proclaimed king, his supporters place on him "the *nezer* and the testimony (*ʿedut*)" (II Kings 11:12).[13] When David conquers the Ammonites, he removes the golden *ʿaṭarah* of the king in Rabbat Ammon and places it on his own head. (2 Sam. 12:30; I Chron. 20:2). *ʿAṭarah* is also used with some frequency in biblical poetry, though not always in a royal context. The removing of a crown indicates loss of kingship (Ps. 89:40; Jer. 13:18; Lam. 5:16). Especially well known among these references is that to the *ʿaṭarah*, marital crown or wreath of Solomon, "with which his mother crowned him on the day of his marriage, the day of his heart's delight" (Cant. 3:11). The Book of Esther contains several references to *keter malkhut*, the royal crown, providing the only biblical usage of the term that becomes the most common one for "crown" in later Hebrew. Clearly, in the Persian context of that book, the crown has become a crucial symbol of royalty, alongside throne and scepter.[14]

The interweaving of royal and priestly motifs in the Bible is further demonstrated by the fact that while both are inaugurated by anointing, priests as well as kings are also depicted as crowned. The *nezer*, or *ṣiṣ*, that Aaron and his sons wore when serving, on which "holy unto YHWH" was inscribed, seems to be a priestly adaptation of the royal crown.[15] The two motifs of anointing and

[12] Anointing is the way priests as well as kings are designated, and its use in the royal traditions is seemingly related to this association. On anointing see M. Jastrow in *Hastings Encyclopedia of Religion and Ethics*, vol. 1, pp. 555ff. and D. Lys, "L'Onction dans la Bible," in *Etudes Theologiques et Religieuses* 29 (1954): 3ff.

[13] See Z. Ben Barak and M. Brettler as cited above in n. 4. On the question of the *ʿedut*, see Z. W. Falk, "Forms of Testimony," in *Vetus Testamentum* 11(1961): 88. It is very possible that *ʿedut* should be emended and read *seʿadot* or *ʾeseʿadot*, "armlets," thus parallel to the II Samuel reference. This view is espoused by J. Gray in *I-II Kings* (Philadelphia: Old Testament Library, 1975), p. 573 and J. Liver in the Hebrew *Biblical Encyclopedia* 4:1099. Brettler (p. 78f.) seems to agree with the emendation. It is opposed by G. Von Rad in *The Problem of the Hexateuch* (Edinburgh: Oliver and Boyd, 1966); S. Yeivin, "King and Covenant," in *Journal of Semitic Studies* 2 (1957): 6f. and De Vaux, *The Bible and the Ancient Near East*, 160f. See also B. Halpern, *The Constitution of the Monarchy in Israel* (Chico, CA: Scholars Press, 1981), 16ff.

[14] *K-t-r* does exist as a verb in earlier biblical Hebrew, usually meaning "to surround." The earliest reference is probably Jud. 20:43.

[15] On *nezer*, its priestly and royal associations, and particularly its relation to the biblical *nazir*, see the doctoral dissertation by Yisrael Knohl (Hebrew University, 1988), p. 140f. and accompanying notes. Knohl also refers there to various Near Eastern sources on crowns of the gods and their relationship to earthly kingship. Throughout both older and more recent discussions of biblical kingship, the question of priestly elements and the relationship between royal and

coronation are further enmeshed in a Levitical description of the high priest (Lev. 21:12), of whom it is said that "the crown of sacred anointing oil" is on him.

It is clear, especially from the uniqueness of the Esther references, that the bestowing of a crown was not the key symbol of royalty in ancient Israel that it was to become in later history. Verbal proclamations of kingship, anointing, and enthronement were the elements central to the royal rites, whether in their heavenly or earthly manifestations.[16]

The Greek and Roman sources have a very different relation to the crown, designated usually as *diadema* or *corona*. Both in the classical age and in the late Hellenistic world that forms much of the direct backdrop for rabbinic literature, wreaths and crowns were commonplace, serving a wide range of roles as signs of honor, obeisance, celebration, and simple adornment. They were used in the private or familial as well as the public domain, and for both secular and religious purposes. Statues of the gods were regularly crowned with leafy diadems. In this case there were appropriate leaves to be chosen: laurel for Apollo, myrtle for Venus, olive branches for Minerva, and of course vines for Bacchus. Lists are available in some detail about the proper composition of a diadem for ritual occasions. Sacrificial victims were crowned as a sign of consecration, and the use of a crown had magical associations in some sources. For those who could afford them, silver and gold crowns were also in use, and these do not seem to have a symbolic value clearly distinguishable from crowns of leaves and branches, other than as an indicator of economic status. For this level of adornment, there were professional crownmakers, and one could order crowns for particular occasions through them. In fact some very lovely Hellenistic crowns have been preserved that consist of leaves wrought in gold, uniting the two traditions.[17] In early Graeco-Roman tradition

---

priestly symbols is widely mentioned. For possible references to a divine crown in Scripture, see M. Mach, *Entwicklungsstadien des jüdischen Engelglaubens in vorrabbinischer Zeit* (Tübingen: Mohr, 1992), p. 201.

[16] There are eight "coronations" of human kings mentioned in the Bible, though not all of these involve crowns. The most fully described is that of Joash, in II Kings 11:4–20 and II Chron. 23. See discussions by Ben Barak and Brettler as cited above. Public proclamation plays a great role in many of these coronations. See I Sam. 10:17–24 (Saul); II Sam. 5:3 (David); II Sam. 15:10 (Absalom); I Kings 1:32–39 (Solomon); II Kings 11:4–12 (Joash). On the use of crowns in the Bible, see S. Yeivin in Hebrew *Biblical Encyclopedia* 4:400–402. See also the brief retrospective on biblical kingship in Stuart Cohen's *The Three Crowns: Structures of Communal Politics in Early Rabbinic Jewry* (Cambridge: Cambridge University Press, 1990). Crowns apparently did play a key role in Babylonian coronation, while anointing did not. See Ben Barak, "The Coronation Ceremonies," who also notes (p. 47) that anointing appears in the earliest biblical kingship tales to be a private event between God, through the prophet, and the king-designate; only with Solomon does it become part of the public ceremony. It may be, however, that this difference is dictated by other aspects of the narrative, and not by a change in the understanding of this rite.

[17] Cf. C. Darenberg and E. Saglio, *Dictionnaire des Antiquités Grecques et Romaines* (Paris, 1877), vol. I, pp. 1521ff., 1528; Ganszyniec in *Paulys Realencyclopädie der Classischen Alter-*

there was no particular association of crowns with royalty, but this changed with the advent of the Roman empire.[18] Julian is the first emperor whose coronation is recorded, but in the late Roman and Byzantine worlds crowning was very much a symbol of royalty. The emperors habitually wore a laurel wreath as a sign of office.[19] This later prevalence of crowns comes to be reflected in Christian iconography, and, as illustrated in the pages that follow, is reflected in the Jewish verbal arts as well as in the synagogue tradition of crowning the Torah, embodiment of legitimate authority in the eyes of Judaism.[20]

For the Jews, the loss of political sovereignty, joined on two occasions to the destruction of the Jerusalem Temple, meant that both royal and priestly traditions were to lose the very base of their onetime existence. The priesthood, with its vast body of learning and tradition, survived the relatively brief Babylonian exile and actually exhibited remarkable vigor during the Second Temple period. History did not give the royal tradition the same chance at reestablishing itself.[21] Already in the Persian period, Jews seem to have begun transferring their love of royalty from earth to heaven, perhaps preserving some bit of faith in this-worldly kingship only for King Messiah, belief in whom was just beginning to develop in this period of Jewish history.

The ancient motifs of royalty are carried over into the rabbinic and later Jewish liturgy on a grand scale, especially on the New Year. The repeated calling out of "The Lord is King!" or the solemn proclamation of the sovereignty verses in the *Mussaf* service recall the cries of tribal chieftains and elders who come together to proclaim the king. The heavenly throne is mentioned with some frequency in the service, on this day when God is said to be seated on the throne of judgment. The royal robes of God are also described in the poetry of the day. Only anointing seems to be missing from this panoply of kingly motifs. God in the Bible was never anointed as King, but neither was He ever crowned. Both of these would have seemed theologically offensive, surely to the prophetic mind. They would have indicated both that God's king-

---

tumswissenschaft (Stuttgart: Metzler, 1922), vol. 22, col. 1588–1607. Fuller treatments are found in L. Deubner, *Die Bedeutung des Kranzes im klassischen Altertum* (*ARW* 30, 1933), pp. 70–104 and M. Blech, *Studien zum Kranz bei den Griechen* (Berlin, De Gruyter, 1982).

[18] Mommsen as quoted by S. Kraus, *Paras we-Romi ba-Talmud uva-Midrashim* (Jerusalem: Mossad Harav Kook, 1948), p. 44f. The distinctions Kraus tries to make there regarding Hebrew terminology do not hold up.

[19] On the coronation of Julian, see Ammianus Marcellinus 20.4.17 and 21.1.4.

[20] For the use of crowns in early Chistian iconography, see J. A. MacCulloch in *Hastings Encyclopedia of Religion and Ethics*, s.v. "crowns."

[21] Crowns were made for the high priest (and for Zerubavel the king?) after the Return to Zion. See Zech. 6:11–15, and the comments of C. Myers and E. Myers in *Haggai, Zechariah 1–8* (Garden City, NY: Doubleday, 1987), pp. 349–53. But the tradition remembered it this way: "When the First Temple was destroyed, kingship was removed from the House of David" (*Tosefta Soṭah* 13).

dom has a beginning and that someone stands over Him to pour the anointing oil, or behind Him to offer the crown. Either of these formulations would have caused difficulty for biblical theology. But in the rabbinic world, one of these will remain out of bounds, while the other becomes quite popular and seemingly unoffensive. We may say that among the rabbis the place of anointing is taken by the offering of the holy crown. Anointing is reserved in postbiblical Judaism for Messiah, whose very title of course means "anointed one." It might be that the appropriate symbol for the offering of kingship to God has in fact evolved with the times; it is the crown of empire, in the Persian and then later Roman/Byzantine mode, that is given to God who is King of Kings, the blessed Holy One. The much simpler and more ancient act of anointing no longer suffices for the Kingdom of Heaven, which now must follow the fashion of the courts of earth's emperors and kings and be yet more glorious than they. Anointing is thus reserved for the more humble human surrogate for Israel's ancient rulers, the one who is still to come.

CHAPTER TWO

Coronation and *Qedushah*

BUT IT IS NOT ONLY on the New Year that divine kingship plays a major role in Jewish worship. The proclamation of God as ruler takes place repeatedly in every daily service. The Talmud in fact insists that each blessing, even if only of a single line, must include reference to the divine name and to God's kingdom, constituting these as some sort of minimal base for a formal act of worship.[1] Each of the three daily services ends with the verse from Zechariah 14:9 that includes this same pair, but in an eschatological setting: "YHWH shall be king over all the earth; on that day shall YHWH be One and His name One."

Surely the most dramatic of all references to divine kingship in the regular weekly liturgy is the introduction to the *qedushah*—or *sanctus*, to use the Latin term familiar both to Christians and to lovers of Western sacred music—as it is recited by Sephardic Jews in the *Mussaf* service on Sabbaths, New Moons, and Festivals. That liturgy reads as follows:

> A crown they give unto You, YHWH our God, angels enthronged above and Your people Israel gathered below. All of them together thrice proclaim Your holiness, as has been spoken by Your prophet's word: "They call out to one another, saying: Holy, holy, holy is the Lord of hosts! The whole earth is filled with His glory!"[2]

This version of the liturgy spells out clearly that recitation of the *qedushah* is an act of daily coronation of God. The *qedushah* to which we refer, recited collectively by the congregation at dawn and dusk services when the reader chants aloud the great *ʿAmidah* prayer, serves as an elaboration to a prior proclamation of divine kingship, a part of the daily morning liturgy in all the traditional rites. In the so-called *qedushah de-yoṣer* (or *qedushah di-meyushav)*, the angelic liturgy inserted into the morning blessing for light,[3]

[1] b. *Berakhot* 12a.

[2] This version of the *qedushah* was recited daily in the Babylonian rite as preserved in *Siddur Rav ʿAmram*. It is the opening used for *qedushah* in all services. Only later, as the Babylonian tradition evolved into the Sephardic rite, was it restricted to Sabbath and festival use.

[3] M. Weinfeld has suggested that this association between *qedushah* themes and praise for the gift of light is found as early as Qumran, i.e., second century B.C.E. See "The Traces of Kedushat Yozer and Pesukey de-Zimra in the Qumran Literature and in Ben Sira," *Tarbiẓ* 45 (1976): 15–26. His findings reopen the question of whether the blessing for light might not in fact be the "original" setting for the *qedushah*, an older view dismissed by Elbogen (*Ha-Tefillah be-Yisraʾel* [Tel

the angels are said to "all open their mouths in holiness and purity, in song and hymn, blessing, praising, exalting, glorifying, sanctifying and ממליכים, proclaiming king . . ." Here the reader breaks for dramatic effect and then continues: "The name of the great, mighty, awesome God and King, holy is He!" In this liturgy Israel recounts an enthronement rite[4] that takes place daily in the upper realms. But in the *qedushah* of the ʿAmidah repetition, which requires a quorum of ten for public recitation, Israel rises to join in with the angels in bestowing the crown upon the divine head, the joint gift to God from His loyal legions above and below. דרי מעלה עם דרי מטה, "dwellers in the upper and lower realms."[5]

The language of these prayers immediately calls to mind the close connection between these sections of the synagogue liturgy and the world of merkavah mysticism. The texts associated with the term *maʿaseh merkavah*, "the work of the chariot," describe ascents[6] to the heavenly chambers (*hekhalot*, hence the other term often applied to this literature), visions of the divine chariot or throne, encounters with angelic beings, and a great host of divine names, prayer fragments, and hymns that accompany these phenomena. This body of literature constitutes the earliest portion of what is now called Jewish mysticism. It is replete with references to the passages from Isaiah and Ezekiel that form the backbone of the synagogue's *qedushah* rite in all its many forms. While known and discussed since the origins of historical scholarship on Judaic sources in the early nineteenth century, these texts have been the subject of particularly intense scholarly scrutiny in the past two decades. A confluence of interests has led to the renewed study of Jewish religion and magic in late antiquity and the reexamination of rabbinic Judaism in the light of such new literary, historical, and phenomenological

Aviv: Dvir, 1972], p. 47ff.) already early in the century. See most recently I. Gruenwald, "Shirat ha-Malʾakhim, ha-Qedushah, u-Veʿayat Ḥibburah shel Sifrut ha-Hekhalot," in *Peraqim be-Toledot Yerushalayim bi-Yemey Bayyit Sheni* (Jerusalem: Ben-Zvi Institute, 1981), pp. 476ff.

4 The Sabbath version adds the phrase *hitʿalah we-yashav ʿal kiseʾ kevodo*. I wonder if the phrasing here is not an intentional inverson of statements elsewhere that prayer causes God to *descend* (from the hidden heights of heaven) to His throne. Cf. the comments by I. Gruenwald in "Shirat ha-Malʾakhim" mentioned in the preceding note.

5 It is customary, when reciting the words "Holy, holy, holy" in the public *qedushah* of the *ʿamidah* repetition, for the worshiper to stand with feet together, imitating the posture of the angels, and to jump upward three times, as though to join in the heavenly chorus. This custom is already mentioned in such medieval sources as *Sefer ha-Manhig*, Laws of prayer 52 and *ʿArugat ha-Bosem*, vol. 1, p. 215.

6 Or "descents," as they are often called in the sources. On this point see Scholem, *Jewish Gnosticism, Merkabah Mysticism, and Talmudic Tradition* (New York: Jewish Theological Seminary, 1960), p. 20n. 1 and Gruenwald's striking explanation of this usage in "Shirat ha-Malʾakhim," pp. 479ff. For the most recent discussion of this terminology, see Elliot R. Wolfson, "*Yeridah la-Merkavah*: Typology of Ecstasy and Enthronement in Ancient Jewish Mysticism." *Mystics of the Book*, ed. R. A. Herrera (New York: Lang, 1993), pp. 13–44.

studies. These interests include the ongoing challenge provided by the Qumran sources and their place in early Judaism, the implications of these and other Jewish sources for various understandings of New Testament and early Christianity, and the great fascination with the newly discovered Gnostic materials and their relationship to both Judaism and Christianity. It has been clear to scholars that the merkavah sources have some place in all this, though their meaning continues to be defined in a wide variety of ways. Thanks to this expanded interest, however (and to the dedication of particular scholars), the key merkavah texts have been edited in a now-standard scholarly edition,[7] and several important monographs as well as a vast array of articles have been published on them.[8]

In contrast to the legal sources of Judaism in late antiquity, the merkavah texts were never granted any sort of canonical status. As a result, they were not codified, were not the objects of extensive commentary by later generations, and many were not even printed until this century, when scholars of ancient Judaism became fascinated by them. Scholarly opinion still varies as to precisely when and where the major collections of these texts were edited, with views ranging from second/third century Ereṣ Israel to seventh/eighth century Babylonia. Related to these questions of location and date is an ongoing scholarly debate concerning the relationship between the merkavah sources that have come down to us in these unedited manuscript collections and the references within the canonical rabbinic corpus to *maʿaseh merkavah* as a body of esoteric teachings.[9] The precise meaning and purpose of the sources has also been much discussed, including their relationship to mysticism and religious experience,[10]

[7] Peter Schaefer, *Synopse zur Hekhalot-Literatur* (Tübingen: J.B.C. Mohr, 1981). This edition, accompanied by a two-volume *Konkordanz zur Hekhalot Literatur* (Tübingen: Mohr, 1986–88), has truly revolutionized the field of *hekhalot* studies and provides an invaluable tool for work such as the present volume.

[8] Key works in this field will be listed throughout the notes below and are found in the bibliography to this volume. For works before 1988, see the very thorough "Reference List" in D. Halperin's *The Faces of the Chariot* (Tübingen: J.C.B. Mohr, 1988), pp. 546–84.

[9] Despite my great respect for the scholarship of David Halperin's *Faces*, I am still not convinced by his insistence on separating the rabbinic references to merkavah from the "later" hekhalot texts. This was the methodology of his prior study, *The Merkabah in Rabbinic Literature* (Leiden: E. J. Brill, 1980), which was legitimate and useful as an academic exercise but did not in itself demonstrate the gap between the two literatures. Taken over into *Faces*, and combined with a truly monumental research effort, it has, I believe, created a somewhat distorted picture that has led him to unwarranted conclusions about the origin and meaning of the hekhalot sources. See the thoughtful review of Halperin's work by Rachel Elior in *Numen* 37 (1990): 233–49.

[10] J. Dan, "The Religious Experience of the Merkavah," in *Jewish Spirituality*, ed. A. Green (New York: Crossroad, 1988), pp. 289–307; I. Chernus, "Visions of God in Merkavah Mysticism," in *Journal for the Study of Judaism* 13 (1982): 123–46; idem, *Mysticism in Rabbinic Judaism* (Berlin: de Gruyter, 1982); R. Elior, "The Concept of God in Hekhalot Mysticism" in

magic,[11] Temple traditions,[12] apocalypse,[13] and the religious phenomenon known as Gnosticism.[14] It is not our intention to review the scholarly debates on these various questions here, particularly since excellent English-language summaries of this discussion are already available.[15] My views on various points in these debates will become clear as we precede.

The important place of prayer in the merkavah literature and in the religious phenomenon it documents[16] is immediately obvious to the reader. The voy-

EJM (Jerusalem Studies in Jewish Thought, 1987), pp. 13–64; idem, "Mysticism, Magic, Angelology: The Perception of Angels in Hekhalot Literature," *JSQ* 1:1 (1993–94): 3–53; M. D. Swartz, *Mystical Prayer in Ancient Judaism* (Tübingen: J.C.B. Mohr, 1992).

[11] See M. Smith, "Some Observations on Hekhalot Rabbati," in *Biblical and Other Studies*, ed. A. Altmann (Cambridge: Harvard Unversity Press, 1963), pp. 142–60. P. Schaefer, "Die Beschwörung des Sar ha-Panim," in *Frankfurter Judaistische Beiträge* 6 (1978): 107–45; idem, "Jewish Magic Literature in Late Antiquity and the Early Middle Ages," in *JJS* 41 (1990): 75–91; Gruenwald, *Apocalyptic and Merkavah Mysticism* (Leiden: Brill, 1980), pp. 102ff.

[12] I. Gruenwald, "The Impact of Priestly Traditions on the Creation of Merkavah Mysticism and the Shiur Komah," in *EJM*, pp. 65–120; Elior, "Mysticism, Magic, Angelology."

[13] A. Saldarini, "Apocalypses and 'Apocalyptic' in Rabbinic Literature and Mysticism," in *Semeia* 4 (1979): 187–205; I. Gruenwald, *Apocalyptic*, pp. 3–72.

[14] Debate on the relationship between Judaism and Gnosticism goes back to the days of Heinrich Graetz, whose *Gnostizismus und Judenthum* (Krotoschin, 1846) was the first substantial treatment of the subject. He was followed by M. Friedländer, *Der vorchristliche jüdische Gnostizismus* (Göttingen, 1898). Writing in a period when Gnostic studies were much advanced by the ongoing publication and discussion of the Nag Hammadi sources, Scholem entered the fray by referring to merkavah mysticism as *Jewish Gnosticism*. Since then an extensive literature has emerged on the relationship, mostly around the question of Jewish influence on the shaping of Gnosticism itself. A few key treatments include I. Gruenwald, "Jewish Sources for the Gnostic Texts from Nag Hammadi?" in *WCJS* 6 (1973) 3: 45–56; idem, "Knowledge and Vision: Towards a Clarification of Two 'Gnostic' Concepts in the Light of Their Alleged Origins," in *Israel Oriental Studies* 3 (1973): 63–107; idem, "Aspects of the Jewish-Gnostic Controversy," in *The Rediscovery of Gnosticism* (Leiden: E. J. Brill, 1981), vol. 2, pp. 713–23; idem, "Jewish Merkavah Mysticism and Gnosticism," in *Studies in Jewish Mysticism*, ed. J. Dan and F. Talmage (Cambridge, MA: AJS, 1982), pp. 41–55; F. T. Fallon, *The Enthronement of Sabaoth: Jewish Elements in Gnostic Creation Myths* (Leiden: E. J. Brill, 1978); P. Alexander, "Comparing Merkavah Mysticism and Gnosticism: An Essay in Method," in *JJS* 35 (1984): 1–18; etc. The term "Jewish Gnosticism" for merkavah literature has not been accepted. A thorough summation of the various positions regarding the relationship of merkavah traditions to Gnosticism has recently been published by Nathaniel Deutch as *The Gnostic Imagination: Gnosticism, Mandaeism, and Merkabah Mysticism*. Leiden: E. J. Brill, 1995.

[15] These are found in Gruenwald's *Apocalyptic*, pp. 98ff.; in Halperin's *Faces*, passim; and in Elior's "Mysticism, Magic, Angelology."

[16] Here I begin to betray my bias. Yes, there is a real religious phenomenon behind the texts. I do not make any "truth" claim, for it is beyond that. I am willing to consider whether these or all other "religious experiences" are delusionary, involve anything beyond the human mind, etc. But I think these experiences, seemingly "bizarre" in our context, deserve that same consideration. I do not believe that these are *only* literary/interpretive/imitative sources. Of course this doesn't apply equally to all texts; I recognize elements of convention, parallel to those found in the language of the prophets, but in neither case does that negate the possibility that experience is

ager into the upper realms hears angels chanting powerfully worded, repetitive, "numinous" hymns. The heavenly traveler himself has to keep in mind prayers, chants, incantations, and adjurations of various sorts that will protect him from the terrible dangers inherent in his voyage. An intense and highly dramatic calling out of prayers and names of God and angels, in which both human and angelic voices take part, may be said to lie at the very heart of the merkavah experience. One scholar has characterized the prayer motif in the merkavah sources this way: "The worship of the angels in the heavenly palaces is the prototype of worship that the *yordey merkavah* are imitating. The ceremony that the angels perform before the throne of glory, including immersion, the offering of praises, the singing of hymns, recitation of prayers, binding of crowns, and mention of the Name, is conceived as the basic ritual structure that the *yordey merkavah* want to learn and imitate."[17]

In what follows I will diverge somewhat from this view, claiming that the relationship between the merkavah voyager, the angels, and the community of Israel at prayer is somewhat more complicated than that portrayed here. But Rachel Elior's well-chosen words can serve us as an appropriate opening formulation.

The existence of a significant relationship between aspects of the liturgy and this body of esoteric writings has long been discussed in historical treatments of Jewish worship. Earlier scholarship in the field saw here an influence of the merkavah "voyagers" on the liturgy. The centrality of the *qedushah* theme, based on the famous prophetic verses that were also key to the merkavah literature, was viewed as a stamp left by the mystics' devotion on what was to become normative prayer for later generations.[18] But with the dating of the merkavah sources still open (though an early dating of the merkavah phenomenon, if not the texts as we have them, is widely accepted), the connection

conveyed in conventionalized language. Often the debate surrounding the question of an experiential core in these sources has not been conducted on a sufficiently clear level of discourse, though that discussion has been raised to a high degree of sophistication in the treatment by Elliot Wolfson in his *Through a Speculum That Shines: Vision and Imagination in Medieval Jewish Mysticism* (Princeton: Princeton University Press, 1994), Chapters 2 and 3. Meanwhile I repeat the wisdom of Ithamar Gruenwald on this subject: "Generally speaking, however, discussions of this kind do not lead very far in any sincere attempt to understand and evaluate the experience once it has been cast as a literary document" (*Apocalyptic*, p. 63). See also the remarks of R. Elior in her review of Halperin, *Faces*, cited above.

[17] Elior, "Mysticism, Magic, Angelology," p. 5. Elior seems to be following Ira Chernus in this view. See his remarks in "The Pilgrimage to the Merkavah: An Interpretation of Early Jewish Mysticism," in *EJM*, p. 10.

[18] See P. Bloch, "Die Yorede Merkabah, die Mystiker der Gaonenzeit, und ihr Einfluss auf die Liturgie," *MGWJ* 37 (1893): 18ff.; I. Elbogen, *Ha-Tefillah be-Yisra'el*, translation of *Der jüdische Gottesdient in seiner geschichtlichen Entwicklung* (Leipzig, 1913, translated and augmented by J. Heinemann. Tel Aviv: Dvir, 1972), p. 282f.; A. Z. Idelsohn, *Jewish Liturgy and Its Development* (New York: Holt, 1932), pp. 32, 47ff.

between the liturgy and the merkavah literature has required reconsideration.[19] It seems likely that most of the merkavah texts as we know them were edited not before Amoraic times (third–sixth century C.E.), and some of them considerably later.

Liturgical use of the *qedushah* theme, on the other hand, has considerable witness at a much earlier date. While the visions recorded in Isaiah 6 and Ezekiel 1–3 seem on their face to describe singular occurrences in the lives of the respective prophets, various authors in the late Second Temple period already seem to understand the angelic calling out of "Holy, Holy, Holy!" as a daily or even constant event. The existence of a heavenly liturgy containing linguistic echoes of the Ezekiel passages and the visions of Daniel is reflected in both the Qumran sources[20] and the Enoch tradition.[21] The prominence of the *qedushah* or *sanctus* theme in the New Testament and in Christian liturgy,

[19] Most important of the recent studies is I. Gruenwald, "Shirat ha-Mal'akhim" mentioned in n. 2 above. See also H. Avenary, "Der Einfluss der jüdischen Mystik auf der Synagogengesang," *Kairos* 16 (1974): 79–87; P. Alexander, "Prayer in the Heikhalot Literature," in *Prière, Mystique et Judaisme*, ed. R. Goetschel (Paris: Presses Universitaires de France, 1987), pp. 43–64; M. Bar-Ilan, *The Mysteries of Jewish Prayer and Hekhalot* (Ramat Gan: Bar Ilan University Press, 1987); and M. Swartz, *Mystical Prayer in Ancient Judaism*. Cf. also the remarks of P. Schaefer, "Gershom Scholem Reconsidered: The Aim and Purpose of Early Jewish Mysticism," *The Twelfth Sacks Lecture* (Oxford: Oxford University Press, 1986), p. 11 and passim. Much of the *hekhalot* literature seems to presuppose Israel's recitation of *qedushah*, in a form that already contains the direct biblical quotations, as an established liturgical reality. P. Alexander, on p. 60f. of the article cited, well describes the mutual character of influence and borrowings between the worlds of *hekhalot* literature and rabbinic prayer.

[20] The key texts are the *Shirot ʿOlat ha-Shabbat*, edited by Carol Newsom (*Songs of the Sabbath Sacrifice*; Atlanta: Scholars Press, 1985). The pioneering study of this material is J. Strugnell's *The Angelic Liturgy* in *Vetus Testamentum*, supp. 7 (1959–60). These hymns and their connection to the merkavah tradition were discussed by Lawrence Schiffman in "*Merkavah* Speculation at Qumran: The 4Q Serekkh Shirot ʾOlat ha-Shabbat," in *Mystics, Philosophers, and Politicians: Essays in Jewish Intellectual History in Honor of Alexander Altmann*, ed. J. Reinharz and D. Swetschinski (Durham: Duke University Press, 1982), pp. 35–45. Schiffman presents these and other related sources in "Hekhalot Mysticism and the Qumran Literature," in *EJM*, pp. 121–38. On the specific evidence of *qedushah* patterns in this material, see M. Weinfeld as cited above in n. 3. While the Isaiah and Ezekiel verses are not quoted in the Qumran materials, Weinfeld (p. 16) brings a prayer that does include several key elements of both ideational content and phrasing that are highly reminiscent of later *qedushah* texts. Most recently see M. Mach, "Qedoshim Malʾakhim: Ha-ʾEl weha-Liturgiyyah ha-Shamayyemit," in *Massuʾot: Studies in Kabbalistic Literature and Jewish Philosophy in Memory of Prof. Ephraim Gottlieb* (Jerusalem: Bialik Institute, 1994), p. 306.

[21] 1 Enoch 39: 12; 2 Enoch 21. This is a strictly angelic liturgy as witnessed by Enoch; there is no talk here of human participation. D. Flusser, "Sanktus und Gloria," in *Abraham unser Vater . . . Festschrift für Otto Michel* (Leiden: E. J. Brill, 1963), p. 139 suggests that in the 1 Enoch text the second stitch is composed of phrases that reflect the nonbiblical *barukh shem kevod malkhuto le-ʿolam waʿed* more than they do Ezek. 3:12. This is of great interest to our discussion below. See also the discussion by Mach as quoted in the preceding note.

including its very earliest documents,[22] bears witness to the fact that it had a significant place in Jewish worship in late Second Temple times, perhaps even in the Temple itself.[23] The received *qedushah* liturgy of the synagogue is most probably a later (perhaps sixth or seventh century)[24] embellishment of an earlier and possibly less fixed core, but one that surely already contained Is. 6:3, Ezek. 3:12, and some verse that proclaimed divine kingship (probably either Ps. 146:10 or Ex. 15:18). In that case the merkavah vision literature we possess may have been influenced by, rather than formative of, the central role of *qadosh* and *barukh*,[25] or *sanctus* and *benedictus*, in early synagogue worship. Perhaps a more nuanced statement of this relationship would be even better: the centrality of belief in angelic worship in late Second Temple and early post-Temple Judaism is reflected in both communal liturgy and records

[22] Reflections of the *qedushah* pattern of worship are to be found in the New Testament in Luke 2:14 and Revelation 4. Both of these documents were presumably composed in the latter part of the first century. The Luke passage stands at the center of the very important study by D. Flusser cited in the preceding note. Flusser demonstrates (successfully, to my mind, though others demur; see E. Werner as quoted in the next note) that this verse is to be seen as an exposition of Is. 6:3, an early parallel to that found in the synagogue's *qedushah de-sidra*ʾ. It is thus also parallel to a merkavah passage and a Gnostic text we examine below. We treat the Revelation 4 passage in Chapter 7. The NT passages thus follow upon the Qumran references and the 1 Enoch and 2 Enoch passages in our attempt to reconstruct an early history of the *qedushah*. They are followed by a reference in the church's *Apostolic Constitutions* 7:33–37, where an early *ʿamidah* version is presented in the Christian context. This is the earliest association of *qedushah* with the *ʿamidah*. This passage was already discussed by K. Kohler in *HUCA* 1 (1924): 387ff. A full *qedushah* very like those of the early synagogue is found in I Clement 34. Cf. treatments by E. Werner, "Hebraisms in Prima Clementis," *H. A. Wolfson Jubilee Volume* (Jerusalem: American Academy for Jewish Research, 1985), 799ff., and Prigent in *Theologische Zeitschrift* 14 (1958): 416–29. These Jewish-Christian sources predate by more than a century the reference in *Tosefta Berakhot* 1:9 (and cf. b. *Berakhot* 21b), which may be considered the rabbinic locus classicus for the *qedushah*. This halakhic reference is followed by such aggadic passages as *Ḥullin* 91b and *Pirqey Rabbi Eliezer*, 4 (end). See S. Lieberman, *Tosefta Ki-Feshuṭah* ad loc. A chapter in Bar-Ilan's book (above, n. 19), promisingly entitled "Kedushat ha-Shem Benediction," deals with the blessing in its various versions but not with the *qedushah* itself. It is hard to see how a book purporting to cover the relationship between Jewish prayer and *hekhalot* manages to avoid this central subject.

[23] E. Werner, in "The Genesis of the *Sanctus* in Jewish and Christian Liturgies" (in his *The Sacred Bridge*, vol. 2; New York: Ktav, 1984, p. 112) agrees to the early date of the *qedushah* as liturgy but sees its origin in the Pharisaic synagogue rather than the Temple. The partly assumed argument is that in the Temple a strong Sadducee influence prevailed, and the well-known Sadducean opposition to angelology would have made recitation of the *qedushah* there less likely. This would contradict the views of J. Maier, *Vom Kultus zur Gnosis* (Salzburg: O. Müller, 1964), p. 134 and I. Gruenwald, who see the Temple as locus of *qedushah* and angelic traditions. Werner also agrees (p. 120) that the *qedushah* in the *yoṣer* predates that of the *ʿamidah*.

[24] The *qedushah* pattern, evidenced in the above-mentioned sources, seems to have existed earlier than the form of *qedushah* that quoted the particular verses. The actual quotation of Scripture in prayer is typical of rabbinic prayer in Amoraic times. It may have come about partly in response to Christian claims and usages.

[25] See Halperin's treatment of Ezek. 3:12 and its relationship to Isa. 6:3 in *Faces*, p. 44f.

of individual visionary experience, which seemed to develop hand in hand throughout the early centuries of the common era.

The presence of a daily enthronement or coronation rite in Jewish liturgy seems well attested by the passages we have quoted. This act has to do both with the role of Israel, those who accept and proclaim God's kingship in this world, and that of the angels, officiants in what is claimed to be the "original" coronation rite on the heavenly plane.[26] In the rites of both of these kingdoms, the heavenly and the earthly, a human legacy that was already of great antiquity and symbolic meaning is being preserved. Israel joins with the angels, humanity joins with the hosts of heaven, in offering a crown to the supreme God.

[26] For the prehistory of the heavenly chorus in ancient Near Eastern sources, see M. Weinfeld, "*Ha-Sifrut ha-shumerit we-Sefer Tehillim: Mavoʾ le-Meḥqar Hashwaʿati*," *Bet Mikra* 19: 2(57) (1974): 136–60 as well as some of the works of G. Widengren listed above (Chapter 1, n.2). Some say that the particular attraction of the Qumran sectarians to this sort of material was the result of their rejection of the earthly temple and its priesthood; leaving behind the defiled earthly chorus in Jerusalem, they now claimed to join into the truer and higher choir of the angels. This explanation seems rather more utilitarian than such attractions usually are. I would treat it with great caution. References to this discussion can be found in Gruenwald, "The Impact of Priestly Traditions," in *EJM*, p. 74f. and in Elior, "Mysticism, Magic, Angelology," nn. 83–85.

CHAPTER THREE

The Heavenly Coronation: Primary Texts

TO UNDERSTAND HOW this rite is seen by the ancient sources and its place within the mythic structure of early Judaism, we turn to a number of sources.[1] Some of these are from the widely known and accepted Talmudic and midrashic collections of aggadah; others are from more obscure works including lesser known midrashim as well as merkavah sources. Dating of any of these materials, or particular reports contained within them, is extremely difficult, and we will not concentrate here on trying to establish dates for particular formulations of what is a rather fluid series of mythic images. Nor shall we hesitate to use rabbinic and merkavah materials to elucidate one another. While I recognize some typological distinctions between these two sets of sources, I believe they are to be read as contiguous, and often overlapping, literary/religious traditions. It may indeed never be clear whether the authors and devotees of the merkavah sources were "rabbis," i.e., whether they were also devotees in the full sense of the norms of praxis and methods of study that were coming to define rabbinic Judaism. But they were Jews, writing in Hebrew, in the same time and place as the classics of rabbinic Judaism were created. The aggadic and merkavah traditions represent varied aspects of an ancient mythic whole, some parts of which may appear in writing (or in authorized oral source collections) as early as the fourth or fifth centuries, and in homilies that later gained great currency and canonicity,[2] while other aspects

[1] This is the place to acknowledge other scholars who have already discussed the key themes of this book. These include Asi Farber, who has written a long note in her doctoral dissertation (*The Concept of the Merkabah in Thirteenth Century Jewish Esotericism* [Jerusalem: Hebrew University: 1986], pp. 231–44) that is a gold mine of information and suggestion. I have followed up on many of her leads and would like to give her full credit for them. Moshe Idel has a section in his *Kabbalah: New Perspectives* (New Haven: Yale, 1988) that reviews this material. As always, Idel adds new texts, insights, and methodological perspectives. Meir Bar-Ilan has written on "The Idea of Crowning God in Hekhalot Mysticism and the Karaite Polemic" in *EJM*, pp. 221–34, dealing with a number of the themes that are treated here. Elliot Wolfson also has a long note containing many sources in his "Mystical-Theurgical Dimensions of Prayer in Sefer ha-Rimmon," in D. Blumenthal, ed., *Approaches to Judaism in Medieval Times*, vol. 3 (Atlanta: Scholars Press, 1988), p. 77f., n. 146. His *Through a Speculum That Shines: Vision and Imagination in Medieval Jewish Mysticism* (Princeton: Princeton University Press, 1994) contains a wealth of material related to our subject. Because it arrived late in the making of this book, I often quote Wolfson's articles rather than the book when the material reappears there. In the final chapter of this book, I deal extensively with the original synthesis of this and others of Wolfson's more recent works.

[2] The "canonicity" of Jewish sources from late antiquity, especially those in the realm of

of the same myth may not show up in textual witness until several centuries later, and then in a version replete with the lists of divine names and adjurations that suggest a "merkavah" image rather than a "rabbinic" one. The fantasies of Jews in late antiquity knew no such lines. It is the network of beliefs, images, and spiritual forms shaping these literary sources that we hope to reconstruct here, by casting our net wide, rather than by seeking to delineate the parameters of our interest too closely.[3]

We begin with a well-known passage in the Babylonian Talmud, telling us of the angel most generally associated with the heavenly coronation. The passage opens with the interpretation of a line from the first chapter of Ezekiel, the chief biblical witness to the *merkavah*, which serves as key to all rabbinic discussion of the upper world:

TEXT #1

"As I gazed on the creatures, I saw one wheel on the ground near the four-faced creatures" (1:15). Said Rabbi Eleazar: This is a certain angel who stands on the earth and whose head reaches near the *ḥayyot*.[4]

---

aggadah rather than halakhah, is quite informal, undefined, and often the result of accidents of literary history. Aggadot that happened to find their way into the pages of the Babylonian Talmud, which also served later as Jewry's normative legal guide, were better known and regarded as more authoritative by later generations than those more "obscure" sources that happened to be recorded only in the Jerusalem Talmud that was so much less studied. Status by age and association with halakhic materials was also accorded to aggadot included within the halakhic midrashim. As for *Midrash Aggadah*, passages in earlier edited collections such as *Bereshit Rabbah*, *Wa-Yiqra' Rabbah*, and *Pesiqta de-Rav Kahana* were sometimes given greater authority than materials of equal or greater age that were only included in later compilations, e.g., *Pirqey Rabbi Eliezer* or *Pesiqta Rabbati*, with others falling somewhere on a continuum between these. Of apparently lower status than all of these are the "lesser" or smaller midrashim, many (but not all!) of which are indeed quite late, and some of which remained unpublished until redeemed (and in some cases "created" as discrete text-units) by such modern scholars as Jellinek, Wertheimer, or Mussaieff. Though texts like the *Shi'ur Qomah* or *Hekhalot Rabbati* might seem to fall into this last group, their antiquity was being championed by some as early as the tenth century (see below for Sa'adya and Hai Gaon on these texts), long before many of the other "late" midrashim were compiled. Collections such as those by the three editors just mentioned contain a great variety of materials, including some that may be quite early.

[3] By reading these groups of sources in a way that makes them contiguous, I also do not mean to utterly identify the practitioners of rabbinic and merkavah religion with one another. Not all rabbis were *yordey merkavah*, by any means, nor vice versa. I believe that these were contemporary, contiguous, and to some unknown degree overlapping circles, going back to the first or second century and extending into the Gaonic period, and sharing a common mythic legacy. This last point is crucial. Many who did not *practice* merkavah techniques nevertheless shared belief in their power and the myths that underlay them, myths that do not differ in essence from those that underlie rabbinic Judaism itself, though there are some shifts of emphasis. I do not think we are capable of much closer delineation than this. On the contiguity of these circles, see Scholem, *Jewish Gnosticism* p. 9ff.; Lieberman in Gruenwald's *Apocalyptic*, p. 241–44, and Idel in "The Concept of the Torah in Heikhalot Literature and in the Kabbalah," *JSJT* 1 (1981), p. 35, commenting on a text from *Midrash Mishle* that is highly significant for this discussion.

[4] This term, the "beasts" or "living creatures" of Ezekiel's vision, will here remain untrans-

> It is taught in a Mishnah[5] that Sandalphon is his name and he is taller than his companion by five hundred years' distance. He stands behind the merkavah and binds (*QoSHeR*) crowns[6] for his Master. Indeed? But does Scripture not say, "Blessed is the glory of God from His place" (Ezek. 3:12), indicating that nobody [including the angels, who speak this verse] knows His place? Rather he recites a name over the crown and it goes and seats itself on His head.[7]

This brief text may serve as our initiation into the realm of *maʿaseh merkavah*. It is short, elliptical, and dialogic in form, as is appropriate to the style of the Babylonian Talmud where it is found. But it is puzzling in a number of ways. Who is this angel Sandalphon and what is it that he does? What does his act of "binding crowns" have to do with God's kingdom, and especially with Israel's coronation of God in their prayers? The answers to these questions are not available in this text, but certain related matters can be cleared up as we begin to seek further knowledge about the relationship of angels, Israel, and the divine crown.

The wheel of Ezekiel's vision is here recast as a giant angel, one who reaches from earth to heaven. While the origins of this specific interpretive transformation may lie in earlier readings of the verse,[8] the gigantic figure of Sandalphon cannot but recall for us other rabbinic passages concerning a giant being who reaches from earth to heaven. One of these reports is in fact recorded on the very preceding folio of b. *Ḥagigah*, in a collection of cosmogonic passages:

---

lated, along with seraphim, cherubim, and ofanim. See Halperin, *The Faces of the Chariot* (Tübingen: J.C.B. Mohr, 1988), pp. 39ff. for discussion.

[5] In fact this is technically a *baraita*, as it does not appear in our Mishnah codex.

[6] The word *keter* can refer to a crown or diadem made of either leaves or precious metal. If the crown is formed of leaves and branches, *q-sh-r* is indeed the appropriate verb. But the term has a long life and is sometimes used for obviously metal crowns as well. On the magical associations of this term, see n. 8 in Chapter 6 below. But *q-sh-r* is also used in connection with earthly crowns, where there is no magic intended. Cf. *Tosefta Soṭah* 3 and Schaefer, *Synopse* #115, Ms. M. 40. There are places where the noun *keter* is replaced by *qesher*. See Schaefer, *Synopse* #29, Ms. V. 228. This may just be a scribal error, however.

[7] b. *Ḥagigah* 13b. This passage is treated in Halperin, *Faces*, pp. 130–36. I have quoted from the standard Vilna edition, which has no significant divergences in this section from the *editio princeps*, Venice, 1520. Ms. Munich (S. Rabbinovicz, *Diqduqey Soferim* [Munich, 1869] b. *Ḥagigah* 13b) reads *gadol me-ḥaveraw* rather than *ḥavero*, which will be significant for our ensuing discussion. R. Joel Sirkis, in *Bayit Ḥadash*, instead of "he recites a name over the crown," has "he binds the crown and adjures it by the explicit name. The crown goes and is seated in its place." A similar reading is found in the *ʿEyn Yaʿaqov*. It is possible that this reading has been influenced by texts we shall see below, or it may be that *ʾamar shem* in the printed text is an attempt to obliterate *mashbiʿa*. Most interesting is a quotation of this passage in *ʿArugat ha-Bosem* 3:481, which adds that Sandalphon binds crowns "from the prayers of Israel." A similar phrase is found in Moshe Taku's account of the heavenly coronation. See his *Ketav Tamim* (ed. Dan), p. 4. Apparently such a manuscript reading was current in Ashkenaz. Of course it could well be an interpretive gloss, based on sources cited below.

[8] See Halperin, *Faces*, pp. 44ff. and 126f. on the Targum to Ezekiel and its role in this process.

TEXT #2

Rabbi Eleazar said: The first human [reached] from earth to heaven, as Scripture says: "Inquire after the first days that came before you, from the day that God created a person on the earth and from one end of the heavens to the other" (Deut. 4:32). But once he sinned, God laid His hand upon him and diminished him, as it says: "You formed me backward and frontward, and placed Your hand upon me" (Ps. 139:5).

Rav Yehudah said in the name of Rav: The first human [reached] from one end of the world to the other . . .[9]

While the attributions of rabbinic traditions to individual teachers are not to be accepted literally, it is certainly noteworthy that this claim about the giant Adam is attributed to the same Tanna, R. Eleazar ben Pedath, as is the interpretation of Ezekiel's wheel as a giant angel. It may be that the oral collection of aggadot, attached to his name by those who conveyed them to the Babylonian academies, contained both of these notions, which were brought forth for recitation by different contexts. It is tempting to wonder, however, whether in their ancient root they are not closely related to one another. The great distance[10] between "heaven" and earth can be traversed, or even filled, by a single giant being. A human was in fact supposed to be that giant but failed the initial test. Instead, the place is taken by a giant angel, the one who stands "behind the merkavah" and binds crowns for his Creator.

Sandalphon, the name of this angel, is clearly of Greek derivation. Contemporary scholars have generally accepted the earlier interpretation of it as *synadelphos*, meaning "brother," "brotherly one," etymologically parallel to the French *confrère*, or "the brother with."[11] Sandalphon is the brother-angel who takes the prayers up to God.

[9] b. *Ḥagigah* 12a. The aggadist has changed the meaning of Ps. 139:5 into a temporal one; instead of "back" and "front," *aḥor wa-qedem* now means "after as well as before [the sin] You formed me." Alexander Altmann deals with related texts in his "The Gnostic Background of the Rabbinic Adam Legends," in *JQR* n.s. 35:4 (1945): 371–91. See also C. H. Kraeling, *Anthropos and the Son of Man; A Study in the Religious Syncretism of the Hellenistic Orient* (New York: Columbia Universty Press, 1927). Following Reitzenstein and others, Kraeling assumes an Iranian origin for the *anthropos* myths that are widespread in Gnostic literature. G. Quispel, "Der Gnostische Anthropos und die jüdische Tradition," in *Eranos Jahrbuch* 22 (1953): 195–234 dismisses this view in favor of Jewish or borderline-Jewish development of the myth. There do not seem to be precise Gnostic parallels to the gigantic size of Adam and his diminishing, though I think Susan Niditsch is a bit too quick in dismissing the value of the Gnostic sources for our understanding of these Jewish speculations. See her "The Cosmic Adam: Man as Mediator in Rabbinic Literature," in *JJS* 34 (1983): 137–46. See also the remarks of M. Idel in "Enoch Is Metatron," in *EJM*, pp. 151ff. and the sources cited there. Of course the diminishing of Adam's size or the reduction of his stature from cosmic *anthropos* to mortal human is a mythic expression parallel to the tale of his moral fall.

[10] On five hundred years as a measure of great distance, see Halperin, *Faces* p. 132f., n. 14.

[11] This etymology of the name Sandalphon was first suggested by Popelauer ("Literaturblatt des Orients," *Orient* 12 (1851): 617). See the dictionaries of J. Lewy, who reads it as we do, and A. Kohut, *ʿArukh Completum*, s.v. Sandalphon, who (as was often his fashion) suggests a Persian

But to whom is he a brother? Here the interpretations diverge. Gershom Scholem understands him as a brother to "his companion," the one than whom he is so much taller. This companion would be Meṭaṭron, the chief of the angelic realms, and the one who stands—or is seated—"before the throne," as his name may indicate. The two chief angels are then seen as two brothers or companions, positioned on either side of the *merkavah*, Meṭaṭron in front of it and Sandalphon behind it. Sandalphon is taller than Meṭaṭron by five hundred years' distance, precisely the figure by which earth is distanced from heaven. His greater height is accounted for by the fact that he is the one who now has to reach from earth to heaven.[12]

David Halperin[13] offers another reading of Sandalphon's "brotherly" status. He sees him rather as a brother to his fellow humans, the friend who (as we shall see) brings their prayers to God.[14] At first reading, this view seems a bit "modern" in tone and out of place in the rabbinic/mythic worldview, where angels are hardly thought of as "brothers" to humans. If there is any "brotherhood" to be found in their relationship, it is only that of sibling rivalry.[15] But there are certain reasons to consider Halperin's reading seriously. Chief among these is the figure of Jesus in New Testament and earliest Christianity. The mythical conceptions being discussed here were the common legacy of those who created Christianity and those who formed rabbinic Judaism. We may assume that both knew legends of a giant angel, one who took the place of giant Adam after the fall. For the Christian this Gestalt is incorporated into the rich stock of symbols associated with the Christ: he is the new Adam, the one who in his person bridges the gap between earth and heaven, the one who is seated at the right side of the Father, and, very commonly, the brother of

---

etymology meaning "exalted master." Lieberman and Scholem affirm Popelauer's reading.

[12] I suggest this despite Moses Cordovero's dismissal of this reading. If Sandalphon and Meṭaṭron are paired, says the great sxiteenth-century Kabbalistic master, Meṭaṭron would have to be the taller one. *Derishot be-ʿInyeney Malʾakhim* 4:7. Cordovero is heir to a later, much-developed Meṭaṭron tradition, while Sandalphon almost disappears from later Jewish angelology. Another late source, Naphtali Bacharach's *ʿEmeq ha-Melekh* (178c; this corrects the reference in Ginzberg, *Legends*, vol. 6, p. 325 n. 40) claims that Sandalphon is to be identified with Elijah, parallel to Meṭaṭron's identity with Enoch. Thus these are indeed two brothers, the two figures who transcend the angelic/human divide. Though there are other texts that speak of Elijah's preexisting as an angel, I have not found this specific identification anywhere earlier than Bacharach, a German Kabbalist of the seventeenth century.

[13] Halperin suggests that Sandalphon needs to be this tall, reaching from earth to heaven, so that he can transmit our prayers (*Faces*, p. 133). See also his references to Sandalphon in the Targum to Ezek. 1:15 and 18 on p. 126f.

[14] Halperin is reading *ha-gadol me-ḥaveraw* instead of *me-ḥavero*. We have already noted in n. 7 above that both readings are to be found. While there is widespread witness to *ḥaveraw*, I do not believe that it is the better reading. In the pair of angels, the referent of *ḥavero* is much clearer.

[15] On angels as "sibling" rivals to humanity, see P. Schaefer, *Rivalität zwischen Englen und Menschen* (Berlin: de Gruyter, 1975) and J. Schultz, "Angelic Opposition to the Ascension of Moses and the Revelation of the Law" in *JQR* n. s. 61 (1970–71): 282–307.

suffering and unredeemed humans who has come to save them.[16] For the early rabbis, these figures did not all coalasce into a single being, and the traditions remain somewhat inchaote. But the notion of a sympathetic angelic "brother" could have pre-Christian roots. Whichever of these explanations of the "brotherly" status of Sandalphon we accept, his role as weaver of crowns or wreaths for the divine head is quite clearly stated.

But what is the relationship between this seemingly purely angelic activity and Israel's coronation of God in worship? Of what materials does the angel form his crowns, and how are they connected to our proclamation of divine kingship? To answer these questions, we shall have to seek out some additional and more amplified versions of the account that has been mentioned only so elliptically in our brief bavli text.

We turn first to a text that is included within the late midrashic collection called *Pesiqta Rabbati*. It occurs there as a digression in a homily on Moses' ascent into heaven, where he encounters the angel Sandalphon. I shall translate the printed text and supply a few interesting variants (in curved brackets) from an Oxford manuscript recently published and discussed by Karl Groezinger.

TEXT #3

They {the sages} said of Sandalphon that he is taller than his companions by five hundred years' [distance]. He serves behind the throne {the curtain} and binds crowns for his Master. But would it occur to you that the ministering angels know where He is? Has it not already been said: "Blessed is the glory of God from His place" (Ez. 3:12), {it does not say "in His place" but "from His place"} but His place [itself] they have not seen. Rather he adjures the crown {by a name}, and it goes and is seated on the head of his Lord. At the time when the crown arrives, all the upper legions quake. The creatures are silent and roar like a lion. Then they all respond and say: "Holy holy holy is YHWH of hosts; the whole earth is filled with His glory."

When it arrives at His throne, the wheels of His throne begin to turn and the feet of the footstool make a great clamor. Trembling overtakes everyone in the heaven. When He passes by all the heavenly legions and His crown (?) {in their crowns} open their mouths and say: "Blessed is the glory of YHWH from His place."

Come and see the praise and greatness of the blessed Holy One: When the crown reaches His head, He strengthens Himself to receive the crown from His servants.

All the creatures, seraphim, ofanim, chariot wheels, and the throne of glory {and all the upper and lower hosts are magnified and beautified; they all offer praise, glory,

[16] Most famous are the references in Matthew 12: 46–50 and Mark 3: 31–35, but there are many others; cf. Matt. 28: 10; Mark 10: 30, Heb. 2: 11, where the disciples are called brothers. See esp. I Cor. 8: 11, "the brother for whom Christ died." See G. Johnston, "Brotherhood," *Interpreter's Dictionary of the Bible*, vol. 1, p. 468f.

and exultation and} say in unison: "May YHWH rule forever, your God O Zion from generation to generation. Halleluyah!" (Ps. 146:10).[17]

Various aspects of this text have been discussed in great detail by other scholars, and there is no need to repeat their work here.[18] Our interest in it is specifically in what it has to teach us, beyond that which we already know from the older Talmudic source, about the angel Sandalphon and the coronation of God. A few changes of wording are first worthy of note. Rather than the Talmudic *ʾamar shem* (he pronounces a name), here we have *mashbiʿa*, "adjures." The interchangeability of these two confirms that we are dwelling in the domain of merkavah mysticism, where the adjuration of angels by the pronunciation of holy names is the chief way in which the visionary reaches his destination protected from harm. Sandalphon does not simply make mention of a divine name over the crown; he uses it in a formula of adjuration that sends the crown on to its proper destination. The crown ascending by means of this oath to "the head of his master" also serves to clarify the crown's destination, keeping us from any ambiguity that might be present in the Talmudic version. It is God, not himself, that Sandalphon is crowning.

But the major innovation of this text is the association of Sandalphon's coronation of God and the heavenly *qedushah* rite. Ezekiel 3:12 is quoted in the Talmudic version in what appears to be a purely homiletical sense; it is the verse that teaches that no one, not even the angels, knows God's place. But in this later version, we find the full group of *qedushah* refrains—Isaiah 6:3, Ezekiel 3:12, and Psalm 146:10—in what is clearly a heavenly liturgy, recited amid great exultation in response to the (daily, as we shall see) coronation of the Creator. The merkavah literature is replete with angels reciting, "Holy, holy, holy," and this midrashic passage (itself embedded in an account of Moses' ascent on high) is a part of that universe of discourse. Here it is clear that the heavenly recitation of *qedushah* and the coronation of God are one and the same event.

The penultimate sentence ("Come and see . . .") seems to be an addition to the text, and one that clearly breaks the liturgical rhythm. The phrase *maḥaziq ʿaṣmo* is difficult and calls for some further clarification.[19] This text also does

[17] *Pesiqta Rabbati* 20 (97a). Compare the Friedmann text to that found of Groezinger, mentioned in the following note. Alternative phrases from the Groezinger text are indicated by rounded brackets {}. See the extensive discussion by Halperin, *Faces*, following his source index, p. 596. Note also the interesting variants to a section of this text quoted in *ʿArugat ha-Bosem*, ed. Urbach, vol. 3, p. 535.

[18] K. Groezinger, *Ich bin der Herr, dein Gott! Eine rabbinische Homilie zum ersten Gebot* (*PesR* 20) (Frankfurt: Lang, 1976) and Halperin, *Faces*, p. 289ff. Halperin treats the printed *Pesiqta* text and the Groezinger manuscript version as two separate sources. Regarding the passage we have studied here, I do not consider that designation to be justified.

[19] For now I am trying to make the best sense possible out of this text. Presently I will prefer another reading of this phrase. But here I am translating the *hifʿil* of *H-Z-Q* to have the same meaning as the *piʿel*, as it does, for example, in Jer. 51:12 or Ezek. 30:25.

not specify the identity of the "servants" who are the true source of God's crown. Sandalphon himself is still their "binder" or "weaver," and yet it is God's "servants," in the plural, who are said to crown Him.

It is not easy to determine the specific relationship between the *Pesiqta* text and the Talmudic version we quoted first. Clearly it is significantly later than the Talmudic passage in its final editing. *Pesiqta Rabbati* is considered a rather late midrashic compilation, probably edited in the ninth century. It is therefore quite safe to assume that the editors of this aggadah knew the Talmudic passage essentially in its final form. But we would be wrong to conclude from this that the *Pesiqta* version is a late expansion of an early Talmudic theme. As David Halperin has correctly suggested,[20] this and other "late" versions of such texts offer us in writing that which must be assumed to already underlie the short Talmudic version, if it is to make any sense. The bavli, as is its way especially when dealing with esoteric matters, is brief and allusive. Though these texts were edited, and maybe even first committed to writing, at a late date, they reflect a myth that was alive and indeed highly developed already in the early centuries after the Temple's destruction.

Closely related to this pair of sources is another text, somewhat more complex both in construction and in elaboration of detail. This text, entitled *Maʿayan Ḥokhmah* (A Font of Wisdom) is included in the first printed collection of merkavah and related late midrashic sources, called *Arzey Levanon*, and printed in Venice in 1601.[21] It too exists in more than one version, but the *Arzey Levanon* text, reprinted by Adolph Jellinek in his *Bet ha-Midrash*, will suffice for our purpose:

Text #4

They said of Sandalphon that he is five hundred years' distance taller than his companion.

Of him Scripture says: "And there was a single wheel on the ground next to the creatures" (Ez. 1:15). This is Sandalphon, standing behind the *merkavah* and binding crowns for his Master.

But would it occur to you that the ministering angels know the place where the blessed Holy One is found? Does Scripture not say, "Blessed is the glory of God from His place"? Not "in His place" but "from His place," teaching that they do not know the Holy One's place. Rather Sandalphon adjures the crown by which the Holy One's place is to be crowned in *qedushot*. The crown ascends on its own and is seated on his Master's head. Immediately all the legions of heaven tremble and

[20] *Faces*, p. 307.

[21] There it immediately follows another work called both *Pirqey Hekhalot* and *Masekhet Hekhalot*. The editor of *Yalquṭ Reʾuveni*, quoting from this collection, mistakenly referred to the *Maʿayan Ḥokhmah* text as *Pirqey Hekhalot*. This accounts for the confusion noted but unexplained by Halperin in *Faces*, p. 219n.45. *Maʿayan Ḥokhmah* is in fact the introduction to the (still unpublished) text entitled *Shimushey Torah*, referring to magical uses of the biblical text.

quake. The holy angels are silent, but the holy seraphim, roaring like lions, call forth: Holy, holy, holy is YHWH of Hosts; the whole earth is filled with His glory.

This is its meaning: Holy above, holy below, holy in all the worlds (*be-khol ha-ʿolamim*), YHWH sanctified by the assembled hosts of Israel.

As soon as the crown reaches the throne, the wheels of the *merkavah* begin to turn and the feet of the footstool make a great clamor. All the heavens are seized with trembling. When the crown passes by the throne to be seated in its place, all the upper[22] hosts burst out and proclaim: "Blessed is the glory of YHWH from His place!"

Come and see the praise of the blessed Holy One. When the crown reaches His head, the Lord holds onto His head to receive the crown from His servants.

All the *ḥayyot*, seraphim, wheels of the chariot, the throne of glory, the upper hosts, the electra, the cherubim, all of them magnified and exalted, join together to proudly ascribe splendor and majesty [to God]. They all proclaim Him King, and call out in unison "YHWH is King, YHWH was King, YHWH shall be King forever!"

And this is its meaning: The Lord was King before creation, the Lord has been King since the world was created, and the Lord shall be King into the world-to-come.

Then the blessed Holy One, praise to His name, agreeing with them, proclaims, "May YHWH rule forever, your God O Zion from generation to generation, Halleluyah!"[23]

The *Pesiqta Rabbati* text is here amplified in a number of ways. Most apparent are two additional explanatory notes that have crept into the text, probably from marginal comments. Each of these begins with "This is its meaning." One explains the *qedushah* verse by reference to three realms of cosmic space, while the other explains the threefold proclamation of God's kingship by referring to the age before creation, the present era, and the future of the world-to-come. The first of these calls to mind the Targumic paraphrase of the

[22] Both *Arzey Levanon* and Jellinek, following it, read *kol ḥayyaley maqom*. I am presuming that it is *marom*, as appears in the *Pesiqta* passage. The phrase *kol ḥayyaley marom* is found in the *Haggadat Shemaʿ Yisraʾel* parallel (see next note) and also in Schaefer *Synopse* #79; its parallel *kol ṣeva marom* is very common.

[23] *Bet ha-Midrash* 1:58–61. Cf. also the shorter form of this version found in Menahem Ṣiyyuni's commentary to *parashat wa-etḥanan*, reprinted in *Bet ha-Midrash* 5:165 with the title *Haggadat Shemaʿ Yisraʾel*. This text is quoted by M. Bar-Ilan in *EJM*, p. 224. See also the interesting variant quoted from an unidentified *Midrash Maʿaseh Bereshit* in *ʿArugat ha-Bosem*, ed. Urbach, vol. 2, p. 184f. That version adds that Sandalphon's "feet reach the lowest depth, while his head is between the seraphim and the *ḥayyot*. . . ." It also says that "he binds crowns for his Master out of the prayers of Israel . . ." and tells us that "when the crown ascends and is seated on the Holy One's head . . . all the angels [above] are seized by trembling . . . and say, "Blessed be the name of His glorious kingdom forever." On the history and use of this formula, see below, Chapter 5 and nn. 17–18. The quotation in *ʿArugat ha-Bosem* reflects the same (and possibly ancient) tradition as the passage in *Devarim Rabbah* 2:36 quoted in Chapter 4, n. 19 below.

qedushah, included also in the *qedushah de-sidra* version of the daily prayer-book.[24] There the two realms of time and space are conflated: the first two repetitions of *qadosh* refer to divine realms above and below, while the third proclaims God holy "forever and ever." One expects there is some confusion here, probably engendered by the double meaning of the word *ʿolam.*

There is also in this text some finer nuancing of the particular participants in this divine liturgy and their respective roles. Note that the *ḥayyot* are silent at the first stage of the crown's ascent. It is only the seraphim who call out, "Holy, holy, holy." This is in accord with the Isaian context of the original vision, where only seraphim are described. But it may also have been influenced by a Talmudic reading[25] of the obscure term *ḥashmal* that appears in Ezekiel 1:4. Rav Yehudah reads this word as an acronym for *ḥayyot esh memalelot*, "fiery creatures that speak." To this reading an anonymous source adds a further pun on *ḥashmal*: sometimes they are silent (*ḤaSHot*) and sometimes they speak (*meMaLelot*). The Talmudic discussion continues that they are silent while God speaks and resume their talk afterward. But this image of partially silent *ḥayyot* seems to have shaped our *Maʿayan Ḥokhmah* text in its own way.[26]

Only in the second phase of the heavenly liturgy, as the crown reaches the throne, are the chariot wheels [*galgalim*] activated. Here the text is again faithful to Scripture, in this case that of Ezekiel 3:13, where the wheels [*ʾofanim*] are said to participate in the sound that accompanies the proclamation of the preceding verse. We are reminded here of the even more precise paraphrase of Ezekiel 3:13 found in our prayerbook's *qedushah de-yoṣer*, where this verse is adapted to make the calling out of "Blessed be the glory of YHWH from His place" a response by the *ʾofanim* and *ḥayyot* to the seraphim's "Holy, holy, holy." *Maʿayan Ḥokhmah* ascribes this second verse of *qedushah* to a rather ill-defined group of "all the upper hosts."

Now another stage is added to the heavenly rite. Where the *Pesiqta* text has all the "creatures" of heaven—*ḥayyot*, seraphim, *ʾofanim*, *galgalim*, and the throne—call out Ps. 146:10, the last verse of our *qedushah*, in *Maʿayan Ḥokhmah* a somewhat different combined chorus calls out the nonbiblical doxology "YHWH is King, YHWH was King, YHWH shall be King forever."[27] Then God Himself responds with the concluding verse. The liturgical purpose of this seemingly gratuitous complication is not clear,[28] but its effect is to

[24] See the discussion in Chapter 2, n. 22 above.

[25] *Ḥagigah* 13b.

[26] Translated by Halperin, *Faces*, p. 131 and referred to later in his discussion. Cf. his index, s.v. *ḥashmal*.

[27] M. Bar-Ilan appropriately refers to this as an "artificial Scripture" in "The Idea of Crowning God," p. 230n.8.

[28] I believe its genesis can be explained in the following way. The text at one point concluded before the last paragraph. Kingship was represented in this version of the *qedushah* by the non-

make for an even more striking union of the *qedushah* rite and the proclamation of divine kingship. The angelic singing of *qadosh* and *barukh* are clearly depicted in this text as the verbal accompaniments, stage by stage, to the essentially theurgic rite of divine coronation, a rite initiated by the angel Sandalphon and continued by the magical flight of the crown itself that rises and sets itself on the divine head.

The *Maʿayan Ḥokhmah* reading also helps by clarifying the phrase *maḥaziq ʿasmo* that was troubling to us in the prior versions. Here the text reads *maḥaziq* YHWH *rosho le-qabbel ha-keter*, "God holds on to His head to receive the crown." The point seems to be that the Holy One is not to be seen as a purely passive participant in the coronation rite. He rather lifts His hands to receive the crown and place it properly on His head, thus indicating His pleasure in receiving the gift that Sandalphon has prepared.

A rather surprising partial parallel to this series of texts is found in a document that lies outside the realm of what are usually considered either Jewish or Christian sources. This is a Gnostic text that was first published more than fifty years ago.[29] Its editor dates it to the second century. It would seem that this text was written in a quasi-Jewish milieu, or in one quite thoroughly influenced by Jewish (possibly Jewish-Christian) ways of thinking. Gershom Scholem and Moshe Idel have each pointed out a link between a passage in this text and an aspect of Jewish esotericism. Scholem found in it "a kind of *Shiʿur Qomah* mysticism," referring to a particular passage about the strands of hair on the divine head.[30] Idel refers to a passage in which the "Father of the universe, the Endless One, sent a crown, the names of these universes being in it" as parallel to the Jewish sources we shall see presently that speak of the divine name or names inscribed on the crown.[31] But in yet another section of that work, the following passage is to be found. It speaks of the cosmic *anthropos*, a figure well known in Gnostic literature:

---

biblical "YHWH is King, YHWH was King, YHWH shall be King forever!" This is in fact the way the *Ṣiyyuni* parallel concludes. The existence of such a *qedushah* version is also witnessed by a quotation in *ʿArugat ha-Bosem* (ed. Urbach, vol. 2, p. 184) from an unidentified earlier source: "I have seen that the *qedushah* verses are found in the prophets. Isaiah heard them saying 'Holy' and Ezekiel heard them saying 'Blessed' . . . but 'YHWH shall be King'—where do we find it said?" If the *qedushah* contained either Psalm 146:10 or Ex. 15:18, the answer to this question would have been obviously either "in a psalm of David" or "in Moses' Torah." Clearly the text is working from a *qedushah* that concluded with a nonbiblical verse, and the author finds that troubling. So did an editor or copyist of the *Maʿayan Ḥokhmah* text, I believe, and he rectified the problem *deus ex machina*, by having the divine voice chime in with an appropriate concluding verse from the Psalter.

[29] *A Coptic Gnostic Treatise Contained in the Codex Brucianus*, transcription and commentary by Charlotte A. Baynes (Cambridge: Cambridge University Press, 1933).

[30] Scholem, *Major Trends in Jewish Mysticism* (New York: Schocken, 1954), pp. 364n.72 and 365n.89.

[31] Idel, "Demut ha-ʾAdam sheme-ʿal la-Sefirot," in *Daʿat* 4 (1980): 46ff.; idem, *Kabbalah*, p. 192. See index for his several other references to that text.

> This is he: the fashioning Word who commanded all things and caused them to work. This is he: the fashioning mind in accordance with the command of God the Father. This same the Creation doth supplicate as God and as Lord and as Saviour and as one to whom all are subject. At his comeliness and beauty all are amazed. All things of the within are as a Crown upon his Head, and all of the Without are underneath his Feet, while those around him and about are those belonging to the Midst—and they bless him saying: Holy holy holy . . . that is to say, Among the living thou art the Living One, among the holies thou art the Holy One, among those who are, thou art the one who is.[32]

The Jewish or Jewish-Christian origins of this passage would be hard to dispute. It concludes with a midrash on the *qedushah* verse, one very like the passage from *Maʿayan Ḥokhmah* just quoted, and not unlike the Aramaic paraphrase found in the *qedushah de-sidra* of the prayerbook or those in the New Testament that we have mentioned. We have in this text a double wordplay on the three "holies." They are sounded forth from the three parts of being: the within, the without, and the middle (parallel to "above," "below," and "in all the worlds" in *Maʿayan Ḥokhmah*).[33] But here each *qadosh* is also given a specific meaning. Translated "back" into Hebrew, they might read something like *qodesh ha-qodashim, ḥay ha-ḥayyim,* YHWH *be-khol ha-hawayot,* a by no means impossible series of formulae for a merkavah hymn. This passage cannot but be called a midrash on the *qedushah* or *tri-shagion,* and one quite close in spirit to those found in rabbinic circles.

But if this passage is taken to be of Jewish origin, as I believe it must, we should have another look at the immediately preceding line. Here we have the great body of the *anthropos,* a figure known as the *yoṣer bereshit* in merkavah sources, which now seem closer in their imaginative thinking to the obviously "heretical" (or entirely non-Jewish) circles in which this text was written. *Yoṣer bereshit* speculation has some undefined relationship to the Sandalphon tradition (the being reaching from earth to heaven) or to related *Adam Qadmon* speculations. Those above are all a crown on his head, those below are beneath his feet, and those in the middle (Might these be humans, denizens of both the upper and the lower worlds?) all join together with them in *qedushah* praise. The prayer here does not form the crown, but the crown itself joins in song, a motif also occasionally to be found in Jewish sources.[34] If this pro-

[32] Baynes (above, n. 29), p. 91ff.

[33] A more direct parallel is in fact found in the prayerbook commentary of Naftali Hirz of Treves (*diqduqey tefillah,* p. 7) in his introduction to the morning service, where he interprets the threefold "holy" as referring to upper, middle, and lower worlds.

[34] See the passage from *ʿArugat ha-Bosem* quoted above in n. 28. The author resolves the dilemna by suggesting that this non-Scripture is sung by the crown itself and is therefore the very highest form of praise. The crown's proclamation of God's kingship, according to that source, is farther "inward" (i.e., closer to God) than either Isaiah's *qadosh* or Ezekiel's *barukh.* See also the parallel in *Sefer Maḥkim,* ed. J. Freimann (Krakow, 1909), which explains why there is no king-

posed reading of the Coptic Gnostic Text is correct, we have here additional confirmation that the stock of images we are discussing, including some association of the divine crown with the *qedushah* rite, goes back to the second century and also existed in "heretical" or syncretistic versions.[35] This means simply that Jews who were to be defined by the later course of events as "heretics" or "dualists"[36] shared with their fellow speculators who would somehow make it under the wire either as "rabbinic" or as "orthodox Christian" a faith in this divine crown and its role in the *qedushah* scene in which they all believed.

---

ship verse in the *qedushah de-yoṣer*: "The angels do not say this, but the crown, which has taken its place on our Creator's head after *qadosh* and *barukh*, says: *yimlokh*." See further *Sefer ha-Navon*, published in Dan, *ʿIyyunim*, p. 129. While these references are late, this motif of the crown singing fits perfectly with early images of other nonpersonal hypostases—the throne of glory or the sabbath day, for example—joining into the chorus of God's praise.

[35] Revelation 4 does not bring us to this conclusion, because it contains no reference to the divine crown. That is why we have not discussed it in this section but will do so below when we deal with crowned humans who appear in the heavens.

[36] On rabbinic references to Gnosticism or dualism, see A. F. Segal, *Two Powers in Heaven: Early Rabbinic Reports about Christianity and Gnosticism* (Leiden: E. J. Brill, 1977), and literature cited in his bibliography, pp. 268ff. On the phenomenon of biblical interpretation in Gnostic sources, though not on this particular text, cf. B. A. Pearson, "Biblical Exegesis in Gnostic Literature," in *Armenian and Biblical Studies*, ed. Michael E. Stone (Jerusalem: St. James, 1976), pp. 70ff.

CHAPTER FOUR

God's Crown and Israel's Prayer

WE RETURN NOW to the more "properly" Jewish sources. From all of the texts thus far quoted, it would seem that the coronation of God is an adjuration rite performed by the heavenly hosts alone. The crown woven by Sandalphon is adjured with the power of heavenly names, rises to seat itself on the divine head, and is received by God who sets it in its place. But such a view is entirely incomplete and indeed distorting. We have already seen that the rite is connected to the human, and specifically Jewish, community of worshipers. Israel's *qedushah* prayer is, at very least, an earthly repetition of that proclaimed on high. "We sanctify Your name in the world as it is sanctified in the highest heavens." The Sephardic introduction to the *qedushah* of *mussaf*, which we have already quoted, says that the crown is offered by angels and Israel joined together. The heavenly *qedushah* exists, we might say as outside readers of these literary and liturgical texts, *in order* that it might be copied on earth. "The kingdom of earth is like the kingdom of heaven."

But there is another and more basic way in which the coronation of God is said to have an earthly component. The "raw materials" of which Sandalphon fashions his crown, according to various rabbinic sources, are nothing other than the prayers of Israel.

TEXT #5

"You who hear prayer, unto You (*ʿadekha*) all flesh will come" (Ps. 63:5). Said Rabbi Phineas in the name of Rabbi Meir, and Rabbi Jeremiah in the name of Rabbi Ḥiyya bar Abba: In the hour when Israel pray, you do not find all of them praying at the same time. Each assembly (or "synagogue") prays on its own, first one and then another. When all of the assemblies have concluded their prayer, the appointed angel takes all the prayers that were said in all the assemblies and makes them into a crown that he places on the head of the blessed Holy One. Of this Scripture says, "Unto You all flesh will come." *ʿadekha* refers only to a crown, as Scripture says, "You shall don them all like jewels (*ʿadi*)" (Is. 49:18) and also "Israel in whom I am glorified" (ibid. 3).[1] The blessed Holy One is crowned with the prayers of Israel, as Scripture says: "A splendid crown upon Your head" (Ezek. 16:12).[2]

[1] We shall see below that the word *peʾer* and this Isaiah verse are directly related to the divine crown. They both have great significance in the materials we are discussing, and their appearance here is hardly coincidental.

[2] *Shemot Rabbah* 21:4; cf. two parallel versions in *Midrash Tehillim* 19:7 (ed. Buber 166f.) and 88:2 (380). The *Midrash Tehillim* version is quoted by R. Ezra of Gerona in his comment to

It is interesting to note that this text represents a rather selective use of our tradition. It seeks to present what we might call a less mythical or more purely rabbinic version of the traditions we have been discussing. The esoteric element is gone; the angel is not named here, nor is there any mention of such activity as "weaving" or "binding" the crown. There is no room in this essentially exoteric text for adjurations or the use of holy names. Hence the question of how the crown finds its way to the divine head simply does not come up. The problem of the unknowability of God's place, already clearly mentioned in the Talmudic version, was most likely known to the editor of this late midrashic compilation, *Shemot Rabbah* 2, but he chose to delete any reference to it. Nevertheless the essential myth, that of the ascent of prayer as a crown to God, is as fully present to this rabbinic source as it is to the parallels dressed in the distinctive garb of merkavah literature.

The motif of coronation is here presented in a carefully crafted mosaic of Scriptural verses. The passages from Psalms and Isaiah both use the relatively unusual word *ʿadi*, ordinarily rendered as "adornment" or "jewel." But this term is understood by the rabbis, both here and elsewhere[3] as referring to a crown, possibly because of an etymological association of the stem *ʿD* with roundness or circularity. The same term and its appearance in Exodus 33:4 is joined to an aggadah about the coronation of Israel at Mount Sinai, as we shall see below. But more closely related to our own tradition is another midrashic reading of the angels' daily glorification of God. This text appears in the much earlier midrash *Wa-Yiqraʾ Rabbah* and depicts Israel as standing on the receiving rather than the giving end of the celestial coronation rite:

Text #6

Thus each day the exalted ones [i.e., the heavenly beings, angels] wreath the blessed Holy One with three "holies," as it says: "Holy, holy, holy." What does the Holy One do? He places one upon His head and two upon the heads of Israel, as Scripture says: "Speak unto the entire congregation of the Children of Israel saying 'You shall be holy for I the Lord your God am holy. Sanctify yourselves and be holy.'" (Lev. 19:1–2)[4]

What is the homiletical basis of this text? What does the passaage in Leviticus have to do with Israel receiving God's wreath or crown? *Wa-Yiqraʾ Rabbah* points to the twice-repeated mention of Israel's holiness, corresponding to the two *qedushot* they receive from God. The text is explaining a para-

Song of Songs 3:11 (*Kitvey RaMBaN*, vol. 2, p. 494f.), an important example of the Kabbalists' appropriation of the earlier merkavah traditions.

[3] b. *Megillah* 12b, end, manuscript versions, where the word *yehudi* is associated with *ʿadi* and thence with *keter*. See *Diqduqqey Soferim*, Megillah 12b and *ʿArukh*, s.v. NMS II. This reading should be kept in mind later when we discuss the identification of Israel and the crown in both Midrashic and medieval sources.

[4] *Wa-Yiqraʾ Rabbah* 24:9; ed. Margaliot, p. 564.

ble in which the king gives a double reward to the more deserving of his servants, in this case a habitual drunk who nevertheless faithfully guards his master's wine. Israel, sinful mortals as they are, are deserving of two crowns for doing good. Apparently the repetition of "be holy" is understood as occasioning the two crowns for Israel. But the word for "congregation" used in this passage, *ʿadat*, is to be homiletically linked with *ʿadi*, the same word for "crown" that is used in these other sources. The homilist (the text is brought in the name of R. Abin) reads the opening verse of Leviticus 19 as though it said, "Speak unto the completely crowned Children of Israel."[5]

The involvement of Israel and their prayers in the heavenly *qedushah*-rite is undoubtedly quite early, even if the best textual evidence for it is often from later sources. In fact I believe this to be the very crux of the entire complex of images and ideas we are studying here. It extends the theurgic act of Sandalphon, in weaving and adjuring the crown, to Israel, their place in the world, and their own prayers. It is the community of Israel, as the liturgical sources clearly state, that offers a daily crown to God in prayer. This act, viewed from one side as a rite of submission to divine power, may also be seen from precisely the opposite point of view. Depicting themselves as the daily offerers of God's crown places Israel in a position of great mythic power, one that makes them nearly equals in the economy of divine/human powers on which the world is based.[6]

[5] This pun, at least a strengthening base for this midrash and very possibly its origin, has been noted by neither M. Margaliot nor the standard traditional commentators. The midrash is quoted by M. Bar Ilan in *EJM*, p. 233n.39, but in a way that does not help one understand it. Not only does he too miss the *ʿadat/ʿadi* pun, but he uses this midrash to demonstrate that the *qedushah* prayer was recited on three separate occasions during the day, a questionable interpretation of the passage. I originally saw no justification for that reading. *Makhtirim shalosh qedushot* seems quite adequately explained by the tripling of the word *qadosh* in the single recitation and need not refer to multiple usages of the *qedushah* in the liturgical day. It is parallel to the phrase *meshaleshim shalosh qedushot* found in the Ashkenazic supplications for each Monday and Thursday. If the meaning of this phrase also seems ambiguous, it is rendered quite clear by the parallel version in *Maḥzor Roma* (ed. Luzzatto, vol. 2f. 12a), where the reference is clearly to the tripling of the word. See however Gruenwald, *Shirat ha-Malʾakhim*, p. 472, where a reference to three daily *qedushot* seems clearly to refer to three separate recitals. Actually it turns out that both readings of *shillush qedushot* are rooted in ancient sources, as R. Judah ben Yaqar (twelfth–thirteenth century) already notes in his *Perush ha-Tefillot weha-Berakhot* (ed. S. Yerushalmi; Jerusalem: Meʾorey Yisraʾel, 1968–69), vol. 1, p. 40.

[6] From a historical point of view, it is not entirely clear to me what the relationship is between the heavenly coronation rite and the earthly role of Israel. Lawrence Schiffman has noted that in the Dead Sea Scroll material that provides the earliest Jewish evidence for a celestial liturgy no link is made between it and the earthly community of worshipers. See his remarks in *EJM*, p. 126. (Note also that on the very next page of that article he quotes sources that show close links between hosts of angels and the "elect" on earth. But those texts are not specifically connected to liturgy.) Certainly the midrashim we have just quoted want to see the heavenly and earthly liturgies as deeply linked, and so they become in the later tradition. But the absence of Israel's role from some key sources, including the early proto-*qedushah* texts—both the Talmudic/*Pesiqta*

I would suggest that the juxtaposition of these last two texts is particularly suggestive. God on the one hand receives the crown from Israel, albeit transmuted through the agency of Sandalphon. On the other hand, in the course of the angelic coronation of God, Israel themselves are blessed and are given crowns by God. Here we have a rabbinic prototype for the sort of ongoing circular exchange of sacred energy between God and Israel that will stand at the very heart of later Kabbalistic religion. The God who "desires"[7] the prayers of Israel or the righteous is in fact dependent on them for His very crown, symbol of God's cosmic authority. The rabbis knew very well, after all, that "there is no King without a people."[8] But the coronation of Israel, also renewed each day, is but an earthly effulgence of the coronation of God, an act of transcendent divine mystery.

The collective power of Israel in the coronation of God is made more explicit by the fact that it is the *communal* prayers of Jews, assembled in their synagogues, that are gathered up by the angel to form God's crown. Another version of our entire aggadah, preserved in the early medieval *Midrash Konen*, refers quite specifically to public worship:

Text #7

On the fifth day . . . He created "a single wheel on the ground" (Ezek. 1:15) whose head [reached so far as to be] parallel to the holy *ḥayyot*. He is an interpreter (*meturgeman*) between Israel and their Father in Heaven, as Scripture says, "And there was a single wheel on the ground next to the creatures." His name is Sandalphon and he binds crowns for the Master of the Glory (*baʿal ha-kavod*) out of the "holy," "blessed be He," and "Amen, may His great name be [blessed]" which Israel offer as responses in the synagogue. He adjures the crown by the explicit name and it ascends to the Lord's head (*rosh ha-ʾadon*). For this reason the sages said that anyone who misses a "holy," blessed be He," or "Amen, may His great name be blessed" causes the crown to be diminished and is liable to be banned until he will repent and bring a sacrifice before the righteous in the future that is to come.[9]

---

sources already quoted (at least in their main versions), and some merkavah texts to be seen below—is noteworthy. I tend to wonder whether we do not have two separate strands of tradition rather carefully woven together here. This possibility was already hinted at by a single word in Asi Farber's note (p. 236) to which I have referred above (Chapter 3, n. 1).

[7] b. *Yevamot* 64a; cf. A. J. Heschel, *Torah min ha-Shamayim*, vol. 1 (London: Soncino Press, 1962), p. 73n.8 and sources quoted there.

[8] This formulation, widely quoted in later Jewish sources, seems to originate with Bahya ben Asher in the thirteenth century. See Chavel's edition of Bahya's collected writings, p. 379 and n. 36. An earlier form of it, "Without an army there is no king" (*im eyn ṣava eyn melekh*), is quoted by Saʿadya (Cf. L. Ginzburg, *Geonica*, vol. 2, p. 88. I am thankful to Avi Gross for this reference), probably as an abbreviation of *Pirqey Rabbi Eliezer* 3: "If the king has no army and no camp, over what does he rule? And if there is no people praising the king, what is that king's glory?"

[9] *Midrash Konen* in Jellinek, *Bet ha-Midrasch* 2:26 and see discussion by Idel, *Kabbalah*, p. 191 and 371n.144. Idel does not mention the public character of these particular prayers. See

Anyone familiar with the synagogue service will recognize that the three prayers referred to here are those parts of the service that require a quorum in order to be recited. "Holy" here refers to the public recitation of the *qedushah* in the repetition of the *ʿAmidah* prayer; "blessed be He" refers to the calling out of that phrase during the reader's recitation of the *ʿamidah* blessings, and "Amen, may His great name be blessed" is the refrain around which the *kaddish*, in all its various versions, was composed. These prayers are collectively referred to in halakhic sources as *devarim shebi-qedushah*, or "words of holiness" that require a quorum. In fact the writer of *Midrash Konen* is using our tradition as a way of admonishing those who either come late to the service or fail to pay attention to the prayer leader, thus missing the opportunity to participate in the coronation rite. Only sacrifice, necessarily postponed until the Temple is rebuilt at the end of time, will suffice to atone for their sin.

The seemingly unusual designations for the deity as wearer of the crown in this text point to a tendency of several later sources to blur the extreme anthropomorphism of the original tradition. *Midrash Konen* is an early medieval text; the designation *baʿal ha-kavod* shows the influence of Saʿadya Gaon (882–942) and concerns raised by his philosophy, to be discussed below. *Rosh ha-ʾadon* also indicates a certain blandness; *ha-ʾadon* is not one of the usual designations for God, and thus its use here allows for some ambiguity and room for interpretation. This same hesitancy is reflected in a comment by Hai Gaon (939–1038), leader of the Babylonian academy in the century following Saʿadya. Commenting on the Sandalphon text in b. *Ḥagigah* 13a, Hai writes: "Not that there is a body or a head upon which the crown rests. Rather they worshiped in this way, binding crowns and sending them forth by the explicit name, unto that place which they were permitted. This is [a way of] worship, but the Creator of all has no image of any sort."[10] Hai seems to be taking the position that such excesses of metaphor are permissible in a devotional context but are not to be taken literally. Other later transmitters of these traditions were bothered more by the adjuration of the crown (to which we return later) than by the image of God as its wearer. Thus *Sefer ha-Ḥesheq*, a medieval Ashkenazic compilation of esoteric traditions around the figure of Meṭaṭron: "When Israel pray to the blessed Holy One with directed hearts, the angel of the presence (=Meṭaṭron) forms a crown out of their prayer. A wind comes forth and carries it to the head of the King of Kings, the blessed Holy One."[11]

---

also the treatment of this passage by Halperin, *Faces* (Tübingen: J.C.B. Mohr, 1988), p. 133f., and in Index VI, s.v. "Midrash Konen."

[10] *Oṣar ha-Geʾonim* ad loc. The reference to worship seems to be to the phrase *keter yittenu*. Hai's contemporary Hananel ben Hushiel ad loc explicitly associates the liturgical phrase *keter yittenu* with the Sandalphon text. For purpose of our later discussion, it is interesting to note that Eleazar of Worms approvingly quotes this comment of Hananel. See his *Shaʿarey ha-Sod ha-Yiḥud weha-ʾEmunah*, ed. Dan in *Ṭemirin* 1, p. 150.

[11] *Sefer ha-Ḥesheq* #67. See J. Dan, "The Seventy Names of Meṭaṭron," in *Proceedings of the*

While our original Talmudic text attributed the act of coronation to Sandalphon, an angel known almost exclusively in this context, we see here that it is associated with Meṭaṭron as well. Meṭaṭron is chief of the angelic hosts, the "angel of the presence" (*sar ha-panim*), also called Yehoel, or the one "whose name is like his master's" (meaning that his angelic name, which typically ends in -*ʾel*, is here joined to the YHW of the tetragrammaton itself). Another passage in the Meṭaṭron-centered *Sefer ha-Ḥesheq* associates this act of coronation with the chief angel's priestly function: "The angel of the presence is the high priest in heaven and he sacrifices the souls of the righteous. He waves the prayers of Israel [like a heave-offering] and he binds a crown for the blessed Holy One."[12] Here again the divine crown seems to be derived from prayers, which are accepted into heaven like a Temple sacrifice. Other sources that derive from the circles of medieval German Hasidism also associate Meṭaṭron with the coronation of God, sometimes in conjunction with Sandalphon.[13] This tradition might serve to strengthen the suggestion mentioned earlier that Sandalphon and Meṭaṭron are brothers or companions to one another, positioned on either side of the merkavah. But all of these associations of Meṭaṭron with God's coronation need to be distinguished from another large body of material, including some rather early sources, that deals with Meṭaṭron's own coronation, related to his acceptance within the heavens as an apotheosis of the human Enoch.[14]

The midrashic sources that speak of Israel's prayers serving as the "materials" of which God's crown is woven are in themselves relatively few. But they are supplemented by a much larger body of materials, from both midrashic and *hekhalot* sources, that speak of Israel's prayers taking precedence over the prayers of the angels. The latter must wait to recite their prayers, morning and evening, until Israel have completed their own devotions. We can see how closely this tradition is related to that which has the prayer-gathering

---

Eighth World Congress of Jewish Studies, vol. 3 (Jerusalem: World Congress of Jewish Studies, 1982), pp. 19–23. Dan dates the text of *Sefer ha-Ḥesheq* to the late-twelfth or early-thirteenth century, though the list of angelic names that forms its basis may be significantly earlier. Parallel lists are found in *Sefer Hekhalot* and *Otiyyot de-Rabbi ʿAqivaʾ*.

[12] *Ḥesheq* #43. Earlier sources (b. *Ḥagigah* 12b, etc.) attribute this to Michael. Origen also knows Michael as the angel of prayer (*De princ.* 1:8:1). See the treatment in Ginzberg, *Legends*, vol. 5 (Philadelphia: Jewish Publications Society), p. 71. See also *Ḥesheq* 22, interpreting *yaʿaleh*, the opening *seliḥah* of the Yom Kippur evening service: "That which we say on Yom Kippur eve, *yaʿaleh taḥanunenu me-ʿerev*, refers to the Angel of the Presence; we supplicate him to take our prayers up to heaven, to the head of the blessed Holy One." The word *yaʿaleh* is here being interpreted as a *hifʿil* (causative) form. Meṭaṭron is the weaver of the crown also in the rabbinic tradition known and opposed by the Karaite Qirqasani. See L. Nemoy, "Al-Qirqasani's Account of the Jewish Sects and Christianity," *HUCA* 7 (1930): 350f.; S. Lieberman, *Sheqiʿin* (Jerusalem: Bamberger and Wahrmann, 1939), p. 13f., and M. Bar-Ilan, in *EJM*, p. 227f.

[13] Cf. Dan, *ʿIyyunim* (Givatayim, 1975), pp. 128–29.

[14] 3 Enoch; Schaefer, *Synopse* 15–17 is the basic source. A small portion of this is quoted below.

angel also wait until the last synagogue has completed its prayers, so that they too may be included within the day's wreathing of the divine head. The angelic prayer thus delayed for the recitation of Israel's prayers is none other than the *qedushah*, the chiefmost prayer of the angels in any case, but also the one that accompanies the coronation of God, as we have seen. The heavenly hosts cannot recite their *qedushah*, which accompanies the coronation of God, until the new day's crown is woven of the prayers of Israel. Israel's prayer is either that same *qedushah*, recited first from below, or the recitation of the *shemaʿ*, Israel's own this-worldly proclamation of faith. In the latter case, another series of aggadot is invoked, one proclaiming the superiority of Israel over the angels, since God's earthly people is permitted to mention the divine name after only two prior words (*shemaʿ Yisraʾel* YHWH) while the angels have to wait until they have completed three (*qadosh qadosh qadosh* YHWH).[15] The traditions that claim the angels are silent while Israel recite their prayers further support this view.[16]

These sources serve to further underscore our sense of the complex interpenetration of divine, angelic, and human elements in the chorus of universal praise that has such a major role in this early Jewish mythic worldview.[17] In this context we should also mention the introduction to *3 Enoch*, a very distinctive text within the *hekhalot* corpus.[18] There R. Ishmael, the classic merkavah voyager, speaks as follows:

TEXT #8

But as soon as the princes of the chariot looked at me and the fiery seraphim fixed their gaze on me, I shrank back trembling and fell down, stunned by the radiant appearance of their eyes and the bright vision of their faces, until the blessed Holy One rebuked them and said, "My servants, my seraphim, my cherubim, and my ofanim, hide your eyes from Ishmael my beloved son and honored friend, so that he

[15] Cf. b. *Ḥullin* 91b and parallels in *Bet ha-Midrasch* 3:24f. and in *Seder Rabbaʾ de-Bereshit, Battey Midrashot* 1:45. The b. *Ḥullin* passage first says that Israel can mention the name after only two words, quoting the *shemaʿ*, but then it goes on to say that the angels recite their "song" above only after Israel has done so below. This seems to refer to Israel's recitation of the *qedushah*; recitation of the *shemaʿ* is not referred to as *shirah*.

[16] Cf. sources quoted by Halperin, *Faces*, p. 399.

[17] The view of the universe as a chorus of unceasing praise to God is also the basis of *Pereq Shirah*, a documentary tradition that ascribes a verse of biblical praise to each of the natural forces, plants, and animals. This tradition is closely linked to the merkavah literature. See the dissertation of M. Beit-Arie (Jerusalem: Hebrew University, 1967), containing a full discussion of this material, its origins, dating, etc.

[18] *3 Enoch* or *Sefer Hekhalot* was first published by H. Odeberg in Cambridge, 1928. The edition has been reprinted with an introduction by J. Greenfield in New York, 1973. The entire text in now included in Schaefer's *Synopse*. A new translation by P. Alexander is found in J. H. Charlesworth's *The Old Testament Pseudepigrapha*, vol. 1 (New York: Doubleday, 1983), pp. 223–53. Alexander's introduction there summarizes the history of scholarly treatments. He dates the text between the fifth and tenth centuries, tentatively suggesting fifth–sixth century as most likely.

> does not shrink and tremble so." At once Meṭaṭron, Prince of the Divine Presence, came and revived me and raised me to my feet, but I still had not strength enough to sing a hymn before the glorious throne of the glorious King, the mightiest of kings, the most splendid of potentates, until an hour had passed. But after an hour the blessed Holy One opened to me the gates of Shekhinah, gates of peace, gates of wisdom, gates of strength, gates of might, gates of speech, gates of song, gates of sanctifying praise, gates of chant. He enlightened my eyes and my heart to utter psalm, praise, jubilation, thanksgiving, song, glory, majesty, laud, and strength. And when I opened my mouth and sang praises before the throne of glory, the holy creatures below the throne of glory and above the throne responded after me, saying, "Holy, holy, holy" and "Blessed be the glory of YHWH from His place."[19]

How far such a passage seems from the once widely accepted scholarly characterization of merkavah mysticism that proclaimed, "The mystic who in his ecstasy has passed through all the gates, braved all the dangers, now stands before the throne; he sees and hears—but that is all."[20] The voyager here has for the moment, at least, become conductor of the cosmic symphony, prayer-leader of the angelic hosts in their *qedushah*-proclamation of God's holiness. One could hardly imagine a more fully participatory and engaged description of the mystic's own transformation as he finds his cosmic role.[21] Here too we see the complex ways in which divine and human prayer meet, to which we have alluded earlier. The voyager does indeed want to learn the prayers of the angels in order to repeat them here on earth. But those very angelic offerings to God themselves have an earthly component. The *qedushah* chorus of the angels cannot be recited until Israel have said their prayers, the crown offered to God in the midst of this chorus is itself made up of prayers from below, and here the earthly voyager into heaven breaks down the barriers between human and angelic song by himself serving as prayer leader for the angelic rites. All of this points to a deep mutual *interpenetration* of the upper and lower realms as the true intent of the merkavah prayer texts. The human is both giver and receiver in this interchange with the upper world.

At least insofar as Israel's role is concerned, the coronation of God seems to

[19] Here and in several places below, I have followed almost completely Philip Alexander's most felicitous translation, to which I have referred in the preceding note. I have allowed myself minor changes in terminology and spelling, so as to avoid inconsistencies.

[20] Scholem, *Major Trends in Jewish Mysticism* (New York: Schocken, 1941), p. 56. See Elliot Wolfson's thorough rejection of Scholem's characterization in *Through a Speculum That Shines: Vision and Imagination in Medieval Jewish Mysticism* (Princeton: Prnceton University Press, 1994), 83f. On this matter my position fully accords with that of Wolfson and Idel. The ultimate goal of the merkavah experience is transformative and "deifying," at least in some of the sources. Merkavah practice thus is, in the most precise sense, truly mystical. Of course the connection between that praxis and the literary expressions that have come down to us remains problematic.

[21] True, the following passage refers to the angels' disputing Ishmael's right to have gazed on the merkavah and not his audacity in conducting the chorus. Seeing or gazing is certainly a very high value in these texts; no reader could dispute that.

be a wholly verbal act.[22] The crown offered to God is made up of words, the words of prescribed prayers, energized, to be sure, by the inner direction of the heart. Vital to this tradition is a certain supraliteralism regarding prayer's "ascent," as though the words themselves actually penetrated the upper gates and entered the heavens, passing into the hands of the proper angel. If they are then "woven" or "tied" into wreaths or crowns, the words would seem to be depicted as quasi-material "objects" that could be linked in such a manner. Here it is important to recall that liturgical prayer remains, for the rabbis, an only partially adequate replacement for Temple sacrifice, the smoke of which was seen as quite literally wafting into the heavens, providing a sweet savor (*reaḥ niḥoaḥ*) that brought pleasure and appeasement (*naḥat ruaḥ*) to the Lord. The Psalter already describes prayer in aromatic terms: "May my prayer stand as incense before You" (Ps. 141:2). An early Jewish-Christian source, belonging to the generation immediately following the Temple's destruction, paraphrases a key prophetic passage on the universality of worship. The prophet Malachai, castigating Israelites who thought that they alone worshiped God, said "everywhere offerings and incense are sent to Me." Now this verse is paraphrased to say that "in every region of the whole earth *the incense of prayer and supplication* is sent up to You."[23] Rabbinic and later Jewish prayers often address the question of verbal worship and its adequacy as a replacement for the sacrificial gift. The ascent of prayer and its placement as a wreath on God's head may itself be a partially unconscious reflex of most ancient associations with the sacrificial smoke that rises to heaven and wreaths itself over the divine throne.[24] Literalist readings of prayer's ascent have a long history in Judaism, as we shall yet see in our further discussion.

22 I am indebted to Asi Farber for this formulation.

23 *Apostolic Constitutions* 7:33, paraphrasing *Malachi* 1:11. Emphasis mine.

24 In an early midrashic interpretation of the ladder in Jacob's dream, R. Eleazar ha-Kappar reads "and its head reached heaven" (Gen. 28:12) to refer to "the sacrifices offered [in the Temple], the smoke of which rises to heaven." *Sifre Be-Midbar* 119, ed. Horovitz, p. 143.

CHAPTER FIVE

The Name on the Crown

BUT CORONATION BY MEANS of the spoken word becomes caught up with another aspect of the description of God's crown in this literature. A great many sources speak of a name of God or another phrase "engraved" or "inscribed" on the crown. Sometimes it seems that the crown itself is altogether made up of words.[1] This association goes back to a very early linking of "name" and "crown," one possibly evidenced as early as the Mishnah. In *Avot* 1:13 Hillel is quoted as saying, "He who uses the crown will pass away," the meaning of which seems somewhat obscure. *Avot de-Rabbi Nathan*, the standard Amoraic commentary to *Avot*, understands him to be speaking of improper use of the divine name. But how does *taga*, a common Aramaic term for "crown," come to be associated with the divine name? An unspoken association is here presupposed,[2] seemingly by the Mishnah passage itself. An early merkavah text

[1] In some cases the precise relationship between "name" and "crown" is unclear. See for example 3 Enoch, Schaefer, *Synopse* #71, where the Holy One's names "go forth in many crowns of fire, in many crowns of flame," etc. There are also destructive letters, "standing parallel to the blessed Holy One's crown," that will come down to burn up the world if one makes improper use of the letters of God's name. See Schaefer, *Synopse* #841, Ms. Oxford 1531. The sword of which the magical work *Ḥarba de-Moshe* speaks is a verbal sword. Apparently the word *ḥerev* (sword) itself in these sources sometimes is to be translated as "magical formula." See *Hekhalot Zuṭarti*, p. 22, line 28, and R. Elior's comments in the notes on p. 62 of her edition. (See below for the relationship of "crowns" and "swords" that Israel receive at Sinai.) See Gaster, *Ḥarba de-Moshe* (London: D. Nutt, 1896), Hebrew text, p. 22.

[2] G. Scholem, *Jewish Gnosticism, Merkabah Mysticism, and Talmudic Tradition* (New York: Jewish Theological Seminary, 1960), p. 54nn.34 and 36. Cf. *Avot de-Rabbi Nathan*, ed. Schechter, p. 56. Cf. also the association of name and crown in Schaefer, *Synopse* #552, ms. Munich 22: *le-hishtammesh be-khitro ule-hazkir shemo*. See also the unusual wording in *Synopse* #71. Moshe Idel has found evidence of a similar terminological association of crown with name in the same anonymous Gnostic text that we have just quoted. See his *Kabbalah*, p. 192. I do not think any of the sources we have quite warrants I. Chernus's assertion (*Mysticism in Rabbinic Judaism*, p. 10) that keter is a name for God. The Samaritan *Memar Marqa* (fourth century) also has Moses crowned with the divine name. See the sources quoted by W. Meeks, *The Prophet-King: Moses Traditions and the Johanine Christology* (Leiden: E. J. Brill, 1967), p. 235. The coronation of Moses and Israel is discussed below in Chapter 8.

Keter and the divine name will be identified later in Kabbalah as well, but there the nature of the identification is somewhat different It is also important to note a structural parallel between these two symbols. If the world that proceeds from God is depicted in anthropic terms, the crown would be the "highest" or first form outside the One; it is the very "top" of the *anthropos*, the highest realm of existence outside the hidden self of the Godhead. But if that same universe is seen as a hierarchy or pyramid of language, the divine name would take that same first place; the highest or first of all verbal expressions can be naught else but the name of God.

depicts the Holy One seated in the midst of His glory, "on His forehead the crown of the explicit name (*keter shem ha-meforash*), composed of fire and hail, and on His head a crown of glory (*ʿateret hod*)."[3] Exactly what *keter shem ha-meforash* means is not clear, but it surely reflects this ancient linkage of crown and name. Does God wear a crown that has the tetragrammaton inscribed on it? Or is the crown identical with the divine name in some more abstract sense? Certainly it is tempting to see God bedecked here like a heavenly high priest (or is it the priest whose headgear imitates that of God?), wearing a *keter* or *ṣiṣ*, a kind of headband, inscribed with a holy name around His forehead, surmounted by an *ʿatarah* (called *miṣnefet* in the priest's case), probably a turban, that rises above it.[4] Such descriptions of the crown or crowns inscribed with the holy name abound in merkavah literature.

The association of crown and holy name is widespread in esoteric sources both early and late and frequently involves divine names considerably more elaborate than the tetragrammaton. We will later find associations with the forty-two-letter name,[5] the seventy-two-letter name,[6] and with God's seventy names in the seventy languages of humanity.[7] According to some sources, the name is inscribed directly on the divine forehead, without the apparent need for a crown at all. But this too is merely a variant of the crown/name tradition.[8]

Let us summarize. The prayers of Israel rise up to heaven and come into the hands of an angel who functions as priest. He weaves these prayers together into a wreath, a crown, a single name, or a garland of names, and causes them to be placed on the divine head. This process seems interestingly parallel to the one that Scripture attributes to the earthly priests who bless Israel: "They shall place My name upon the Children of Israel, and I will bless them" (Num. 6:27). Blessing comes about through the presence of the name, and the almost physical placing of the name upon the one to be blessed.[9] In God's case too,

[3] *Hekhalot Zuṭarti*, line 274; ed. Elior, p. 30.

[4] See Schaefer, *Synopse* #697, ms. Oxford 1531. For a late midrashic version of this same formula, see *Pirqey Rabbi Eliezer* 4: "A crown (*ʿaṭarah*) is placed on His head and a diadem (*keter*) with the tetragrammaton on His forehead."

[5] See the anonymous "Commentary on the Forty-Two Letter Name," included in Eleazar of Worms's *Sefer ha-Ḥokhmah*, quoted by Dan in *Torat ha-Sod*, p. 120. On this name cf. L. Schiffman, "A Forty-Two Letter Divine Name in the Aramaic Magic Bowls," *Bulletin of the Institute of Jewish Studies* 1 (1973): 97–102. It is mentioned in b. *Qiddushin* 71a as well as other later rabbinic sources.

[6] Schaefer, *Synopse* #949; cf. also #698. On the seventy-two-letter name, see A. Hoffer in *Ha-Ṣofeh* 2 (1912): 127ff. On both of these names, see also Trachtenberg, *Jewish Magic and Superstition* (New York: Behrman's Jewish Book House, 1939), pp. 93ff. and sources quoted there.

[7] Schaefer, *Synopse* #46, Ms. V228. This may be related to the reconstruction of a lost passage we have suggested from a reading in *ʿArugat ha-Bosem*. See below, chapter 12, n. 35.

[8] Schaefer, *Synopse* #949.

[9] Jacob Milgrom comments on Num. 6:27 (*JPS Commentary* [Philadelphia: Jewish Publication Society, 1989], p. 52) that the "placing" of the name could be quite physical, as in the form of

that which is given to Him as a gift from below, offered in the form of words, turns out to be a crown of the holy name itself, a crown that He helps to place firmly on His head. But how does the crown of prayers become the crown that is the name? Is it the angel who takes the "lesser" human words and transforms them into the name of God? Or might our chain of associations be pointing to something else, an esoteric form of worship lost to (or even intentionally hidden by) the later transmitters of this material, in which the community of worshipers actually pronounced the name (or names) of God in prayer?

We know that God's name is pronounced by the angels. In fact the pronouncement of the explicit name and various esoteric elaborations of it seems to form the very heart of the heavenly prayer service as described in the old merkavah texts. There the recitation of the name is linked directly to the heavenly *qedushah* chorus.[10] When it comes to earthly mention of the divine name in prayer, however, we seem to run into a halakhic problem. According to the rabbis it was forbidden to mention God's explicit name in prayer outside the Temple.[11] This applied even to the priestly blessing, where the verse just quoted might indicate some special license for use of God's name, and where such a usage certainly would have lent the blessing an extra measure of solemnity and power.

But not all rabbis agreed with this ban. A debate is recorded between two second-century figures, R. Jonathan and R. Josaiah, on this question.[12] Josaiah, if we accept Louis Finkelstein's reading, believed that the name might still be mentioned after the destruction and outside Temple precincts. The attribution of such a view to a well-known Tannaitic authority who lived in the second century may indicate that there were groups, even later, in which recitation of the name was permitted within certain ritual contexts. The Talmud finds precedent for use of the divine name in extraordinary situations, even

---

an amulet, or it could be meant metaphorically. Something midway between the two seems to be happening here with regard to Israel's giving the holy names to God. The placing of the crown is quite "physical" as an image, though it of course does not happen in a literally physical sense. The reciting of liturgy, especially if it includes holy names, is more than metaphoric coronation; it is a *real* act, even an ultimately real one as far as the worshiper is concerned. We would call it symbolic, but only in a far-reaching use of that term.

[10] Cf. Schaefer, *Synopse* #168, 390, 590; #961, Ms. M40. Discussed by Farber, *The Concept of the Merkabah*, doctoral dissertation (Jerusalem: Hebrew University, 1986), pp. 231–44n.40.

[11] *Tosefta Soṭah* 13:8 says the avoidance of mentioning the name in the priestly blessing (outside the Temple?) began after the time of Simeon the Righteous, while others say it continued to be used until the destruction. See discussion by S. Lieberman, *Tosefta Ki-Feshuṭah* on *Tosefta Soṭah* 13:8, including consideration of the identity of this Simeon ha-Ṣaddiq. Cf. *Sifre Be-Midbar* 39 and parallel in *Sifre Zuṭa* ad loc. (*Naso*' 27); *Sifre Devarim* 62; b. *Soṭah* 38a; b. *Qiddushin* 71a. Cf. also *Tosefta Yadayim* 2:5, clearly referring to a "real" mention of the name, but possibly in Temple times. On the ban on pronouncing the name outside the Temple, see also Philo, *2 Moses*, p. 114. Philo's mention would seem to confirm the view that the ban was earlier. See discussion by G. Alon in *Tarbiẓ* 21 (1950): 34ff.

[12] See Finkelstein on *Sifre Devarim*, p. 129, proposing an emendation to *Sifre Be-Midbar* 39.

outside the Temple, in the prayer of Ezra (Neh. 8:6).[13] Other passages within the rabbinic discussions of prayer even in their own day seem to indicate quite clearly that they are discussing a situation where the name of God is mentioned.

TEXT #9

Whence is it derived that the ministering angels do not mention (*mazkirim*) the name of the blessed Holy One from above until Israel make mention (*yazkiru*) from below? Since it says: "Hear O Israel YHWH our God, YHWH is One" (Deut. 6:4) and also "When the morning stars rejoiced together," followed by "Then all the sons of God raised a shout" (Job 38:7). "The morning stars" refers to Israel, who are likened to stars, as in "I will surely multiply your seed like the stars of heaven" (Gen. 22:17). "Then all the sons of God raised a shout"—these are the ministering angels, as Scripture says, "All the sons of God came to stand before YHWH" (Job 1:6).[14]

The use of the same term to refer here to both human and angelic mention of God's name in the context of worship makes it hard to imagine that the human *azkarah* is anything less than what this word means in connection with the angels and what it would mean in so many other contexts as well: actual pronunciation of the four-letter name of God. We should further note that the liturgy recited in the synagogue to this day, in introducing the morning Psalm-cycle, still says explicitly that "we will mention Your name and proclaim You King," even though we do not go on to recite the explicit name in prayer. That introductory blessing, called by its opening words *Barukh she-ʾamar*, in fact overlaps considerably with prayer-formulae found in the *hekhalot* literature.[15] Those sources make frequent reference to the mentioning of God's name, often followed by long series of esoteric and incomprehensible phrases, sometimes featuring permutations of the tetragrammaton among them.[16]

The confluence of these associations leads me to suspect that there existed in early post-Temple times an esoteric form of worship, practiced among those circles who sought out visions of the merkavah, in which the name of God was in fact pronounced.[17] This might have occurred in the recitation of the *shemaʿ*,

[13] b. *Yomaʾ* 69b. See the discussion of this passage by R. Hai Gaon in *ʾOṣar ha-Geʾonim, Ḥagigah, teshuvot*, p. 22f.

[14] *Sifre Devarim* 306; ed. Finkelstein p. 343. This is a parallel to *Bereshit Rabbah* 65:21, much discussed by D. Halperin, and is discussed below.

[15] On *barukh she-ʾamar*, cf. Elbogen and Heinemann, *Ha-Tefillah be-Yisraʾel* (Tel Aviv: Dvir, 1972), p. 65f. and sources quoted in n. 4 on p. 404; Heinemann, *ʿIyyuney Tefillah* (Jerusalem: Magnes, 1983), p. 112f.; Bar-Ilan, *The Mysteries of Jewish Prayer and Hekhalot* (Ramat Gan: Bar Ilan University, 1987), pp. 100ff.

[16] See Scholem, *Jewish Gnosticism*, p. 108 for one of a great many examples.

[17] A late reflex of this tradition is found in *Sefer ha-Bahir* #111, a section that in its language reflects a combination of earlier midrashic and *hekhalot* sources:

What is the meaning of "YHWH is King, YHWH was King, YHWH shall be King forever!" [See above, chapter 3, n. 28]. This is the explicit name, which it is permitted to recombine and mention (*le-ṣaref ule-hazkir*). Thus Scripture says, "They will place My name upon the Chil-

depicted in the Mishnah as a central pillar of Israel's worship. The *shemaʿ* serves, as we have seen, as Israel's prayer that takes precedence over the angels' *qedushah*. Pronunciation of the tetragrammaton in the *shemaʿ* would explain the otherwise surprising presence of the whispered formula "Blessed be the name of His glorious kingdom forever!" that immediately follows the *shemaʿ* in traditional Jewish worship. This formula, as it is known from Mishnaic sources, was spoken by the Israelites in the Temple courtyards when they heard the priest recite the name of God on the Day of Atonement. Its presence in the liturgy following the opening verse of the *shemaʿ* is a puzzle that has been explained in extraordinarily complicated and esoteric ways by a long series of modern studies.[18] But perhaps there is a rather simple explanation for

---

> dren of Israel and I will bless them." [Num. 6:27; see above, n. 9] This is the name of twelve letters, [contained] within the name of the priestly blessing . . . whoever guards it (*ha-shomero*; probably to be emended to *ha-ʾomero*, "whoever pronounces it") and mentions it (*mazkiro*) in holiness and purity will have all his prayers accepted. Not only that, but he will be beloved above and beloved below, a delight above and a delight below. He will receive a response and be aided forthwith. This is the holy name written on Aaron's forehead.

This text must be compared to b. *Qiddushin* 71a, to which it stands as an esoteric countertext. This problem deserves consideration in its own right, and this is not the place. But clearly in the circles represented by this passage, there was no taboo on reciting the name. The problem is chiefly one of identifying and dating those circles as well as determining their relationship to the rather more cautious editors of the b. *Qiddushin* passage.

[18] On the antiquity of this usage, see y. *Pesaḥim* 31b, commenting on M. *Pesaḥim* 4:8. The classic legendary explanation of the whisper of *barukh shem* is found in b. *Pesaḥim* 56a. The key studies are those by L. Blau in *REJ* 31 (1895): 186–88, M. Liber, "La Récitation du schema et des Bénédictions," *REJ* 58 (1909): 18–22, and V. Aptowitzer in *MGWJ* 73 (1929): 93–118. Cf. also Elbogen, *Ha-Tefillah*, p. 386n.19 as well as the debate between Elbogen and Blau in the pages of *REJ* 55 and 56 (1908). More recently see J. Heinemann, *Prayer in the Period of the Tannaʾim and the Amoraʾim* (Jerusalem: Magnes, 1966) pp. 84ff. Cf. also the article by Norman Lamm in *Sefer Yovel li-Khevod . . . Yosef Dov ha-Levi Soloveichik* (Jerusalem/New York: Mossad ha-Rav Kook, 1984) p. 320ff. (h.), reprinted in his *Halakhot we-Halikhot* (Jerusalem: Mossad ha-Rav Kook, 1990). Lamm ignores the entire earlier discussion but offers some interesting views. M. *Yoma* (3:8; 4:1) tells us that *barukh shem* was said after *widdui* on Yom Kippur, following the pronunciation of the divine name in the confessional's *anaʾ ha-shem*; it is still used this way in the synagogue's *ʿavodah* service. B. *Yomaʾ* 37a says it was used in response to *azkarot* in the Temple. According to b. *Taʿanit* 16b, the people answered amen after each *berakhah* by *ḥazzan ha-kenesset*, but in the Temple they said *barukh shem* instead of amen (presumably because in the Temple the divine name was pronounced in these blessings.) *Taʿanit* there offers the verse Neh. 9:5 to explain the difference between prayers in the Temple and elsewhere; Neh. 9:5 includes the phrase *vi-yevarekhu shem kevodekha* (and they will bless Your holy name). That is precisely what *barukh shem* is: a blessing on God's holy name, recited when one hears the name pronounced, but replaced by amen when the name is not pronounced. Lamm (p. 327) interprets the use of this verse differently, but I think he has missed the point. Outside its usage following the *shemaʿ*, the *barukh shem* formula is found *only* in response to pronunciation of the divine name. It is still used in precisely this way as a conclusion to the late prayer *anaʾ be-koaḥ*, which is a verbalization of the ancient forty-two-letter name of God. On *anaʾ be-koaḥ* see S. Tal in *Sinai* 92 (1982–83): 287f. The article by Y. Urbach in that same volume, which explains *barukh shem* by means of *Gematria*, is not one I am capable of taking seriously.

this custom. Its placement after the *shema*ᶜ may bear witness to a practice among some circles of Jews to recite the name aloud at this crucial moment in the prayers, at a time and place when this was no longer done elsewhere in the liturgy.[19]

The name might also have been recited in the *qedushah* formula itself, which in later Jewish prayer is recited standing during the reader's repetition of the ᶜ*amidah* and where the worshiper claims to be participating in, rather than observing, the angelic liturgy. In this *qedushah*, or some esoteric version of it, the circle of elite worshipers below now directly imitate the language of the angels, offering to God the pronounced name that itself will become the verbal wreath with which God is to be crowned in the highest heavens. But here our claim goes beyond speculation. The practice of reciting the divine name in this liturgical context is evidenced by a very well known source, but one generally overlooked in this context. I refer to the famous responsum of R. Hai Gaon with regard to mystical and esoteric practices. In the context of a lengthy discussion of the name and its uses, he says: "All our rabbis and ancestors forbid mentioning the explicit name in Babylonia. But when it is

---

Of course it is possible that *barukh shem* in the *shema*ᶜ does indeed reflect a response to pronunciation of the name, but a pronunciation that took place only in Temple times. The name was replaced by ʾ*adonai* after the destruction, but the *barukh shem* refrain was in this case preserved. That seems to have been the view of Ludwig Blau (*REJ*, as quoted above). But this would not explain why *barukh shem* remained only here, since the recitation of God's name in the Temple was not limited to the *shema*ᶜ.

For some further halakhic sources on the recitation of *barukh shem*, see Carmi Horowitz in *JSJT* 5 (1986): 125n.46. Horowitz is not interested there in the historic origins of the practice.

[19] Here we should note an interesting alternative tradition on the origin of this phrase:

> When Moses went up into heaven, he heard the ministering angels saying to the blessed Holy One: "Blessed be the name of His glorious kingdom forever." He brought it down to Israel. Why do Israel not say it right out in the open? Said Rabbi Yosi: "To what may this be compared? To one who stole jewelry from the king's palace. He gave it to his wife but said to her: 'Do not wear it in public, but only inside your house.' But on Yom Kippur, when they are as pure as the ministering angels, they say right out loud: 'Blessed is the name of His glorious kingdom forever.'" *Devarim Rabbah* 2:36

This tradition associates *barukh shem* with the angelic worship, perhaps reflecting that its original use in post-Temple times was in circles of merkavah-related prayer. Cf. *Aggadat Shir ha-Shirim*, ed. Schechter, line 220. The midrashic sources here may be quite late, but if Flusser is right in his interpretation of the passage in *1 Enoch*, to which we referred above in Chapter Two, n.21, what we have here is a late midrashic preservation of an extremely early tradition! This reading makes this doxology one of the several esoteric gifts that Moses received and "took captive," discussed below in Chapter 8.

The name seems to have been used, under some unspecified circumstances, also in the call to worship (*barekhu*). See the discussion in *Mekhilta Pisḥa* 16 (Horovitz/Rabin p. 61) and *Sifre Devarim* 306. This too seems to be a discussion referring to prayer services after the destruction of the Temple, as was already noted by A. Büchler, *Types of Jewish-Palestinian Piety* (London: Jews' College, 1922), p. 226f.

mentioned, it is only done in a transformed manner,[20] since it is transformed in its reading and pronunciation. This [transformed name] is passed on [esoterically] from one to another. It is recited only in *qedushah* and in times of trouble, but not at any [other] times."[21] This very important text tells us first that pronunciation of the name in Babylonia, where R. Hai lived, was universally frowned upon by the legal authorities. But he then makes it clear that a circumvention had been found to deal with this opposition. The *eʿeteq*, whatever it was, allowed for a sort of pronunciation, one that could still be considered *hazkarat ha-shem*. Liturgically one dared to engage in this practice only at this dramatic highpoint. The fact that it was used only in these two situations—the recitation of *qedushah* and "times of trouble," in other words, in emergencies—shows the great efficacy attributed to mentioning the name and confirms the associations in this study between the *qedushah* as liturgical event and the magical tradition of divine names and their "use." The divine name—and perhaps in many forms—was mentioned in worship, and this recital of the name was seen as an apex of the prayer experience. Originating as early as the time when the Second Temple still stood, this practice was still in force at least within esoteric circles in Babylonia in the time of R. Hai Gaon, nearly a millennium later.[22]

[20] The Aramaism אעתק is quite obscure. I take it to refer to some system of letter substitution, either a reversal or a code of some other sort.

[21] Quoted in *Oṣar ha-Geʾonim, Ḥagigah, teshuvot* p. 22f. Cf. I. Gruenwald's discussion of this passage, in a different context, in his "*Ha-Ketav, Ha-Mikhtav, weha-Shem Ha-Meforash*," in *Massuʾot: Studies in Kabbalistic Literature and Jewish Philosophy in Memory of Prof. Ephraim Gottlieb* (Jerusalem: Bialik Institute, 1994), p. 87.

[22] See the suggestion of I. Gruenwald ("Shirat ha-Malʾakhim," *Peraqim be-Toledot Yerushalayim bi-Yemey Bayyit Sheni* [Jerusalem: Ben Zvi, 1981], p. 474f.) and P. Alexander ("Prayer in the Heikhalot Literature," in *Prière, Mystique et Judaïsme*, ed. R. Goetschel [Paris: Presses Universitaires de France, 1984], pp. 43–64) that the *yordey merkavah* had their own liturgical rules, differing from those of the rest of the rabbinic community in Ereṣ Yisraʾel. Gruenwald specifically suggests that the mystics recited the *qedushah* each day, while other Jews did so only on the Sabbath. This *qedushah* was probably the setting for the use of the tetragrammaton; the same need that would have led them to the daily *qedushah* also would have made them want to say it with the *shem*, as do the angels. Such a practice in early merkavah circles would fit with Gruenwald's theory that sees a certain continuity between priestly, and especially unofficial priestly, esotericism in the second Temple period and the emergence of merkavah practices within early Tannaitic circles after the destruction. If Gruenwald is right in his claim that such practice had to do with the assertion of the new group's leadership claim, the continued pronunciation of the four-letter name in esoteric prayer-circles might have been an assertion of esoteric "priesthood" in the heavenly Temple by its practitioners. See his discussion in *EJM*, pp. 86f., 96ff. The text quoted in note 19 above, though found only in late sources, is also an interesting attribution of what was clearly a Temple tradition to an esoteric realm. Alexander's view of prayer is considerably more radical than Gruenwald's. He sees the merkavah texts themselves as comprising a liturgy, one that was used by both individuals and conventicles of mystics, and standing in contradistinction to the rabbinic liturgy. This view is in keeping with Schaefer, Halperin, and others who see the merkavah texts as reflecting a group that was quite tangential to the rabbinic community.

CHAPTER SIX

Crowns, *Tefillin*, and Magic Seals

AT LEAST TWO OTHER TRADITIONS exist as to the inscription on God's holy crown. One says that it is the letters of the Hebrew alphabet that adorn the crown.[1] This view calls to mind the opening of *Sefer Yeṣirah*, a work that sees the twenty-two letters of the Hebrew alphabet and the ten primal numbers as the essential building blocks of the cosmos. The alphabet retains great theurgic power even after Creation, and knowledge of its secrets can give that power to humans.[2] One is reminded immediately of the aggadah about

[1] *Otiyyot de-Rabbi ʿAkivaʾ*, version 2, in Wertheimer, *Battey Midrashot*, vol. 2, p. 396. In 3 Enoch 13 (Schaefer, *Synopse* #16) the letters of the alphabet are inscribed on the crown of Meṭaṭron. The sword given to Moses, according to the magical *Ḥarba de-Moshe* (see above, Chapter 5, n. 1), is inscribed with the "twenty-four letters that are on the crown" (ed. Gaster, Hebrew text, p. 3, line 8). Twenty-four letters comprise the Greek rather than the Hebrew alphabet. Could this text have it that God's crown is inscribed in Greek? Here we need to compare the Hebrew source to a passage in Marcus the Gnostic, as Gaster did a century ago. See the reference to his work by K. Groezinger in *EJM*, p. 64n. 12. Cf. also Groezinger's interesting comment (p. 54) that letters may themselves be a form of name. His comments, with which I am in general agreement, also have to be read in conjunction with rabbinic views on the divine name and its pronunciation and writing. Two of many may be briefly mentioned here. One is the warning of either Ishmael or Akiva to the scribe that he take special care in his work, "for if you add or detract a single letter, you will destroy the entire world." This statement (b. *ʿEruvin* 13a) has already been quoted by Scholem in his essay on "The Meaning of Torah in Jewish Mysticism" (in *On the Kabbalah and Its Symbolism* [New York: Schocken, 1969], p. 39). In *Be-Midbar Rabbah* 2:3, we find a very direct statement about names: "Said Rabbi Ḥanina: In former times, whoever pointed with his finger at a statue of the king was executed. But [nowadays] children go to the House of Study and point to mentions (*azkarot*) of God's name with their fingers." A name is an image of the King. For rabbinic Jews—who forbade images of clay or stone—these were verbal icons. *Ḥarba de-Moshe* has been the subject of a recent M.A. thesis at the Hebrew University by Y. Harari. I have not yet had a chance to examine this work.

[2] I can not offer a full bibliography here on *Sefer Yeṣirah*. Significant work has been done by Ithamar Gruenwald, Israel Weinstock, and Nehemia Aloni. See Gruenwald's "Preliminary Critical Edition of Sefer Yezira," in *Israel Oriental Studies* 1 (1971): 154ff. and the several studies by Weinstock and Aloni in *Ṭemirin* 1 (1972) and 2 (1981). In addition to Gruenwald's text edition, the most important recent studies are those by A. P. Hayman in *EJM*, pp. 71–85 and Yehuda Liebes. Liebes has conclusively shown that at least an initial portion of *Sefer Yeṣirah* belongs to the world of Greek grammatical reflections. This will firmly anchor some part of the work to a third-century date, the earliest end of the range once proposed by Scholem. *Sefer Yeṣirah* makes its own cosmological use of the term *keter*; each of the three primal letters, aleph, mem, and shin, is given dominion over a particular set of dimensions and is "crowned" accordingly. This does not mean, however, that *Sefer Yeṣirah* shares in the image-world of the merkavah writers; on this

Bezalel, architect of the tabernacle, who was said to "know how to combine the letters through which heaven and earth were created."[3] The combination and permutation of letters plays a major role in Jewish mysticism throughout its history; it is hardly surprising that its early advocates would have seen the entire alphabet as engraved on God's crown. This tradition is certainly related to the reading we have discussed earlier of Hillel's "he who uses the crown will pass away." The permutation of letters and the particular fascination with the letters of God's name may in fact have originated as separate traditions, but they were joined together at a fairly early point. But where is the border between such licit knowledge of combining the letters as Bezalel's and the illegitimate "use"[4] of the crown and its secrets? Here we are operating in the border areas of mysticism, theurgy, and magic, and the lines are by no means clearly drawn. Of course it is easy to say that Bezalel is using the power of the letters to fulfill a divine command, that of erecting the tabernacle, whereas the magician is drawing on that same knowledge and power to effect his own desires. But this hopeful formulation does not fully satisfy as a means of distinction between the two, certainly not when one reads the sources themselves. This is especially true if one includes among these sources such a blatantly magical work as *Sefer ha-Razim*,[5] which shares quite extensively in the vocabulary, structure, and spiritual atmosphere of the entire *merkavah/hekhalot* tradition. There the most obviously magical uses of divine names, seemingly the precise object of Hillel's indictment, are crowned with a lofty mystical vision of God in the seventh heaven. The need to distinguish the mystical from the theurgic or the theurgic from the magical is in fact quite alien to the literature we are discussing.

In fact it is clear that this entire tradition is quite closely related to the world

---

matter I am in agreement with Hayman. Here it may be again that *keter* is being used more as "seal" than as "crown" in the pictorial sense. Cf. Gruenwald, *Apocalyptic*, pp. 154f., 159.

[3] b. *Berakhot* 55a; *Sefer Hekhalot*, ed. Odeberg, chapter 41 (=Schaefer, *Synopse* #59); Gruenwald, *Apocalyptic*, p. 11. The *Sefer Hekhalot* passage depicts the letters engraved on the throne rather than the crown.

[4] On the magical meaning of names, see Idel, "The Concept of the Torah in Heikhalot Literature and in the Kabbalah," in *JSJT* 1(1981): 29n.23. For some other treatments of magic in Judaism in Idel's work, see his "Defining Kabbalah: The Kabbalah of the Divine Names," in *Mystics of the Book: Themes, Topics, and Typology*, ed. R. A. Herrera (New York: Lang, 1993), pp. 97–122; idem, "Jewish Magic from the Renaissance Period to Early Hasidism," in *Religion, Science, and Magic, in Concert and in Conflict*, ed. J. Neusner et al. (New York: Oxford University Press, 1989), pp. 82–117.

[5] *Sefer ha-Razim*, ed. Mordecai Margulies (Jerusalem: American Academy for Jewish Research, 1966). This important book, which represents a scholarly reconstruction from many fragmentary sources rather than a continuous single text tradition, has been quite controversial. Cf. the reviews by Ch. Merhavya in *Kirjath Sefer* 42 (1967): 297–303 and J. Dan in *Tarbiẓ* 37 (1968): 208–14.

of Jewish magic in late antiquity.[6] The association of the crown and its names or letters with the term *shamesh* already indicates that we are operating in the magical/theurgic realm. The crown itself is a symbol often used by magicians, perhaps because of its round shape and its relation to the magic circle.[7] The somewhat peculiar word *qashar*, here translated as "bind," is the verb most commonly associated with the accounts of Sandalphon and the preparation of the crown. True, if the "crowns" were in fact wreaths of leaves and flowers, qashar is an appropriate choice. But this same verb, and especially its Aramaic parallel *qaṭar*, also means "to cast a spell" or to "bind" by magical means.[8] Now if the crown offered by the angels is made up of the words of Israel's prayers, or perhaps especially of their pronunciation of divine names, "prayer" and "spell" are rather difficult to distinguish here. In fact they are quite identical in structure: both are ritualized verbal exercises that have power through the formation of a holy and binding circle. It is true that no text in this tradition ever goes so far as to claim that Israel's coronation of God binds the deity to

[6] For primary sources and publications before 1939, see the bibliography in J. Trachtenberg's *Jewish Magic and Superstition* (New York: Behrman's Jewish Book House, 1939), pp. 315–32. For early materials, the bibliography of Naveh and Shaked, *Amulets and Magic Bowls* (Jerusalem: Magnes, 1985), pp. 243–64 is also useful.

[7] On the magical associations of *shammesh* see Scholem, *Jewish Gnosticism* (New York: Jewish Theological Seminary, 1960), p. 54n. 36. For the use of crowns in Greek magic, see Ganszyniec in *Paulys Realencyclopädie*, vol. 22, col. 1588ff. On circles in merkavah literature, see Schaefer, *Synopse* #562. The drawing of circles is well-known as a magical device from ancient times. Its prototype is already found in Assyrian ritual texts. See the quotation by R. Campbell Thompson, *Semitic Magic* (London, Luzac, 1908), pp. lviii ff. On the use of circles in preparing magical healings, etc. in the Graeco-Roman world, see Pliny's *Natural History* 21:19; 25:21, 55, 94 for a few of many examples. See also Lynn Thorndike, *A History of Magic and Experimental Science* (London, Macmillan, 1923), index s.v. "circles." The drawing of circles plays a prominent role in the magical *Mafteaḥ Shelomo*. See the references in H. Gollancz's introduction, *Sepher Maphteah Shelomo* (Oxford: Oxford University Press, 1914), p. 10. See also S. Daiches, *Babylonian Oil Magic in the Talmud and in the Later Jewish Literature* (London: Jews' College, 1913), p. 32ff. For further treatment of circles in Jewish magic, see the references in J. Trachtenberg, *Jewish Magic and Superstition*, p. 121. On Honi, see G. Vermes, *Jesus the Jew: A Historian's Reading of the Gospels* (New York: Macmillan, 1974), pp. 69–72, 210–13. The now-dated apologetic discussion of Honi's circles by A. Büchler in *Types of Palestinian-Jewish Piety* (London: Jews' College, 1922), p. 246f. is not helpful.

[8] The magical association of this verb was noted by J. N. Epstein in *REJ* 73 (1921): 33. See also discussion by A. Marmorstein, "Binden und Lösen im Zauber," in *Jahrbuch für jüdische Volkskunde* 1 (1923): 291ff. See the use of *qitrin* in a purely magical sense in Scholem's edition of Havdalah de-Rabbi *ʿAkivaʾ*, in *Tarbiẓ* 50 (1981): 262. There the word can mean only "spells." Cf. the uses of *isra* or *hitma* in *Hekhalot Zuṭarti*, p. 28, lines 223ff. All of these refer to the act of binding that lies at the core of the "spell" as a magical device. *Q-t-r* is also found in the magical incantation bowls with Aramaic inscriptions, though *asar* and *isra* alternate as the more common operative magical term in the bowl texts. See Montgomery, *Aramaic Incantation Texts* (Philadelphia: University Museum, 1913), p. 52 and C. H. Gordon in *Orientalia* 10 (1941): 272. The magical meaning of *q-t-r* is also discussed by Y. Liebes in his *Sections of the Zohar Lexicon* (Jerusalem: doctoral dissertation, Hebrew University, 1976), p. 397, s.v. "*QiSHRaʾ*" #10.

do their will. The coronation remains an essentially devotional rather than magical act. But the magical or quasi-magical implications are never far behind. The fact that the term *keter* in a number of early texts turns out to be interchangeable with *hoṭam*, or "seal," another well-known magical term, serves to underscore this aspect of the rite's meaning.[9]

The magical side of divine coronation is also underscored by the other major tradition concerning the inscription on the crown. A very ancient series of passages, appearing specifically in the *shiʿur qomah* texts, claims that it is the word "Israel" or the phrase "Israel My people is Mine" (*Yisraʾel ʿami li*) that is inscribed on the crown. In one *shiʿur qomah* text we read:

TEXT #10

The circumference of His head extends 3,003,033 parasangs. The height of His crown (*ʿaṭarah*)—*Yaʾ DURiYaH* is its name, and the crown (*keter*) on His head, Israel is its name—is 3,000,000 by 3,000,000 parasangs.[10]

Another version renders a somewhat more "modest" size for the crown:

TEXT #11

The crown (*keter*) on His head is 500,000 by 500,000; Israel is its name. On the precious stone between its staves *Yisraʾel ʿami li* is inscribed. "My beloved is clear-skinned and ruddy, preeminent among ten thousand. His head is like finest gold . . . his eyes are like doves by watercourses" (Cant. 5:10–11).[11]

[9] *Keter* and *ḥotam* are frequently associated in the merkavah literature. See, for two of many examples, Schaefer, *Synopse* #298 and 651. For a clearly magical usage, see #318, Ms. Oxford 1531. For some history of mystical associations with the word *ḥotam*, see M. Idel, *Golem: Jewish Magical and Mystical Traditions on the Artificial Anthropoid* (Albany: SUNY, 1990), p. 154n. 9.

The magical meaning and setting of Jewish prayer in the rabbinic period is the central theme of I. Gruenwald's "Ha-Ketav, ha-Mikhtav, weha-Shem ha-Meforash," (in *Massuʾot* [Jerusalem: Bialik Institute, 1994]), to which I have referred in Chapter 5, n. 21 above. Some of Gruenwald's conclusions in that article seem a bit extreme to me. In identifying the power of the righteous people's prayers quite entirely with magic, I wonder if he is not too much diminishing the personalist dimension in the relationship between God and the *ṣaddiqim*. God *loves* the righteous; God pays attention to the *merits* of the righteous; "God *longs for* the prayers of the righteous." What is the relationship between these well-known locutions, familiar to any student of the rabbinic corpus, and the magical meaning that Gruenwald (quite properly) finds in the identification of the *ṣaddiq*'s power to negate divine decrees and the obviously magical circle-drawing of Ḥoni? We need a more nuanced articulation of the subtle relationship between prayer, to which God responds out of love and compassion, and theurgy/magic, which works because the hierophant knows the proper divine names.

[10] M. Cohen, *Shiʿur Qomah: Texts and Recensions* (Tübingen: Mohr, 1985), p. 64 (=Schaefer, *Synopse* #679, Ms. Oxford 1531). The details are quite different in the parallel Schaefer shows from N.Y. 8128.

[11] This wording is found in the text called *Sefer ha-Qomah*, published by Cohen, p. 149f. See parallels on pp. 41, 45, and 96. Cf. Schaefer, *Synopse* #951, Ms. Munich 40. See parallel in ibid., #487.

Sometimes the connection between the crown and Israel is indicated not by inscription, but by the actual size or appearance of the crown. I take this to be a variant of the same tradition. Thus we are told in one manuscript that "the crown on His head is six hundred thousand [?], parallel to the six hundred thousand of Israel."[12]

It should here be recalled that the entire *Shiʿur Qomah* tradition is seen by Talmudic scholar Saul Lieberman as related to an ancient esoteric midrash on the Song of Songs, and especially on these verses in chapter 5 of the Canticle.[13] Here discourse on the measurements of the divine "body" reaches its climax in the description of the crown, after which the speaker, presumably at the height of ecstatic trance, lapses back into the familiar biblical idiom. One wonders whether the closeness in sound between *ketem*, one of the two words used for "gold" in 5:10, and *keter* did not play a role in this midrash.

The notion that either the word *Israel* or the phrase *Yisraʾel ʿami li* is inscribed on the crown takes us to another interesting parallel in a well-known rabbinic source. The Talmud[14] records an aggadah concerning the *tefillin*, or "phylacteries," of God.

Text #12

R. Abin son of R. Ada said in the name of R. Isaac: Whence is it derived that the blessed Holy One dons *tefillin*? From the Scripture: "The Lord has sworn by His right hand and by the arm of His strength" (Is. 62:8). "His right hand" refers to Torah, as in "By His right hand, a fiery law for them" (Deut. 33:2); "the arm of His strength" refers to [God's] *tefillin*, as in "The Lord will give strength to His people" (Ps. 29:11). But how do we know that *tefillin* constitute a strength for Israel? Because Scripture also says, "All the peoples of the earth shall see that the name of the Lord is called upon you, and they shall fear you" (Deut. 28:10). It has been taught: R. Eliezer says [that this verse refers to] the *tefillin* on the head.

R. Nahman b. Isaac said to R. Hiyya b. Abin: What is written in these *tefillin* of the Master of the Universe? He replied: "Who is like Your people Israel, a singular nation in the earth?" (1 Chron. 17:21).

This type of boldly anthropomorphic aggadah, held in such disdain first by Karaite mockers of the rabbinic corpus and later also by rabbanite medieval philosophic preachers and then rationalist apologists for Judaism, was precisely the sort of rabbinic text most loved by the Kabbalists, and it has a long tradition of explication within the various later mystical traditions. But its

[12] Schaefer, *Synopse* #376, Ms. N.Y. 8128. This makes God's crown interestingly parallel to the six hundred thousand crowns that were given to Israel at Sinai. Cf. *Midrash Shir ha-Shirim Rabbah* 4:4 (ed. Donski p. 103). The coronation of Israel will be treated below.

[13] This has been disputed by Martin Cohen (*Shiʿur Qomah* [Lanham: University Press, 1983], introduction, p. 1) and Daniel Boyarin. I deal below with Boyarin's objections and why I disagree with certain of his claims.

[14] b. *Berakhot* 6a.

plain meaning can be understood only within the context of the sources we have been discussing.[15] "Who is like Your people Israel" inscribed in God's head-*tefillin* sounds quite a bit like "Israel My people is Mine" engraved on God's crown or on the divine forehead. But here again we need not be satisfied with suspicions aroused by structural or verbal similarities. There is evidence in the sources that makes the connection quite explicit. In the text Scholem calls *Maᶜaseh Merkavah*,[16] an important variant of the Sandalphon tale occurs. That passage reads: "Sandalphon binds *tefillin* on the head of the Eternal Rock YWYH God of Israel, blessings to His name." In commenting on this passage, Scholem makes reference to a parallel from an otherwise lost version of the b. *Ḥagigah* passage preserved in the writings of Eleazar of Worms, where the word *tefillin* is substituted for *ketarim*. This version of the Talmudic text[17] is also parallelled by two important fragments preserved in the writings of Karaite authors and polemicists. In their battle against the rabbinic tradition, Karaite writers were quick to pounce on these seemingly bizarre aggadot, using them to demonstrate the naive and dangerously anthropomorphic quality of the rabbis' theology. A passage in the writings of Jacob Qirqisani, a tenth-century author, reads:

> That which they say in the *Shiᶜur Qomah* . . . that Michael binds *tefillin* to His head each day . . . and they say in the Book of Ishmael[18] that Meṭaṭron binds *tefillin* each morning to the head of the Creator.

A second reference occurs in *The Wars of the Lord*, by Qirqisani's contemporary, Salmon ben Yeruham:

> They said further that the blessed Holy One binds *tefillin* and frontlets, that the name Israel is engraved on his turban, that the name Jacob is inscribed on His seat.[19]

[15] See M. Bar-Ilan, "The Idea of Crowning God in Hekhalot Mysticism and the Karaite Polemic," in *EJM*, pp. 221–33.

[16] Published in his *Jewish Gnosticism*, p. 112; Schaefer, *Synopse* #582.

[17] This version of the *Ḥagigah* passage was discovered and discussed by S. Lieberman in *Sheqiᶜin* (Jerusalem: Bamberger & Wahrmann, 1939), p. 13.

[18] This refers to one of the merkavah texts, several of which could be designated by the name of the frequent speaker in them.

[19] Cf. Lieberman, *Sheqiᶜin*, p. 11; Bar Ilan in *EJM*, pp. 227–28. I see no basis for Bar-Ilan's claim that *tefillin* here is a later substitution for *keter*, in an attempt to "judaize," a worldly rite. This reading reflects an overly narrow notion of the need to "judaize," something that might be appropriate to much later centuries. I similarly disagree with the historical reconstruction he proposes, in which coronation by the angels came first, leading to a belief in coronation by Israel, and finally to the myth of God's *tefillin*. I do not think we are capable of tracing the history in that way. God's *tefillin* may in fact be the oldest element here, going back to amulets worn by pre-Israelite dieties. But I would not like to have to compare the dating of deity-worn amulets to that of sacred coronation!

The final phrase reflects a variant on the well-known midrashic theme that an image of Jacob is engraved on God's Throne of Glory. On this theme and its later interpretation, see the important

These passages taken together make it quite clear that what we have here are variants of a single tradition, one that depicts God as bearing the name of Israel on His head, whether written directly on His forehead, inscribed on a crown or diadem, or contained within *tefillin*.[20] In most versions this headgear is given Him by a chief angel, named Sandalphon, Michael, or Meṭaṭron. Interestingly we have no version of the tradition that combines the notion that Israel are givers of the crown, or that the crown is made up of Israel's prayers, with the belief that "Israel" is inscribed on the crown or the *tefillin*. There might have been a sense of impropriety that forbade this combination. I suspect that such a sensibility might also have to do with magic. The theurgic/magical power of divine names is well known. For the suppliant-magicians (the community of Israel, in this case) to come into the angelic realm bearing the name(s) of God was a way of depicting them as powerful participants in the cosmic rites, co-givers of God's own crown of names. A much more daring version of the magical tradition[21] has the magician use his own name as the object of power. This would have been more audacious, in the context of discussing God's crown, than any textual tradition could permit. No one may place his own name on the head of God. If Israel were givers of God's crown, it had to bear His name, not theirs. If the crown was to bear the name of Israel, it could be given only by the angels. That is not to say, of course, that the implications of the "forbidden" combination do not lurk somewhere in the background.

One of the most unusual merkavah texts, generally called by the name *Merkavah Rabbah*, opens with another reference to the *tefillin* of God, but in an even more obscure context. The passage reads as follows:

TEXT #13

Said Rabbi Ishmael: I saw the cosmic King seated on the high and exalted throne, [accompanied by] a single troop that stood [reaching] from earth to heaven. Its name is Sandalphon. At the time when He seeks—*Rozey* YHWH the God of Israel—to

---

study by E. Wolfson, "Demut Yaʿaqov," in *Massuʾot: Studies in Kabbalistic Literature and Jewish Philosophy in Memory of Prof. Ephraim Gottlieb* (Jerusalem: Bialik Institute, 1994).

20 M. *Megillah* 4:8 contains a somewhat surprising prohibition against the wearing of round *tefillin*. This is usually read as having been a defensive measure used during times of persecution, the round *tefillah* not being recognizable as such to the enemy. But this explanation hardly seems realistic. The Babylonian Talmud (b. *Megillah* 24b; cf. also b. *Menaḥot* 35a) interprets the wearing of round *tefillin* as a "way of heresy." Could it be that such *tefillin*, or something looking like them, were used by magicians?

21 On the use of the magician's own name in magical operations, see the discussion by M. Idel in *Hasidism: Between Ecstasy and Magic* (Albany: SUNY, 1995) and in his "Jewish Magic from the Renaissance to Early Hasidism," in *Religion, Science, and Magic*, ed. J. Neusner et al., pp. 101–2. He refers there to a well-known story of the Baʿal Shem Tov, one of whose amulets was opened, only to reveal his own name.

swear by His *tefillin* and to cast an oath by His hand, He takes the *tefillin* from His head and He nullifies decrees from the earth.[22]

This text is difficult in a number of ways. Though I have capitalized the third-person pronouns throughout, it is not entirely clear whether the subject of the key sentence is Sandalphon or *Rozey* YHWH, the latter a designation for the deity found in other merkavah sources as well. Probably it is *Rozey* YHWH who wants to take an oath. For this purpose He needs to have a sacred object (one bearing a divine name) held in His hand. Here God follows the exact procedure described for oath-taking in the rabbinic courts.[23] He takes the *tefillah* off His head, holds it in His hand, and swears.

Exactly what is meant by "and he nullifies decrees from the earth" (*u-mevaṭṭel gezerot min ha-ʾareṣ*) remains obscure. Perhaps God is swearing to cancel a previously issued decree that caused some plague or other destructive force to be unleashed against earth's inhabitants. The point that is not made here but is frequently understood in the merkavah sources, is that the righteous human practitioner, armed with proper knowledge of the upper worlds, can administer such an oath, can *mashbiʿa* (the causative of *sh-b-ʿ*, the root for "oath taking"), or "adjure," the heavenly forces to avert such decrees. This technique of adjuration is generally practiced on angels, rather than on God Himself. Although the theological distinction between those two is important, the purpose is the same. It is also noteworthy that the phrase *mevaṭṭel gezerot* is reminiscent of another Talmudic statement, one claiming that "the blessed Holy One issues a decree, but the righteous one nullifies it."[24] Is the power of human righteousness alone equivalent to the force of powerful adjurations? Or is the *ṣaddiq* here actually one who combines his personal righteousness with the use of powerful prayer and "techniques" designed to affect the upper realms? An attempt to answer these questions would take us far afield, into the realm of rabbinic views of "the righteous" and their powers altogether.[25]

[22] Schaefer, *Synopse* #655, from Ms. NY 8128. See the related reference to *tefillin* in ibid., #550, which we discuss in another context below. Interestingly an eleventh-century *payyeṭan*, Benjamin ben Zerah, says just the opposite, in a liturgical composition included in the Sukkot liturgy:

> The angel Sandalphon, placed within His innermost chambers,
> When an oath goes forth to destroy His creatures,
> Receives a crown. For its sake [the decree] is annulled.

Here God is given the crown, rather than removing it, to annull His oath (*Maḥzor Sukkot*, ed. D. Goldschmidt [Jerusalem: Koren, 1981, p. 89]).

[23] Cf. b. *Shevuʿot* 38b; *Maimonides' Code*, Laws of Oaths 11:11–12.

[24] *Moʿed Qaṭan* 16b and parallels.

[25] R. Mach, *Der Zaddik in Talmud und Midrasch* (Leiden: Brill, 1957), part 2, pp. 51ff.; Scholem, "Tsaddik, the Righteous One," in *On the Mystical Shape of the Godhead* (New York: Schocken, 1991), pp. 88–139; and my comments in *Tormented Master* (Tuscaloosa, AL: Univer-

Here we might do well to summarize the series of themes we have been discussing and their role in the religious life of Israel in late antiquity and rabbinic times. This role is reflected in sources from the synagogue liturgy, the aggadah, and the merkavah literature; it is especially apparent when these sources are placed side by side with one another. Israel's prayers are seen as ascending into the heavens, passing into the hands of an angel who weaves of them a crown that he places on the head of God. This is said especially of such public prayers as *qedushah* in the synagogue. The prayer-life that underlies this tradition may include an ancient practice of pronouncing the divine name in the context of public or private worship. We have here a daily enactment of a coronation rite, performed by Israel in conjunction with the great coronation that takes place daily in the heavens above. Israel proclaim themselves to be not mere observers of, but full and indispensible participants in, this cosmic ritual event. This daily coronation reaches its greatest liturgical moments in the New Year[26] and Day of Atonement, given their most ancient associations with both divine kingship and the reenactment of the Temple service. The ascent of prayer to form God's crown replaces the earlier ascent of sacrificial smoke and bears with it both the loyalty of Israel as subjects in the Kingdom of Heaven and an assertion of their special power as God's chosen beloved on earth. The coronation of God is in the fullest sense theurgic, an act that dwells in the undefinable border areas in which religion and magic so deeply overlap. The crown is a gift that Israel and the angels give to God, one that binds them in submission to the divine will. In a way less clearly spoken but no less deeply meant, it hopefully binds the ultimate divine power to their will as well. Devotion and magic, submission to the King and assertion of power to offer the crown, are here all bound together as one.

sity of Alabama Press, 1979), pp. 116–23 and "The Zaddik as Axis Mundi in Later Judaism" in *JAAR* 45 (1977): 327–47.

[26] A text preserved in *Merkavah Rabbah* (*Merkavah Shelemah* 25b = Schaefer, *Synopse* #33), undoubtedly of German Hasidic origin, notes that Sandalphon is also the angel in charge of bringing the first shofar-sound of the New Year to God. *TeQiʿaH* (the name of this type of blast) is numerically equivalent (if you drop its final heh) both to *seraph* and to *tefillin*. "This teaches that [Sandalphon] leads the shofar-sound[s] to the blessed Holy One's head, in place of the *tefillin*, and makes of them a crown." Rosh Ha-Shanah is, after all, a holiday, when God would not wear *tefillin*. But He has a crown nevertheless.

CHAPTER SEVEN

The Angels Crowned

CROWNS PLAY A MAJOR ROLE throughout the rich imagery of the merkavah sources and the related aggadot. Having explored the key motif of the coronation of God, we should now place this most sublime crown into the context of some broader uses of the theme. We shall first turn our attention to other crowns, in addition to the crown of God, envisioned in the heavens by merkavah voyagers. By far the richest source for these descriptions is *Sefer Hekhalot* or *3 Enoch.* Its author(s) allowed freer rein to the imagination than did others, and it often offers significantly more expansive descriptions of heavenly beings than those found elsewhere. After dealing with angels and their crowns, we shall discuss two passages that refer to crowned humans who are encountered in the course of merkavah "visits" to the upper realms. Later we also consider the crowning of humans in this world as described primarily in certain aggadic passages, showing how these relate to the heavenly coronation already under discussion.

We have already seen that Meṭaṭron, the chief of the angelic hosts, is the wearer of a crown. According to some sources, it was Meṭaṭron's crowned and enthroned status that caused Elisha ben Abuyah, called Aḥer or "the other," the Talmud's classic heretic, to be misled into proclaiming, "two domains in heaven." Following is the account from Sefer Hekhalot:

TEXT #14

Rabbi Ishmael said: The angel Meṭaṭron, prince of the Divine Presence, the glory of highest heaven, said to me:

At first I sat upon a great throne at the door of the seventh palace, and I judged all the denizens of the heights on the authority of the blessed Holy One. I assigned greatness, royalty, rank, sovereignty, glory, praise, diadem, crown, and honor to all the princes of kingdoms when I sat in the heavenly court. The princes of kingdoms stood beside me, to my right and to my left, by authority of the blessed Holy One. But when Aḥer came to behold the vision of the chariot and set eyes upon me, he was afraid and trembled before me. His soul was alarmed to the point of leaving him because of his fear, dread, and terror of me, when he saw me seated upon a throne like a king, with ministering angels standing beside me as servants and all the princes of kingdoms crowned with crowns surrounding me. Then he opened his mouth and said: "There are indeed two powers in heaven!" Immediately a divine voice came out from the presence of the Shekhinah and said, "Come back to Me, apostate sons—apart from Aḥer!" Then ʿAnafiel YHWH, the glorified, beloved, wonderful, terrible, and dreadful Prince, came at the command of the blessed Holy One, and struck me with sixty lashes of fire and made me to stand on my feet.[1]

An earlier passage in that same text describes the original coronation of Meṭaṭron, after he was translated from his earthly existence as Enoch into his supreme heavenly role.

TEXT #15

The blessed Holy One fashioned for me a majestic robe, in which all kinds of luminaries were set, and He clothed me in it. He fashioned for me a glorious cloak in which brightness, brilliance, splendor and lustre of every kind were fixed, and He wrapped me in it. He fashioned for me a kingly crown in which 49 refulgent stones were placed, each like the sun's orb, and its brilliance shone into the four quarters of the heaven of ʿAravot, into the seven heavens, and into the four quarters of the world. He set it upon my head and He called me "The lesser YHWH" in the presence of His whole household in the height, as it is written: "My name is in him." (Ex. 23:21)[2]

No wonder Aḥer erred as he did! Not even any other angel can look directly at Meṭaṭron because of the brilliance of the crown upon his head.[3] This tale of Meṭaṭron's investiture has earlier roots in the Enoch tradition, as one would expect. But there the element of coronation is not yet present. The Second (or Slavonic) Enoch has the new ruler of heaven invested by the older Israelite tradition of anointing, as he is also dressed in heavenly rainment.[4] The crown does not seem to play an important role in the apocalyptic visions of the Second Temple period; it is in the transition of this Enoch material from apocalypse to merkavah fantasy that the crown comes into the picture.

After Meṭaṭron tells the heavenly voyager (and narrator) of *Sefer Hekhalot* the tale of his own ascent, he takes his visitor on a tour through the heavens. Here the author is following in a Jewish-esoteric narrative tradition that was

[1] *3 Enoch* 16; Schaefer, *Synopse* #20. Regarding the translation, see above, Chapter 4, n. 19. The better-known parallel to this text is found in b. *Ḥagigah* 15a. Interestingly the other parallel, found in Schaefer, *Synopse* #597 and translated and discussed in Halperin, *The Faces of the Chariot* (Tübingen: J.C.B. Mohr, 1988), p. 410, as well as by Scholem, *Jewish Gnosticism*, p. 52f., has Elisha encountering Akhtariel, about whom we shall have more to say presently. There Akhtariel, who elsewhere is usually a manifestation of the Deity, seems to take the form of a "separate" being, surrounded by a host of angels. The only reference to any crown in this passage is that included in his mysterious name. For prior discussion of this passage, cf. J. Dan, "Anafiel, Metatron, and the Creator," in *Tarbiẓ* 52 (1983): p. 455n.27, and the previous treatments quoted there.

[2] *3 Enoch* 12; Schaefer, *Synopse* #15.

[3] *3 Enoch* 14, end; Schaefer, *Synopse* #18. A great deal has been written on Aḥer and his sin. See Gedaliahu G. Stroumza, "Aḥer: A Gnostic," in *The Rediscovery of Gnosticism*, vol. 2 (Leiden: E. J. Brill, 1981), pp. 808–18 and the extensive bibliography provided in his notes, as well as the more recent treament by Y. Liebes, *Ḥetʾo shel Elisha* (Jerusalem: Akademon, 1990).

[4] 2 Enoch 22:8–10.

by his time perhaps nearly a thousand years old.[5] As they go through the upper realms, the voyager is soon shown a being called Keruviel, who, as his name indicates, is head of the cherubim in heaven.

TEXT #16

Above them is a prince, noble, wonderful, mighty, praised with all manner of praise: Keruviel YHWH is his name, a valiant prince, full of boundless power; a majestic prince, with whom is majesty; a righteous prince, with whom is righteousness; a holy prince, with whom is holiness; a prince glorified by thousands of hosts, a prince extolled by countless legions.

A crown of holiness is on his head, with the sacred name engraved upon it, from which lightning flickers. The bow of the Shekhinah is across his shoulders; his sword, like a lightning flash, is on his thigh; his arrows, like lightning flashes, are in his belt; a breastplate of consuming fire hangs round his neck, and coals of juniper encompass him. The splendor of the Shekhinah is on his face; horns of majesty are on his wheels, and a royal turban crowns his head.[6]

This description is immediately followed by a lovely poem, in which attention is given to Keruviel's relation to his charges and all he does for them. The poem opens by noting that

He glorifies the crowns on their heads;
He polishes the diadems on their foreheads.[7]

The double crown, or the combination of crown on the head and some sort of frontlet on the forehead, seems here to be worn throughout the heavens.

Parallel to Keruviel (at least terminologically) in the *3 Enoch* description, is Sarafiel, the head of the fiery angels called seraphim and the one who teaches them their song of praise. His crown is described in terms that recall the language of *Shi*ᶜ*ur Qomah*:

TEXT #17

The crown on his head is radiant like the throne of glory, and the height of the crown is a journey of 502 years. There is no kind of radiance, no kind of splendor, no kind of brilliance, no kind of light in the world that is not placed in that crown.

[5] See M. Himmelfarb, *Ascent to Heaven in Jewish and Christian Apocalypses* (New York: Oxford University Press, 1993). Himmelfarb dates the *Book of the Watchers*, an early link in the chain of apocalyptic ascent-texts, to no later than the first quarter of the second century B.C.E. Her work, combined with that of I. Gruenwald and D. Halperin, provides for a line of historical and literary influences stretching from Ezekiel, through the Jewish and Jewish-Christian apocalyptic works, into the merkavah tradition, the later Hebrew apocalypses, and the quasi-esoteric midrash (*Pirqey Rabbi Eliezer*; *Otiyyot de-Rabbi ʿAqivaʾ*) of the Gaonic period.

[6] *3 Enoch* 22; Schaefer, *Synopse* #33. After text: cf. parallel in the text called *Hilkhot Kiseʾ* in Mussaieff's *Merkavah Rabbah* 27b.

[7] *3 Enoch* 22; Schaefer, *Synopse* #34 (my translation).

Serafiel is the name of that prince, and the name of the crown on his head is "Prince of Peace."[8]

While the crown of Keruviel was said to bear the divine name as an inscription, a motif we have already encountered, here in the case of Sarafiel we meet a crown that itself has a name. It is not clear whether or not *sar shalom* is inscribed on Sarafiel's crown; the wording we have seems rather to indicate that this crown is itself a distinct "being," one that is called by its own name.

The crowns of these chiefs of the angelic brigades are described in particularly colorful language in this text. But each and every one of the angels beneath them is also wearer of a crown. 3 Enoch describes an elaborate ceremony wherein each of these angels removes his crown and bows to the ground (lit., "falls on his face") as a sign of respect for the angel above him. Here the listing of the various angels and their realms, presumably the real purpose of such a passage, is accompanied by the notation that each one doffs his crown in the proper order.

Parallel to these elaborate descriptions in 3 Enoch (and possibly a source of inspiration for them) is a description in Hekhalot Rabbati[9] of the distribution of crowns to the heavenly hosts. Here it is the vast numbers of crowns indicated that gives to the passage its typically "numinous," or mysterious and imposing quality. Each of the Ofanim is crowned with a thousand thousand (a million?) crowns, each of the Cherubim with two thousand (thousand?), each of the *Ḥayyot* with three, and so forth. The Angel of the Presence is the one who distributes all these crowns. As he gives each one to the being who receives it, he bends his kneee, bows, and prostrates himself before that particular angel. Thus here too we have the description of a heavenly ceremony, one that involves a combination of crowns and elaborate bowing. The ceremony of *3 Enoch* was one of the doffing of crowns, where each being showed respect to those above him in the heavenly hierarchy. Here, in what can only be described as an act of intentional heavenly lèse majesté, it is the being at the head of that hierarchy who bows to acknowledge the nobility of each of his subjects as he crowns them. The reader of such passages cannot but be reminded of the crowded and elaborately hierarchical heavens described in some Buddhist traditions and, somewhat closer to home, in a number of the Gnostic sources.

The richly filled heavens of the merkavah are described with such a luxurious use of religious language that one ultimately becomes hard-pressed to find a specific and unique place for that which we thought was central to any Jewish vision of the upper worlds, the figure of God. The fact is that the language and images used to describe God in the biblical and rabbinic sources are used here for certain of the angels as well. This is surely true for Meṭaṭron, the chief of the angels (hence leading to Elisha's confusion), but it applies to

[8] *3 Enoch* 26; Schaefer, *Synopse* #41–42.

[9] Schaefer, *Synopse* #170–71.

others as well. The figure ʿAnafiel is described with his crown in *Hekhalot Rabbati*[10] in language that seems, according to expected usages, to describe "God Himself."[11] Such descriptions may include terms like *yoṣer bereshit, elohey Yisraʾel,* and frequently even the tetragrammaton itself, often combined with the being's own "angelic" name. In an important note commenting on this material,[12] Joseph Dan has suggested that the term *angel* for such heavenly figures as fill the imagination of merkavah writers is misleading. We tend to hear in the word *angel* a being clearly distinguished from "God," as is the case in medieval and later Jewish theology (reflecting the usage in Scripture itself). But in these much earlier and doctrinally rather amorphous sources, the lines do not seem to be so clearly drawn. As Rachel Elior has pointed out,[13] these sources represent a strange combination of highly elaborated hierarchy in the heavenly realms and a nearly total obliteration of any clear lines of distinction between the divine and the semidivine, or "angelic" domains. Elior's suggestion that we have evidence here of an only partially absorbed late encounter of the Jewish-biblical tradition with a Hellenistic polytheist view of divinity seems very much to the point.

This problem comes into especially sharp focus when we encounter the term Akhtariel (or Akatriel), seemingly an angel name that combines with the word *keter* in the same way that *el* is added to *keruv, saraf,* or *ʿAnaf* to create the names of those beings we have most recently discussed.[14]

The name Akhtariel is familiar from a most extraordinary Talmudic passage in which the following story is told:

TEXT #18

Rabbi Ishmael ben Elisha said: I once went to offer incense in the innermost [chamber of the Temple]. There I saw *Akhtariel YaH YHWH Ṣevaʾot,* seated on a high and glorious throne. He said to me, "Ishmael my son, bless Me!" I replied, "May it be Your will that Your compassion overcome Your wrath. May Your compassion prevail over Your other attributes, so that You deal compassionately with Your children, and You be more gracious to them than the law demands." And He nodded His head toward me [in agreement to this blessing.][15]

10 Ibid., #243ff.

11 See Dan's explanation of this in "ʿAnafiel," pp. 447–57. Regarding the name ʿAnafiel itself, I wonder whether the key might not be found in the phrase *ʿanaf ketaraw* in *3 Enoch* 22 (=Schaefer, *Synopse* #244), quoted by Dan on p. 449f. "Crowns," we recall, may still actually be wreaths in this period, fashioned from woven branches. On ʿAnafiel see also Schaefer, *The Hidden and Manifest God* (Albany: SUNY, 1992), pp. 30 ff.

12 Dan, "ʿAnafiel," p. 448n.5.

13 R. Elior, "Mysticism, Magic and Angelology: Angels in Merkavah Mysticism," *JSQ* 1 (1993): 29.

14 According to a midrashic source, each angel carries "a tablet over his heart, on which is the name of God combined with that of the angel: *Micha-el, Rapha-el,* and so forth." *Tanḥuma Buber Yitro* 14, in the name of R. Simeon ben Lakish.

15 b. *Berakhot* 7a. This is a strange passage in many ways. The offering of incense on the

There is no doubt in this tale that we are dealing with a manifestation of "God," and not a separate "angelic" presence. It is the blessed Holy One, not an angel, who relates to humanity as His "children," who has an "Attribute of Compassion," and all the rest. I confidently see the subject of this tale as "God Himself" despite the fact that the earliest commentators, for their own apologetic reasons, are somewhat divided on this matter.[16]

We have already had occasion to refer to another passage in which Akhtariel is mentioned. This is the *hekhalot*-related fragment called *The Secret of Sandalphon*, where Elisha ben Abuyah encounters Akhtariel YaH YHWH Ṣevaʾot seated at the entrance to the seventh heaven. Now we shall have to quote that passage in full:

TEXT #19

Elisha ben Abuyah said: When I ascended into the *pardes*, ["Orchard" of mystical experience] I saw Akhtariel YaH [Ms. New York adds: *Elohey Yisraʾel*] YHWH Ṣevaʾot seated at the entranceway of the *pardes*. 1,200,000 ministering angels surrounded him, as Scripture says: "A thousand thousands served Him, and ten thousand times ten thousands stood before Him" (Dan. 7:10), and so forth. When I saw them, I was astonished and taken aback. I pushed myself in before the blessed Holy One. I said to Him: Master of the Universe! You have written in Your Torah: "The heavens and heavens of heavens belong to the Lord your God" (Deut. 10:14), and also "The firmament proclaims His handiwork" (Ps. 19:2). Only One! He said to me: Elisha my son, have you come to doubt My qualities? Have you not heard the parable people tell . . .[17]

This text as it stands is extremely difficult. Just what did Elisha see that led him to heresy? There is nothing necessarily dualistic about Akhtariel; the

---

innermost altar would have to be performed by the high priest, but there is no high priest recorded with the name Ishmael ben Elisha. The tale must be considered in tandem with what may be called its postdestruction version, told by R. Yosi in b. *Berakhot* 3a. The use of the name Ishmael here seems adjacent to its frequent employment in the *hekhalot* sources; this text seems to be a *hekhalot*-related fragment of aggadah that has entered the bavli. As Y. Liebes has shown (see next note), however, it is deeply interwoven with other aggadic sources playing on related motifs. This is another example of the close relationship between aggadic and *hekhalot* sources.

[16] See R. Hananel ben Hushiel as quoted by Scholem, *Jewish Gnosticism*, p. 51n.26. Those who saw this Akhtariel vision as that of an angel were protecting against too anthropomorphic a reading, a protection quite inappropriate to the original setting of this passage. The same is true of the one occasion when *Akhtariel YaH YHWH Ṣevaʾot* is mentioned in *Sefer Hekhalot*, as Scholem has already shown (ibid., p. 52). On this passage see also discussion by Y. Liebes in "De Natura Dei: On the Development of Jewish Myth" in his *Studies in Jewish Myth and Jewish Messianism* (Albany: SUNY, 1993), pp. 10ff. (Hebrew original in the Gottlieb memorial volume *Massuʾot*). On Akhtariel see also W. Rosenau, "Some Notes on Akteriel," in *Paul Haupt Festschrift* (Leipzig: Hinrichs, 1926), pp. 103–5.

[17] Schaefer, *Synopse* #597. The number of 1,200,000 angels, which we shall encounter soon again, is double the number of Jews (adult males) who left Egypt and stood at Sinai. The midrashic tradition to be discussed below indicates that each was attended by two angels.

vision of Akhtariel is not considered too "improper" to be included prominently in the Talmud, when it comes to the case of R. Ishmael. Nor was R. Ishmael himself, to compare story to story, taken aback by seeing this divine figure. A precise reading of this text as it stands seems to indicate that it was the angels surrounding and waiting on Akhtariel that unnerved Elisha; it was when he saw *them* that he was cast into doubt. It seemed as though these angels were waiting on someone other than "God Himself." But why should Elisha have thought that about Akhtariel YaH YHWH Ṣevaʾot? Who told him that there was something "other" than God here? Such an assumption makes no sense when the only other references we have to Akhtariel clearly refer to a manifestation of the divine Self.

For this reason, I believe that the text as we have it is an imperfect one. I would suggest that this text, just like its parallel in b. *Ḥagigah* 15a, originally referred to Meṭaṭron. At some point in the text's history, a copyist was too offended by the notion that Elisha had actually seen a vision that could indeed be interpreted dualistically, especially when this version contained no account of the demotion or punishment of Meṭaṭron. He therefore changed "Meṭaṭron" into "Akhtariel YaH YHWH Ṣevaʾot," hoping to show that Elisha was mistaken in what he thought he saw. In fact he saw a vision of "God," but he, because of his own inadequacy, thought it was something "other."[18]

This suggestion that the Akhtariel name was substituted for that of Meṭaṭron is substantiated by a similar substitution that has probably taken place in another text, noted by Gershom Scholem. In an obscure apocalyptic fragment first published over a century ago,[19] R. Ishmael tells of a revelation of this same being: Akhtariel YaH. But as the text continues, suddenly the name changes, and he calls back to Meṭaṭron, who had not been previously mentioned. This seems to offer another case where Akhtariel YaH has been substituted for Meṭaṭron by a scribe who hoped to protect some notion of theological orthodoxy. He did it somewhat clumsily in this case, however, and his tracks remain visible.

If these two texts are explained in this way, we have almost no case in either the rabbinic or the *hekhalot* literature where the name Akhtariel refers to anything but a visioned manifestation of God.[20] The name always appears together with the tetragrammaton, something that is surely not the case for any

[18] Scholem, in *Jewish Gnosticism*, p. 53, has already said that the name Akhtariel is "substituting here for Meṭaṭron," but he interprets this as evidence of an "original" variant tradition, rather than as a later emendation.

[19] Chaim M. Horowitz, ed., *Bet ʿEqed ha-Aggadot* (Frankfurt-am-Main: E. Slovottski, 1881); 1881; discussed by Scholem in *Jewish Gnosticism*, p. 53n.32. I follow Scholem's reading of this text, though I am somewhat less sure than he of the interpretation offered. The text was reprinted in Ibn-Shmuel's *Midreshey Geʾulah* (Jerusalem: Mossad Bialik, 1954), pp. 144–52.

[20] The one exception seems to be the magical fragment appended to *Ḥarba de-Moshe*, Schaefer, *Synopse* #667. There Akhtariel (without the rest of the name) is an angel located in the fourth heaven. I do not know how to acount for this reference.

others among the "angelic" names. Akhtariel YaH YHWH Ṣeva'ot is the crowned deity, God as receiver/wearer of the crown, seen by Moses as he ascended into heaven and by the high priest in the Holy of Holies. If we now examine the single reference to this figure in *Sefer Hekhalot* (actually in what is generally thought to be an addendum to that work), we find that this is precisely the case.

TEXT #20

When Moses ascended to heaven . . . he sought mercy, first for Israel and then for himself. The one seated on the merkavah opened the windows above the heads of the cherubim. . . . They received the prayers of Israel and placed them as a crown on the head of the blessed Holy One. He [Moses] recited "Hear O Israel." . . . At that time Akhtariel YaH YHWH Ṣeva'ot turned to Meṭaṭron, angel of the presence, and said, Whatever he asks of Me, see that he not be turned away empty-handed.[21]

Note that the term Akhtariel appears only after—and quite immediately after—the crown is placed on the head of the *Qadosh Barukh Hu*. I would suggest that Akhtariel YaH YHWH Ṣeva'ot is apparantly a title or technical term that can only be used after the coronation rite, when the Gestalt of the blessed Holy One has been transformed into the figure of Akhtariel by the addition of the crown. This gives us some idea of the theurgic power of the crown, and ultimately of the prayers of Israel.

The merkavah literature contains one other mention of Akhtariel to which attention should be called. This passage too has been translated and discussed by Scholem,[22] an incantation text that refers to "Akhtariel YHWH Elohey Yisra'el sealed upon the crown and engraved upon His throne." Here we have another reading of the name written on God's crown, one that is obviously of particular appropriateness. It may be that when God is manifest in this particular visionary embodiment as Akhtariel, it is this name that is seen written on the holy crown.

If the borders between angel and deity are somewhat blurred at one end of the heavenly spectrum, one is tempted to say the same of those between angels and humans, at the other. The merkavah sources sometimes include encounters with various human figures in the course of visionary experiences. Although none of these humans is transposed into a heavenly being like Meṭaṭron, their status is not quite clear. Are these encounters perhaps visions

[21] Chapter 15b, ed. Odeberg, p. 21f. (h.).

[22] *Jewish Gnosticism*, p. 53f. It is now Schaefer, *Synopse* #501. My reading of Akhtariel as a name for God as a crowned manifestation is a refinement of Scholem's rather strange idea (ibid., p. 54) that Akhtariel is the name of the crown itself, "one of the secret names of His various paraphernalia as He appears upon the throne." The texts are quite clear in referring to a (crowned) being, rather than to the crown as sacred object.

of *gan ʿeden* ["The Garden of Eden"; "Paradise"], where souls await the final resurrection of the dead? Is this "paradise" identical with the realms of the *reqiʿim* ["firmaments"] that are the usual haunts of the merkavah traveler? Of course such questions are partly inappropriate, as they indicate an overly literal reading or an overly determined set of boundaries in a realm that is in fact quite fluid.

This is most clearly the case in a highly original text to which we shall now turn our attention. This is an apocalyptic vision text, found in the key manuscripts of *Hekhalot Rabbati.*[23] It is a text in which crowns and coronation play a key role, though here they are the crowns of once earthly kings, rather than those of God or the angels.

Text #21

[After showing me the tribulations that await Israel, Hadariel] brought me into the treasuries of consolation and salvation. There I saw bands of ministering angels sitting and weaving garments of salvation, making crowns of life (*ʿosim kitrey ḥayyim*), setting precious stones and pearls into them. [They were also] mixing all kinds of perfumes and sweetening wines for the righteous.[24] I saw one crown different from all the others; it had sun, moon, and the twelve constellations fixed on it.

I said to him: "O glorious heavenly light! For whom are these crowns?" He said to me, "For Israel." "And for whom is this special crown?" He said to me, "For David, King of Israel." I said to him: "O glorious heavenly light! Show me David's glory!" He said to me, "Wait here, my beloved, until David arrives, and you will see his greatness."

He took hold of me and seated me in his bosom. He said to me, "What do you see?" I said to him, "I see seven bolts of lightning, running about as one." He said to me, "Hide your eyes, my son, that you not be shaken by these, which have come forth to greet David." Immediately there came forth all the Ofanim, Seraphim, *Ḥayyot*, the treasuries of hail and snow, the clouds of glory, the stars and constellations, the ministering angels and fiery beings of Zebul, saying: "For the conductor, a Psalm of David. The Heavens declare the glory of God" (Ps. 19: 1–2) and so forth. I heard the sound of a great noise coming from Eden, saying, "May YHWH rule forever!" [I saw] David King of Israel at their head and all the kings of the House of David following him. Each of them had his crown on his head, but the crown of David was more

[23] The text constitutes Schaefer, *Synopse* #122–26, found in Mss. NY 8128 and Budapest 238. The latter is the basis of the translation here of 124–26. The apocalypse is found in Ibn Shmuel, *Midreshey Geʾulah*, pp. 8–10. Cf. his bibliography, p. 7, for prior publication history. A fuller translation is found in my article "Religion and Mysticism: The Case of Judaism," in *Take Judaism for Example*, ed. J. Neusner (Chicago: University of Chicago Press, 1983), pp. 67–91.

[24] To be drunk at the messianic banquet. Cf. b. *Berakhot* 34b and Ginzberg, *Legends*, vol. 5, p. 29n.79. To those of us who still anticipate redemption, it is distressing to note that the Jewish predilection for "specially sweetened" wines will not diminish even "on that Day."

brilliant and glorious than all the others, its radiance extending from one end of the world to the other . . .

Once David had entered the great House of Study (*bet ha-midrash ha-gadol*) in the firmament, a fiery throne was awaiting him, forty parasangs high and double that in width and length. When David came and was seated on the throne prepared for him, facing the throne of his Master, with all the kings of the House of David seated before him and all the kings of Israel standing behind him, David immediately began to recite hymns and praises like no ear had ever heard. Once he opened with: "May YHWH rule forever!" Meṭaṭron and his entire retinue began to say: "Holy, holy, holy is *YHWH Ṣevaʾot*." The *Ḥayyot* recited praise and said, "Blessed is the glory of YHWH from His place." The firmaments said, "May YHWH rule forever." Earth said, "YHWH is King, YHWH was King, YHWH shall be King forever." And all the kings of the House of David said: "YHWH shall be King over all the earth; on that day will YHWH be one and His name one."

A most interesting text, for a number of reasons. Here we have an enthronement ceremony in the heavens, almost precisely like those we have discussed earlier. The throne is established, the glorious crown is given (though here we do not actually see it *placed* on David's head), and the angels follow Israel's lead in singing *qedushah*. What is different is that the enthronement is that of David in the heavenly *bet ha-midrash*, rather that that of God in the seventh heaven! There is great religious daring in this text, one that is willing to take the *qedushah*/coronation of God and apply it to the king of Israel. David, or his future descendant to come, is no longer merely the anointed representative of God on earth; here he participates quite fully in the ritual event of cosmic kingship. This text takes us back to the saying with which we began this study, but with a new twist. The earthly kingdom is not only *like* the heavenly kingdom; sometimes the figures of earthly rule are themselves transferred to the upper realms.

It would be interesting to know the date of this text and the political context in which it was composed. The earlier portion (not translated here) foretells a time of terrible suffering for Israel, as is the way of such apocalypses. Yehudah Ibn Shmuel, who included it among his *Midreshey Geʾulah*, dates it in the middle sixth century,[25] though I see no reason to be more certain about that date than we are of so many others regarding this sort of material. This thoroughly Jewish apocalypse ascribes to David a place so parallel to God in the upper ceremonial rights that he could quite rightly be described as "the lesser YHWH," a role generally thought to be given to a human (of Davidic descent) only in Christian sources.

Whatever the date and specific setting of this strange fragment, reading it recalls a key passage in an earlier and much better known apocalyptic work. I

[25] *Midreshey Geʾulah*, p. 7.

refer to the fourth chapter of the New Testament apocalypse, generally known as the Book of Revelation. This chapter has been much discussed in scholarly literature, most recently by David Halperin,[26] and we have made brief mention of it above. Verses 8–10 contain a full if abbreviated *qedushah* sequence,[27] making this one of the earlier written sources for the full three-part (holiness, glory, and kingship) series of refrains. But reminiscent of our David apocalypse are the twenty-four crowned elders, each clad in white garments, seated on a throne, and wearing a golden crown on his head. They are seated surrounding the throne of God, and as the *qedushah* is recited they "cast their crowns before the throne" as a sign of homage before the Creator. This act reminds us of the angels in *Sefer Hekhalot*, who doff their crowns out of respect for those above them. But the presence of presumably human "elders" in this heavenly scene is surprising. There has been much discussion of the identity of these figures.[28] Whatever turns out to be the case, they are humans who have entered the realm of heavenly vision. Like the kings of Israel in the later apocalypse, they show how thin are the presumed borders between the upper and lower worlds. And the contiguity of motifs between this New Testament apocalypse and Jewish Hebrew-language sources of several centuries later shows that yet another presumed border, that between Jews and Christians, was also crossed rather freely by the shapers of these texts.

[26] *Faces*, pp. 87–96. See also Gruenwald, *Apocalyptic and Merkavah Mysticism* (Leiden: Brill, 1980), pp. 62–69.

[27] This text has been discussed by Flusser, "Sanktus und Gloria," in *Abraham unser Vater* (Leiden: Brill, 1963), pp. 129–52.

[28] On the number 24, see J. M. Baumgarten, "The Duodecimal Courts of Qumran, Revelation, and the Sanhedrin," in *JBL* 95 (1976): 59–78 and Andre Feuillet, "Les Vingt-Quatre Vieillards de l'Apocalypse," in *Revue Biblique* 65 (1958): 5–32.

CHAPTER EIGHT

Israel Crowned at Sinai

HAVING SURVEYED SOMETHING of the widespread use of crowns and the coronation motif throughout the upper worlds, including the crowns of humans who are seen there, we are ready to return to this world and to encounter the sacred coronation of certain humans who are still more or less resident in the earthly realm. We can begin our reentry into this world nowhere else but at Sinai, where we arrive to celebrate Israel's coronation by the angels. We begin with the best-known text witness to this event, recorded in the Babylonian Talmud.

TEXT #22

"The Israelites stripped themselves of their adornment from Mount Horeb" (Ex. 33:6). Rabbi Simlai expounded, When Israel said "We shall do" before "We shall listen" (Ex. 24:7), six hundred thousand ministering angels came forth, each of them binding two crowns for each one of Israel. One was for "we shall do" and one was for "we shall listen." But when Israel sinned, one hundred twenty thousand punishing angels came down and took them apart, as this verse indicates. Said R. Ḥama ben Rabbi Ḥanina: At Horeb they were put on and at Horeb taken off. . . . Rabbi Johanan said: And Moses merited to acquire them all, since this verse is followed by, "And Moses took the tent (*ohel*)" (Ex. 33:7).[1]

The coronation of Israel at Sinai is witnessed widely in the midrashic literature.[2] It is part of a broader theme telling of gifts that were received by Moses and Israel along with the Torah. The attempt is to glorify this greatest of all moments and finest of all gifts with additions of a magical or supernatural quality, thus also lending an added dimension to the supernaturalist reading of the Sinai event itself.[3] Another version of the tale, attested by several Midrashic references, tells it this way:

[1] b. *Shabbat* 88a. Here RaSHI suggests that the Talmud understands *ohel* not as "tent," but as an obscure word for "light," related to the root *H-L-L*. It may well be that the etymologically aware preacher thought of this root, which appears in Job 29:3 and 31:26. But I believe he also had in mind a play with the Greek word *halo*, used in both pagan and early Christian contexts for a sacred aura, as is well manifest in Christian art of the earliest periods. Moses took their crowns of light, their *ohel/halo*, and that is why he shone so brightly (see below).

[2] See *Tanḥuma Teṣawweh* 11, *Shelaḥ* 13; *Tanhuma Buber Wa-'era'* 9; *Teṣawweh* 7; *Shelaḥ* addendum 1; *Shemot Rabbah* 45:2, 51:8, and parallels.

[3] This attempt is most widespread in the aggadah. A. J. Heschel identifies it with the school of R. Akiva. Cf. his *Torah min ha-Shamayim*, vol. 2 (London: Soncino, 1965), pp. 3ff., 38ff., etc.

TEXT #23

When they stood at Sinai and said, "We shall do and we shall listen," a crown was placed on their heads. Said Rabbi Abba bar Kahana in the name of Rabbi Levi: Once Israel had accepted the Ten Commandments, one hundred twenty thousand ministering angels came down with belts [*zonniyot*, "armor" or "belts," = b.h. *ḥagorot*] and crowns in their hands. Two of them attended to each one of Israel; one gave him a crown and the other girded him with a belt.[4]

To this version there is often added a tradition ascribed to R. Simeon ben Yoḥai: They gave each of them a weapon with the name of God engraved on it.[5] This added gift seems related to motifs attached by the midrash to Moses' staff, depicted already in the biblical text itself as an instrument for performing wonders. The staff had been in Moses' hands since his period of wandering before the Exodus, when he had found it growing, according to some, in Jethro's garden.[6] All the magical gifts of Sinai were taken away from Israel in response to the sin of the Golden Calf. In the case of the weapon inscribed with the divine name, question is raised as to how it could be taken away, presumably since it might have been used against any emissary who came to remove it. Thus R. Aibo says: It [the name] peeled off of its own accord.[7] God's own magic cannot be used to best the divine will!

For our purposes, the most interesting version of these midrashic traditions is that of *Pirqey Rabbi Eliezer*. It is hardly surprising that we find a new formulation of this sort of tradition in that probably eighth-century text. Its editors had a strong instinctive feeling for the mythic elements of Jewish tradition, and they sought out sources, including apocalyptic and merkavah

[4] *Pesiqta Rabbati* 10 (37a), 21 (103b); *Shir ha-Shirim Rabbah* 4:4 (ed. Donsky p. 103); *M. Tehillim* 103 (435).

[5] *Pesiqta Rabbati* 33 (154a); *M. Tehillim* 91 (397), 103 (435); *Tanḥuma Buber* 4:76. See the extended note of Meir Ish Shalom (Friedmann) to the *Pesiqta Rabbati* passage, where he suggests that the "belts" (*zoniyyot*) and weapons (*zayyenot*) are probably alternative readings for the same "gift." Assuming Israel are given two gifts, crowns and swords, might it be that there is a hierarchy among powers here? The magician is given a sword (or staff, wand) for *use;* the verbal sword is the divine name available for magical *shimmush*. But the *keter* or *taga*, sometimes also an aura, is too high to use; this is a "mystical" rather than a "magical" gift. Therefore *de-ishtemmesh ba-taga ḥalaf*, for the crime of misappropriating or demeaning a divine gift, "using" it for lowly magical purposes. On the gifts of crowns and swords at Sinai, see also I. Chernus, *Mysticism in Rabbinic Judaism* (Berlin: de Gruyther, 1982), p. 25f.

[6] On the rod of Moses see the sources cited in Ginzberg, *Legends*, p. 411n.88. See also the appendix to *Ḥarba de-Moshe*, to which we have referred above in Chapter 6 (Hebrew text, ed. M. Gaster, p. 22, line 2). The author refers to a sword "that was revealed to Moses at the bush." In the body of the text, the sword is given him at Sinai. Here we see two traditions combine. One says that he had it from the days of his lone wanderings, either from Jethro's garden or from the burning bush encounter. This allows the staff used to work wonders in Egypt to be that same magic rod. The other tradition, more closely related to those we are discussing here, has him receive it at Sinai, perhaps on his ascent to heaven.

[7] *Shir ha-Shirim Rabbah* 5:4; ed. Donsky, p. 130.

materials that had not made it into the earlier midrashic collections, to reward that sense. There we read:

TEXT #24

Rabbi Eleazar ben ʿArakh says that when the blessed Holy One came down to give Israel His Torah, sixty myriads of ministering angels, parallel to the sixty brave myriads of Israel, came down with Him. In their hands were weapons and crowns. They crowned Israel with the crown of the explicit name (*we-ʿiṭeru et Yisraʾel be-keter shem ha-meforash*). For all the days until they did that deed [made the Golden Calf], God considered them superior to the ministering angels, and the angel of death had no rule over them. They also did not have to attend to bodily functions like human beings. But once they had done that deed, the blessed Holy One became angered at them, saying: I had thought you were like angels before Me. Thus Scripture says: "I had taken you for divine beings, sons of the Most High, all of you. But you shall die as men do, fall as any prince" (Ps. 82:6–7).[8]

What Israel are given at Sinai is a taste of eternity. Bearing either the sword or the crown with God's name (these appear to be variant traditions), they have become immortals. They need have no fear of the angel of death. Here they stand apart from all other humans—even their own forebears—who have lived since the expulsion from Eden. It might not be going too far to say that all of them are now on the same rung as was the newly translated Enoch/Meṭaṭron: they are immortals who wear the crown of the explicit name and they are higher in God's sight than any angel.[9] The coronation of Israel at Sinai is indeed "a foretaste of the world to come." But this remarkable transformation happens to them while they are yet alive in this world. Perhaps for that reason it cannot last. Enoch is transformed and taken up into the heavens; he can reside there forever in his angelic garb, no longer having to contend with the temptations of life on earth. Israel are left in this world, and it is to this world they must belong after all. They are consoled only by the promise that the gifts of Sinai will finally be restored to them in the world to come, the time when "the righteous will sit with crowns upon their heads and bask in the glory of the Presence."[10]

[8] *Pirqey Rabbi Eliezer* 47. See also the references quoted by M. Idel in *JSJT* 1 (1981), pp. 29n.22 and 30n.24.

[9] This theme of Israel's erstwhile perfection at the moment of receiving the Torah has a long life in Jewish religious literature. It is emphasized in the Zohar (1:52b, 131b; 2:45b, etc.) and thence it travels into Hasidic literature. Even so late a text as the *Sefat Emet* by Judah Loeb Alter of Gur (1847–1904) makes frequent use of this tradition, noting that had it not been for Israel's sin, the final redemption would have been immediately adjacent to the giving of the Torah.

[10] *Sifre Devarim*, 356 (ed. Finkelstein, p. 424). As is often the case with *ʿolam ha-baʾ* ["world to come"] or *le-ʿatid la-voʾ* ["in the future"] references, it is not clear whether the various depictions of the souls of the righteous as crowned are eschatological or refer also to the fate of the individual soul after death. For the latter view, see *Tanḥuma Pequdey* 3, where each soul before birth is taken round to see the crowned *ṣaddiqim* in Eden. This view is developed in such passages

The idea that Moses inherited Israel's lost gifts, mentioned in our original Talmudic source, also deserves some further discussion. Scripture tells us of Moses, in the very next chapter, that "he was not aware that the skin of his face shone" (Ex. 34:29). Might it be possible that the radiance of Moses' face as he descended from Sinai (the second time, after the sin had been forgiven) is related somehow to the "gifts" of Israel that had now been given to him? Some midrashic sources do associate Moses' shining face with the motif of coronation,[11] or the coronation of Israel with the bestowing on them of God's own radiant glory.[12] Especially interesting among these is a text still recited in the *Shabbat* morning liturgy, where it is said:

> Moses shone at the giving of his portion, for You called him a faithful servant. A crown of glory You placed upon his head as he stood before You on Mount Sinai. He brought down two tablets in his hand, and in them is written the Sabbath command.[13]

---

as *Sefer ha-Ḥesheq* 14, where the crowning of the soul is joined to the notion of an Edenic garment that the soul wears after death. Probably reflecting the other (if indeed it may be called "other" at all) view is the well-known passage in b. *Sanhedrin* 111b and b. *Megillah* 15b, where the righteous are seen seated "with crowns on their heads," basking in the splendor of *shekhinah*.

[11] See *Midrash Tehillim* 8:7 (78); *Pesiqta Rabbati* 21 (102a); *Pirqey Rabbi Eliezer* 41 (end). See also Ginzberg, *Legends*, vol. 5, p. 397. According to Zohar 3:243a, Moses *is* the crown of all Israel. Traditions surrounding the coronation of Moses have been studied quite thoroughly by W. Meeks in *The Prophet-King: Moses Traditions and the Johanine Christology* (Leiden: Brill, 1967), which includes consideration of Hellenistic, rabbinic, and Samaritan materials. Meeks (p. 193ff.) quotes *Tanḥuma Buber* 4:15, where Moses is seen as crowned with God's own crown, and notes the parallel to Philo's Moses, who is also depicted as king, though in an entirely different cultural context. Meeks also notes the parallels between Moses' coronation and that of Enoch. Because he is interested in the parallel to Johanine Christology, however, he concentrates on Moses', rather than Israel's, coronation.

[12] In *Pesiqta DRK* 4:4 (ed. Mandelbaum, p. 67); in *Pesiqta Rabbati* 14 (62b) it is illumination of their faces by *ziw ha-shekhinah* rather than actual coronation that takes place at Sinai. This brings us particularly close to the "halo" traditions of Christian iconography, a parallel that has often suggsted itself in the course of this study. See also nn. 1 above and 13 below.

[13] A. Mirsky has suggested (in *Sinai* 57 [1965]: 127ff.) that *yismaḥ Moshe* is a fragment of an old alphabetical *piyyuṭ*, only three verses of which are here preserved. It is found, according to Elbogen-Heinemann, *Ha-Tefillah be-Yisra'el* (Tel Aviv: Dvir, 1972), p. 87, in all the rites. Cf. also the more complete treatment by Naphtali Wieder, "The Controversy about the Liturgical Composition 'Yismaḥ Moshe'—Opposition and Defence," in *Studies in Aggadah, Targum, and Jewish Liturgy in Memory of Joseph Heinemann*, ed. J. Petuchowski and E. Fleischer (Jerusalem: Magnes, 1981), pp. 75–99. For the translation "Moses shone," cf. the comments of J. Greenfield on the root שמח in *HUCA* 30 (1959): 141–51, where he offers many biblical (see for example Ps. 19:9, Prov. 13:9) examples where it means "shine." Read this way, the two verses of the prayer are parallel to one another: Moses "shines"; he receives a diadem of light. On Moses' shining countenance and its relationship to God's own shining face, see M. Haran, "The Shining of Moses' Face: A Case Study of Biblical and Ancient Near Eastern Iconography," in *In the Shelter of Elyon: Essays . . . in honor of G. W. Ahlstrom*, ed. W. B. Barrick (Sheffield: JSOT, 1984): 159–73; J. Morgenstern, "Moses with the Shining Face," in *HUCA* 2 (1925): 1–27.

The term used here for "crown" is *kalil*, a somewhat unusual word and one not generally used in connection with either the divine crown or those of Israel.[14] But the choice of term can be accounted for by the typically lofty tone of the liturgical prose-poem, and it does not necessarily mean something other than *keter* or *ʿaṭarah*. The passage is a poetic expression of the midrashic claim that Moses' descent from Sinai with glowing countenance indicated that he had been given a divine crown or an aureole of holy light. This "coronation" has its own witness in Scripture and is separate from the traditions concerning the angels' crowning all of Israel. But the two traditions sometimes seem to be conflated: Moses, who descended from Sinai in a crown of light, and who did not sin at the Golden Calf, draws to himself all the crowns, which are now to be removed from the people.[15]

The gifts received by Israel at Sinai are often related to the exegesis of Psalm 68:19: "You went to the heights and took a captive; you took gifts for humankind." The "captive" here is understood to be Torah (sometimes personified as God's daughter), taken from the heavens and forced to dwell on earth. But along with this victory of humans comes a series of gifts. In a tale that follows a page after our above-quoted passage from b. *Shabbat*, the angels argue with God to keep His hidden treasure, extant since before Creation, with them in the heavens.[16] After they are bested in argument (Why do you unembodied and sinless beings need Torah?), they concede to support its earthward journey:

TEXT #25

Immediately each and every one of them became Moses' friend. Each gave him something, as Scripture says: "You went to the heights and took a captive; you took

[14] There are some exceptions. It is found in Schaefer, *Synopse* #73 (= Odeberg, at 3 Enoch 48C) together with *keter* and in #490, in an Aramaic passage.

[15] The crowned Moses does very much exist in the Samaritan sources, which generally deify him at every opportunity. See Montgomery, *The Samaritans* (New York: Ktav, 1968), p. 228 and the discussion by Meeks, as cited in n. 11 above, pp. 232ff. Meeks comments that in the Samaritan sources both coronation and enthronement of Moses are "more common and more extensively elaborated." The crowned Moses is also to be found in Jewish-Hellenistic literature. Ezekiel the Tragedian (2nd century BCE; preserved by Eusebius), records a vision (in the form of a dream of Moses) in which a heavenly personage, seated on a throne, wearing a crown, and bearing a sceptre, rises and gives them all to Moses. The text is preserved in Eusebius's *De Praeparatio Evangelica*, ed. K. Mras (Berlin: Akademie Verlag, 1954), p. 529. English translation in E. H. Gifford, *Eusebii Pamphili, Evangelicae Praeparatione*, vol. 3, pt. 1 (Oxford: Oxford University Press, 1903), p. 470. Cf. Meeks, *The Prophet-King*, pp. 146ff. *The Crown of Moses*, incidentally, is the name of a magical book referred to in Greek magical papyri. See Frederick G. Kenyon, *Greek Papyri in the British Museum* (London: British Museum, 1898), 96, p. 104, line 619 and note.

[16] This is part of a larger literature on the theme of rivalry between humans—or Israel—and the angels, beginning with the creation of Adam and aggravated particularly by God's decision to give the Torah to Israel and Moses' ascent into the heavens. See the treaments mentioned in Chapter 3, n. 15 above.

> gifts for humankind." Because they called you a human (*adam*; for the angels had earlier quoted Ps. 8:5 in their argument), you took gifts. Even the angel of death gave him something, as Scripture says: "He put on the incense and made expiation for the people; he stood between the dead and the living until the plague was checked" (Num. 17:12f).[17]

The reference here is to the plague that followed the rebellion of Korah. The implication derived from "the incense" is that the secret of this particular incense offering, one effective in stopping death in a plague, was given to Moses at Sinai by the Angel of Death. Here we have another gift of a supernatural order accompanying the great gift of Torah. But the offering formula for stopping a plague surely is related to that gift we have already mentioned, the great and explicit name of God on the crown or the sword, that which makes one no longer fear the Angel of Death.

If we once again allow ourselves to step beyond the somewhat more conservatively worded Talmudic text and enter the realm of esoteric aggadah, we immediately find an expanded version of this tale. Here we enter briefly into the literature associated with *Sar ha-Torah* (the prince of Torah), a group of writings that has attracted considerable recent attention.[18] In the text called *Maʿayan Ḥokhmah*, from which we quoted one version of the coronation event, we read in reference to Moses' ascent to heaven:

TEXT #26

> Immediately the blessed Holy One called to Yefehfiyah the prince of Torah and he gave Moses the Torah, edited and bounded (*ʿarukhah u-shemurah*). All the ministering angels became his friends and each one gave him some healing formula or secret names (*refuʾah we-sod shemot*) that proceed from each *parashah*, along with their applications (*shimusheyhen*). . . . This is the glorious application [of Torah] which the angels gave him through Yefehfiyah, prince of Torah, and through Meṭaṭron, angel of the Presence. Moses gave it to Eleazar, and Eleazar to Pinhas his son, who is Elijah the glorious high priest, may he be remembered for good.[19]

Maʿayan Ḥokhmah served as an introduction to a longer text known by the name *Shimushey Torah*, now lost to us. This text was presumably an esoteric commentary on the Torah, one that listed the magical names, healing formulae, and similarly usable combinations of letters that proceeded from each *parashah*. A classical and still-used example of such names would be the seventy-two-letter name of God, composed of the letters of three verses in Exodus 14, read backward, forward, and backward. Torah is filled with such names, as this text must have taught. Moses is given the exoteric Torah, con-

[17] b. *Shabbat* 88b–89a.

[18] See Gruenwald, *Apocalyptic and Merkavah Mysticism* (Leiden: Brill, 1980), index s.v. "Sar Torah," and Halperin, *The Faces of the Chariot* (Tübingen: J.C.B. Mohr, 1988), pp. 376ff; 427ff.

[19] *Bet Ha-Midrasch*, ed. Jellinek (Jerusalem: Bamberger and Wahrmann, 1938), vol. 1, p. 61; see discussion by Idel in *JSJT* 1 (1981): 27ff.

taining laws, statutes, and narratives, to be read to and studied by the people. But the angels give him the additional gift of being able to read this same Torah "in the way of names," to appropriate a medieval term for such a reading. This level of Torah exegesis is to be taught only to those who are properly initiated into the realms of secret lore.

The body of aggadah with which we are dealing seems to carry us yet another step, especially if we follow along with Moshe Idel's reading of this material. Devotees of the merkavah traditions among the rabbis[20] had their own ways of studying the Torah text. Like both halakhists and aggadists, they were close readers of the divinely revealed Word. But rather than seeing Torah as a corpus of hints at legal structures and as a source of precedents for a legal system, as did the halakhist, or alternatively as the blueprint out of which to fashion an elaborate castle of literary and homiletic fantasy, as did the aggadist, these circles within Judaism saw Torah as a mysterious underground labyrinth of divine names and mysterious letters that served also as magical formulae and healing incantations. It was this unique combination of the fantastic and the practical that was revealed at Sinai, either through a supernaturally given "commentary" on the text or as the true heart of the revelation itself.

The aggadot that deal with Israel's coronation at Sinai are linked to this tradition, representing a tie-in between this esoteric reading of Torah and the world of exoteric aggadah. Various scholars[21] have amply demonstrated complex and sometimes ambiguous connections between merkavah visions and rabbinic understandings of the events at Sinai. I am here suggesting that the theme of coronation plays a key role, though an often understated one, in this linkage.

We have seen God depicted as wearing a crown that bears divine names and/or holy letters. We have encountered God as the wearer of phylacteries, crowns, or seals that contain the name Israel or the praise of Israel as God's own people. We have also seen Israel crowned once at Sinai, and again each day, with crowns containing the name of God and thereby bearing supernatural powers. The crown given to God is made up of the prayers of Israel, and it is placed on the divine head at the moment when the angels sing *qedushah*, a key element also in the liturgical life of Israel, who join into the angelic chorus.

[20] I hope the overlap between rabbinic and merkavah circles (see above, Chapter 3, n. 3) is well demonstrated by the midrashic passages quoted here and their obvious relationship to key themes of merkavah literature.

[21] Gruenwald, Groezinger, Chernus, Idel, etc. This link is the very heart of Halperin's *Faces*. While I share his belief that these sets of sources should be read in tandem with one another, I do not share in his rather radical conclusions regarding the ox of the merkavah and the Golden Calf. The link between those two is indeed made in the sources he quotes, but I find his view of this link as the key to the real meaning of the merkavah to be overly contrived and exaggerated. See the review of his work by Elior cited above in Chapter 2, n. 9.

Israel's participation in this mutual cosmic cycle of both worship and empowerment begins at Sinai. Moses calls out, "Hear O Israel" and the people call it out after him.[22] The heavens open and Israel see the angelic hosts.[23] God is crowned by the angels who receive the prayers of a perfect and immortal Israel, themselves newly crowned with the holy name of God.

The act of coronation is a bestowal of power, an investiture of authority. When Israel pray, put on *tefillin*, or cry out, "The Lord is King!" they are "accepting the yoke of the kingdom of heaven" or giving to God the crown of glory, woven of their devotions. When God or the angels crown Israel, the latter are given dominon over this world, including both the authority to interpret and develop God's law (itself adorned with crowns, upon which they will expound!) and the mastery of certain supernatural tools useful in the combating of plague, demons, and other evil forces that may block their path.

Israel's coronation at Sinai should also be seen in the broader context of symbolic acts of union or intimacy indicated by the sharing of a garment, cloak, or hat. The best-known example of this widespread motif in late antiquity is that found in Esther 6: 6–9:

> Haman entered, and the king asked him, "What should be done for a man whom the king desires to honor?" Haman said to himself, "Whom would the king desire to honor more than me?" So Haman said to the king, "For the man whom the king desires to honor, let royal garb that the king has worn be brought, and a horse the king has ridden, and on whose head a royal diadem has been set; and let the attire and the horse be put in the charge of one of the king's noble courtiers. And then let the man whom the king desires to honor be attired and paraded on the horse through the city square, while they proclaim before him, This is what is done for the man whom the king desires to honor!"

Honor is bestowed on the king's loyal subject by his wearing of one of the king's own royal robes and by the temporary right to wear a kingly crown (here perhaps placed on the horse's head in the spirit of the Purim-tale parody!). There are a number of biblical passages in which Israel either is or wears God's garment as a sign of intimate relationship. These have been analyzed by Yochanan Muffs in a brief but most illuminating study[24] that touches also on the matter of *tefillin*. Muffs claims that "the wearing of the hat/phylactery/tattoo is a means of 'wearing' the divinity. One 'wears' God on one's head; one 'wraps' God on one's arm; one 'imprints' God on one's

[22] *Sefer Hekhalot* 15b, part of which has been translated above. The text is poorly preserved, to the point that the speakers are not clear. But this is a rare use of the *shema*ʿ in the heavenly prayer context.

[23] *Pesiqta Rabbati* 20 (98b) and the various midrashic interpretations of Ps. 68:18, several of which have been listed above. A more "tame" (or at least less visual) version of this tradition is that of b. *Shabbat* 88b and parallels, where Israel faint at the sound of God's voice.

[24] "As a Cloak Clings to Its Owner: Aspects of Divine-Human Reciprocity," in *Love and Joy: Law, Language, and Religion in Ancient Israel* (New York: JTSA, 1992), pp. 49–60.

flesh. The same meaning of coming close to the beloved is available to God, who wears Israel on His head and wraps Israel around His arm."[25] This understanding of *tefillin*, very much in tune with (in fact almost paraphrasing) the later Kabbalistic interpretations, will also shed light on the coronation of both Moses and Israel at Sinai. The newly appointed viceroys of God for this world are given the honor of being dressed in royal robes and kingly crowns, an honor quickly taken away from them as they besmirch this glory by their worship of the Golden Calf. The dream of future restoration of this privilege is then a restatement of the intimacy that Israel will again have with God "on that day" which is inter alia a new Sinai, a moment of renewed revelation and love restored.

[25] Ibid., p. 53.

CHAPTER NINE

Coronation and Marriage

BUT THERE IS ANOTHER ASPECT to the mutual coronation of God and Israel that we have not yet treated, and this too relates specifically to Sinai. "Go forth, O maidens of Zion," says the author of the Song of Songs, "and gaze upon King Solomon, wearing the crown with which his mother crowned him on the day of his marriage, the day of his heart's delight" (3:11). "The day of his marriage," says the Talmud[1] refers to "the giving of the Torah." Sinai is frequently depicted in the rabbinic imagination as the day of God's marriage to Israel, a tradition that has a long history, represented even today in Sephardic synagogues by the reading of a symbolic marriage contract between God the Bridegroom and Israel His bride on the holiday of Shavuʿot.

In fact our Talmudic reference is but the tip of a much greater mass of material on this verse and the crown of Solomon's marriage. We should remember, of course, that the rabbis generally read the Song of Songs as referring to the marriage of God and Israel. It was this reading that had permitted the Canticle to be included in Scripture altogether. Still a matter of debate in the early second century, the inclusion of the Song was assured by the position of R. Akiva, the great mystic/romantic of early rabbinism, who supposedly said regarding an earlier debate over this matter: "They never were divided regarding the Song of Songs. The whole world is not worthy of the day when the Song of Songs was given to Israel. All of Scripture is holy, but the Song of Songs is the Holy of Holies."[2]

Saul Lieberman has noted that the word *given* is of special interest here. Only the Torah, and in this passage the Canticle, are referred to in this way. He suggested this reflected an ancient belief that the Song of Songs was in fact "given" along with the Torah—indeed as a secret inner level of Torah—at Sinai. This would accord with the view of Akiva, recorded elsewhere, that the Song of Songs was first "spoken" at Sinai.[3]

[1] b. *Taʿanit* 26b.

[2] M. *Yadayim* 3:5. Cf. my discussion in "The Song of Songs in Early Jewish Mysticism," in *Orim: A Jewish Journal at Yale* 2 (1987): 49–63.

[3] Lieberman, "Mishnat Shir ha-Shirim," in *Jewish Gnosticism, Merkavah Mysticism, and Talmudic Tradition*, ed. G. Scholem (New York: Jewish Theological Seminary, 1960), pp. 118–26. Here Akiva differs from other *tanaʾim*, or early sages, who claim the Sea of Reeds, the Tent of Meeting, or the Temple as the original locus of the Song. See Lieberman, and my treatment of this theme in *Judaism* 24 (1975): 446–56. I am aware of the attempt by D. Boyarin to refute Lieber-

The rabbis tell us elsewhere[4] that every "Solomon" in the Song of Songs but one is "holy," that is, it calls God the King of Peace, rather than the mortal Solomon. So the king crowned in 3:11 is none other than the blessed Holy One, wedded to His beloved Israel. Sinai is "the day of his marriage"—the day of God's marriage to Israel.

But now our verse gets us into difficulty of another sort. If Solomon here is the King of Peace or God Himself, what are we to make of "the crown with which his mother crowned him"? To answer this and other questions, we had best look at the midrashic comments on this phrase as recorded in several sources:

man in his "Two Introductions to the Midrash on Song of Songs," in *Tarbiz* 56 (1987): 479–500. Though I very much appreciate Boyarin's work generally, I believe several of his arguments there are seriously flawed, and as a result I do not accept his conclusions. I shall try to briefly state my objections here, though they are of a somewhat technical nature. Boyarin's claim that *kol ha-ketuvim* is the original wording of the Akiva statement, and that *kol ha-shirim* is an emendation made to fit the setting of *Midrash Shir ha-Shirim* is at very least unprovable. The fact is that *kol ha-shirim* is the language most fitting the verse (Cant. 1:1) upon which the midrash is commenting. It would more likely seem that this is the original homiletic statement, of which *kol ha-ketuvim* is an expansion to fit the point being made by the Mishnah and its parallels. Boyarin's reading of an admittedly difficult *Shir ha-Shirim Zuṭa* text (p. 495) also fails to convince me. The text is making the point that the Song of Songs is the choicest of all the Scriptures. I think Boyarin is reading the elevation of Hagiographa over prophets, and prophets over Torah, too seriously, when it is chiefly an adjunct to this key point, and I certainly do not see the Midrash indicating that the Canticle is of the same origin or "ontological" status as the other writings. I further disagree with his reading of *ba-yam neʾemerah* to mean "referring to the sea" rather than "at the sea." The verses quoted there, especially Ps. 68:26, are much more suited to describing an actual event than they are to pointing to a more abstract reference. Finally and most important, Boyarin's claim that the early Midrash on the Song of Songs is "not mystical" (p. 499) because it refers to descriptions of God as experienced in the past rather than the present, could equally be applied to nearly all the sources of Jewish mysticism. The Zohar and all the other classical texts of Kabbalah speak almost exclusively of such "past" experiences, often cloaking the authors' own experiences within that garb. I believe that is precisely the case in this early material on the Song of Songs as well, and I see no reason to thereby disqualify it as "mysticism." Some greater refinement of categories is needed for this discussion. This last point is noted also by Marc Hirshman in his article on the Song of Songs in *Mikra and Midrash: A Comparison of Rabbinics and Patristics* ([Israel]: Hakibbutz Hameuchad, 1992), pp. 65–73. Fortunately Boyarin's later and much more interesting work on *Midrash Shir ha-Shirim* (*Intertextuality and the Reading of Midrash* [Bloomington: Indiana University Press, 1990, 105–16] is not dependent on this early article).

These reservations about the Boyarin criticism do not mean that I accept all of Lieberman's claims in the "Mishnat Shir ha-Shirim" article in Scholem's book. The utter identification of *Shiʿur Qomah* with *Midrash Shir ha-Shirim* is overstated. I have tried to refer in this work to a midrashic understanding of the Canticle as the "setting" in which *Shiʿur Qomah* took place or found a home. This is perhaps as close as we can come to an appropriate formulation of the still-mysterious relationship between these elements of Judaism in the early centuries of the Common Era.

[4] b. *Shevuʿot* 35b. The one exception is Cant. 8:12.

TEXT #27

"The crown with which his mother crowned him." This refers to the Tabernacle. Why is it called a crown? Just as a crown is elaborately decorated (*meṣuyyeret*), so is the Tabernacle. . . .

Rabbi Isaac said, I have searched through the entire Scripture, and I have not found anywhere that Bathsheba made a crown for Solomon. Rabbi Simeon ben Yoḥai asked Rabbi Eleazar ben R. Yose, Might you have heard from your father the meaning of "the crown with which his mother crowned him"? He replied Yes [and offered] a parable of a king who had an only daughter. He loved her very much and called her "my daughter." He kept on loving her until he called her "my sister," and then until he called her "my mother." The blessed Holy One first called Israel "daughter," as in "Hear O daughter and give ear; forget your people and your father's house" (Ps. 45:11). He kept on loving them until He called them "my sister" as in "Open for me, my sister, my love, my perfect dove, for my head is filled with dew, my locks with drops of night" (Cant. 5:2). He kept on loving them further until He called them "my mother" as in "Listen to Me, My people, and My mother (*le'umi*/"my nation" = *le-'imi*/"my mother") hear Me. . . ." (Is. 51:4) Rabbi Simeon ben Yoḥai stood up and kissed him on his head.[5]

This midrash is noteworthy for a number of reasons. The reference to the king and his beloved whom he sees first as daughter, then as sister, and finally as mother, could be taught as a classic of devotional psychology; the several female figures combine with one another in a way that almost smacks of a "spiritual incest." The hesitancy that creates the midrash may have to do with early Jewish-Christian polemics and an attempt to respond to a seeming scriptural "opening" to the figure of God's mother, who was in fact to play a major role in later Christian mystical readings of the Song.[6] This parable was eagerly taken up in the Middle Ages by *Sefer ha-Bahir*, the late pseudo-midrash that forms the basis for Kabbalistic symbolism. We discuss this further below. The thought of the tabernacle placed as a crown on God's head may have helped to inspire one of the oddest images in that often puzzling book. This text was to be quoted and discussed very frequently by Kabbalists who would find in it an important rabbinic precedent for their assertion of the feminine within divin-

[5] The version quoted is that of *Shemot Rabbah* 52:5, but see the earlier parallel in *Pesiqta DRK* 1:3 (ed. Mandelbaum, p. 7) and other parallels listed there. The association of tabernacle and crown is quite early; cf. *Sifra Shemini* 15. I believe that the kiss on the head with which this aggadah ends may be a sign of initiation, and not just a spontaneous response to fine preaching. In that it is related to the conclusion of *Sefer Yeṣirah*, where God kisses Abraham on the head, the teaching of Eleazar ben Arakh before Yohanan ben Zakkai in b. *Ḥagigah* 14b, and other sources. I hope to deal with this theme elsewhere.

[6] Cf. E. Ann Matter, *The Voice of My Beloved: The Song of Songs in Western Medieval Christianity* (Philadelphia: University of Pennsylvania Press, 1990), chapter 6, "The Woman Who Is the All: The Virgin Mary and the Song of Songs."

ity, and especially for the multiple grades of feminine potencies that they will expound. This text claims, after all, that all these feminine figures are one, differentiated only by the expansive language of each lover's affections. This would prove most helpful to the Kabbalist who would try to demonstrate that his seemingly multiple *sefirot*, or symbol-clusters within divinity, do not contravene his monotheistic faith.[7]

The main alternative tradition with regard to the original "setting" of the Song of Songs also offers an accounting of Cant. 3:11. Here we see a particularly frank statement concerning the meaning of coronation:

TEXT #28

"The crown with which his mother crowned him." At the Sea, as it is written: "The Lord shall reign for ever and ever" (Ex. 15:18). The blessed Holy One said to them: You have bound a royal crown to My head. . . . "Go forth and see," all you nations, the wondrous miracles He has wrought for His children, and the glorious crown with which He will be crowned on the day the exiles are gathered in, as it says: "The Lord will rule over them on Mount Zion from now and forever" (Mic. 4:7). But is the kingdom not really God's [in the first place]? . . . Yes, but the blessed Holy One says to Israel, "I had neither kingship nor legions, as it were, until you established Me and proclaimed My rule."[8]

The reader will notice that no accounting is given for "his mother" in this interpretation. While in the previous midrash we saw an Isaian reference to *le'umi* read as *le-'imi*, here the opposite has taken place, and "my mother" in our verse has been read as "my people".[9] Cant. 3:11 is taken to mean that the people crown God. Though God truly could be considered ruler of the world since Creation, He insists that divine kingship depends entirely on Israel's proclamation of it, beginning with their song at the Sea of Reeds. Only then is He crowned.

An interesting reversal has taken place in the course of our ongoing discussion of these midrashic sources. We thought we had turned away from the coronation of God to deal with the coronation of Israel at Sinai or perhaps at the Sea. Yet now it turns out to be God who is being crowned there as well, whether by "mother," "sister," "daughter," or people. The relationship between these two coronations will now take us another step, from the purely aggadic realm into one that also involves ancient religious custom.

[7] The key passage is *Bahir* #63. I should perhaps make it clear that I do not "believe" the Kabbalists' claims about the meaning of this passage. "Daughter," "sister," and "mother" here are appelations for Israel, indicating God's great love for them, perhaps showing different modes of relationship in which God and Israel stand. There is no indication that they have referents in the realm of ontology, as the *sefirot* do in the eyes of the Kabbalist, nor are they interchangable with other symbol-terms in a fixed way, as are the Kabbalist's *sefirot*.

[8] *Aggadat Shir ha-Shirim*, line 1000. See the treatment by Idel, *Kabbalah*, p. 192.

[9] *'immi* is understood as *'umati*.

What is the plain meaning of Cant. 3:11? It would seem that in late biblical times both bridegroom and bride would wear a wreath or crown on their wedding day.[10] Perhaps it was even usual for a mother to weave such a crown for her bridegroom son. In the Song, a very much post-Solomonic author tries to imagine how great a crown would have been woven by the legendary king's mother for the greatest of all royal weddings.

Unfortunately, we do not know exactly where these crowns fit into the marriage rites; it may well be that bridegroom and bride exchanged them with one another. Marriage was very much a time for the use of crowns or weaths in the Graeco-Roman world. Both bridegroom and bride were crowned, the latter generally with a crown given her by her new husband. These crowns were made of myrtle, laurel, olive, or other branches and were sometimes seen as representing fruitfulness. That ancient practice is followed to this day in the Greek and other Orthodox churches, though with metal crowns, and the marriage ceremony altogether is sometimes referred to as *stefanos*, or "coronation." Among the Greeks, the prospective husband first crowns his bride in the name of the trinity, and then she does the same to him. When both are crowned, the priest blesses them by reciting three times, "O Lord our God, crown them with glory and honor!"[11]

That which survives in this latter-day Greek rite can be traced to the very earliest days of Christianity, when it was the subject of some controversy. Tertullian devoted a treatise (*De Corona*) to his opposition to the wearing of crowns by Christians.[12] Concerned about what he considered pagan influences on Christian life, he wanted the new Christians to distinguish themselves from their pagan neighbors by not wearing the ubiquitous *diadema* at all. When it came to weddings, he insisted that no flowers be worn on the head at all, as a clear demonstration of separation from what he considered to be pagan practice. He even recommended to Christian men, in the days of the movement's rapid spread, that they avoid marrying pagan women who might lead them to wearing coronas at the wedding![13] The Western church seems eventually to

[10] For other biblical evidence of this practice, see Is. 61:10 and, regarding the bride, Ezek. 16:12.

[11] See discussion in *Paulys Realencyclopädie*, vol. 22, col. 1594f. and Goodenough, *Jewish Symbols*, vol. 7 (New York: Pantheon, 1968), p. 155.

[12] *De Corona*, and see especially chapter 13, where crowns on the occasion of marriage are opposed. The entire treatise is concerned with teaching Christians not to wear wreaths or crowns at all, largely because of the pagan associations. Chapter 7 of Tertullian's work contains a very interesting mythic history of crowns and their place in the Roman pantheon.

[13] Cf. the treatment by K. Baus, *Der Kranz in Antike und Christentum* (Bonn: P. Hanstein, 1940) as cited by Goodenough, *Jewish Symbols*, vol. 7, p. 155. The use of crowns of "laurel, flowers, or other plants" is also condemned in a sermon of Ephrem the Syrian (fourth century) as a "custom of Greeks and Jews." See the citation in Goodenough, vol. 7, p. 152. The crown under discussion is being used to decorate a house. It is not clear here whether this is related to marriage (see vol. 7, p. 155).

have followed Tertullian's warning, and the practice of marriage crowns fell out of use at some point. But Christian sources report that in the East marriage crowns were widely in use in the days of John Chrysostom (c. 345–407), and they are central to the marriage ceremony even in the very ancient Nestorian Syriac rite.[14]

The Talmudic sources regarding marital crowns are fragmentary, and many of them turn around the suspension or restriction of a popular custom; only in this backward way can we come to understand how much it flourished. "In the battle against Vespasian," we are told, "a decree was issued against bridegrooms' crowns. . . . In the battle against Titus, they decreed regarding the brides' crowns."[15] Titus, the son of Vespasian, came with him to put down the Judean revolt in the year 66 C.E. When Vespasian was named emperor in 69, Titus stayed on and became commander. Thus the "battle of Vespasian" here refers to the Judean revolt, and the "battle of Titus" is the last critical stage, during which Jerusalem was sacked. We seem to have before us a poignant record of increasingly severe restrictions on frivolity in a time of national crisis. Alternatively, assuming that these "crowns" were actually wreaths of leaves and flowers, we may see here warnings of increasing intensity against unnecessary destruction of plant life in a city under seige. As far as the brides were concerned, another source seems to indicate that it was just those particularly ornate crowns known as *ʿir shel zahav*, or "golden towers," that were forbidden, while more modest marital wreaths were permitted even after the destruction.[16]

The fact that such adornments, including the *ʿir shel zahav*, were alive and well again among Jewish women (perhaps not only brides) by the time of the Mishnah makes it clear that the trauma of the destruction did not permanently erase them from use in Jewish life. The Mishnah worries about which of them may be worn in the public domain on the Sabbath. The Talmud limits the restrictions against men's crowns and permits those of myrtle and of roses.[17] Gaonic and early medieval sources preserve several cases in which *ga'onim* were asked whether Torah crowns might be used for adorning bridegrooms during the week of their wedding-feast.[18] The authorities generally disap-

[14] Bedjan, *Breviarium Chaldaicum*, cited by G. P. Badger, *The Nestorians and Their Rituals* (London: J. Master, 1852). See also Wm. Smith and S. Cheetham, *Dictionary of Christian Antiquities* (London, 1875), vol. 1, p. 511.

[15] M. *Soṭah* 9:14; *Tosefta Soṭah* 15:8.

[16] See S. Lieberman, *Tosefta Ki-Feshuṭah* (New York: Jewish Theological Seminary, 1950), "*Soṭah*," p. 766f., based on S. Paul in *Israel Exploration Journal* 17:4 (1967): 259ff.

[17] Cf. *Mishnah Shabbat* 5:1; b. *Soṭah* 49a-b. See also the references to R. Jeremiah in y. *Soṭah* 9 (24b, end) and *Echah Rabbah* 94b (?), where he is described as having used crowns to entertain at weddings. See E. G. Hirsch in *Jewish Encyclopedia*, vol. 4, p. 372.

[18] Cf. A. Yaʿari, *Toledot Ḥag Simḥat Torah* (Jerusalem: Mossad Ha-Rav Kook, 1964), p. 25. He refers to such sources as Rabbenu Nissim, published with Alfasi on b. *Megillah* 3; Gaonic Responsa *Shaʿarey Teshuvah* 287; Responsa of Ibn Adret attributed to Nahmanides 260. I was led

proved of this usage, citing the diminution of holiness that would result, on the principle, "We raise [use of objects] in holiness but do not diminish."[19] But the fact that they were not permitted the use of Torah crowns hardly means that they did not make special crowns or wreaths for this occasion. The practice was apparently quite common in the Middle Ages, and there is evidence of opposition to it by leading rabbis in both Ashkenaz (northern France) and Spain.[20] Nevertheless, R. David Abudarham (Seville, fourteenth century), recording customs current in his day, tells us that "it is customary in most places in Spain to place on the heads of bridegroom and bride two crowns (he calls them קרונש) made of olive branches covered with silver leaves and silken threads."[21]

What happens at Sinai is just this: a mutual coronation of God and Israel. Israel crown the blessed Holy One as their God, ruler, husband. The Holy One crowns Israel as His unique beloved bride. What we have here is rather clear testimony to the historicized sacred marriage myth that lies at the heart of Israelite faith, both in biblical and later times. This is the moment when God first says to His chosen people: "You made Me into a unique love-object in the world; I shall make you into a unique love-object in the world."[22] The heavenly kingdom is like the earthly kingdom; God takes a bride the same way men do, by a solemn exchange of crowns.

We mentioned only briefly in the opening paragraphs of this study that ancient Near Eastern enthronement or coronation ceremonies contained an element of *hieros gamos*, a dramatic representation of the divine marriage,

---

to this material thanks to Elliot Wolfson's "Female Imaging of the Torah," in *From Ancient Israel to Modern Judaism: Essays in Honor of Marvin Fox* (Atlanta: Scholars Press, 1989), vol. 2, p. 284n.47.

[19] b. *Berakhot* 28a.

[20] See the comments of Rabbenu Tam in *Tosafot* to *Shabbat* 59a and *Sefer ha-Yashar* (ed. Schlesinger), p. 204. He is the chief source for the extended treament by Nahmanides near the end of his *Torat ha-ʾAdam* (in *Kitvey RaMBaN*, ed. Chavel, vol. 1, p. 262).

[21] *Sefer Aburdarham*, ed. Jerusalem, 1963, p. 361f. He goes on to suggest, very much in contrast to the usual spirit of marital crowns, that the olive branch was chosen for its fruit's bitter taste, as a reminder of mourning for Jerusalem's destruction. This sounds like an after-the-fact etiology that probably has little to do with the custom's origins. The source of it seems to be *Tosafot ad Pes.* 36a, on the bitterness of the olive, and *Ṭur Even ha-ʿEzer* 65, for the custom itself. (The ox leading the first-fruits procession was crowned with olive branches in Temple times. Cf. M. *Bikkurim* 3.) While I have not been able to find reference to marital crown in the various *minhag*-compendia of early Ashkenaz, I do have reason to believe they existed there as well. *Maḥzor Vitry* (#491; p. 599) records a hymn in honor of the bridegroom that clearly was written to one wearing a crown. See also the passage from *Sefer ha-Navon* to be discussed in Chapter 10, where Old French or German terms for such crowns are mentioned, as well as two passages in *Sefer ha-Bahir* that may indicate a familiarity with marital crowns, to be discussed in Chapter 13. The *Ṭur* (*Even ha-ʿEzer* 65), however, records the custom of placing ashes on the forehead of the bridegroom, in the place of *tefillin*, as the Ashkenazic alternative to the Sephardic crowning custom.

[22] b. *Berakhot* 6a, following the aggadah on God's *tefillin*.

typically acted out by the earthly king. These traditions of sacred eros were received by Israel from the cultural surroundings in which they lived, either directly in Canaan or very possibly through contact in exile with remains of the neo-Babylonian religious culture. The great passion aroused by their own religious teaching, one of love and loyalty to the God who had liberated and forged them as a people, could not but seek out expression in erotic terms. But with the heavens containing but a single God, One described almost exclusively in masculine terms, the only possible object for a divine love relationship is the human community or the individual human soul. I believe that this change in erotic situation is the very essence of Israel's monotheistic revolution: there is now no one other for God to love than His chosen human creatures. In a narrowly conceived sense, there of course can be no *hieros gamos* in Israel, and it is no surprise that scholars have come to deny the extravagant claims once made in this regard.[23] But in a transformed sense that is still more than metaphor, the marriage of God and Israel is a "real" one. Seen in this light, the use of the Song of Songs as an account of the divine courtship and marriage with Israel is not an incidental bit of midrash but the very essence of early Judaism,[24] indeed the "holy of holies," as Akiva so well understood. It is in fact the narrative version of what was artistically represented in the Temple's holy of holies: the two cherubim intertwined with one another "like the love of man and woman."[25] There *is* in fact *hieros gamos* in Israel, though ritual performance of it was not to be fully articulated until the emergence of Kabbalah in the Middle Ages.

In dealing with the sacred marriage of God and Israel, we might seem to be back on the secure ground of relatively exoteric aggadah. Faith in this marriage and its celebration is certainly well-attested in the classic early midrashim,[26] and it greatly influences later Jewish poetic and mystical expression as well. But I trust that by now it will be clear to the reader that I believe the exoteric and esoteric traditions of Jews in late antiquity and rabbinic times must be treated as a spectrum or continuum, rather than as clearly demarcated realms. Neither is "earlier" than the other (I am referring to the traditions, not their textual forms), nor can either be understood as more "mainstream."

[23] See the reference to I. Wheatley's dissertation in Chapter 1, n. 7 above.

[24] I have written about this previously in "The Song of Songs in Early Jewish Mysticism," in *Orim*. See above, n. 2. Cf. also the discussion by Tikva Frymer-Kensky, *In the Wake of the Goddess*.

[25] b. *Yoma*ʾ 21b, 54a. See the discussion and sources cited in Heschel, *Torah min ha-Shamayim*, vol. 1, pp. 62ff.

[26] The best-known of these passages is probably the opening homily in *Pesiqta DRK*. A great deal of material is to be found there and in the cross-references of the Mandelbaum edition. The several midrashim on Canticles are also obvious places to look for this material. On the marriage metaphor in rabbinic Judaism, see G. D. Cohen, "The Song of Songs and the Jewish Religious Mentality," in *The Samuel Friedland Lectures: 1960–1966* (New York: Jewish Theological Seminary of America, 1966), pp. 1–21.

While exoteric teachings are by definition to be made more available to the general public, it is not at all clear, as Jacob Neusner and others have emphasized, what the general (and mostly unlettered) Jewish public of ancient Judea or Babylonia believed about the rabbis and their powers, about the relationship of the upper and lower universes, or about the Torah and its secret meanings. It may well be that aspects of belief or practice that were relegated to the "esoteric" tradition by those who later copied and controlled the documents in fact reflect more widespread forms of religious consensus than that which came to be seen, by the standards of a later era, as the Jewish "mainstream." The marriage of God and Israel, and the exchange of crowns that is its symbolic expression, surely had a wide range of meanings that extended across the lines that we moderns might use to demarcate the devotional, the theurgic, and the magical. Some surely saw Israel's crown mostly as a magic seal, while others viewed it more as a sign of their faith in God or of the Holy One's affection for Israel. But none of these usages is exclusive of the others. We are given no sense by the sources that the faithful Jew, ever seeking to be numbered among those righteous who can rescind the decrees of heaven, was not at once both faithful servant and powerful agent, engaged in a devotional life that included both surrender to the kingdom of heaven and the ability to affect God's will and shape it to the needs of His faithful, with no sense that these values were in conflict with one another.

All parts of this spectrum saw the events at Sinai as paradigm and justification for their own chosen sorts of religious activity, as we have indicated. The merkavah voyager saw himself to be repeating the journey of Moses, who stepped off the mountaintop and entered into the heavenly chambers. The merkavah journey is a way in which the individual repeats the ascent of Moses.[27] Akiva's entry into the *pardes* serves to legitimate this attempt, to show that one who lives in our own postarchaic times can succeed in such a journey. This is why the aggadic sources tell the same tales of Moses and Akiva in their heavenly adventures. Like Moses before him, Akiva too meets the angels who want to destroy him with their fiery breath. He too is told to hold onto the heavenly throne, as the Holy One calls out, "Leave this elder alone, for he is deserving to gaze upon My glory."[28] Of course Akiva is the

[27] See *Pesiqta Rabbati* 20 (97a), already discussed above in another context. The parallel between the ascents of Moses and Akiva, as well as a more general sense that the merkavah voyage is a private repetition of Moses' Sinai experience and entry in heaven, have been discussed by M. Idel in *JSJT* 1 (1981): 23ff. See also the references by Y. Liebes in *Het'o shel Elisha*, p. 98 and by Schaefer in *The Hidden and Manifest God: Some Major Themes in Early Jewish Mysticism* (Albany: SUNY, 1992), pp. 67ff.

[28] b. *Ḥagigah* 15b (end). According to *Maʿaseh Merkavah* (Schaefer, *Synopse* #550), Akiva sees the knot of God's *tefillin*, thus repeating the vision of Moses on Sinai. The relationship between the aggadic treatments of the Sinaitic revelation and the merkavah experiences of the rabbis has been treated from a somewhat different point of view by I. Chernus, *Mysticism in Rabbinic Judaism* (Berlin: de Gruyter, 1982), pp. 1ff.

new Moses in some other ways as well, having discovered Torah after tending his father-in-law's flock for forty years and having revealed to him "things that were not revealed to Moses our Teacher."[29] Perhaps it is no coincidence that these secrets had to do with interpreting the crowns that God was tying to the letters. Here we have another piece of imagery that helps to complete our cycle: the crowned God, whose crown contains the divine name, gives to His crowned bride a Torah replete with mysterious names, itself decorated with crowns that serve as the keys to unlocking its secrets.[30]

[29] *Tanḥuma Buber Ḥuqqat* 4; *Be-Midbar Rabbah* 19:4.

[30] In order not to extend this work beyond its present length, I have avoided dealing with both the crowns of letters and the crowns placed on the Torah scroll itself. These seem to be rather separate subjects, the one relating more to letter speculations than to coronation traditions, and the other belonging more to the realm of ritual art and its history. But for a full picture of the crown and its uses in the Jewish religious imagination, these would of course have to be considered as well.

Regarding the crowns on the letters, the crucial passage is the very puzzling one on b. *Shabbat* 89a. I am not completely satisfied with Y. Liebes's explanation in his "De Natura Dei," but I do not have a better solution to this problem.

CHAPTER TEN

Medieval Reconsiderations

THE BODY OF MATERIAL with which we have dealt until this point may be said to originate roughly in the Judaism of the first millennium of the common era. I have made relatively few attempts to date particular traditions, mostly out of a belief that such specific dating of ideas or literary images is rarely possible, considerably more difficult than the already daunting task of dating the texts in which they appear. Believing that the culture of Jews in this era was a highly conservative one, and that later generations saw themselves mostly as transmitters rather than creators of sacred traditions, I am generally a supporter of the early dating of these esoteric materials. In the specific body of images with which we have dealt, I have tried to show that this bias in favor of early dating is supported by the presence of similar associations within Jewish-Christian and, in one case, Gnostic materials, which had to have derived them from existing Jewish traditions at rather early points. It is true that some of the sources I have quoted were edited only during the period we generally call the Middle Ages (tenth century and later, in the case of Jewish materials), and some even in Europe rather than the Near East. But I have tried to this point to remain within the bounds of texts and traditions that *typologically* reflect the Judaism of that first millennium, what may broadly be called the rabbinic/Gaonic milieu. I believe there is nothing quoted to this point that could not have had its origins—and thus very probably had at least its oral origins—in the pre-tenth-century period, or in a Judaism uninfluenced by typically medieval concerns.

We turn our attention now to the discussion and expansion of these traditions by medieval Jews, who saw themselves even in this highly amorphous realm of the esoteric as receivers of a firmly established tradition. We have already begun to see how early medievals found aspects of these esoteric traditions unsettling. Karaites had attacked the rabbis as fools for their tales of God's *tefillin*, and R. Hai Gaon, staunch defender of rabbinism, had to apologetically "cover" for those traditions by saying that they were expressions of worship that surely did not contain a claim to representing actual descriptions of the divine self.

This willingness to deny the literal truth-value of such aggadic passages characterized certain philosophers of the Middle Ages, their tradition perhaps reaching its apex in Maimonides, who determined that the *Shiʿur Qomah* tradition altogether could not be seen as an authentic part of the rabbinic corpus and must be the work of "some Greek preacher."[1] This may be seen as an early example of Jewish openness to form criticism, though here such willingness to treat texts critically surely serves as a "handmaiden" to a particular philosophic view of what might or might not be considered an acceptable part of the rabbinic tradition.

But it was not only rationalists who were troubled by these early esoteric sources. Mystical teachers of the Middle Ages had themselves accepted a good deal of the antianthropomorphic theological ground of medieval religious discourse. They too found these texts to be something of an embarrassment, but they could not dismiss them so handily. Not only were they generally of the more theologically conservative sectors of Jewry, naturally loath to deny or criticize anything inherited from earlier ages. In many cases their mystical turn of mind was instinctively attracted to these seemingly "bizarre" or "wild" claims of the early aggadah. It was precisely in these theologically outlandish statements that the deepest truth seemed to lie buried.[2] As we shall see, their general strategy was to attribute the various anthropomorphic descriptions to a being lower than God Himself. Aggadic preachers might have most feared this move, because of the Gnostic or Christian challenges and the question of "two domains in heaven." Meṭaṭron had to be given lashes and Adam had to be pushed out of the divine carriage, according to the earlier traditions, so that no one would think that God had an equal or a rival. But the medievals were no longer so concerned with the issue of dualism. Their greater concern was the creation (which they saw as "preservation") of a pure and nonanthropomorphic notion of the deity. In order to do that, while preserving the value of these inherited and revered sources, the attribution of both biblical and other anthropomorphisms to an angelic or quasi-divine being often seemed to be the best alternative. This approach, almost universal in the early Middle Ages, is rejected both by Maimonides, who devotes the first portion of his *Guide* to an explanation of the seeming anthropomorphisms as homonyms, and by Nahmanides (1194–1270), who uses Kabbalistic method as a way to deny both anthropomorphism and dualism at the same time.

There are two major streams of esoteric or mythic/mystical thought among Jews in the high Middle Ages. In northern Europe small circles of Jews developed a somewhat diversified group of secret teachings. These are known to us collectively as the esoteric lore of German Hasidism, despite the fact that not

[1] The statement is found in a responsum published in the collection of Maimonides' *Teshuvot* edited by A. Freimann, #373, p. 343. The Arabic original is included in the edition of Maimonides' Commentary to *Mishnah Sanhedrin*, ed. Gottlieb (Hanover, 1906), p. 97. On the complicated history of Maimonides' attitude toward *Shiʿur Qomah*, see the remarks of S. Lieberman in his appendix to Scholem, *Jewish Gnosticism*, p. 124.

[2] See the remarks of G. Scholem, "Kabbalah and Myth," in *On the Kabbalah and Its Symbolism* (New York: Schocken, 1969) and of Y. Liebes in "De Natura Dei."

all of them were necessarily associated with those groups called *ḥasidim* in their own day, and some of them in fact originated from circles that flourished in France and England as well as Germany.[3] The leading figures associated with German Hasidism are Judah the Ḥasid (c. 1150–1217), who lived in Regensburg, and his disciple Eleazar of Worms (c. 1165-c.1230), the latter author of some of the most important esoteric treatises concerning this area, a large number of which still remain unpublished.[4] The other stream, first identified in Provence in the latter half of the twelfth century, passed quickly over the Pyrenees and is known primarily in its Catalonian and Castilian incarnations. This is the tradition known to us as Kabbalah, but it too is a highly complex phenomenon with several different subschools and stages within its early development.[5] It is generally accepted that medieval Kabbalah reached its greatest heights in the Zohar, composed in Castile in the last decades of the thirteenth century.

Both the Ashkenazic and the Kabbalistic circles received the traditions of divine coronation as part of their shared legacy from the sacred past, a legacy they revered unquestioningly. Their own religious worldviews were formed by their encounters with that legacy, one that both shaped them and was itself reshaped as they sought to integrate it into their own emerging new forms of religious discourse. In fact that legacy was essentially identical until the late twelfth century, when Kabbalah split off from the shared late midrashic/ esoteric realm to create its own symbolic universe. We shall be interested here in seeing how this process of reworking the ancient legacy was undertaken with regard to the traditions of sacred coronation in German Hasidism and in developments that created the symbolism of *Sefer ha-Bahir*, a document that stands in a unique place between these intellectual and spiritual worlds. We shall then go on to treat briefly the evolution of crown symbolism within Kabbalah up to the period of the Zohar.

We turn our attention first to the esoteric world of Ashkenaz in the twelfth and thirteenth centuries. The pietistic authors of Rhineland Jewry saw themselves largely as religious conservators. Leaders of small and somewhat isolated communities, they had received from their ancestors esoteric traditions, associated particularly with the meaning of prayer, and it was their task to transmit these from one generation to the next, passing them on to appropriately learned and

[3] For clarification regarding the various circles of esoteric creativity among the *Ḥasidey Ashkenaz*, see J. Dan, "The 'Exceptional Cherub' Sect in the Literature of Medieval German Hasidim" (*Tarbiẓ* 35 [1966]: 349–72), reprinted in his *ʿIyyunim*, pp. 89–111.

[4] The most important scholarly syntheses regarding Ashkenazi Hasidism are those by I. Marcus, *Piety and Society: The Jewish Pietists of Medieval Germany* (Leiden: E. J. Brill, 1981) and Joseph Dan, *The Esoteric Theology of Ashkenazi Hasidism* (= *Torat ha-Sod*) (Jerusalem: Bialik Institute, 1981). Marcus's work contains an excellent bibliography (pp. 178–89) for publications up to that time. Dan has concentrated more on the mystical/esoteric writings of the group, and his books and many articles will be cited frequently in the following pages.

[5] See Scholem, *Origins*. For further detail, see below, Chapter 12, n. 1.

pious leaders of the community. Especially after their decimation in the wake of the first Crusade, this mission of cultural and spiritual self-preservation seemed all the more vital to them.[6] Among the sources treated in this reverential way by Ḥasidey Ashkenaz were the merkavah texts and some quasi-esoteric midrashim, a number of which are known to us only through manuscript traditions that passed through west-central Europe. These sources, clearly Near Eastern in origin, came to that area via one of a number of channels of transmission, but quite possibly through Lombardy, the region to which the all-important Kalonymide family of the Rhine area traced its own origins.

We do not know what the preservation of these texts meant to the early Ashkenazic pietists in terms of their own religious practice. I generally follow Joseph Dan, the leading scholar of Ashkenazic esotericism, on this question. Dan claims that the merkavah traditions were no longer living for them as they had been for the original practitioners of this art, for whom experiences of some sort lay behind the texts. These sources were collected and cherished in the West in the same way that early midrashim were held dear: they were a part of the teachings of the ancient rabbis, objects of study and comment, but not particularly of "practice." At the same time, Dan notes, the merkavah sources were among the key elements that helped to forge the emerging new religio-speculative literature of the *ḥasidim* themselves.

The difficulties in reading the literature of *Ḥasidey Ashkenaz* are enormous. It is the absolute antithesis of a systematic body of teachings, its insights scattered in scores of little treatises, many of which exist only in obscure manuscripts. The treatises are themselves often collections of short fragments, seldom concentrating on any one subject for more than a few pages. Moreover, as a highly conservative literature, the writings of *Ḥasidey Ashkenaz* often copy old texts or parts of old texts, interweaving them with bits of commentary. In this way the Ashkenazic teachers apparently sought to present their own views as integral to received tradition. When it happens that the original text itself is preserved only in such Ashkenazic versions, we understand that the complexities of sorting ancient material from medieval commentary or rearrangement can themselves be quite severe.

The first source we shall examine well exemplifies this situation. It is a passage from *Sefer ha-Navon*, an anonymous text that Dan dates to the late twelfth or early thirteenth century. This is one of several German Hasidic sources that exist more or less in textual isolation. It is not a part of the corpus known to and used by Judah or Eleazar in composing the most important esoteric writings of this area. Nevertheless, Dan affirms that it is quite close in origins to this "main" circle of Ashkenazic pietists.

Following various quotations from the *Shiʿur Qomah* sources, *Sefer ha-*

[6] See the famous document in which Eleazar gives his own history of the Ashkenazic leadership, published by Dan in *Torat ha-Sod*, p. 15f., as well as the discussion in chapter 1 of that work.

Navon comes to discuss the physiognomy of God's head, then gets to the letters inscribed on the divine forehead, and thence to God's *tefillin*. None of this sequence will seem surprising to us. After this the text quotes the passage from b. *Ḥagigah* 13b with which we began our discussion. It continues as follows (I have omitted several explanatory parallels from Talmudic sources that do not add to the original discussion here):

TEXT #29

Weha-Keter is numerically equivalent to *shel esh* (of fire) and to *weha-ruḥot* (and the winds),[7] for the winds lead the crown to Meṭaṭron. Meṭaṭron adjures it so that it goes to the blessed Holy One's head. Therefore the crown is *GaNaZ* (= sixty) thousand myriad parasangs,[8] which is *GaNUZ* and *NiGeNaZ* (secret and hidden). . . . And the crown, which is named Israel, is numerically equal to *u-tefillah* (and the prayer), written defectively, with the yod. . . .[9] The prayers of Israel are tied to the crown. Thus Qallir[10] established in the concluding hymn of Rosh Ha-Shanah: "They will receive the kingly prayers that arrive/ and will place them upon the head of the God of hosts." The crown praises the blessed Holy One, saying: "May YHWH rule forever, your God O Zion from generation to generation, Halleluyah!" (Ps. 146:10)

In the book *Hekheley Qodesh* and in *Midrash Abba Gurion*:[11] As the crown ascends, "[the angels] run and bow, leaving their crowns in the heavenly plains (*ʿaravot*) and granting kingship to Him." Of this King Solomon has said, "His head is pure gold, his locks are curly, black as a raven" (Cant. 5:11).[12] There are *KaBOD* letters

[7] Each equals 631. This corrects the interpretation of Dan in *ʿIyyunim*, p. 128n.84 from *ha-keter* to *weha-keter*. Idel, in *Kabbalah*, p. 194 translates *ruḥot* here as "spirits." I prefer "winds," because the *ruaḥ*, along with fire, is an element that ascends, that carries the crown upward. The properties of *ruaḥ*, *esh*, and *mayyim* are much discussed in the commentaries to *Sefer Yeṣirah*, well known to *Ḥasidey Ashkenaz*. See also the opening section of the text from *Sodey Razaya*ʾ to be quoted below. The same meaning of *ruaḥ* is evidenced in *Sefer ha-Ḥesheq* #67, as quoted above at chapter 4, n. 11, where the wind carries the crown to the head.

[8] This seems here to be a measurement of size, but sixty myriads—the word *thousands* does not add to the count—is the number of Israelite males who came out of Egypt, and, at least according to later Kabbalists, the fixed number of Israelite souls at any given time. The way in which the crown "corresponds" to this number is unclear here as it is in the *Shiʿur Qomah* sources from which this count is taken. See above, Chapter 6, n. 12.

[9] ותפילה written this way is numerically 531, corresponding to שראל, or Israel without its initial yod, as it is sometimes found in these sources. This corrects Dan, *ʿIyyunim*, p. 129n.88.

[10] R. Eleazar ha-Qallir, probably the most famous of early Hebrew liturgical poets, lived in Ereṣ Israel, possibly in the seventh or eighth century. His work was very popular in early Ashkenaz, and his *piyyuṭim* were the subject of much commentary.

[11] The former is his designation for several *hekhalot* sources, and the latter is a late midrashic work on Esther, published by Salomon Buber in Vilna, 1886. Dan notes that the only extant parallel is in *Otiyyot de-Rabbi ʿAkiva*ʾ, ed. Wertheimer, in *Battey Midrashot*, vol. 2, p. 378f. It is reasonable to assume confusion of these two late midrashic compilations.

[12] Of course this is the passage from Song of Songs that we have discussed above on p. 53, the section of the Canticle to which Lieberman claims *Shiʿur Qomah* is a midrash.

here,[13] the power of the ministering angels who give glory to the blessed Holy One. And we, Israel, crown [Him] each morning with the eighty-seven (*PaZ*, "gold") words of *barukh she-ʾamar*. "His head is pure gold, his locks are curly, black as a raven" is numerically equivalent to "And the crown of YHWH: Sandalphon, this one binds it to the Rock, the Master of mercy, the gracious and merciful YHWH and He is unique, Shaddai."[14] Meṭaṭron and Sandalphon are the ones appointed over the crown. Sandalphon has five names: Yagidiel, Ḥaviviel, ʿir we-qadish (cf. Daniel 4:10), and some say Hadraniel [plus Sandalphon itself]. He praises his Master. Thus Rabbi Simeon the Great ben Isaac[15] established in the *ofan*[16] for Shavuʿot: "Crowned with woven song, enwrapped and glorified." . . . The crown opens wide its mouth and praises the blessed Holy One, saying, "May YHWH reign forever!". . .[17]

Ten angels are inscribed upon the crown: Akhtariel, Ahaviel, Ḥaniel, Ḥasdiel, Raḥmiel, Shemuʿiel, Yehudahiel, Nikhbadiel, Sariel, Shoshaniel. Shoshaniel stands on the top of the crown in front, as it is said: "I will be as the dew to Israel; he shall blossom like the lily (*shoshanah*) and cast forth his roots like the Lebanon" (Hosea 14:6). It stands there like that which in the vernacular[18] is called *boṭon*, standing like a diadem on the bride's head, called a *kuṣaʾ*[19] in German. The ten angels inscribed on the crown parallel the ten places where Israel is compared to a bride, as it says in the *Midrash Pesiqta* on "Surely I will rejoice" (Is. 61:10).[20] In ten places Israel are called "bride," as it says: "You have ravished my heart, my sister, O bride" (Cant. 4:9); "a locked garden is my sister, the bride" (Cant. 4:12); "come with me from Lebanon, O bride (ibid. 5); "as a bridegroom rejoices over a bride" (Is. 62:5); "surely I will rejoice" and so forth on to "as a bride wears her adornments" (Is. 61:9); "the sound of gladness, the sound of joy; the voice of bridegroom and of bride" (Jer. 7:34).

Whoever answers "Amen" after a blessing in the prayer (*birkat ha-tefillah*) forms a link in the crown of the blessed Holy One. Without that link, every single letter and word of the Prayer will fall from the crown.[21]

[13] "Glory" = 32. Cant. 5:11 contains thirty-two letters. This is obscured by the plene spelling in the manuscript from which Dan prints.

[14] I have had no more success than Dan in getting this long *gemaṭria* to work.

[15] Payyetan, born c. 950. His works were widely published in the Ashkenazi *Maḥzor*.

[16] An *ofan* in this context is a liturgical hymn written for insertion into the Sabbath or festival liturgy during the *qedushah de-yoṣer*, immediately following the recitation of Is. 6:3. It is named for the next word in the liturgy (*weha-ʾofanim*), before which it is inserted.

[17] Here I have cut a brief passage on ʿAnafiel, taken from *Hekhalot Rabbati* chapter 23 (= Schaefer, *Synopse* #244).

[18] Old French. The word means "bud" or "knop" and is the source of modern French *bouton* and English *button*. See *Oxford English Dictionary* (Compact Edition; Oxford: Oxford University Press, 1971), s.v. "button."

[19] Possibly a scribal corruption of *Kranz*.

[20] *Pesiqta de-Rav Kahana* 9:1 (ed. Mandelbaum 147).

[21] Dan, *ʿIyyunim*, p. 128ff. See the discussion and shorter quotation by Idel in *Kabbalah*, p. 194.

From here the text wanders off into a long series of quotations on the importance of "Amen" and leaves our subject.

Sefer ha-Navon's author shows in this passage complete familiarity with the earlier traditions of divine coronation. He appreciates the connection between the angelic coronation of God and the prayers of Israel, particularly their public worship. He also articulates quite clearly the *hieros gamos* aspect of this myth, both by quoting Cant. 5:11 and by linking the crown of God to the ten places in Scripture where Israel is described as bride. Clearly in his day the custom of crowning brides is still well known,[22] and there are common vernacular terms that refer to such crowns. It is with these that he chooses to identify the crown of God. To the biblical, midrashic, and merkavah sources he adds quotations from the early *payyeṭanim*, whose works were the object of much veneration and commentary in medieval Ashkenaz. At the same time that the author combines all these older elements of the tradition, he adds the new and typically German Hasidic method of linking everything by *gemaṭriot* or numerical equivalencies, often of the most obscure sort. This type of reading may be characterized as the "trademark" of *Ḥasidey Ashkenaz*, giving their works an unmistakably recognizable stamp and distinguishing them both from earlier sources and from the writings of most Sephardic Kabbalists.

We shall have occasion to return to this text in the course of our further deliberations. For now we should especially note that ten angels are inscribed on the crown, a claim we have not seen elsewhere, that Shoshaniel is the central one of these, and that they are associated with Israel's status as the bride of God. We should also note that it is the crown itself that sings God's praises. One has the clear impression here that the crown is a living entity, a hypostasis quite as fully developed in this text as, for example, the heavenly throne was in the earlier sources. What distinguishes this heavenly entity, however, is its entire dependence on Israel and their prayers. Here the historic origins of this crown remain apparent; it was originally nothing other than the prayers themselves. The future role it will play in the Kabbalistic realm, if I may jump ahead, is also predicted here. It is fully a part of the divine pleroma (see Chap. 13, n. 7), reaching up to the greatest heights within the divine world. But its ability to do so depends entirely on the quality of human effort.

Similar in tone to the *Sefer ha-Navon* passage is another text, found in several manuscripts attributed to Eleazar of Worms. While this source has already been the subject of some scholarly attention,[23] it is important enough that we need to discuss it here as well:

[22] I presume this means that it was current among Jews in his day. See the discussion and sources above, Chapter 9 and n. 15ff. It is possible but less likely that he is referring to a non-Jewish practice. See N. Feuchtwanger, "The Coronation of the Virgin and the Bride," *Jewish Art* 12–13 (1987), for discussion of the Jewish/Christian parallels. I am grateful to Elliot Wolfson for this reference.

[23] Idel, *Kabbalah*, p. 193.

TEXT #30

HWH[*H*] is numerically equal to *BYṬ*[24] and *HYH*, since it is a name of the Shekhinah, as Scripture says: "I was [*wa-ʾHYH*][25] with Him [*eṣlo*] as a nursling (Prov. 8:30)." She is prayer [*ṣelotaʾ*] and the sound of prayer [*tefillah*] rising upward. Thus RaSHI interprets the verse: "There was a sound from the firmament above their heads; as they stood, their wings were set at rest" (Ezek. 1:25). He comments: "'There was a sound' refers to Israel's prayer, for Israel's prayer rises beyond 'the firmament above their heads' and goes and seats itself on the head of the blessed Holy One, becoming His crown." . . . for prayer sits like a crown . . . for when the *ṣelotaʾ* and the *tefillah* rises [!] upward, they whisper with one another and cause the *ḥashmal* to whisper, parallel to our prayer.[26] . . . The *ʿaṭarah*[27] of the blessed Holy One is 600,000 parasangs, parallel to the 600,000 of Israel. The name Sariel[28] is on the crown, numerically equal to *tefillah av eḥad* [prayer; one father], because one father arranges a crown [*ʿaṭarah*] out of the prayers. When the crown [*keter*] ascends, they rush to prostrate themselves and lay down their crowns in the *ʿAravot* and they ascribe kingship to Him.[29] "And above the firmament that is upon his head is an appearance like that of sapphire stone in the image of a throne, and on the throne an appearance in the image of a man" (Ezek. 1:26). So the prayers [and?] crowns that rise unto the throne are like the throne, which is made of sapphire stone.[30]

Here too the crown engages in dynamic movement of its own accord. The sound of Israel's rising prayers accompanies Ezekiel's vision, fully a continuation of themes we saw in the much earlier aggadic sources. But several mysterious elements have been added. HYH is designated as a name of "the Shekhinah." But what is "Shekhinah" here? Is it a term for God when present in the world, as in the old rabbinic sources, or rather a proto-Kabbalistic usage of Shekhinah,[31] as an element disinguished from a higher God-figure? The ensuing scriptural proof-text makes it clear that here we have the latter; it is being read to mean "HYH [or "shekhinah"] was with Him [God] as a nursling." The nursling of Prov. 8:30 is understood in the midrash to be Torah in the earlier sources;[32] here that figure (the daughter of God, in equally well-known ag-

[24] The significance of *BYṬ* is unclear to me.

[25] Correcting Idel's rendering as "I will be."

[26] I am not convinced by Idel's "and they instigate the *ḥashmal* against our prayer." *Ke-neged* can at least as well refer to a parallel movement as to an opposing one. I would like to see some clearer examples of such usage of *ḥashmal* before assuming that it is here a mythic antiprayer force.

[27] The following three sentences, down to "kingship to Him," constitute a *Shiʿur Qomah* fragment that has been incorporated into this text. For its sources see Idel, *Kabbalah*, p. 373n.170.

[28] An anagram of Yisra'el.

[29] This reads much like the descriptions in the early chapters of *3 Enoch*.

[30] Ms. New York, JTS 1786 fol. 43a; Ms. Oxford 1812, fol. 101b-102a.

[31] See the discussion by Scholem in *On the Mystical Shape of the Godhead* (New York: Schocken, 1991), pp. 141–57 and our further consideration below in Chapters 12 and 13.

[32] M. *Bereshit Rabbah* 1:1 and its many parallels. See my prior discussion of this and other

gadic passages[33]) is identified with Shekhinah. And Shekhinah is identified with prayer: the *ṣelota*ʾ (prayer) was formerly *eṣlo* (with him) as Shekhinah/nursling. This means that the ascent of prayer as crown is its return to its former place (though now risen from His bosom to His head?), making this a proto-Kabbalistic passage indeed. The play of *eṣlo* and *ṣelota*ʾ is one we will see again in this literature,[34] combined with the third element of *ṣel*, or "shadow." A possible distinction is being made here between *ṣelota*ʾ and *tefillah*, two terms for prayer, which whisper with one another as they rise. But *ṣelota*ʾ was just identified with *shekhinah*! Is it possible that *ṣelota*ʾ and *tefillah* are Shekhinah and Israel's prayers, rising together to be God's crown, divine and human elements that combine in ascending prayer?

Neither the *Sefer ha-Navon* treatment nor this one, anonymous but likely to be attributed to Eleazar of Worms, reflected any sense of theological hesitancy about the coronation traditions, nor any need to defend them in an apologetic manner. That is not by any means the case for a great many other Ḥasidut Ashkenaz sources, as we have already indicated. Certain key features may be said to characterize the intellectual speculations of this group and period. Most relevant for our purposes here is a preoccupation with the question of identifying the true object of anthropomorphic descriptions of God in the received biblical and rabbinic sources. Aware by means of an eleventh-century Hebrew paraphrase[35] of Saʿadya Gaon's *Book of Beliefs and Opinions* (written c. 935), the first major work of medieval Jewish philosophy, they were much influenced by his teachings concerning the divine glory. Saʿadya had been challenged by both Muslim and Karaite critiques of anthropomorphism in biblical and rabbinic views of God. To account for the obviously anthropomorphic descriptions found in biblical texts of prophetic vision, he developed a theory of "glory," or manifestation of the deity.[36] It is this glory, created especially

sources in "Bride, Spouse, Daughter: Images of the Feminine in Classical Jewish Sources," in Susannah Heschel's *On Being a Jewish Feminist: A Reader* (New York: Schocken, 1983) and Elliot Wolfson's in "Female Imaging of the Torah: From Literary Metaphor to Religious Symbol," in *From Ancient Israel to Modern Judaism—Intellect in Quest of Understanding: Essays in Honor of Marvin Fox*, vol. 2 (Atlanta: Scholars Press, 1989).

[33] *Shemot Rabbah* 33:1 and parallels, discussed in the two articles referred to in the preceding note.

[34] In Chapter 12.

[35] The paraphrase, often referred to as *Pitron Sefer Emunot*, was probably undertaken in the Byzantine region in the mid-eleventh century. This is the conclusion of Ronald Kiener, who is currently preparing a critical edition of this text, a portion of which comprised his doctoral dissertation at the University of Pennsylvania (1984). See his article in *AJS Review* 11 (1987). The paraphrase, which presents Saʿadya as much more of a mystic than seems the case from the Arabic original of his work, has a particulary important place in the development of both thought and terminology in early medieval Jewish theological discussion in Europe.

[36] Saʿadya's major philosophical work is *Kitāb al-Amānāt waʾl-ʿItiqādāt*, edited by S. Landauer (Leiden: E. J. Brill, 1880). The complete English translation is by S. Rosenthal, *The Book of Beliefs and Opinions* (New Haven: Yale Univerity Press, 1948). The *kavod* is dealt with in the second treatise. See also *Oṣar ha-Geʾonim, Berakhot, teshuvot*, p. 16.

for the purpose of revelation, that the prophets see. The first light God created at the creation of the world, it has neither premundane status nor any function as an intermediary between God and humans. It exists in order to offer a pictorial element in prophecy that will strengthen the prophet's faith, and that of his hearers, in the content revealed.[37]

In addition to dealing with anthropomorphic accounts in the prophets, however, Saʿadya was also challenged specifically with regard to the *shiʿur qomah* traditions. While he had his own doubts as to the authenticity of these sources, he felt a need to defend them from the barbs of Karaite authors, in particular. He thus proposed the existence of a higher *kavod*, one visible to the angels alone. This glory, also created by God, was what the angels saw seated on the throne and transmitted to the authors of the *Shiʿur Qomah* texts. Insofar as texts discussing the inner life of God in the heavens have any validity at all, they must refer to this "first glory," rather than the Creator Himself. Sometimes this is depicted as a higher angelic presence, knowable only to other angels.[38]

Saʿadya thus gives us a "double-glory" theory, one that was later used in ways he would hardly have found acceptable or might not even have comprehended. Over the course of some two hundred years of translation, interpretation, and expansion, Saʿadya was converted from rationalist into mystic. The steps in this process have largely been traced by Dan, Kiener, and others and need not be repeated here. One interesting passage does deserve mention, however. In the Talmudic dictionary by Nathan of Rome (1035–1110), Saʿadya's higher glory is referred to as being "close to the Shekhinah; unseen by any human." As Dan has noted, this passage is widely quoted in the later texts on Shekhinah and *kavod*. Though the author of the ʿArukh may have simply meant "God" when he said Shekhinah here, the passage was later used to indicate yet another realm. Saʿadya thus becomes the purported source of a hierarchy of created light-realms, creating a precedent for both neo-Platonic and "Gnostic" or Kabbalistic conceptions that were soon to come. It has been

[37] For Saʿadya's views on revelation, see A. Altmann, "Saadya's Theory of Revelation: Its Origin and Background," in *Saadya Studies: In Commemoration of the One Thousandth Anniversary of the Death of R. Saadya Gaon* (Manchester: University Press, 1943), pp. 4–25.

[38] On Saʿadya and *shiʿur qomah*, see J. Kapah's "Sarid me-Ḥibbur Temani ʿAtiq be-ʿInyeney Sefer Shiʿur Qomah," in *Yahadut Teman: Pirqey Mehqar we-ʿIyyun* (Jerusalem: Ben Zvi Institute, 1976), pp. 407–10. This Arabic original of the Saʿadya passage still needs to be read alongside the quotation in Judah ben Barzilai's *Commentary on Sefer Yeṣirah* (Berlin: Mekize Nirdamim, 1885), p. 21. See also p. 31, for the view that not even the angels can see this higher *kavod*. See also the important material in the *Oṣar ha-Geʾonim* source mentioned above in n. 36, p. 17f. There Saʿadya claims that the lesser light (or *kavod*), created for the prophets, is big enough to fill a house, as Isaiah notes in his vision (6:2). The greater light was made only for the angels, and this fills the heavens (presumably their *hekhal*). This would account for the vast numbers used in the *Shiʿur Qomah* descriptions; the angels told the prophets or sages what they saw without readjusting the numbers to human dimensions.

noted, however,[39] that part of Saʿadya's terminology for drawing this distinction was itself taken from the earlier merkavah literature. He thus may be seen as a rationalist who served as a strange bridge between mysticisms, using the terminology of one and helping to create the terminology of another.

Less critical in temperament than Saʿadya, the German *ḥasidim* revered and initially seem to have believed in the merkavah sources in quite literal fashion. That certainly seems to be true of the *Sefer ha-Navon* text we have just seen. There is no hint there that the heavenly accounts are to be taken with anything less than total and literal seriousness. In other sources, however, we see them struggling to develop a sense of metaphor, partly in response to their understanding of Saʿadya and other philosophical influences. These included the writings of Sabbatai Donnolo, the Neoplatonists Abraham bar Ḥiyya and Abraham Ibn Ezra, and, perhaps especially important for our materials, the *Sefer Yeṣirah* commentary of Judah ben Barzilai of Barcelona, whose struggles with notions of truth and metaphor in religious language are very much worthy of study.[40]

At the very heart of the problem created by this dual acceptance of the merkavah traditions and the Saʿadyanic theology lies our body of material referring to the coronation of God, God's *tefillin*, and the throne of glory. The essential response of *Ḥasidey Ashkenaz* was to preserve faith in the truth of the merkavah sources, but to apply them to the *kavod*, sometimes identified as Shekhinah and in some cases as an angelic presence. In a functional sense this redefinition of the object of earlier descriptions is tantamount to the creation of metaphor. Rather than redefining the use of language, however, as would both the Maimonideans and the Kabbalists, *Ḥasidey Ashkenaz*, following their understanding of Saʿadya, redesignated the object to which such language referred. The *Shiʿur Qomah* descriptions were still "literally" true, insofar as they were concerned. But the one of whom they were true was no longer the blessed Holy One, Creator of heaven and earth, but rather a secondary divine manifestation, characterized as "glory," "cherub," or by some other angelic terminology.

Sometimes this changing of the referent is done with a degree of subtlety:

Text #31

When Moses prayed for Israel and for himself, the one who is seated on the merkavah opened the windows that are above the heads of the cherubim, and one thousand eight hundred defenders came forth. Meṭaṭron the angel of the presence

[39] By Alexander Altmann, in the article cited in pp. 17ff, and n. 26. See also the remarks by M. Fishbane in his "Some Forms of Divine Appearance in Ancient Jewish Thought," in *From Ancient Israel to Modern Judaism . . . Essays in Honor of Marvin Fox* (Atlanta: Scholar's Press, 1989), pp. 261–70 and especially 270.

[40] See Wolfson's important discussions both of the early medieval philosophical materials in themselves and as elements within the intellectual/religious universe of *Ḥasidut Ashkenaz* in *Speculum*, chapters 4 and 5.

was with them. They received the prayers and placed them on the head of Akhtariel.[41]

Here it is clear that "the one who is seated on the merkavah" is a figure of less than ultimate stature in the upper worlds. That figure is involved in the ascent of prayer to the head of Akhtariel, who is presumably a "higher" configuration. As we have seen in *Sefer ha-Navon*, however, for at least some German Hasidic writers this is the name of an angel, rather than a designation for God. The referent of the word *Akhtariel* here is simply left unstated.

There was much that separated the intellectual worlds of Jews in Ashkenaz from their brethren in Provence and Catalonia; these are generally seen as quite distinct realms in the cultural geography of medieval Jewry. It will be interesting, then, to look at our next text, written by none other than R. Abraham ben David of Posquieres (c. 1125–1198), a major Provençal thinker and halakhist, and the earliest figure historically associated with the tradition that would come to be called Kabbalah. Here we turn again to the question of God's *tefillin*, and the question of how those seemingly strange aggadot in the Talmud were to be understood. The fact that these passages were found in the by-now canonized Babylonian Talmud made it seem all the more important to find an acceptable reading of them. These could hardly be dismissed as not belonging to the "real" rabbinic corpus, as some might do with a strange idea found only in a *hekhalot* source. Abraham ben David here transfers this *tefillin* association to Meṭaṭron; he is the wearer of the *tefillin* whom Moses sees.[42] This was meant to take some of the anthropomorphic sting out of the tradition, assigning the pictorial image to a being lower than God Himself. Here is his comment on the b. *Berakhot* passage:

TEXT #32

This [the aggadah concerning God's *tefillin*] refers to the angel of the presence [Meṭaṭron], whose name is like his Master's. Or perhaps there is another one above him, emanated from the primal cause. This being has supreme power, and it was this one who appeared to Moses and to Ezekiel "in the form of a man from above" (Ezek. 1:26). That is what appeared to the prophets. But the Cause of Causes has not appeared to any person, neither by right nor by left, by front nor by back. This is the secret [spoken of] in *Maʿaseh Bereshit*:[43] "Whoever knows the measure of the *yoṣer bereshit* will surely partake of the world-to-come." Of this Scripture says, "Let us make man in our image."[44]

[41] *Sodey Razaya'*, ed. Jerusalem., p. 109. Compare with Text #20 above.

[42] Meṭaṭron had already been associated with the divine *tefillin* as the one who ties them—instead of Sandalphon—and as the one who shows the *tefillin*-knot to Moses, when he seeks to see the divine glory. See *Sefer ha-Ḥesheq* 39 and 46 and the discussion in Chapter 5 above.

[43] This is the concluding line of several *Shiʿur Qomah* texts. See M. Cohen, *The Shiʿur Qomah: Texts and Recensions* (Tübingen: Mohr, 1985), p. 53, l. 144; Schaefer #952.

[44] Quoted by Scholem in *Reshit ha-Qabbalah* (Jerusalem: Schocken, 1948), p. 75f. This

Here we clearly see, even in one so prominently associated with esoteric lore, the medieval attempt to obliterate what is quite clear in our earlier tradition, namely that the wearer of the crown, seal, or *tefillin* is the Holy One and none other. RABaD is clearly influenced here by the German Hasidic tradition, and in turn by the double *kavod* theory of Saʿadya.

Some of these concerns will also be reflected in the longer passage we are now about to examine. Here we are looking at a section of *Sodey Razaya*ʾ,[45] a text written by Eleazar of Worms, the most important and prolific of the esoteric masters in Ashkenaz. In this text we shall see a desire to faithfully preserve and continue the old merkavah traditions, combined with considerable hesitancy about stating them in their most bold and unvarnished form. While there is a good bit of new midrash here, there are also several references to the *kavod* and some ambiguity as to exactly whose head the crown is to reach. This text has just recently been published for the first time and has not previously been considered in this context.

TEXT #33

When Israel pray with their hearts [properly] directed, Sandalphon selects those praises [or: words] that come from the heart and establishes the crown. The crown is alive, because the breath of speech is a dew of air and fire. Know that the human voice brings forth air, and speech contains moisture. You can see this on winter days on the skin of [your hand, placed] in front of your mouth. Speech too is hot, and hence it rises upward. It passes through[46] all the heavens and is more beloved than the breath of the ministering angels, which issues forth as fiery torches.

He is called Sandalphon. *Sandalphon* are precious stones, the goodly objects within prayer.[47] *Phon* is after "He has turned (*panah*) to the prayer of the destitute" (Ps.

passage is found in the writings of R. Asher ben David, who is quoting his grandfather R. Abraham ben David. See I. Twersky, *Rabad of Posquieres* (Cambridge, Harvard University Press, 1962), p. 269 f., where the passage is quoted and discussed. See also Twersky's brief discussion on the preceding page of Rabad's mention of *taga de-malka* and the polemical response of R. Zerachiah ha-Levi.

45 The various sections of this complex work have been listed and discussed by J. Dan in *Torat ha-Sod*, pp. 61ff. Since that treatment the first part of *Sodey Razaya*ʾ has been published from manuscript by S. Weiss in Jerusalem, 1991, and the Kamelhar edition of the second part has appeared in an undated reprint.

46 I am emending the impossible *ḥaver* in the Weiss edition to *ʿover*.

47 The words *Sandalkhon*, defined as a "precious stone," and *Sandalphon* are adjacent in the *ʿArukh*. These two words are confused in many manuscripts of the rabbinic sources; cf. Lewy and Jastrow, s.v. "*sandalkin*," "*sandalkonim*." Their confusion, or in this case their probably intentional association, is quite to be expected. This interpretation of the angel's name, based on a corruption of the Greek word *sardonyx*, a precious stone, seems to indicate that the angel himself is a symbol for the glowing nuggets of good *kawwanah* within the prayer, and it is those that make it rise. See further discussion below. For another interesting etymology of the name Sandalphon, see R. Jacob ben Jacob's *Commentary to the Chariot of Ezekiel* (ed. A. Farber; Jerusalem: Hebrew University, 1978), p. 35, line 22.

102:18), but His rule is in the heavens (*sheḥaqim*), the place where song is recited. This means that no song is acceptable to God like the song of Israel; the letters of *YISRA'EL are SHIR'EL* [the Song of God]. Since God is one, Israel is a single nation, and Sandalphon is called "a single wheel upon the ground" (Ez. 1:15); let the one receive the prayers of the one for the one God.

Sheḥaqim is an honored heaven, and Sandalphon rules over it. . . . [Here follows a version of the *Pesiqta Rabbati* 20:4 text translated above in Chapter 3]

Behold they [also] said: "Sandalphon stands behind the merkavah, binding crowns."[48] Why does he stand behind the merkavah? So that if a person prays without direction, Shemu'iel the Gatekeeper and the other gatekeepers will not allow that prayer to rise upward. But a prayer [spoken] with direction of the heart comes before Him, as it says, "My cry is before Him; it reaches His ears" (Ps. 18:7). So the prayer is there before the *kavod*. Since it is deserving, it has come by way of behind the *kavod* to Him.[49] Sandalphon selects the prayer the way that a person selects among silver, gold, and precious stones to make a crown. Thus he selects that which is proper; this is "He has turned to the prayer of the destitute." If the gatekeepers and angels see that the prayer is deserving, they open the gate [or: windows] of prayer, and it comes before the [throne of] glory. He causes it to pass on from before Him and dresses it in light. [The prayer descends] from chamber to chamber until it reaches Sandalphon. He receives it and knows on which side of the crown to affix it: whether it should go in front, as Scripture says, "Pour out your heart like water before the face of the Lord" (Lam. 2:19), or whether it should go behind the *kavod*, as Scripture says, "My cry is before Him; it reaches His ears," meaning [that it should go] near the ears. When the blessed Holy One finds that prayer acceptable (*roṣeh be-'oto* [!] *ha-tefillah*), He adds to it light, brilliance, and beauty. An angel receives it and leads it to Sandalphon. Since it is crowned with beauty and brilliance, he fixes it in the crown before the face of the *kavod*. Sandalphon distinguishes which prayer is whose. This is, "Understand my meditation" (Ps. 5:2). This is, "That which comes out of my lips is before Your face" (Jer. 17:16).

When the blessed Holy One sends that shining light upon the prayer to the voice of the righteous, this light gives joy to the voice of the person above, and, parallel to this, the person's heart below rejoices in the love of God. This is, "Beauty upon the awesome God" (Job. 37:22). The crown,[50] this is "Light gives joy to the righteous" (Prov. 13:9). When the prayer is lit up, then "the heart of those who seek God rejoices" (1 Chron 16:10). It is further written: "They walk in the light of Your

[48] This is our original b. *Ḥagigah* 13b text.

[49] The text is quite confusing here, and I have some hesitation about capitalizing this "Him." One could read "him" as Sandalphon, who here receives the prayer and prepares it to become a jewel in the divine crown. But because of the following lines, I prefer to read that the prayer comes up the rear channel, that of Sandalphon, to the *kavod* (Him) and then is passed back down to Sandalphon.

[50] The Hebrew here is also quite awkward.

countenance," and therefore "they rejoice in Your name all the day . . . for You are the glory of their strength" (Ps. 89:16ff.). For the brilliant light of His crown is upon the heads of the righteous, as Scripture says, "On that day shall YHWH of Hosts be a crown of beauty and a diadem of glory to the remnant of His people" (Is. 28:5), referring to "those who make themselves like remnants"[51] to the rest of the world, being last, the tail that follows all. "He will glorify the humble in salvation" (Ps. 149:4), in a crown of light.

Now why does He make armor out of righteousness and a crown out of praises? For it is written: "I put on righteousness and it clothed me" (Job. 29:14) and "Righteousness shall be the girding of his loins, and faith shall gird his reins" (Is. 11:5). He makes crowns out of praises because praise spoken aloud is said by the person's head and the head of the *kavod* is glorified,[52] and it is written, "[He wears righteousness as armor and] a helmet of salvation upon His head" (Is. 59:17).

For salvation one offers thanksgiving. In the *tefillin* above is inscribed: "A people saved in YHWH" (Deut. 33:29), and also "to set you above all the nations that He has made for praise, for name, and for glory" (Deut. 26:19). "To set you above"—what is most "above"? Surely it is the crown of the One above (*ʿaṭarah shel ʿelyon*). And it is written "for praise" and "for name"—for it [comes about by] adjuring the name. "And for glory"—this refers to the *tefillin* of the One above.[53] Why does it speak of the "helmet of salvation upon His head?" In order to refer to the *tefillin* in which it says: "A people saved in YHWH." . . .

[further discussion of the *tefillin* and the armor follows] . . .

Thus He showed the prophet of His garments and the crown of praise upon the head,[54] as Scripture says, "Remove from upon Me the multitude of your songs" (Am. 5:23). This shows that the praise is upon Him [i.e., as a crown], as it is written: "Israel in whom I am glorified" (Is. 49:3), the glory of praises. This is, "His head is fine gold; his locks are curls (*taltalim*)." (Cant. 5:ll) *Tal* would stand for one tefillah,[55] *talim* means there are two. Each crown is set aside before its neighbor.

In the future each righteous one will be shown the crown he made with his prayers and the praises he recited while directing his heart. Then his heart will rejoice.[56]

[51] b. *Megillah* 15b.

[52] *rosh shel adam omer we-rosh ha-kavod mitkabbed.* This strange phrase should be recalled when we come to our later discussions of the divine head as an object of mystic contemplation.

[53] See below (Chapter 11, n. 11) on the associations of *tifʾeret* or *peʾer* and *tefillin.* There are long-standing messianic associations to Deut. 33:29 ("A people saved in YHWH"), often linked with Is. 45:17 ("Israel saved in YHWH in eternal salvation") . Cf. *Tanḥuma, aḥarey*, end. The joining of this verse to the Isaiah 59:17 passage seems to view *tefillin* as protective "weapons" in the ongoing battle against the heathen that will culminate in the messianic victory.

[54] *wa-ʿaṭeret tehilah ba-rosh* (probably should read *be-rosho*).

[55] Meaning either "prayer" or "singular phylactery." In the ellipted section there was some discussion about two *tefillin* on the head.

[56] The text is quite difficult here, but this seems to be the point of it.

When a person directs his heart in reciting those blessings coined by the sages, the *kavod* adds shining brilliance [to them]. In the future he will merit that light: "YHWH will shine upon you" (Is. 60:2). For the glory (*kavod*) and brilliance will increase in blessing, as it is written: "And Your pious ones shall bless You. They shall speak of the *kavod* of Your kingdom . . . and the glorious *kavod* of His kingdom" (Ps. 145:10ff.).

When a righteous person prays with direction, eighteen hundred angels go forth to receive it, as the poet R. Eliezer Qalir wrote: "A thousand eight hundred angels went forth/Receiving prayers that came from the heart/And placed them upon the head of the God of hosts."[57] For the angel affirms and joins together every prayer that comes from the heart, preparing the crown of beauteous glory that goes upon the head of the *kavod*. And every song that [is sung with] direction and love of heaven in the heart, the angel forms into a tablet.[58] [He forms] one from the prayer of one *ṣaddiq*, and another from another righteous one's prayer. The name of the *ṣaddiq* is upon it, "all who are inscribed for life" (Is. 4:3). He joins them together in a welding of beauteous glory, and that ascends to the head of the *kavod* by the time of prayer. He removes the former [crown] before the latest one. Each day He receives a new one, as it is written: "Renewed each morning, great is Your faithfulness" (Lam. 3:23). The former one is hidden away for the *ṣaddiq*. This is, "On that day shall YHWH of hosts be a crown of beauty and a diadem of glory to the remnant of His people."[59]

This passage can only be characterized as boldly anthropomorphic and hesitant at the same time. It makes rich use of the older pictorial materials and even adds to them. The claim that the crown is alive, something we suspected in the *Sefer ha-Navon* text, is here made quite openly, and we shall have much more to say about it later on. One wonders, however, whether the need to state it in just that way does not itself reflect a certain distance from the mythic realm in which such "life" might be rather taken for granted. The quasi-scientific explanation of why verbal prayer should rise is also new and reflects the complex "package" of medieval knowledge, including the scientific, which all became part of the informational background for the pious musings of an Eleazar of Worms. One can also see here a typically medieval need to explain aspects of the ancient tradition that seem to have lost their original meanings. The etymology of the name Sandalphon, the explanation of why he stands behind the throne, and the final passage that seems puzzled by the verb *QaSHaR* in connection with the crown, all belong to this category.

The fifth paragraph, as the translation is divided here, is particularly inter-

[57] The reference is to R. Eleazar ha-Qallir. See above, n. 10 in this chapter.

[58] *Ṭas* is a thin sheet of metal or a foil. See the many references to it in *Sefer ha-Razim*, where Michael Morgan in his English translation (*Sepher ha-Razim: The Book of the Mysteries* [Chico, CA: Scholars' Press, 1983]) renders it as *lamella*. The point is that each of these is added successively to form the crown.

[59] *Sodey Razaya*ʾ, part one, letter nun; ed. Weiss, p. 89ff.

esting. It speaks of the reward to be experienced by the one who prays as the overflow of light, added by God to the accepted prayer, shines back on him and fills his heart with love. This is quite a new motif in our tracing of prayer as coronation. One is tempted to see in it a highly mythicized Neoplatonism, in which the light of the heavenly crown reflects back on those who have contributed by their prayers to its making. There is an immediate sense of mutuality in the moment of coronation here, one that in the older midrashic sources was reserved either for the unique moment of Sinai or perhaps reflected only in the ritual form of *tefillin*. Here the faithful are themselves crowned in holy light and glory. Though the verse from Isaiah 28:5 is eschatological in its original setting, here it seems to be used in quite an immediate sense. Only later in the passage, in the penultimate paragraph, is eschatological assurance added to immediate reward. There the worshiper is assured that *kawwanah* will be stored up for the future also, and the rewards of piety during this life will make for future blessedness as well. At the very end of the section quoted here, the same Isaiah verse is repeated, this time with its eschatological meaning restored.

Another important motif that we have also not yet encountered is the "physical" description of the way the divine crown is formed. Here all traces of the crown-as-garland have disappeared; we are clearly dealing with a highly ornate metal crown, something that might be worn by the God of the Holy Roman Empire in the thirteenth century. Since God is given new crowns each day, the former ones are kept aside, presumably with the names still legible on each thin metal *ṭas*, so that reward can be merited out in the future to the appropriate soul. The description of these metal plates, welded together to form the crown, is a strikingly graphic statement of theurgy, a quasi-physical way in which each *ṣaddiq* makes a distinctive contribution to the crown of God.[60]

The passage seems to reflect two major strategies for dealing with the theological problems caused by this material, which obviously still excites the religious imagination of R. Eleazar. The term *kavod* is used frequently in the passage, leading to quite thorough confusion as to whether the crown actually goes to God or is placed on the head of this secondary apparition. I would suggest that the ambiguity here is intentional, reflecting the depth of Eleazar's theological predicament. In order for the myth to have its true power, that

[60] This reference is all the more striking when we recall that the *ṭas* has frequent applications in Hebrew magical texts. M. Margaliot notes (in his introduction to *Sefer ha-Razim*, p. 3) that its Greek parallel, *epi*, is common in the magical papyri. The *ṭas* in *Sefer ha-Razim* may be made of iron, lead, tin, copper, silver, gold, or pure gold, depending on the particular usage. It is parallel, Margaliot notes, to *luaḥ* or *tabla*. Usually, but not always, it has magical words or angel names written on it.

Here we have a good example of the convergence of magic and mysticism. The *ṭas* here is used solely to form the crown of God, without reference to magical intent. Yet it hardly seems possible that the reader of such a text would not have made the magical association. Then the point might be that magical tools should best be used for the theurgic purpose of making God's crown.

which attracts him to it in the first place, it must be the blessed Holy One Himself who is crowned by prayer. For human prayer to be so very powerful and holy that it reaches the head of a less-than-Godly heavenly figure would seem quite insufficient, a diminishing of the ancient traditions that would leave him cold. But the theological objections raised by Saʿadya and other critics are real to him and cannot be ignored. Helped by the two-gender language (*kavod* being a masculine noun) and retreating frequently to spoken or understood pronouns, Eleazar is to some degree able to have it both ways. The reader is intentionally left confused as to whether God or the *kavod* is the wearer of this crown.

The emphasis on recompense, both immediate and eschatological, is also a way of avoiding the problems raised by this tradition. There is nothing theologically offensive in the notion that God rewards with light and grace, or even with crowns of light, those who pray with intense devotion. This pious sentiment becomes a central message of the text, something that was very much not the case in earlier treatments of the coronation theme.[61] There the emphasis was on giving to God and on the power reflected by the ability of human prayer to reach God's head. While we have speculated that there too hope of reward was not absent from the act of prayer, the shift of emphasis here is certainly dramatic, and I believe this theological awkwardness of the material is at least a partial reason for it.

The medieval texts we have seen to this point show a living tradition that lent great significance to the divine coronation and the crown of God. But another subtle shift has taken place in the ongoing evolution of this tradition. In the aggadic and *hekhalot* sources, we saw great emphasis on the *event* of God's coronation. The arrival of the crown, timed to the angelic singing of *qedushah*, was the main focus of the myth. Around this main concern, secondary traditions were also developed, describing the crown, the names written upon it, and so forth. In the *Ḥasidey Ashkenaz* materials, the balance seems to tip in favor of this latter body of material. The flight of the crown is described somewhat more briefly, and the scene of its arrival is simply copied from the old midrashim, no longer an object of current speculative creativity. It is the crown as an *object*, as a symbolic being or hypostasis within the divine world, that now begins to take center stage. We might characterize this as the emergence of a somewhat changed religious phenomenon, one that we would call *crown*-mysticism, as distinct from *coronation* mysticism in the older sources.

[61] See also *ʿArugat ha-Bosem* 3:81, quoting Eleazar: "'In the future God will place a crown on the head of each and every *ṣaddiq*' (b. *Sanhedrin* 111b). This refers to the crowns that Israel give to God in this world with their hymns and praises. The blessed Holy One will return those very crowns to them, saying: 'Take of what is yours.'" This notion of the crown as reward draws it close to the *ḥaluqaʾ de-rabbanan*, the otherworldly garment that the righteous weave through fulfilling the commandments. On this see Scholem, "Levush ha-Neshamot we-Ḥaluqa de-Rabbanan," in *Tarbiẓ* 24 (1955): 290–306.

CHAPTER ELEVEN

The Hymn of Glory

CONSIDERATIONS RAISED BY THE DISCUSSION of these several texts have now prepared us for a reading of the best-known document in all the literature of *Ḥasidey Ashkenaz*. I refer to that poetic masterpiece known as Shir ha-Kavod (The Song of the Glory), written by an anonymous Hasidic author probably in the thirteenth century and popularly attributed to Judah he-Ḥasid.[1] This song is still sung in the Sabbath liturgy of the traditional Ashkenazic synagogue.[2]

The author of this boldly anthropomorphic hymn, shocking in its highly pictorial depictions of a radiant, youthful, masculine God-figure is deeply engaged, perhaps even infatuated, with images of the divine head[3] and crown. After an apologetic introduction of some ten stanzas (in which some form of the word *kavod* is introduced five times and *demut*, or "image," four times), reassuring the reader repeatedly that what follows lies within the realm of the

[1] *Shir ha-Kavod* is presented in many printed texts as the concluding section of the *Shirey ha-Yiḥud*. It is lacking, however, in the oldest manuscripts of that work, as was noted already by Seligmann Baer in *ʿAvodat Yisraʾel* (Roedelheim, 1868), p. 250. Baer did see a manuscript that attributed it to Judah he-Ḥasid, and he notes that this attribution is accepted by *Sefer Yuḥasin* (by Abraham Zacuto, 1452-c. 1515), which is probably the source of its popular attribution to Judah.

[2] The hymn was first included in the prayerbook printed in Venice, 1549, and thence was copied in almost all prayerbooks of both the Western Ashkenazic and the Polish rite. See Elbogen and Heinemann, *Ha-Tefillah be-Yisraʾel* (Tel Aviv: Dvir, 1972), p. 64. There were communities where the Song was recited every day. See the quotation from the Venice 1549 prayerbook in A. M. Habermann's edition of *Shirey ha-Yiḥud weha-Kavod* (Jerusalem: Mossad Harav Kook, 1949), p. 198. For objections to this daily recitation on grounds of overfamiliarity, see *Siddur Oṣar ha-Tefillot* (Vilna, 1915; rpt. New York: Sefer, 1946), p. 748.

[3] Note the following comment by R. Eleazar of Worms: "It is known that the human being is the most glorious of the creatures, and the head of a human the most glorious of all the limbs, and so it is above." Quoted and translated from Eleazar's *Commentary on the Merkavah of Ezekiel* by Elliot Wolfson, in "Images of God's Feet: Some Observations on the Divine Body in Judaism," in *People of the Body: Jews and Judaism from an Embodied Perspective*, ed. H. Eilberg-Schwartz. (Albany: SUNY, 1992), p. 157. See also *Sodey Razayaʾ*, ed. Weiss, p. 147f. and Wolfson's comments in his "Demut Yaʿaqov Ḥaquqah be-Kise ha-Kavod," in *Massuʾot: Studies in Kabbalistic Literature and Jewish Philosophy in Memory of Prof. Ephraim Gottlieb* (Jerusalem: Bialik Institute, 1994), pp. 164–65, and in English in the revised "The Image of Jacob Engraved upon the Throne," in his *Along the Path: Studies in Kabbalistic Myth, Symbolism, and Hermeneutics* (Albany: SUNY, 1995), 32–33. For Eleazar's defense of the use of the word *head* in referring to God, see his *Shaʿarey ha-Sod, ha-Yiḥud weha-Emunah*, ed. Dan in *Ṭemirin* I, p. 144f. If this seeming fascination with the head (see also Chapter 10, n.52, above) were a characteristic unique to Eleazar, I would be tempted to attribute the *Shir ha-Kavod* to him. But *Sefer ha-Bahir*, which is certainly not by Eleazar, shows the same fascination. See *Bahir* #17, 79, 90, 141, etc. This has been noticed by H. Pedaya in *JSJT* 9 (1990): 150n.37.

theologically permissible, the poet sets free his imagination to describe a figure who combines the lover of the Song of Songs, the warrior of the ancient prophets, and the crowned God of the merkavah tradition. The only English translation that begins to do this song justice is that of Israel Zangwill, translator laureate of Anglo-Jewry in the late nineteenth century. Of course it is in the nature of such translations not to be entirely literal, and sometimes to mislead. But even a literal prose rendition would not pick up all the complicated allusions the poet makes to the head and crown, and would have its own more severe inadequacies. The word *rosh* (head) appears no fewer than twelve times, beginning in the tenth verse, and there are about as many referencs to crowns, diadems, *tefillin*, and other associated terms. In general, the poetic technique here is one of extraordinarily rich allusion to biblical verses. It is often only by recalling the context from which a particular phrase is chosen that one understands what seems to be the poet's intent. The reader might want to read the poem through without notes for effect and then refer to the detailed annotations.

אַנְעִים זְמִירוֹת וְשִׁירִים אֶאֱרֹג, כִּי אֵלֶיךָ נַפְשִׁי תַעֲרֹג:
נַפְשִׁי חִמְּדָה בְּצֵל יָדֶךָ, לָדַעַת כָּל רָז סוֹדֶךָ:
מִדֵּי דַבְּרִי בִּכְבוֹדֶךָ, הוֹמֶה לִבִּי אֶל דּוֹדֶיךָ:
עַל כֵּן אֲדַבֵּר בְּךָ נִכְבָּדוֹת, וְשִׁמְךָ אֲכַבֵּד בְּשִׁירֵי יְדִידוֹת:
אֲסַפְּרָה כְבוֹדְךָ וְלֹא רְאִיתִיךָ, אֲדַמְּךָ אֲכַנְּךָ וְלֹא יְדַעְתִּיךָ:
בְּיַד נְבִיאֶיךָ בְּסוֹד עֲבָדֶיךָ, דִּמִּיתָ הֲדַר כְּבוֹד הוֹדֶךָ:
גְּדֻלָּתְךָ וּגְבוּרָתֶךָ, כִּנּוּ לְתֹקֶף פְּעֻלָּתֶךָ:
דִּמּוּ אוֹתְךָ וְלֹא כְּפִי יֶשְׁךָ, וַיְשַׁוּוּךָ לְפִי מַעֲשֶׂיךָ:
הִמְשִׁילוּךָ בְּרֹב חֶזְיוֹנוֹת, הִנְּךָ אֶחָד בְּכָל דִּמְיוֹנוֹת:
וַיֶּחֱזוּ בְךָ זִקְנָה וּבַחֲרוּת, וּשְׂעַר רֹאשְׁךָ בְּשֵׂיבָה וְשַׁחֲרוּת:
זִקְנָה בְּיוֹם דִּין וּבַחֲרוּת בְּיוֹם קְרָב, כְּאִישׁ מִלְחָמוֹת יָדָיו לוֹ רָב:
חָבַשׁ כּוֹבַע יְשׁוּעָה בְּרֹאשׁוֹ, הוֹשִׁיעָה לּוֹ יְמִינוֹ וּזְרוֹעַ קָדְשׁוֹ:
טַלְלֵי אוֹרוֹת רֹאשׁוֹ נִמְלָא, וּקְוֻצּוֹתָיו רְסִיסֵי לָיְלָה:
יִתְפָּאֵר בִּי כִּי חָפֵץ בִּי, וְהוּא יִהְיֶה לִּי לַעֲטֶרֶת צְבִי:
כֶּתֶם טָהוֹר פָּז דְּמוּת רֹאשׁוֹ, וְחַק עַל מֵצַח כְּבוֹד שֵׁם קָדְשׁוֹ:
לְחֵן וּלְכָבוֹד צְבִי תִפְאָרָה, אֻמָּתוֹ לוֹ עִטְּרָה עֲטָרָה:
מַחְלְפוֹת רֹאשׁוֹ כְּבִימֵי בְחֻרוֹת, קְוֻצּוֹתָיו תַּלְתַּלִּים שְׁחוֹרוֹת:
נְוֵה הַצֶּדֶק צְבִי תִפְאַרְתּוֹ, יַעֲלֶה נָּא עַל רֹאשׁ שִׂמְחָתוֹ:
סְגֻלָּתוֹ תְּהִי בְיָדוֹ עֲטֶרֶת, וּצְנִיף מְלוּכָה צְבִי תִפְאֶרֶת:
עֲמוּסִים נְשָׂאָם עֲטֶרֶת עִנְּדָם, מֵאֲשֶׁר יָקְרוּ בְעֵינָיו כִּבְּדָם:
פְּאֵרוֹ עָלַי וּפְאֵרִי עָלָיו, וְקָרוֹב אֵלַי בְּקָרְאִי אֵלָיו:
צַח וְאָדוֹם לִלְבוּשׁוֹ אָדֹם, פּוּרָה בְּדָרְכוֹ בְּבוֹאוֹ מֵאֱדוֹם:
קֶשֶׁר תְּפִלִּין הֶרְאָה לֶעָנָו, תְּמוּנַת יְיָ לְנֶגֶד עֵינָיו:
רוֹצֶה בְעַמּוֹ עֲנָוִים יְפָאֵר, יוֹשֵׁב תְּהִלּוֹת בָּם לְהִתְפָּאֵר:
רֹאשׁ דְּבָרְךָ אֱמֶת, קוֹרֵא מֵרֹאשׁ דּוֹר וָדוֹר, עַם דּוֹרֶשְׁךָ דְּרוֹשׁ:
שִׁית הֲמוֹן שִׁירַי נָא עָלֶיךָ, וְרִנָּתִי תִּקְרַב אֵלֶיךָ:

תְּהִלָּתִי תְּהִי לְרֹאשְׁךָ עֲטֶרֶת, וּתְפִלָּתִי תִּכּוֹן קְטֹרֶת:
תִּיקַר שִׁירַת רָשׁ בְּעֵינֶיךָ, כַּשִּׁיר יוּשַׁר עַל קָרְבָּנֶיךָ:
בִּרְכָתִי תַעֲלֶה לְרֹאשׁ מַשְׁבִּיר, מְחוֹלֵל וּמוֹלִיד צַדִּיק כַּבִּיר:
וּבְבִרְכָתִי תְנַעֲנַע לִי רֹאשׁ, וְאוֹתָהּ קַח לְךָ כִּבְשָׂמִים רֹאשׁ:
יֶעֱרַב נָא שִׂיחִי עָלֶיךָ, כִּי נַפְשִׁי תַעֲרֹג אֵלֶיךָ:
מִי יְמַלֵּל גְּבוּרוֹת יְיָ, יַשְׁמִיעַ כָּל תְּהִלָּתוֹ:

Sweet hymns shall be my chant and woven songs,
For Thou art all for which my spirit longs—

To be within the shadow of Thy hand
And all Thy mystery to understand.

The while Thy glory is upon my tongue,
My inmost heart with love of Thee is wrung.

So though Thy mighty marvels I proclaim,
'Tis songs of love wherewith I greet Thy name.

I have not seen Thee, yet I tell Thy praise,
Nor known Thee, yet I image forth Thy ways.

For by Thy seers' and servants' mystic speech
Thou didst Thy sov'ran splendor darkly teach,

And from the grandeur of Thy work they drew
The measure of Thy inner greatness, too.

They told of Thee, but not as Thou must be,
Since from Thy work they tried to body Thee.

To countless visions did their pictures run,
Behold through all the visions Thou art one.

In Thee old age and youth at once were drawn,
The grey of eld, the flowing locks of dawn,

The ancient judge, the youthful warrior,
The man of battles, terrible in war,

The helmet of salvation on His head,
And by His hand and arm the triumph led,

His head all shining with the dew of light,
His locks all dripping with the drops of night.

I glorify Him, for He joys in me,
My crown of beauty He shall ever be!

His head is like pure gold; His forehead's flame
Is graven glory of His holy name.

And with that lovely diadem 'tis graced,
The coronal His people there have placed.

His hair as on the head of youth is twined,
In wealth of raven curls it flows behind.

His circlet is the home of righteousness;
May He not love His highest rapture less!

And be His treasured people in His hand
A diadem His kingly brow to band.

By Him they were uplifted, carried, crowned,
Thus honored inasmuch as precious found.

His glory is on me, and mine on Him,
And when I call He is not far or dim.

Ruddy in red apparel, bright He glows
When He from treading Edom's winepress goes.

Phylacteried the vision Moses viewed
The day he gazed on God's similitude.

He loves His folk; the meek will glorify,
And, shrined in prayer, draw their rapt reply.

Truth is Thy primal word; at Thy behest
The generations pass—O aid our quest

For Thee, and set my host of songs on high,
And let my psalmody come very nigh.

My praises as a coronal account,
And let my prayer as Thine incense mount.

Deem precious unto Thee the poor man's song
As those that to Thine altar did belong.

Rise, O my blessing, to the Lord of birth,
The breeding, quickening, righteous force of earth.

Do Thou receive it with acceptant nod,
My choicest incense offered to my God.

And let my meditation grateful be,
For all my being is athirst for Thee.

Comments

Note: numbers in the left margin of the commentary that follows refer to lines referenced from the preceding poem.

1. אנעים זמירות (sweet hymns) Cf. 2 Sam. 23:1 where David is called נעים זמירות, traditionally understood as "sweet singer." The poet seeks to liken his song to those of David.

1. נפשי תערוג (my spirit longs) Cf. Ps. 42:2: "As the hart pants after streams of water, so does my soul long for You, O God." The erotic character of the poem is already revealed in this opening line.

2. נפשי חמדה (within the shadow) Cf. Cant. 2:3: "Like the apple among the trees of the forest, so is my beloved among young men. I delight to sit beneath his shadow, and his fruit is sweet to my taste." And also Is. 51:16: "I have placed My words in your mouth and covered you with the shadow of My hand." The author seeks to be both God's beloved and the one who speaks His word.

2. בצל ידיך (the shadow of Thy hand) As we shall see presently, there is much material in *Ḥasidut Ashkenaz* on the word *ṣel*, especially around the exegesis of Ps. 91:1, where *ṣel shaddai* (the shadow of the Almighty) is parallel to *seter ʿelyon* (the secret of the Most High).[4] The choice of this image here is hardly accidental.

2. כל רז סודך (all Thy mystery) The words *raz* and *sod* may be seen as synonyms, both meaning "secret." *Raz*, a postbiblical term, is especially favored by early esoteric writers. But *sod* also means "council" or "assembly" (Cf. esp. Ps. 89:8); this strophe could be read "to know the full secret revealed in Your angelic council." *Sod* also plays a significant role in the *Sefer ha-Ḥokhmah* text to be discussed below. If *sod* does refer to a secret council here, the whole stanza could reveal a picture of the author as a merkavah voyager, one who seeks to be protected by God's own hand as he learns the secrets of the heavenly council.

3. מדי דברי (is upon my tongue) Cf. Jer. 31:19: "Is Ephraim My beloved son, My child of delight? Whenever I speak of him I remember him well; My very innards long for him. Surely I love him, says YHWH."

3. בכבודך (Thy glory) This term will be repeated several times in the next few verses, indicating that the subject of the author's passion is the kavod. Of course the attempt to distinguish such a passion from the love of "God Himself" is already undercut by the ubiquitous Biblical allusions, which clearly admit of no such fine distinctions.

3. אל דודיך (with love of Thee) "For Your love" is the proper translation here. Cf. Cant. 1:2: "For Your love is better than wine."

4. אדבר בך נכבדות (Thy mighty marvels I proclaim) Cf. Ps. 87:3: "Glorious things are spoken of thee, O city of God."

4. בשירי ידידות (Songs of love) The phrase is used in Ps. 45:1.

5. אספרה כבודך (I tell Thy praise) A possible echo of Ps. 19:2: "The heavens tell the glory of God." The heavens, and the angels within them, also tell it without having seen it.

[4] Cf. the *Sefer ha-Ḥokhmah* text to be discussed shortly.

5. ארמך אכנך (I image forth) The reader cannot but here acknowledge in this attempt a counterforce to several Isaiah passages, including: "To whom can you liken Me?" (40:25).

6. ביד נביאיך . . . דמית (For by Thy seers' and servants') The poet's sense of inadequacy to image God is lessened by the fact that God has already revealed such images to the prophets, and he can rely on these. "Great is the power of the prophets who liken the formed to its Former."[5] The prophets are permitted to depict God in human terms, and the poet seeks his license in them.

7. גדולתך וגבורתך (The grandeur of your work) There are several places in these opening lines that are reminiscent of the opening verses of Psalm 145, also a grand alphabetic acrostic that tells of God's glory. The parallels are somewhat unspecific, but the language of this psalm certainly underlies that of *Shir ha-Kavod.*

8. דמו אותך (And from the grandeur of Thy work) The argument here is that biblical descriptions of God are only derivative from divine actions and do not describe the essence of God. This view was to be associated with Maimonides, whose philosophy would limit positive description of the Deity to such "attributes of action."[6]

9. המשילוך (To countless visions) The author over the next several strophes refers to a well-known aggadah in which Israel, having seen God as youths at the Sea of Reeds and as elders at Sinai, thinks these visions might represent two distinct deities. The divine voice reassures them by beginning the Sinai revelation with, "'I am YHWH your God' (Ex. 20:1)—so as not to allow the nations of the world to say, 'There are two powers.' I was in Egypt; I was at the Sea. I was in the past; I shall be in the future. I am in this world; I am in the world to come."[7]

11. זקנה ביום דין (The ancient judge, the youthful warrior) The point is that God's appearance changes as is appropriate to human need in each particular situation. The rest of the poem will be devoted to God as He appeared at the Sea, the youthful image that combines aspects of God as warrior and lover.

The evocation of this aggadah, along with the various references to *kavod* and *demut*, has now given our poet license to fully release his vision in its

[5] *Bereshit Rabbah* 27:1 and parallels.

[6] Cf. H. A. Wolfson, "Maimonides on Negative Attributes," in *Louis Ginzberg Jubilee Volume* (New York, JTSA, 1945), pp. 411–46.

[7] *Mekhilta ba-Ḥodesh* 5, *Shirta* 4; main parallels in *Mekhilta de-Rabbi Shimʿon ben Yoḥai, be-shalaḥ* 15 (p. 81) and *Pesiqta Rabbati* 21 (f. 100b). See the treatment by A. Segal in *Two Powers in Heaven* (Leiden: E. J. Brill, 1977), pp. 33–59. I have considered this aggadic motif previously in "The Children in Egypt and the Theophany at the Sea," in *Judaism* 24 (1975): 446–56. For discussion of this aggadah in another *Ḥasidut Ashkenaz* source, see Dan, *ʿIyyunim*, p. 152 There R. Judah he-Hasid is reported to have said: "They saw that image that is visible to human eyes. If one prophet saw black [hair] and another pure white, [God] does not change, as it says in the *Mekhilta*, etc."

boldest form. The body of the poem may be said to begin here, with the stanza that opens with the letter *ḥet*.

12. כובע ישועה (The helmet of salvation) The description opens with the warrior-aspect of the youthful divine self. Cf. Is. 59:17: "He wears righteousness as a breastplate and a helmet of salvation upon His head; He puts on garments of vengeance for clothing and is clad with zeal as a cloak."[8] These references to God's warrior-like qualities, including such elements as zeal and vengeance, are appropriate to a poet of the decimated Jewish communities living in the shadow of the Crusades and the horror they wreaked on Rhineland Jewry. Calls for vengeance are quite frequent in the elegies for the various communities. The martyrs' elegy "*Av ha-Raḥamim*," also composed in this era and widely accepted throughout the Ashkenazic communities, is a mosaic of biblical verses most of which represent a call for vengeance. The "salvation" of God's helmet seems to be primarily the historical salvation of Israel from the pains of exile and foreign domination.

12. הושיעה לו (And by His hand) Ps. 98:1.

13. טללי אורות (the dew of light) Here two verses are combined. Cant. 5:2: "The sound of my beloved knocking: Open for me my sister-love, my dove, my perfect one, for my head is filled with dew, my locks with drops of night" and Isa. 26:5: "Awake and sing, you who dwell in the dust, for Your dew is a dew of light and earth will cast forth the shades."

From war the author turns quickly to love, choosing one of the most passionate verses of the Song of Songs. The lover is aroused and calls on his beloved to allow him to enter.[9] That this sexual arousal should include a reference to the dew with which God will resurrect the dead is also not surprising. This dew, we will recall, was present at Sinai and was used to revive Israel when they passed out in ecstasy due to the great fragrance with which

[8] This verse also plays a major role in the *Sodey Razaya'* passage we have just quoted, especially in the ellipted section on God's armor. See also our comments in Chapter 10, n.41. The battle helmet of God here is identical with His *tefillin*, hence also His crown, etc.

For another reference, see *Sha'avey ha-Sod ha-Yiḥud weha-Emunah*, by Eleazar of Worms, edited by Dan in *Ṭemirin* 1, p. 151.

[9] It is likely that in the original meaning of this verse of Song of Songs "head" stands in place of the phallus, and the description is altogether one of the male approaching sexual climax. It seems possible to me that our author is influenced by this, though he understands it only semiconsciously. The preoccupation with "head" throughout the rest of the poem has an obsessive and almost sexual quality about it. An unconscious or semiconscious displacement, where "head" represents the phallus, is certainly possible here. In this connection we should note that *'aṭarah*, the term for "crown" most frequently employed here, also refers in Hebrew to the corona of the penis, and is a term well known in halakhic discussions of circumcision. On mystical use of this term in the Zohar, see E. Wolfson, "Circumcision, Vision of God, and Textual Interpretation: From Midrashic Trope to Mystical Symbol," in *History of Religion* 27: 2 (1987): 205. See also his expanded discussion in *Speculum* and elsewhere, along with my review of *Speculum* in *History of Religions* (February, 1997).

the world was filled as God gave the Torah. "When God resurrects the dead, He shakes out His locks and the dew falls."[10]

14. יתפאר בי ((I glorify Him) Cf. Isa. 49:3: "You are My servant, Israel, in whom I am glorified."

14. לעטרת צבי (My crown of beauty) Cf. Is. 28:5: "On that day will YHWH of hosts be a crown of glory and a diadem of beauty for the remnant of His people." Note that here God is the crown of Israel. This will be discussed below.

1–14. In this first descriptive section of the poem, the mutuality of coronation is already emphasized. יתפאר בי means that God wears Israel, the object of His desire, as a crown (further evidence of this usage below); in the second strophe Israel wears God as a crown, following the verse in Isaiah.

15. כתם טהור פז (like pure gold) This is of course Cant. 5:11, a passage by now quite familiar to us from frequent reference to it throughout this literature. Its use here is a good reminder of the link between this depiction and the ancient *Shiʿur Qomah* traditions. See also Ps. 21:4: "You place a golden crown (עטרת פז) on his head."

15. וחק על מצח (Is graven glory of His holy name) Here the name seems to be inscribed directly on the divine forehead, as we have seen and discussed above.

16. אמתו לו עטרה (The coronal His people there have placed) This is a reference to the midrash discussed above on Cant. 3:11, wherein "the crown his [Solomon's] mother made for him" is made not by *ʾimmo* (his mother), but by *ʾummato* (his people).

17. מחלפות ראשו (His hair . . . is twined) The word *maḥlefot* is used in the Bible only twice, both times in reference to Samson (Jud. 16:13, 19). They seem actually to be "braids." The term is combined in this stanza with *qevuṣot*, or "locks," from Cant. 5:11 to give the impression of the rich, thick, dark hair of a virile young man. The inference that God's hair is like that of Samson, or that the *qevuṣot* and *taltalim* of the Canticle's lover and the *maḥlefot* of this very human hero can be homologized, is important to our reading of the poem as a whole.

18. נוה הצדק (the home of righteousness) This is Jerusalem. Cf. Jer. 31:22. The poet asks God, in the language of Ps. 137:6, to keep her at the *head* of His delights.

19. סגולתו (His treasured people) Israel, God's chosen people. Cf. Isa. 62:3: "You will be a crown of glory in the hand of YHWH, a royal diadem in the palm of your God." Again, Israel themselves *are* the crown of God.

[10] b. *Shabbat* 88b and *Midrash Shir ha-Shirim* (ed. Gruenhuet) 5:2, p. 38a.

20. עמוסים נשאם (they were uplifted) Cf. Isa. 46:3: ". . . O house of Israel, borne from the belly, carried from the womb." God has known and cared for Israel since before their birth.

20. עטרת ענדם (carried, crowned) The verb ענד is used only twice in the Bible. Here the reference is to Job 31:36: "I would take it upon my shoulder and bind it as a crown to me."

20. מאשר יקרו (Thus honored inasmuch) Cf. Is 43:4: "Since you were precious in My sight, you were honored."

21. פארו עלי פארי עליו (His glory is on me) Here the poet returns to the mutual crowns of glory. Halakhic sources refer to *tefillin* as "a commandment that contains *pe*ʾ*er* (glory)," so these crowns may also be seen as the respective *tefillin* of God and Israel.[11]

22. צח ואדום (Ruddy in red) Here the images of lover and warrior are most fully combined. "My beloved is white and ruddy" opens the description of the male lover in Cant. 5:10, directly preceding the passage we have seen earlier. But this is immediately combined with images of Is. 63:1–4, verses used also in the *Sodey Razaya*ʾ passage: "Who is this that comes from Edom, with crimsoned garments from Bozra? . . . Why is Your garment red, Your clothing like that of one who treads grapes? I have trodden the winepress alone . . . for I have trodden them in My anger, trampled them in My fury; their blood is sprinkled upon My garments, and I have stained all My rainment. For the day of vengeance is in My heart, and the year of My redemption has come." The poet envisions the pure white lover-God reddened with the blood of Edom, the well-known medieval cipher for Christendom, which He will trample out as one who stomps the grapes.

23. קשר תפילין (Phylacteried) Moses saw the back of God's head (Ex. 33:23), the place where His *tefillin*-knot is tied.[12]

23. תמונת יְיָ (The day he gazed) From Moses' point of view, however, he was looking at the very image of God, as in Num. 12:8: "He sees the similitude of YHWH."[13]

[11] b. *Berakhot* 11a, b. *Ketubot* 6b, and parallels. For a discussion of the meaning of wearing *tefillin*, comparing their human wearer to the cherubim who have God's name written on their forehead, cf. *Sodey Razaya*ʾ (ed. Jerusalem), p. 167.

[12] See also the reference in *Sefer ha-Ḥokhmah*, to be quoted below.

[13] This distinction between what God may show and what the prophet experiences is based on the complex and subtle discussions of revelation in Judah ben Barzilai's *Commentary on Sefer Yeṣirah*. There is also a passage in *Sefer ha-Ḥesheq* (#46) that refers to Meṭaṭron as "God's rear side." In the literature of *Hasidey Ashkenaz*, it is common for Meṭaṭron to be identified with the *kavod*. The point would be that Moses saw only the rear of God's head, the place of the *tefillin* knot. From the viewpoint of human potential, however, his experience was of the highest order.

An important and puzzling parallel to this verse is found in Ms. Bod. 1812, 63a, quoted by

24. רוצה בעמו (He loves His folk) Cf. Ps. 149:4. This psalm too is a mixture of joy and call for violent destruction of enemies.

24. יושב תהלות (enshrined in prayer) Ps. 22:4 describes God as "You holy One, seated amid the praises of Israel." This verse of enthronement immediately precedes the *qedushah* verses in the daily morning liturgy's final recitation of them, the *qedushah de-sidra.*

25. ראש דברך (Truth is Thy primal word) Literally: the head of Your word is truth. Ps. 119:160. The "head of God's word," the first three words in Genesis, end with the letters that comprise the word *emet* or "truth."[14]

25. קורא מראש (at Thy behest the generations pass) Cf. Is. 41:4: "He calls the generations from the beginning."

25. עם דורשך (O aid our quest) Lit.: "Seek out the people who seek You."

26. שית המון (and set my host of songs on high) The antithesis of Amos 5:23: "Remove from upon Me your multitude of songs."

26. ורנתי תקרב אליך (And let my psalmody) Ps. 119:169: "May my joyous sound come near to You."

27. תהלתי (My praises as a coronal account) Lit: "May my praise be a crown upon Your head."

27. ותפלתי (my prayer as Thine incense mount) Ps. 141:2: "May my prayer be fixed as incense before You." I proposed earlier a relationship between prayer as crown and the curling upward of sacrificial smoke. The juxtaposition of

---

Wolfson in *Demut Ya*ʿ*aqov*, p. 168n.165, and discussed in his "Images of God's Feet: Some Observations on the Divine Body in Judaism," in *People of the Body*, p. 159f.:

> "When Moses asked of the blessed Holy One: "Show me Your glory" (Ex. 33:18), He replied, "No person may see Me and live" (vs. 20). "Nevertheless [the divine voice continues], because you have found favor in My sight, I will reveal My boot to you, something I have never shown to any prophet." Of this Scripture says: "Mouth to mouth I speak to him; visually and without riddles; he gazes upon the similitude of God" (Num. 12:8). This is because it was by way of a polished glass that He showed him His boot, which is *keter* ʿ*elyon*, the tenth kingdom.

The meaning of this offer to show Moses the divine boot seems quite obscure. It may have to do with the fact that the Byzantine emperors wore unique purple boots; along with their crowns and purple robes, these constituted "the imperial insignia par excellence." "Showing Moses the boot" was then precisely showing His *malkhut*, the insignia of divine authority. See *Oxford Dictionary of Byzantium* (New York, Oxford University Press, 1991), s.v. "crown." We will return to this text, from Eleazar's *Sefer ha-Ḥokhmah*, when we discuss another passage from that work below. I introduce it here only for the notion that God shows Moses only something lowly, when considered from the divine point of view, but which for the prophet becomes the very similitude of God.

[14] In an article published just a century ago in *MGWJ* 37 (1893): 463–67, D. Simonsen pointed to this and three other verses near the end of the song as "Unechte Verse in שיר הכבוד". His arguments, largely based on an assumed sophistication of style that a skilled author would not violate, are not particularly convincing to me. He does call attention, however, to the otherwise unexplained doubling of the *resh* and *tav* in this alphabetical work.

these two in the same stanza suggests that this may have been seen by our poet.

29. לראש משביר (to the Lord of birth) Cf. Prov. 11:26: "blessing to the head of the provider." But cf. also Prov. 10:6: "blessings to the head of the righteous."[15] The worshiper asks that his blessing affect the head of the mashbir, the one who brings about birth. Since seed was seen as flowing from the father's mind and that seed contained the fully formed homunculus, this may also be a call for the birth of the messianic soul.

29. צדיק כביר Cf. Job 34:17: "Will you condemn one who is very just?" The phrase refers there to an innocent man; here it is applied to God. Or could *ṣaddiq kabir* here be the object rather than the subject of *meḥolel u-molid* and thus refer to the Messiah rather than to God?

30. תנענע לי ראש (with acceptant nod) This is a reference to the passage in b. *Berakhot* 7a, where "Rabbi Ishmael the High Priest" encounters Akhtariel YaH in the ruins of Jerusalem. God seeks the blessing of the priest, who prays that God's mercies overpower the forces of divine wrath. God accepts this blessing and nods His head in approval of it. The author seems to hope that his prayer will find similar acceptance and perhaps bring about the same result. This would also fit in with the messianic reading of the preceding stanza. It is when God's mercies finally succeed in overcoming His wrath that He will bring forth the messianic soul.

30. בשמים ראש (My choicest incense) Cf. Ex. 30:23. The translation is correct in meaning, but the phrase is being read supraliterally to mean, "Incense for Your head."[16]

31. יערב נא (Let my meditation grateful be) Cf. Ps. 104:34: "May my meditation be pleasing to Him."

The combination of images that makes for this poem's power is particularly interesting. The full joining of the "young God" imagery of Judaism, in both its erotic and warlike manifestations, to the already pictorial merkavah traditions, creates a powerful and startling effect. The depiction here makes us aware in a new way of just what we find and do not find in the earlier sources. There is a strikingly powerful masculinity here that is rare in postbiblical and medieval Jewish descriptions of God (before Kabbalah). One may claim a precedent for "*Shir ha-Kavod*" in the attention merkavah sources pay to *beauty* as a feature of both God Himself and the angels. They are not at all hesitant about referring to the *yofi* (beauty) of God; this is an important element of His praise. The term *yofi*, almost always in a theophonic context,

[15] On this see *Midrash Tehillim* 19:7 (p. 166f.), end, which associates Prov. 10:6 with the crown fashioned of Israel's prayers.

[16] On the plain meaning of *besamim rosh*, see N. Sarna in *The JPS Torah: Exodus* (Philadelphia: Jewish Publication Society, 1989), p. 260, chapter 30, n. 35.

appears in more than forty separate references in Schaefer's *Concordance to the Hekhalot Literature*.[17] But the beauty described there has a different quality than that of "*Shir ha-Kavod*." Here we are offered a series of rather realistic and earthy descriptions, based on the Scriptures: black curls, bloody clothes, and so forth. The beauty in the older merkavah texts is much more ethereal; *yofi* goes with such words as *ziw*, *zohar*, *hadar* and is often part of a series of similar terms. It is the beauty of infinite light, and the divine countenance seems to be the source of that light, itself not given to description in anything but luminescent terms.[18] The physical description of God in the erotic idiom of the Song of Songs is not characteristic of merkavah literature, except for direct quotations. But here we have a much more concrete sort of beauty. Once the author of "*Shir ha-Kavod*" finishes with his extensive apologia, the *kavod* he has in mind turns out to be a figure of rather rugged masculine appearance, the sort of king or young prince one could picture in a Teutonic fairy tale of his own time and place. The crowned head is that of King/Defender/Lover, and Israel, in the person of the poet, longs for nothing other than to be given totally to Him.

I do not mean to say, of course, that this poem is completely without precedent. God is Lover of Israel, a love sometimes expressed in terms by no means shy of passion, in the Hebrew poetry of Jews in Spain. Both Gabirol and Halevi, to take the two best-known figures, could provide us with many examples of such sacred eros.[19] There is also some precedent in payyetanic compo-

[17] Incidentally, this represents more than twice as many references as there are in the entire Babylonian Talmud, according to the concordance of Kosovsky, s. v. "yofi." The Talmudic examples refer to men, women, and inanimate objects (e.g., Jerusalem), but never to God or an angel. S. Pines has noted this concern for *yofi* in the merkavah sources in his "Points of Similarity between the Doctrine of the *Sefirot* in the *Sefer Yezirah* and a Text from the Pseudo-Clementine *Homilies*: The Implications of This Resemblance," *Israel Academy of Sciences and Humanities* 7:3 (1989): 106, but his concern there is primarily that of comparison to an early Christian text. Both the Pseudo-Clementine text and these merkavah references are exceptional within their respective traditions. The emphasis on beauty in some merkavah texts has also been noted by M. Cohen in *The Shiʿur Qomah: Liturgy and Theurgy in Pre-Kabbalistic Jewish Mysticism* (Lanham: University Press, 1983), p. 173. He makes the interesting suggestion that beauty functioned for some merkavah writers the way bigness did for the authors of the *Shiʿur Qomah*: as the key impressive attribute of the deity. Contrast this feature of merkavah religion with the single biblical reference to divine *yofi* in Is. 33:17. Cf. the remark of M. Brettler in *God Is King* (Sheffield: JSOT Press, 1989), p. 73: "After Israelite worship of God became aniconic, God was not called handsome since this attribute would encourage visualizing God." There are verbal as well as plastic icons (cf. *Be-Midbar Rabbah* 3:2), and merkavah literature shows us just how visual these can be! On beauty as an attribute of God in merkavah sources, see also the remarks of R. Elior in *EJM*, pp. 18f., 27ff. and P. Schaefer, *The Hidden and Manifest God: Some Major Themes in Early Jewish Mysticism* (Albany: SUNY, 1992), index s.v. "beauty."

[18] For reference to ancient Near Eastern sources on the radiant face of the deity as the source of blessing, see the passages cited by J. Milgrom, *The JPS Torah: Numbers* (Philadelphia: Jewish Publication Society, 1989), p. 360.

[19] See the treatment of such religious love poems (based on an understanding of the Song of

sitions, including those of tenth- and eleventh-century Ashkenaz, quite a number of which are woven around verses or phrases from the Canticle.[20] The *payyeṭanim* were also very fond of references to the coronation theme, as we have mentioned.[21] Given the veneration of *piyyuṭ* in *Ḥasidey Ashkenaz* circles, it seems right to say that these would be a direct source of influence on "*Shir ha-Kavod*," which itself is not written in typical payyetanic style.

Two other points are especially worthy of mention in connection with a "*Shir ha-Kavod*." The reader will notice that for the first time we see a full and avid presentation of the crown tradition without even a single mention of the angels. There are no intermediaries in this poem, and no heavenly hosts or luminaries, as one finds so frequently in the older merkavah hymns. There is of course a poetic reason for this. Our author wants his lovers to stand out, to be alone in the world; the intensity of this passion would be diminished if Sandalphon or Meṭaṭron had to step in and pass the crown from one to the other! We may see in this omission that our poet works rather freely with his inherited tradition, shaping it to his own creative will. But we may also take this lack as indicative of a tendency that is emerging in the medieval materials to remove the crown as a symbol from its context in the elaborate heavenly coronation scene, and thus to disengage it from its once total integration with the angelic theology. This is an important stage, as I shall suggest below, as we move toward the emergence of the crown as a key symbol in Kabbalah.

The other point to note is that about half the references to God's crown and coronation in this poem show Israel as *being* rather than making or offering the crown of God. The two themes are in fact deeply intertwined here, as though to insist that their meaning is one. The idea that Israel are, or will one day themselves become, God's crown immediately strikes one as more metaphoric than literal. It may even be seen as metaphor in such a biblical verse as Isaiah 62:3: "You shall be a crown of glory in the hand of your Lord, a royal

---

Songs) in Gabirol, by A. Mirsky, *Ha'Piyuṭ* (Jerusalem: Magnes, 1990), pp. 653ff. On the role of Arabic love potry in the evolution of this genre, see the remarks by R. Scheindlin in *The Gazelle: Medieval Hebrew Poems on God, Israel, and the Soul* (Philadelphia: Jewish Publication Society, 1991), pp. 36ff.

20 Verses from the Canticle are used especially in *piyyuṭim* for Pesah and Shavuʿot. The Canticle is read in the synagogue on the seventh day of Pesah, but its motif of marriage is also much associated with Shavuʿot. See Z. M. Rabinovitz, *Piyyuṭey Rabbi Yannai*, vol. 2, pp. 267–87 and the editor's comments on p. 272.

21 Yannai's לך דודי /חן עטרה בראשך (2, 286), "Come, my beloved/Place a crown upon your head," is a reference to a marital crown for God and is one of a great many references one could find in the *piyyuṭim* where eros and coronation imagery are joined. In addition to the *ofan*, mentioned above, the concluding verse, or *silluq*, of the *qerovah* was also a choice location for images of the divine crown. A *qerovah* is a long *piyyuṭ*, inserted into the reader's repetition of the *ʿamidah*. These insertions alternate with portions of the fixed liturgy through the first two *ʿamidah* blessings. Thus the *silluq* ("departure" or conclusion) serves also as an introduction to the third blessing, where the *qedushah* is contained.

diadem in the hand of your God."[22] But this theme is developed in the aggadah, and there it receives its usual semiliteralist flavor:

TEXT #34

Thus the blessed Holy One desires to mention Israel always. Said Rabbi Judah ben Simon: This is like someone who was fashioning a crown. Another person happened by and saw it. He said, As much as you can adorn that crown with precious stones and pearls, do so, for it is one day to be placed upon the head of the king. Thus the blessed Holy One said to Moses, As much as you can praise and glorify Israel before Me, do so, because in them I am glorified. Thus Scripture says: "He said to me, 'You are my servant Israel, in whom I am glorified.' " (Is. 49:3)[23]

One might note a certain hesitancy about this midrash that makes for an especially awkward fit between the parable and its meaning. God, after all, is no idle passer-by in Moses' glorification of Israel in the Torah! The midrash also refuses to close the frame of the explanation as one might want, and say: "Because one day they will be placed as a crown upon My head." But for us the association is close enough. We have already seen Is. 49:3 quoted in connection with God's *tefillin*, containing the praise of Israel, and the *tefillin* are the crown. His crown contains their praises, but this does not quite openly say that they *are* the crown of God. It is interesting to note a certain shyness in the midrash, possibly because of the magical/theurgic associations linked to the crown image.

"*Shir ha-Kavod*" makes use of this midrashic tradition, but without a hint of shyness. The verse beginning with *yod* that Zangwill translated, "I glorify Him, for He joys in me" should more properly be rendered, "He is glorified [or crowned] with me, for He desires me." The *ʿayin* verse literally reads: "He raises them, His burden, and wears them as a crown." Throughout the song the author returns to this theme: it is themselves, as well as their prayers, that Israel seek to raise up to the head of God. This theme also will be crucial in the turn toward Kabbalah.[24]

But if Israel are themselves God's crown, the one He places on His head, the motif of coronation has gone a significant step beyond the magical/theurgic meaning we saw in the merkavah and related midrashic sources.

[22] Second Isaiah is saying that this is in intentional contrast with first Is. 28:5, where God is depicted, in the same eschatological context, as the crown of Israel!

[23] *Tanḥuma, Tissa*ʾ 8. In the passage just above this one, Israel is God's royal cloak, so close to Him that "they cleave to My loins." Cf. Idel, *Kabbalah*, p. 373n.168. Parallels in *Wa-Yiqra*ʾ *Rabbah* 2:5; *Pesiqta DRK* 2:7 (ed. Mandelbaum, p. 29); *Pesiqta Rabbati* 10 (38b), etc. See discussion of this text by S. Kraus, *Paras we-Romi ba-Talmud uva-Midrashim* (Jerusalem: Mossad Ha-Rav Kook, 1948), p. 46.

[24] In mentioning these two themes here, I am not claiming that "*Shir ha-Kavod*" itself played a crucial role in the turn toward Kabbalah, but only that it serves as an unusually fine illustration of themes that were current in its time and place and that did play such a role.

The power of Israel and their prayers, the ability to proclaim God's kingship, now reveals itself once again to be tied to Israel's status as God's beloved, as the one with whom He is united in a sacred marriage act. The mutual act of coronation, seen here as the core of religious longing and fulfillment, is also an act of marital union. Whether or not the crown and head references in the poem are specifically sexual, as I have suggested in a note above, "*Shir ha-Kavod*" provides clear testimony that *hieros gamos*, as a literary and devotional theme, is alive and well among Jews in the Middle Ages.

"*Shir ha-Kavod*," I would suggest, represents a culmination of the ancient tradition of divine coronation, before that symbol begins the transformation it will undergo in the evolution that leads to Kabbalah. It joins together, with a great sense of pageantry, images of divine power and authority, a sense of Israel's intimate and unique relationship to her God, a touching portrayal of this all-powerful God's love and care for His people, as well as His wrath for those who have caused her harm. We see reaffirmed in it our awareness that the traditions of coronation unite a sense of submission to God's unquestioned authority and an assertion of His beloved Israel's unique and vital role in the balance of God's universe.

CHAPTER TWELVE

The Way to Kabbalah

No single issue in the history of Jewish mysticism has more fascinated and preoccupied scholars than the origins of Kabbalah, and the relationship of this seemingly new and highly original type of thinking to older strands of Jewish and other esoteric tradition. Gershom Scholem wrote the early history of Kabbalah at least three times in the course of his career.[1] In recent years a host of other scholars have made important contributions to our still somewhat dim understanding of this critical transition period in the history of Judaism.[2]

It is now widely agreed that the most important part of this puzzle is to be deciphered around the relationship between *Ḥasidut Ashkenaz,* or at least between works known and preserved in Ashkenazi Hasidic circles, and the authors/editors of *Sefer ha-Bahir,* a text that played a crucial role in the development of Kabbalistic myth and symbolism. At what point can clear lines be drawn between these two movements, which are readily recognizable as quite distinct in their more developed stages? How much were they created out of common sources, some of which are now unknown to us? What specifically makes for Kabbalah, distinguishing it as religious phenomenon and as an intellectual system, from that which existed earlier? As it happens, the coronation of God has played a key role in the investigation of this relationship, for reasons that will presently become clear. In tracing a history and phenomenology of the coronation motif, we enter directly into the question of how the earliest Kabbalistic symbols evolved.

[1] *Reshit ha-Qabbalah* (1948); *Ursprung und Anfänge der Kabbala* (1962); *Origins of the Kabbalah* (1987). The English version was published posthumously, edited by R.J.Z. Werblowsky. See his introductory comments there, which also include mention of the various Hebrew University lectures that Scholem allowed to be published for internal use by the university's Akademon press. The various articles Scholem wrote on early Kabbalah for the English-language *Encyclopedia Judaica*, published afterward as *Kabbalah*, also belong to this last stratum.

[2] J. Dan, *Ḥuggey ha-Mequbbalim ha-Rishonim* (Jerusalem: Akademon, 1977 Hebrew University lectures); Shahar, "Catharism and the Beginnings of the Kabbalah in Languedoc," *Tarbiẓ* 40 (1971): 483–507; I. Gruenwald, "Jewish Mysticism's Transition from *Sefer Yesira* to the Bahir," *JSJT* 6 (1987): 15–54; M. Idel, "The Problem of the Sources of the Bahir," ibid., 55–72; H. Pedaya, "'Flaw' and 'Correction' in the Concept of the Godhead in the Teachings of Rabbi Isaac the Blind," ibid., 157–286; idem, "The Provençal Stratum in the Redaction of Sefer ha-Bahir," *JSJT* 9 (Pines Volume) (1990): 139–64. This list is surely not exhaustive. Many other studies by these authors and others, including Rachel Elior, Asi Farber, and Elliot Wolfson have contributed to our understanding of this problem. For a full bibliography of Bahir-related studies, see D. Abrams's edition, *The Book Bahir* (Los Angeles: Cherub Press, 1994), pp. 293–336.

We have already seen in the opening lines of our *Sodey Razaya*ʾ passage the rather startling assertion that the crown is alive. This statement is given more substance by an interesting quotation from the the writings of Eleazar of Worms found in *ʿArugat ha-Bosem*, a commentary on the *piyyuṭim* written under the influence of *Ḥasidey Ashkenaz*.[3] Because the *payyeṭanim* so loved the coronation symbol, it is not surprising that we find important discussions of it in a commentary on their work:

TEXT #35

As [the crown] ascends, an angel in the first heaven receives it and adorns it. It expands (*mitraḥev*) and becomes glorious. Then a second angel receives and adorns it, and it expands further. The same [takes place] in each of the heavens: the crown becomes more and more glorious and expansive until it reaches the image of Jacob that is engraved on the throne of glory. Then it expands as befits the *kavod*, and it becomes glorious altogether. Of this it is said: "Israel, in you am I glorified" (Is. 49:3). . . . When the crown is altogether glorious, the blessed Holy One brings light into it and illuminates it with a brilliance unlike any other. Of this it is said, "By the light of the countenance of the King of life" (Ps. 16:15). As soon as the crown is illuminated, it goes and is seated on the head of the *kavod*.[4]

Here we see clearly what it means that the crown is "alive." It acts as an independent entity, growing in size and glory as it passes through each of the heavenly realms. The angels have been reduced to a rather secondary role here, as glorifiers or adorners of the crown. We can see how far we have come here from the entirely passive crown, a gift for God being woven by an angel out of Israel's prayers.

The process of this evolution is not entirely clear to us; some factors that motivated it may remain unknown. But surely a large part of the process may be accounted for by an underlying tension that inhabited this myth from the beginning: that between the power of men and angels to crown God, on the one hand, and the undiminished and increasing need to assert the transcendence of God, on the other. This tension grew ever greater with the coming of the Middle Ages, combining as it did with the need for a less anthropomorphic and more intellectually "pure" notion of the deity.[5] As early as the Talmudic

[3] *ʿArugat ha-Bosem*, vol. 3, p. 80f. The ellipse is the parallel to the passage discussed below in n. 35.

[4] This "expanding" crown is closely related to the *kavod mitraḥev* (expanding glory) that is found in the several passages mentioned by E. Wolfson in "Demut Yaʿaqov," p. 167n.158, mostly from R. Eleazar's commentary on the liturgy. One of these (*ʿArugat ha-Bosem*, vol. 3, p. 481) is discussed at length in n. 35 below. See also the comments by Dan in "Ashkenazi Hasidic Commentaries on the Hymn *Ha-Aderet Weha-Emunah*," *Tarbiẓ* 50 (1981): 396–404, and Wolfson, "Demut," p. 180n.219.

[5] For one familiar with some of the discussions of ancient Israelite kingship to which we referred at the very opening of this study, these medieval discussions have a strangely familiar ring. Whose throne is it, "really," and whose crown? Is the king seated on the throne of God?

source, we will recall, there was a problem as to how the crown was to reach God's head. Sandalphon himself, the tallest among the angels and weaver of the crown, could not see God. The angels are not given to see or know "the place of His glory." Even the one who is five hundred years' distance taller than all the others seems to be far too short to reach the head of the One whose greatness is "measured," after all, in terms of indescribable height. All he can do is have recourse to angelic magic; he adjures the crown by a holy name and it flies up to its proper place. But if a name is what is needed to bring the crown to God, what is the power of the angel? His power seems mostly to lie outside himself, in the powerful name that he knows (and that the avid student of merkavah secrets might also hope to learn!). But then if the crown itself is inscribed with God's name, or is woven of names and letters altogether, the power seems to lie more in crown and names than it does in the angels themselves.

The angels are still frequently mentioned in the Ashkenazic texts that deal with the crown, and the texts would be almost unthinkable without them. The magical element or the adjuration is also still present in these sources.[6] But another element has become more important in the pietistic context of *Ḥasidut Ashkenaz. Sodey Razaya*ʾ spoke of *kawwanat ha-lev* (the direction of the heart); it was this that ultimately caused the prayer to rise to God. In the earlier sources, we are not told that prayers recited with a greater degree of *kawwanah* are more likely to be used in the making of God's crown. The angel goes about to the synagogues and picks up the "Amens" and other words that make for public worship. We are not told that he rejects them if they were recited without *kawwanah*. The magical/pneumatic character of merkavah religion is not especially concerned, so it would seem, with this dimension of piety.[7] For *Ḥasidey Ashkenaz*, on the other hand, *kawwanah* and devotional attitudes play a central role in the religious life. Even the name Sandalphon was awkwardly reinterpreted as referring to the "precious gems" of *kawwanah* that lay within the prayers. We should recall here, as stated above, that the author of "*Shir ha-Kavod*" was able to make very extensive use of the coronation theme without a single reference to an angel. In the *ʿArugat ha-Bosem* passage, the angels each adorn the crown as it passes through their respective heavens, but its movement seems essentially independent of them, that of a living entity that grows in size and grandeur as it flies upward through the

---

Could someone dare to day that in an Israelite context? (See 1 Chron. 28:5 compared, for example, with 2 Chron. 23:20.) Or is this some lesser form of kingship, having divine sanction, to be sure, but not truly representing "God Himself"? It would be interesting to reread the lovely description in G. Widengren, *Sakrales Königtum in Alten Testament* (Stuttgart: W. Kohlhammer, 1955), pp. 44–45, for example, with the merkavah materials and this medieval discussion (*rather than* biblical Israel!) in mind.

[6] See *Sodey Razaya*ʾ 88, immediately preceding the passage translated.

[7] The term *kawwanah* or *kawwanat ha-lev* is not entirely absent from the merkavah literature (see for example Schaefer, *Synopse* #560, Ms. Oxford 1531), but it is quite rare.

celestial realms. As in *Sodey Razaya*ʾ, its ultimate light will come from God; it is the Holy One Himself, not an angel, who finally makes it into a fitting crown for the *kavod*.[8]

In the world of *Ḥasidut Ashkenaz*, we seem to have an new understanding of and emphasis on the ascent of the crown itself, an ascent that remained quite obscure in the earlier materials. The crown has become a distinct heavenly entity or hypostasis, one that ascends and descends,[9] expands and diminishes,[10] quite independent of angelic actions or adjurations. Key to its role is its dynamic movement; it represents the rise of human energy, in the form of Israel's devotion, into the highest heavens. Received by God, that crown is blessed with divine light, some of which (at least in the *Sodey Razaya*ʾ passage) will shine back on those whose prayers formed the crown.

In preparing for the transition of our theme into the Kabbalistic mode, we should mention again the numerous passages where Israel themselves *are* the crown of God. This motif has its roots, as we have seen, in earlier materials, evident in both the aggadic and the esoteric sources. Surely it is related to the older *hieros gamos* references, and especially to the mutual exchange of *tefillin* between God and Israel. The reference to Isaiah 49:3 in connection with *tefillin* almost sounds as though God's wearing *tefillin* is something like His placing Israel directly upon His head. The tradition that the crown contains the name of Israel or the words *Yisraʾel ʿami li* also serves as a precedent for this image of Israel themselves as the crown of God.[11] In a certain way it may be said that this reading cuts through the mythic images and recreates, with the directness of Biblical language, the effect that is sought here.

We have thus seen two key elements of Kabbalistic symbolism already within texts created in the realm of *Ḥasidey Ashkenaz*. The crown is a dynamic entity, rising or falling in accord with the degree to which it is energized from both below and above. That crown may itself be identified with the Community of Israel, who collectively ascend by means of God's love and their own devotions to become a crown upon the holy head of the *kavod*. In order to see the emergence of some other key elements, we will need to turn to a somewhat longer text that will require our careful attention. I refer to a passage included within Eleazar of Worms's *Sefer ha-Ḥokhmah*[12] that has been discussed throughout the recent literature on the origins of Kabbalah. Though smaller sections of this text have been translated by several scholars,

8 The relative diminishing in importance of the angels is also reflected in Text #30 in Chapter 10, also discussed in M. Idel's *Kabbalah*, p. 193.

9 Cf. the *Sodey Razaya*ʾ passage quoted above.

10 Midrash Konen, quoted above; see Idel's treatment in *Kabbalah*, p. 191f.

11 This tradition continues into the writings of *Ḥasidey Ashkenaz*. See *Sefer ha-Navon* in Dan, *ʿIyyunim*, p. 128: "Crown—Israel is its name. Between its staves (?) is engraved on precious stone *ʿami li Yisraʾel*, in the name of Israel, the letters of Israel."

12 Though probably not written by Eleazar himself. See J. Dan, *Torat ha-Sod* (Jerusalem, 1968), p. 118ff. Farber, however, questions Dan on this point. See her *Concept*, p. 237n.40.

it has not yet been discussed in the context of a history of the coronation symbol. For this purpose, somewhat more of the text must be presented.

Text #36

"And YHWH His countenance unto you" (cf. Num. 6:25). Dot the letters Yofi'el priest. So too "May YHWH lift His countenance unto you and grant you . . ." (ibid. 26), the first letters of each word reads [by rearrangement] as Yofiʾel. Thus you have learned that this priest recites the priestly blessing as he begins his ascent, receiving from the eighteen hundred angels who receive the song of Israel . . . Baraqiʾel, who offers it as sacrifice upon the altar above. Of him Moses said: "He approaches the altar" (cf. Lev. 9:8);[13] dot the letters Baraqiʾel. And that angel has *SHaGaM* (=343) types of lights, like the ball of the sun, according to the numerical value of Baraqiʾel (=343). He is in charge of the rain. . . . He is the one who gives it [the song of Israel] to Sandalphon, who is taller than a thousand camps [of angels], by five hundred years' distance. He is called by God's name, and he [was revealed] to Moses from the Tent of Meeting, as it says, "He called unto Moses" (Lev. 1:1). That is why the aleph of *wa-yiqra*ʾ (he called) is written small, because "the small aleph" numerically equals "Sandalphon" and Yofiʿel (?), because that small aleph is five hundred years' distance taller than any of them.

And the crown sits on the Creator's head by the forty-two-letter name.[14] Of him[15] Ezekiel said, "Behold one wheel upon the earth" (1:15). *Ofan* (wheel) numerically equals Yofiʾel. . . . As soon as he puts the crown [in its place], Peniʾel and Uriʾel immediately come forward, inside the seven camps and the four creatures. They faint and bow because [it is] upon Him (?). Of this Moses said, "My face will not be seen" (Ex. 33:23). The letters [of *lo*ʾ *yera*ʾ*u*] are those of Uriʾel, and going back [*panai lo*ʾ], those of Peniʾel [meaning that neither of these two may see the crowned figure].

When the crown (*ʿaṭarah*) is on the Creator's head, the crown is called Akhtariel. Then the crown (*keter*) is hidden from all the holy angels, hidden in five hundred thousand myriad parasangs.[16] Then they ask one another: "Where is the place of His glory?"[17] Of this David says: "He [or "it"—the crown?] dwells in the secret of the Most High; he is sheltered in the shadow of the Almighty" (Ps. 91:1); in the prayer [=shadow] of the Almighty we take shelter.[18] It also contains the letters of "*our prayer*" because the Prayer (the *ʿamidah*) is a prayer to the blessed Holy One. It is

[13] Correcting J. Dan, *Torat ha-Sod*, p. 119n.16.

[14] See above, Chapter 5, n. 5.

[15] The text ignores the preceding sentence and goes on to discuss the angel.

[16] It has apparently ascended that distance higher than their ability to see, the same distance by which Sandalphon is taller than the other angels.

[17] This is a quotation from the *qedushah* liturgy in the *Mussaf* service.

[18] This represents a rearrangement of the Hebrew letters. See *Be-Midbar Rabbah* 12:3, where *seter ʿelyon* is used as a name for, or is at least identified with, the cloud that Moses entered at Sinai.

seated at the blessed Holy One's left,[19] like a bride next to the bridegroom. It is called "daughter of the king." Sometimes, because of its mission, it is called *bat qol* (daughter-voice). Of this Solomon said: "I—Shekhinah—was (*eHYeH*) with him" (Prov. 8:30).[20] The name of Shekhinah is *eHYeH*, and the Aramaic translation of "with him" is *TaRBeYH*, the same letters as *BaRTeYH* (his daughter), because she is called the king's daughter,[21] since Shekhinah is with Him in His house. This is "he is sheltered in the shadow of the Almighty," meaning, He has a prayer [a shadow?] that is called "with Him." She is the tenth kingdom, the secret of all secrets.

Know that the hidden numerical value of sod.[22] . . . There are royal crowns about every side of the Shekhinah. It in itself is two hundred thirty-six thousand myriad parasangs in size. Of it David has said: "Great [or "large"] is our Lord and of great strength" (Ps. 147:5); *we-rav koaḥ* numerically equals 236, and [the verse continues] "there is no keeping count of His understanding." Jeremiah said of it, "And YHWH God is truth; He is the living God and the eternal King" (10:10). Two hundred thirty-six; she conducts the world by her say. She is called an angel of God, according to her mission, but there is no separation in her [i.e., she is never fully separate from the divine Self].

Of this Scripture says: "Behold I send an angel before you" (Ex. 23:20). This was the Shekhinah, because "my angel," fully written out, numerically equals Shekhinah. This is what the sages said on "Moses fell on his face" (cf. Num. 16:4)—This teaches that the Shekhinah was prostrated before the blessed Holy One.[23] The

[19] In the Jewish amulets published by Naveh and Shaked (#7, p. 70), we find an amulet that reads: *Be-shimekha elah de-Yisraʾel li-reqiʿah milleyh saleqaʾ bi-setar de-ʾelah rabbah* (In Your name, O God of Israel, may his [the wearer's] prayer rise to heaven, at the side of the great God's throne). Here we have prayer seated at God's side—but certainly in a magical rather than a mystical key.

[20] Note the phonemic resemblance of *eṣlo* to *ṣel*—"shadow"—and *ṣelotaʾ*—"prayer." The associations of *eṣlo* and *ṣelotaʾ* we have already seen, in the anonymous (but probably authored by R. Eleazar) text discussed in Chapter 10. There too we found the association of Shekhinah with a reading of Prov. 8:30. It seems almost certain that these are two texts by the same hand.

[21] The nonexistent Targum of *TaRBeYH* for *eṣlo* only comes about through yet another play on this word, one that associates it with the verb *ʾṢL*, meaning "emanate" in medieval philosophical Hebrew. This verb is rendered as *RBY* (increase) by the Targum to Num. 11:17 and 25. See Scholem, *Origins of the Kabbalah* (Philadelphia: Jewish Publication Society, 1987), p. 185n.213.

[22] Here the text seems to break off in midsentence.

[23] Though the text is somewhat awkward, this seems to be its meaning. Thus Scholem explained it in his *Reshit ha-Qabbalah*, p. 51, n. 1. There he connected it to the passage in *Midrash Mishle* 47a, where Shekhinah stands before the blessed Holy One, the first time Shekhinah appears as a figure separate from God. See also the parallel thirteenth-century references to the Shekhinah bowing down on pp. 202 and 208. But in the German expansion of *Reshit ha-Qabbalah* (*Ursprung und Anfänge der Kabbala*, p. 163, followed by *Origins*, p. 185) Scholem has changed his mind about this passage. There he has "Moses fell on his face, that is, because the Shekhinah was [there]." I surmise that he made this change because he saw that there was no connection between this passage and that in midrash Mishle, and therefore that his rather radical interpretation was without precedent. But in making this change, he left behind the two other references quoted in *Reshit ha-*

prophets saw the Shekhinah because she is emanated. Thus it says in *Sefer Hekhalot* that the Shekhinah dwelt beneath the cherub, and both angels and men saw her. Once the generation of Enosh sinned, the Shekhinah ascended upward. But the Creator, the Shekhinah's Master, is hidden from all. He has neither measure nor likeness, and no eye has ever see him. When Scripture says, "Mouth to mouth [I speak to him]" (Num. 12:18), or that [a prophet] saw him, each time that was through a polished looking-glass, as it says: "And for all the great awe (*mora*ʾ, but read here as *mar*ʾ*eh*, "appearance"), this numerically equals Shekhinah.

He [Moses] also saw the great crown (*keter*) from behind Him, as it is written: "You may see My back" (Ex. 33:22)—this teaches that He showed him the *tefillin* knot. But He also showed him the crown, as it says: "I shall place you in the cleft of the rock." The final letters of those words spell out *keter*. His mouth is fire, His tongue is fire, and He Himself is a pond of fire. He conducts the world and she conducts the world. But because she is the tenth kingdom, the same letters as "world of two crowns," the Shekhinah has two thrones, two crowns, and two wheels, one below and one above. Each of them is five hundred [parasangs] higher than creation. Of this Solomon said: "Intellect upon" (Prov. 16:20)—numerically five hundred . . .

[There follows a paragraph about God's qualities of judgment and mercy, including references to the forty-two-letter name and to ten names or names of ten letters] . . .

This is the secret of the crown and the secret of the Shekhinah. Whoever knows them has a place in the World to Come. He inherits two worlds and is saved from the judgment of Gehenna; [he is] beloved above and is the object of delight below.[24]

This text has had so much to say that we had best begin by summarizing it. A priest-angel named Yofiel receives the prayers of Israel. They are given to Yofiel by eighteen hundred angels, presumably those who have been out gath-

Qabbalah, which are quite unambiguous. For that reason and because of the following line here, I prefer a version of Scholem's earlier reading. Eleazar is here interpreting the lack of a separate subject for "fell on his face" (the Torah does not say "Moses" here!) in Num. 16:4 to mean that Shekhinah fell on its face in horror at the sin of Korah. If there was a precedent for this reading (which Eleazar quotes in the name of "sages"), I have not been able to find it.

24 The Hebrew text is found in Dan, *Torat ha-Sod*, p. 119ff.; printed from Ms. Oxford 1568. See discussions also by Scholem, in *Origins*, p. 184ff.; Idel, *Kabbalah*, p. 195; Wolfson, "*Demut Ya*ʿ*aqov*;" idem, "Images of God's Feet: Some Observations on the Divine Body in Judaism," in *People of the Body*, ed. H. Eilberg-Schwartz (Albany: SUNY, 1992), p. 159, etc. See also J. Dan, "The Emergence of Mystical Prayer," in *Studies in Jewish Mysticism*, ed. Dan and Talmage (Cambridge, MA: Association for Jewish Studies, 1982), pp. 112–15. On p. 115 he notes that "human prayer becomes here a lower manifestation of the divine prayer." This theme is taken up by Asi Farber (*Concept*, p. 237f.), who writes: "The crown/prayer concept underwent a process of reification to become a dynamic, many-faceted pleromatic power. It was symbolized by prayer below, which was substantially linked with it and strengthened by this bond. . . . Against the background of such a possible theological development, I believe one can explain the nature of 'the secrets of prayer' in the circle of R. Judah he-Ḥasid, meaning the incredible importance placed upon taking care that the proper wording be used."

ering them from Israel's houses of prayer and study.[25] As Yofiel ascends with the prayers, he recites the priestly blessing. He then passes them on to Baraqiʾel, a sacrificing angel (a fellow priest?) who offers Israel's song as a sacrifice on his altar. Apparently in this way the prayers reach Sandalphon, who dwells at a much greater height. The crown ascends to God's head by means of the forty-two-letter name and is then called Akhtariel. Much is made of the fact that none of the angels can see the crown.

Up to this point, our text does not diverge from anything we might have expected; it is in every way like the other *Ḥasidey Ashkenaz* texts we have seen, fully absorbed within the mythic universe of the crown and the angels. But now it begins to take a radical turn. First it becomes involved in a complicated and somewhat obscure wordplay around the words *ṣel* (shadow), *ṣelotaʾ* (prayer), *eṣel* (near), and *aṣal* (emanate), some parts of which we have seen earlier. In the midst of this exercise, as though out of nowhere, a little vignette is drawn. Prayer sits at God's left side like a bride next to her bridegroom. She is God's bride and God's daughter. Sometimes, however, instead of being the king's daughter she is a *bat qol* (lit.: "daughter of a voice"), an ancient term referring both to an echo and to a form of revelation, possibly meaning a barely heard voice.[26] She is also identified with the Shekhinah, who is in God's house, an altogether bizarre statement according to the older meaning of the term *shekhinah*, the presence of God as it interacts with humans and with the lower world. She conducts the world along with God, and she has two thrones, two crowns, and two holy wheels!

Here we clearly seem to have gone through a door that leads into a new universe. It is not only that the crown is fully a part of the divine pleroma; that would be hardly even a small stretch from what we have already seen. Nor is it the "dynamic" character of the crown; we have already seen that the crown ascends and expands of its own accord, though that dynamism will increase significantly as we enter the realm of Kabbalah. What is really new here is that symbols and images work in a new way. There is a change in the flash of an instant—from crown to bride, from bride to *bat qol*, from *bat qol*, which is a divine voice, back to human prayer—that needs and receives no explanation or comment. Here we were talking about a crown, and suddenly we find that "she" is a princess. In another moment she will be an angel, then a crown, then the tenth kingdom. How did all this happen? Nothing in the wordplay forced us to go in that direction, nor does the author bother with providing biblical verses to prove most of his points. The seemingly senseless or meaningless associations here only work if there is some underlying pattern that is partially

[25] We have already encountered these eighteen hundred angels above in the *Sodey Razayaʾ* text, and in the quotation from Qallir included there.

[26] On the term *bat qol*, cf. S. Lieberman, *Hellenism in Jewish Palestine* (New York: JTSA, 1950), pp. 194–99.

known, and partially being revealed to the reader, as though for the very first time. *It is that pattern of associations that makes for Kabbalah.*

The most important creation of the Kabbalists lies in the realm of religious language. Kabbalah utilizes the unique language that it creates in order to penetrate deep within the human mind as well as into the Torah text to discover, and then to retell in countless ways, its essential myth of a Godhead/cosmos rent asunder and in search of reunion. This language is created around a tenfold grid of associative clusters. Each of the ten *sefirot*, ostensibly "aspects" of the divine self or stages in the flow of God's self-revealing emanation, is *in function* a group of terms and verbal pictures, each member of the cluster identified with all the others. While talking about the same *sefirah* or pair of *sefirot* in union, the Kabbalist will quite casually let his symbolic imagination flow from water imagery to that of light, from sexual metaphors to those of one or another of the commandments, and thence on to beasts and birds or Jerusalem and the history of the Jews. Within a given cluster all the symbols, whether drawn from nature or from tradition, are supposed to bear the same valance. Thus there is created a symbolically enriched language, a linguistic entity given a new profundity by this network of associations across the bounds of nature, Torah text, and Jewish religious tradition. Where such a pattern of associations may be seen to underlie a text, we are dealing with Kabbalah. The very earliest evidence of such assumed associative links (though not yet the grid-pattern of ten) are to be found in sources written by or deriving from the circle of Eleazar of Worms, including this text and the one previously quoted in Chapter 10.

Let us try to define more specifically the associations we have here. The crown, representing the prayer (*ṣelota*ʾ) of Israel, now dwells in the shadow (*ṣel*) of the Almighty. It is called Akhtariel, but it is also Shekhinah, God's daughter. It dwells sometimes at His left side, as a bride sits next to her bridegroom, or in His shadow.[27] But sometimes it is sent forth as His emissary, to accomplish some mission in the world. Then it may be called *bat qol* (as though to retain the daughter-association) but sometimes "angel" (or "messenger") as well. Originally its dwelling-place was "beneath the cherub,"[28] whence it was visible to both angels and humans.[29] In response to the emer-

[27] We will recall that the crown was associated both with the motif of Israel as God's bride and with the number 10 also in the *Sefer ha-Navon* passage we translated above. It is impossible to say which of these texts is earlier, but they clearly reflect some of the same traditions. "Crown" and "prayer" are identified with one another also in Eleazar's *Commentary to the Song of Songs*, 3:11. There it is also made explicit that the "prayer" referred to is the *ʿamidah*; *ʿaṭarah* is mentioned twice in that verse parallel to the two obligatory *ʿamidot* recited each day.

[28] This is a quotation from 3 Enoch 5. See Scholem, *Origins*, p. 185n.211.

[29] In Saʿadyanic terms, this seems to refer our crown symbol to the lower *kavod*, since the upper is seen, if at all, by angels alone.

gence of human sinfulness in the world, it began to retreat upward.[30] It seems to be identical also with the "back" of God that Moses was shown in the Sinai-vision.[31] It is the tenth kingdom.[32]

We see before us a cluster of symbolic associations around a figure who is somehow a secondary deity or a highest representation of the unknowable God.[33] Several of the elements present here belong to the feminine-leaning group of symbols that will eventually emerge in Kabbalah as the tenth *sefirah*, the "lowest" of the symbolic configurations. Later Kabbalists will understand this element of divinity to have a liminal role. Though it is never fully separate from divinity,[34] it does sometimes appear to take on the garb of "angel" or "lad," sent into the world to do God's bidding.

But the group of symbols here presented as one cluster also includes a key symbol that will be associated with the very highest supernal realms in Kabbalistic thought: the crown of God, called *kete*r or sometimes *keter ʿelyon.* The association of the crown with the shadow drew upon Psalm 91:1, "He dwells in the secret of the Most High." The Hebrew phrase is *seter ʿelyon*, identical with *keter ʿelyon* except for a single letter. Whether or not this linguistic closeness is the source of the Kabbalistic term,[35] we certainly have a reference here

[30] Cf. *Pesiqta DRK* 1: 1 (ed. Mandelbaum 2f.) and parallels.

[31] There is some awkwardness in the text as to how the crown, which is the *tefillah shel rosh*, can be identical with the *qesher shel tefillin*, but that is what it seems to want to say.

[32] There is some relationship between this assertion, the ten kings mentioned in *Bahir* #49 (itself derived from *Pirqey R. Eliezer* 11), and the fact that *malkhut* will be the tenth *sefirah* as Kabbalah emerges. The precise nature of this relationship among developing symbols remains unclear.

[33] I agree with Wolfson that this single grouping of symbols found in Eleazar is reminiscent of Judah Ha-Levi's second definition of *kavod* in *Kuzari* 4:3. See his "Merkavah Traditions in Philosophical Garb: Judah Halevi Reconsidered," *PAAJR* 57 (1991): 194–95 and sources mentioned in n. 49.

[34] See Nahmanides' sometimes sharply worded insistences on this, for example in his commentary to Genesis 46:1 (ed. Chavel, p. 250).

[35] The locution *keter ʿelyon* is first found in *Midrash Shir ha-Shirim* (ed. Gruenhuet; Jerusalem, 1897, f. 39b) to Cant. 5:11, a verse to which we have made frequent reference. There we find "'His head is of pure gold'—these are the letters of the supreme crown." In that instance I do not believe that *keter ʿelyon* has a specific meaning requiring explanation; *ʿelyon* could as well be rendered "sublime" or "most high," without any thought that it implies the parallel existence of a "lower" crown or crowns. The phrase is picked up in the medieval esoteric literature, particularly in the writings of R. Eleazar, as Scholem notes in *Origins*, p. 125n.129. But why is it called this? Is the phonetic closeness to *seter ʿelyon* the key here? Or is it that this *keter* is surrounded or followed by other crowns, as our *S. Ḥokhmah* text has it, and stands above them? That is what Scholem seems to say in *Origins*, p. 185n.208, but I am not completely satisfied with that explanation, particularly in face of *Sefer ha-Ḥokhmah*'s identification of *keter ʿelyon* with *malkhut ʿasirit.* I would suggest that the usage has to do with the bifurcation of symbols that I shall discuss below, toward the end of Chapter 13. As the crown is divided, *keter ʿelyon* becomes the term for the static crown, as distinct from *keter/ʿaṭarah*, which is the dynamic one. *Sefer ha-Ḥokhmah* would then already know of this separation but would be trying to make the point that both of these are one.

The relationship between *keter ʿelyon* and *seter ʿelyon* is complicated by the added presence of

to a high and hidden realm, not to an angel-like emissary who appears in this world. Why should symbols connected with God's crown turn out to be here associated with a figure that exists at the very margins of the divine world? Is not the crown on God's head as high as one can be, far beyond the reach or sight of the highest angels? And what of Shekhinah? How is it that this term, originally referring to God's own presence, should now belong to this same "lowest" group of symbols? And what are her two crowns and her two thrones? The text remains extremely difficult, especially when seen in light of the Kabbalistic usages found in *Sefer ha-Bahir*.

It would seem that our text reflects a very early stage in the development of Kabbalistic language, or possibly an early variant tradition. Here the symbols to be associated with the "first" and "tenth" *sefirot* are one, not yet divided from one another. There is no hierarchy of hypostases here, but rather a chain of symbolic terms that are all identified with one another. Specifically, the crown symbol has not yet been divided into two, as it will be in the *Bahir* and throughout later Kabbalah.[36]

Throughout the long history of crown symbolism as we have seen it, the various Hebrew terms for "crown" were readily interchangeable. Occasionally, in the older texts, God seemed to wear a two-part crown, parallel to the headband and turban of the ancient priest. But nothing of symbolic value was made of the distinction between those two. The two most common terms for "crown" throughout this literature in all its forms are *keter* and *ʿaṭarah*. There is no basis for distinguishing between the two as they are used in any text that is not specifically associated with the symbolism of Kabbalah.

For the Kabbalist the distinction between these two will be completely

---

ṣad ʿelyon, found in the *ʿIyyun* literature. This term has an independent source, translated from the Aramaic of Daniel 7:25. See M. Verman, *Books of Contemplation* (Albany: SUNY, 1992), p. 43n.27. Azriel of Gerona will identify *ṣad ʿelyon* with the highest *sefirah*. See his Commentary on *Sefer Yeṣirah*, p. 455.

Another possible meaning of *keter ʿelyon* emerges from an interesting passage on the crown found in *ʿArugat ha-Bosem*, vol. 3, p. 481. When the crown reaches the image of Jacob engraved on the divine throne, according to that passage, it "expands fully," and Is. 49:3 is quoted. But then the text adds, "Of this it says: "to place you supreme (*ʿelyon*) (Deut. 26:19) over all the nations." This quotation seems to make no particular sense at this point. But if we look slightly above in the source, we find another sentence that also seems out of place: "that [crown] which is formed by the songs of Israel is *ʿelyon*." It would seem that here a sentence has fallen out, most likely at the hands of a censor. All the nations (or perhaps "the princes of the seventy nations") were said to make crowns for God, (as the parallel passage in 3:80f. makes clear), but Israel's crown was *ʿelyon*, "highest of all." This reconstruction is based on an old textual witness (cf. Schaefer, *Synopse* #46) to the crown of God being inscribed with the seventy names of the angels representing the seventy nations. If my reconstruction here is correct, this would be an interesting association of Israel with *keter ʿelyon*.

[36] Perhaps there is some hint at this in the "two crowns" mentioned here, but that reference needs to be explained in conjunction with the two thrones and two wheels (or *ofanim*, "angelic beings") that accompany it.

clear, and they are no longer to be casually associated with one another. *Keter* is a member of the "first" symbol-group, that which is said to be highest in the hierarchical arrangement of *sefirot*. It will there be associated, in the Kabbalah of Gerona and later, with such terms of abstraction as *ether*, *nothingness*, the *One of ones*, *will*, *pure compassion*, *primal cause*, and so forth. In fact *keter* is virtually the only pictorial symbol that the classical Kabbalists[37] permitted in this cluster, one that mostly has to do with reconditeness and abstraction. *ʿAṭarah*, on the other hand, is a well-known member of the tenth symbol-group, the liminal cluster at the other "end" of the hierarchy, the one often associated with femininity.[38]

The presence of *keter* amid the highest cluster makes complete symbolic sense. One of the chief symbolic "orderings" of the *sefirot* is that which arranges them as parts of the divine "body." In this reading the first three *sefirot* are related to the divine "head," the fourth and fifth are arms, the sixth the torso, etc. Of course this sounds very much like a Kabbalistic adaptation of *shiʿur qomah*, the ancient "measuring" of the gigantic divine body, and it has generally been understood in that way.[39] Given this ordering, it is quite "natural" that *keter* would be at the head of the hierarchy, occupying the same place it did in those much more ancient sources. Of course the cosmic *anthropos* (here reconceived as an arrangement of inner divine entities) should be crowned. The problem with this understanding is that it does not quite fit the texts as we have them. In the *Bahir*, the key earliest presentation of Kabbalistic symbols, the crown and the body occur in different sections and do not seem to belong to one another.[40] The crown symbol also carries over into the

[37] See the list of symbolic terms for *keter* in Gikatilla's *Shaʿarey Orah*, chapter 10, ed. Ben Shlomo, vol. 2, p. 107ff. The only other pictorial image listed there for the first *sefirah* is "the white [hoary] head." Note also the abstract quality of all the terms for the highest *sefirah* found in the list in Tishby's edition of *Perush ha-ʾAggadot le-Rabbi Azriel*, p. 134. Jehiel Luria in the sixteenth century is able to add a few more verbal pictures to the list: "sealed spring," "font of blessings," "goodly oil," and "roof of the canopy." See his *Hekhal ha-Shem* (Venice, n.d.), f. 6a.

[38] Scholem noticed the importance of this fact early in his career. See his German translation of *Sefer ha-Bahir*, p. 62n.6: "God's crown and its symbolism is also a central feature of Gaonic Hekhalot mysticism, and the transition to sefirotic thought here is revealed with unusual clarity. The concept of the first sefirah as 'highest crown' derives from this conceptual circle. That the first and last sefirot are both originally called 'crowns' is no coincidence." Of course the later Scholem saw this tradition as much earlier than Gaonic.

The early stage in the development of crown symbolism may still be reflected in the comment of R. Ezra of Gerona to Song of Songs 3:11 (*Kitvey RaMBaN*, vol. 2, p. 494), where *keter* and *ʿaṭarah* are synonyms, both standing for that which flows directly from *afisat ha-maḥashavah*. For an exception to the clear distinction made in Kabbalistic sources between *keter* and *ʿaṭarah* see the important passage in R. Jacob ben Jacob's *Commentary to the Chariot of Ezekiel* (ed. A Farber; Jerusalem: Hebrew University, 1978) p. 35, to be discussed below in Chapter 14.

[39] See also Scholem, *On the Mystical Shape of the Godhead* (New York: Schocken, 1991), pp. 37ff.

[40] Body symbolism is chiefly in #117; crown symbolism appears in several other places, as we detail below, but not there.

rather more abstract, including neo-Platonic Kabbalistic authors, who would make almost no use of these bodily symbols. Historically it sometimes almost seems that the process is reversed: the presence of "crown" symbolism is a fixture of Kabbalah from the beginning, firmly rooted in the tradition we have been tracing here. It has developed a life of its own within the symbolic universe of medieval Jews that has made it quite independent of the ancient—and often attacked—*Shi*ʿ*ur Qomah* traditions. It may be that this crown symbol, once established, had a formative role in legitimating or re-creating for the Kabbalists the head and body configurations that go beneath it.[41]

But we are running ahead of ourselves. Our next task is to examine the symbol of the crown in the *Bahir* itself, as it will set the stage for further developments of crown symbolism within Kabbalah. It is to the crown(s) in the *Bahir* that we now turn our attention.

[41] Note the passage in *Sha*ʿ*arey Orah* (vol. 1, p. 172; see parallels in Ben-Shlomo's notes) that says *keter* is above the ten *sefirot*; the ten are in the form of Adam, but *keter* is higher, "the place that is not called *adam*," beyond being *demut ke-mar*ʾ*eh adam*.

CHAPTER THIRTEEN

Sefer ha-Bahir

Sefer ha-Bahir, one of the strangest documents in the history of Jewish literature,[1] is a book that begins in the midst of nowhere and seems to wend its way through a path of highly disjointed midrashic fragments,[2] also to nowhere in particular. In the course of its meanderings, however, it gives voice to a dazzling array of myths and symbols; it specializes in a unique and remarkably arcane form of dialogic rhetoric.

Gershom Scholem's several treatments of Kabbalistic origins, to which we have referred above, point to various parallels between the *Bahir* and esoteric works composed by *Ḥasidey Ashkenaz* and especially to fragments of possibly earlier oriental works preserved in their circles. The closeness of the *Bahir*, and thus of the first Kabbalistic symbols, to some combination of such works as *Sefer ha-Navon* and *Sefer ha-Hokhmah* should also be fairly clear. The ten angels and ten references to Israel as God's bride associated with the crown in one source and the strange association of prayer, bride, daughter, and two crowns in the other both bring us to the very edge of the symbolic world now so much more richly embellished in the *Bahir*.

About three-quarters of the way through its text, the *Bahir* tries to organize its lush symbolic garden into a series of ten clusters, hanging these on the frame of the "ten utterances" by which God is alleged to have spoken the world into being.[3] The attempt begins with crown symbolism:

Text #37

What are the ten utterances? First is most high crown (*keter ʿelyon*), blessed, blessed be its name and its people. And who are its people? Israel, as it is written:

[1] Daniel Abrams has recently published a critical edition of *Sefer ha-Bahir* (Los Angeles [!]: Cherub Press, 1994). It arrived too late to serve as the original basis for this chapter, though I have now consulted it and corrected accordingly. Scholem's German translation, based on the Munich manuscript and a host of quotations from the *Bahir* found in Kabbalistic sources, also remains useful. By now a large number of *Bahir* passages have been commented on in scholarly literature, and a compendium of such comments would be of great value. For scholarly literature on the *Bahir*, see Chapter 12, n. 2 above.

[2] Reuven Margaliot divided his edition of the *Bahir* into two hundred paragraphs; these divisions are in no way original to the text and are often misleading. Scholem also numbered the sections in his German translation, but he divided the text quite differently. His numbering is now used also by Abrams and I have followed their lead. An appendix to the Abrams edition (p. 337) gives a guide for coordinating the two sets of numbers.

[3] See *Avot* 5:1 and b. *Rosh Ha-Shanah* 32a.

"Know that He is God; He has made us and not we, His people . . ." (Ps. 100:3). [We belong to the aleph], to recognize and know the One of ones, singular in all His names.[4]

A most puzzling text, and one extremely rich in nuance, much of which is difficult to translate. The first of the utterances, presumably the highest in a hierarchical arrangement, is most high crown. This much, and only this much, is quite straightforward. The blessings pronounced upon "its" (or should this be translated "His"?) name are quite surprising. Indeed we have seen at times that the crown itself has a name,[5] but this formula of blessing is one that the classical Hebrew reader would expect to be used exclusively for God.[6] Are we being told here that the crown *is* God? As we shall see, exactly what we mean by the word *God* will again become problematic in the *Bahir* context, as it was amid the lush angelology of the merkavah. Where "God" fits into the cosmic realm or "pleroma"[7] of the *Bahir* is by no means a simple matter. Might "its name and its people" refer to the tradition that "Israel" is inscribed on the crown? Or might this be "His" name, either YHWH or some more complex formulation, *and* His people Israel, two entities quite distinct from one another?

The quotation from Psalm 100 is filled with complicated allusions. The written Bible text contains the word ולא, "and not." But the Masoretes read this word as ולו, meaning "are His." The verse then reads: "He has made us, and we are His." The *Bahir* now suggests a third reading of this short word as ולא, meaning "to aleph," so that the verse would mean, "He has made us, and we belong to aleph," or to the One. To complicate the reading further, the word עמו, "His people," could also be vocalized עמו, or "with Him," meaning "He has made us, and we were not [partners] with Him [in Creation]."

The concluding two phrases, "One of ones" and "singular (or "united?) in

4 *Bahir* #96. "We belong to the Aleph" is indicated in the Munich manuscript by a single line over the aleph of *we-lo*ʾ; Margaliot adds it as a separate interpretive phrase.

5 See the discussion in Chapter 6 above.

6 See discussion by Scholem, *Origins*, p. 125, where he claims that this particular phrasing of the blessing is based on a formulation found in *Sefer Yeṣirah*.

7 The term *pleroma* is used in Gnostic writings to describe the "fullness," the divine world out of which the fallen one has been cast in the Gnostic myth. Noting the frequent use of the odd term *ha-male*ʾ in the *Bahir*, Scholem came to explain it as related to pleroma and spoke of the sefirotic world of the *Bahir* as its pleroma. On this usage cf. the comments of M. Idel in *JSJT* 6 (1987): 67ff.

There are passages in the *Bahir* that seem to well fit Y. Liebes's formulation "that the Bahir is aware of a divine personal essence transcending the attributes and the sefirot, attesting to this book's special status between Midrash and Kabbala" ("De Natura Dei," p. 26), though this "transcendence" should be distinguished from the Neoplatonic *Eyn Sof* language of thirteenth-century Kabbalists. Elsewhere in the *Bahir*, God seems to be elusively present *among* the *sefirot*, or to comprise them to one degree or another.

all His names" are unusually abstract language for the *Bahir*. Scholem has already suggested that these represent a late stratum in the text's complicated editing process,[8] and they are probably addenda to the original homily here.

The phrase *keter ᶜelyon* appears once more in the *Bahir*, this time in an explanation of Is. 6:3, the *qedushah* verse.

TEXT #38

And what is "Holy, holy, holy"? Holy—most high crown; holy—root of the tree; holy—attached and united with them all. "Lord of hosts"—the entire host is filled with His Glory. And what is the "holy" that is united [with them all]? To what may this be likened? To a king who had sons and whose sons had sons. At the time when the sons do his will, he enters into their midst, granting status to all, satisfying all, causing goodness to flow upon them, so that both fathers and sons are sated. When the children do not do his will, he lets flow to the fathers sufficient for their need [but no more].[9]

Here we have a typically strange Bahir passage, a joining of two mythic images and a perhaps philosophical formulation that seem to make no sense in conjunction with one another. The latter formulation is then explained by a parable. The *qedushah* is being interpreted as referring to the entire realm of the pleroma. First is the crown, second is the root of the tree that is to become the tree of divine powers, perhaps the best-known symbol of the *Bahir*.[10] Using the later and more clearly defined language of Kabbalah, the "root" here might include together the second and third *sefirot*. The third "holy," described in somewhat abstract and "late"-seeming Bahiric terms, is one that is united with all the "lower" powers. The parable makes it clear that God as "father" and "grandfather" of the pleromatic world controls the flow of divine bounty or energy into the lower *sefirot* in accord with His "children's" fulfillment of His will. Ostensibly these are the sefirotic children referred to in the parable, but they might (on the basis of other passages) mean His human children as well. The *qedushah* itself is the utterance of the entire heavenly host, all of which is filled with His glory. This passage on the threefold meaning of *qadosh* is introduced by a typically liturgical passage[11] that concludes, "They crown [Him] with three "holies."[12]

[8] Scholem, *Origins*, pp. 67n.28, and 125f. on the possible Saᶜadyanic origin of the phrase. See also Pedaya, "The Provençal Stratum in the Redaction of Sefer ha-Bahir," *JSJT* 9, part. 2 (= Pines Jubilee Volume), pp. 139–64.

[9] *Bahir* #89.

[10] Scholem, *Origins*, pp. 71ff.

[11] *Bahir* #88.

[12] It is noteworthy that both references to *keter ᶜelyon* are in places adjoining such "late" language. In this case that language has been noted by J. Dan, *Torat ha-Sod*, p. 116, who suggests the influence of Ibn Ezra. It is by no means impossible that the use of this phrase itself represents a later stage of the *Bahir*'s symbolic development.

In both of these passages, *keter* is defined by the adjective *ᶜelyon*, and the realm being discussed is to be considered "first," whether first of the ten utterances or first of the three "holies." Readily distinguished from these two references are several others, in which the crown is neither highest nor stationary in position at all. We begin with a comment on the names of certain musical tropes used in cantillation:

TEXT #39

Rabbi Amorai was seated and expounded: Why is it called *segol*? *Seggulah* is its [proper] name. [It is thus called] when it comes above [at the beginning of the list of tropes], following *zarqa*ʾ. What is the meaning of *zarqa*ʾ? It is like its name, thrown (*niZRaQ*). It like is something that has been thrown, and in its wake comes a treasure (Seggulah) of kings and provinces.[13]

And what is the meaning of *zarqa*ʾ? That which is written:[14] "Blessed is the glory of YHWH from His place" (Ez. 3:12), indicating that nobody knows His place. We recite a name over the crown and it goes to the Master's head, as is written: "Master of heaven and earth" (Gen. 14:19). As it goes it is like a *zarqa*ʾ with a *seggulah* following it, and it comes to be at the head of all the letters.[15]

[13] I am in this case preferring Margaliot's reading *nizraq* over the difficult *nevarekh* found in the Munich text. Orthographically they are quite close. This interpretation of *zarqa*ʾ is of great antiquity. Something is thrown, and following it comes the treasure of kings and provinces. This sequence is reminiscent of an unusual usage in the language of Hebrew liturgical poetry. We have seemingly unexplained references to "throwing" with regard to royalty in early *piyyuṭim* from Ereṣ Yisraʾel. See *Piyyuṭey Yosi ben Yosi* (Jerusalem, Mossad Bialik, 1991), p. 94; *le-mi nizreqah melukhah*; and also Yannai's *zer lekha zoreqet*, in Z. M. Rabinowitz, *The Liturgical Poems of Rabbi Yannai* (Jerusalem, Mossad Bialik, 1987), vol. 2, p. 199f. M. Zulay commented on this latter passage in his "*ᶜIyyuney Lashon be-Fiyyuṭey Yannai*," in *Studies of the Research Institute for Hebrew Poetry in Jerusalem*, vol. 6 (Jerusalem: Schocken, 1945), p. 220f. He suggested that the tossing of a wreath or some object of value was part of the way a coronation was celebrated, presumably in Byzantine times. This claim is supported by reference to two aggadic passages: the *Targum Yerushalmi* to Gen. 49:22, where the cheering crowd throws all sorts of gold objects at Joseph as he is made Pharoah's second, and a Midrash (*Yelammedenu* fragments from the *Yalqut*; Jellinek, *Bet ha-Midrasch* 6:89) in which a king says, "I will ride the horse I rode on the day when I was made king, and I will wear the cloak that was thrown upon me when I was made emperor (*augustos*)." Zulay cites S. Krauss, *Talmudische Archaeologie*, vol. 2 (Leipzig: G. Fock, 1911), p. 475n.321, where more sources are given, including both classical and New Testament parallels. (On the purple cloak as symbol of empire, see O. Seyffert, *A Dictionary of Classical Antiquities*, s.v. "purpura" and S. Krauss, *Paras we-Romi ba-Talmud uva-Midrashim* [Jerusalem: Mossad Ha-Rav Kood, 1948], p. 44.) *Zarqa*ʾ is here being interpreted in this way: an act of throwing that makes for kingship. In the *Bahir*, this interpretation immediately leads into the quotation from b. *Ḥagigah* 13b. The ascent of the crown to God's head, it is hinted, should be seen in light of this custom.

[14] From here to "the Master's head" is a quotation from b. *Ḥagigah* 13b. See above, Chapter 3.

[15] Treatment of the symbolization of the musical notations is outside the scope of our concerns here. This should be undertaken in conjunction with manuscript research that will show the physical form of the signs as indicated in the appropriate manuscripts. There might be some key here to dating or locating this portion of the *Bahir*.

> And why is it [the *zarqa*ʾ written] at the end of a word and not at its head? To teach you that this crown ascends upward, upward. And what is the nature of this crown? It is a precious stone, perfectly set in a crown, of which it is written, "The stone the builders rejected has become the headstone [i.e., cornerstone]" (Ps. 118: 22). It ascends to the place from which it was hewn, as is written, "From there the shepherd, stone of Israel" (Gen. 49:24).[16]

The term used for "crown" throughout this passage is the Aramaic *taga*, following the usage in the Talmudic quotation. The image is one of a flying crown that ascends ever upward by the motion of a projectile pushing it on until it reaches its elevated destination. This destination is "the place from which it was hewn." We might think this is the third element, the one sometimes referred to as "quarry." But there are suffcient hints here regarding "head" to tell us that the crown goes to the very top and is seated on the Master's head, which is also the "head" of all the letters and the "head" stone out of which this symbolic universe of the pleroma is constructed.[17]

What we have here is a return of a lower crown to its uppermost source, presumably the "other" crown that stands at the head of this entire realm. We are given no explanation of how it came to be that the "crown" has to come up from below, nor are we specifically told that there are two crowns here. It is only by reading this passage in conjunction with our *keter ʿelyon* passages that we get an idea of a crown above that is the place of origin of a lower crown, one that seeks to rise upward and return to its source. The crown described here is the one involved in movement upward, recalling especially the crown as described in the *ʿArugat ha-Bosem* passage, ascending through the heavens to reach God's head. Notice that even though the *Ḥagigah* passage is quoted here, the angel Sandalphon is conspicuously missing. It is *we* who "recite a name" over the crown and help it rise to the Master's head. This is a very interesting change in the Talmudic text. The *Bahir* has no shame about revealing the human-driven theurgic intent of this passage and the entire myth that stands behind it.

This "crown" that ascends to the divine head, or to the head of the pleromatic world, becomes a key symbol of the *Bahir*'s universe and is sometimes still visible even when the word *crown* itself is not mentioned. First we see a passage based on the identification that has already been made of "crown" with "precious stone":

[16] *Bahir* #61. See the discussion of this passage by E. Wolfson, in "Biblical Accentuation in a Mystical Key: Kabbalistic Interpretation of the Teʿamim," *Journal of Jewish Music and Liturgy* 11 (1988–89), pp. 4–5.

[17] See the parallel use in this verse in *Sefer ha-Qomah*, included in Scholem's *Reshit ha-Qabbalah* (Jerusalem: Schocken, 1948), p. 221. There *even* is identified both with "the Holy One" and (numerologically) with "garden," or with symbols that might fit both the "top" and "bottom" of the sefirotic ladder.

TEXT #40

Another interpretation of "Revive Your work in the midst of the years" (Hab. 3:2). To what may this be compared? To a king who had a goodly pearl, the delight of his [entire] kingdom. In his hour of joy he would embrace it and kiss it, place it upon his head and love it. Said Habakkuk: Even though the angels are with You, that pearl is the delight of Your world. Therefore "revive it in the midst of the years. . . ."[18]

The pearl referred to here reflects a well-known Gnostic symbol, as Scholem has pointed out.[19] There it is the precious *pneuma*, hidden in the depths of the defiled lower world. For the *Bahir*, the pearl is God's beloved treasure that He places upon His head. Surely this is the crown as well as the pearl. But it is also Israel, His *ḥemdah* or *seggulah* (delight or treasure), whom He raises up to the highest place. Here we recall those passages in *Shir ha-Kavod* where Israel themselves were seen as the crown of God, the ones placed upon His head.

This also explains the statement attributed here to the prophet Habakkuk: "Even though the angels are with You. . . ." Israel are the delight of God that is higher than the angels. Though the angels surround God in the merkavah traditions, only Israel goes higher than they stand, placed above them all as the crown or pearl upon God's head.

The motif of the precious object placed upon the king's head is also central to the following passage, reconnected from two widely separated locations in the very poorly (or strangely) edited *Bahir* text.

TEXT #41

. . . like a king who had a throne. Sometimes he carried it in his arm and sometimes on his head. [The students] asked [the master]: "Why?" [He replied:] "Because it was beautiful and he was hesitant to sit on it." They asked: "And where did he put it?" "On his head. . . ."[20]

You said, "His throne?" But we have said that this is the crown (*keter*) of the blessed Holy One. Thus we have said, "With three crowns are Israel crowned: the priestly crown, the royal crown, and the crown of Torah above them."[21] Indeed, the crown of priesthood, the royal crown is above it, but the crown of Torah is above them both. To what may this be compared? To a king who had a beautiful and fragrant vessel that he loved greatly. Sometimes he put it on his head. These are the *tefillin* of the head. Sometimes he carried it in his arm, in the knot of the *tefillin* on

[18] *Bahir* #49 and see Wolfson, "Biblical Accentuation."

[19] Cf. Scholem, *Origins*, p. 174f. and the important discussion by H. Jonas, *The Gnostic Religion* (Boston: Beacon Press, 1958), pp. 125ff.

[20] *Bahir* #25.

[21] Cf. *Avot* 4:13, where the crown of a good name is above the three others.

the arm. Sometimes he lends it to his son to sit with him. Sometimes it is called his throne, because in his arm he carries it like an amulet, a kind of cup.[22]

Here the symbol has become somewhat more complex and obscure. Crown and throne are assimilated to one another, two ancient symbols of divine royalty. The image of the chair on the king's head is there for shock value, or possibly even as a bit of humor.[23] The image is still in large part one of Israel, as the crown or *tefillin* (the references to *tefillin* may be marginalia that have been added to the text) of God, placed upon His head. We also note that the terminological distinction between *keter* and *ʿaṭarah* is not yet absolute in the *Bahir*. The reference here is to the crown that moves in dynamic fashion, called only *ʿaṭarah* in the post-*Bahir* tradition. But here, probably because of the influence of the *Avot* passage on the three crowns, the term *keter* is used without any hesitation.

Exactly how this fits in with the throne, however, is a bit puzzling. And who is the son, to whom He lends the throne? This must have been a rather daring image for Jews living in medieval Christian Europe, if we recall whose throne is next to that of the Father. Here it would seem that this daring image is being used to give us a glimpse of an inner pleromatic development. The highest being has a precious object that is symbolically manifest as his throne or

[22] *Bahir* #101. According to R. Yedudah ben Pazi in *Yerushalmi Ḥagigah*, Chapter 2, beginning, God wears "the storm wind containing . . . the entire world" as an amulet on His arm. See parallels to this in Schaefer, *Synopse* #784: "The entire world is suspended from His great arm like an amulet on the hero's arm" and further in ibid., #727 and #840. See L. Ginzberg's remarks on this passage in *Legends*, vol. 5, p. 12. According to another (probably related) tradition, the primordial Torah was written on God's arm. See sources cited and discussion by M. Idel in "The Concept of the Torah in Heikhalot Literature and in the Kabbalah," *JSJT* 1 (1981): 43–44.

My translation of the final word as "cup" rather than "throne" relies on the several references to *kasa de-kaspaʾ*, connected to an amulet on the left arm, found in *Maʿaseh Merkavah* in Scholem, *Jewish Gnosticism*, p. 111. My thanks to Rachel Elior for this reference. The cup as a magical figure is well-known in the ancient Near East. The biblical cup of Joseph (Gen. 44:5) is the first example that comes to mind. Cf. also Is. 51:17. There is some reference to cups in incantation texts from Nippur. See Montgomery, *Aramaic Incantation Texts* (Philadelphia: University Museum, 1913), pp. 7, 13. See also the brief discussion by J. Obermann in "Two Magic Bowls: New Incantations Texts from Babylonia," *American Journal of Semitic Languages and Literatures* 57 (1940): 12, and the charm quoted and discussed by Goodenough, *Jewish Symbols in the Greco-Roman World*, vol. 2 (New York: Pantheon, 1954), p. 172f. Closer to home is the reference in the *Sar ha-Torah* fragment, Schaefer, *Synopse* #564, to Moses writing a divine name in a cup (the paper burned and its ashes included in liquid?) which he then gave Joshua to drink, presumably so that he would take the secret name into his own person. I recognize, however, that this reading of the text as a play between *kisseʿ* and *kasaʿ* ("throne" and "cup") is awkward. I would be happy to learn of evidence of a throne- or chair-shaped amulet worn on the arm; this would allow for a more straightforward understanding of the passage.

[23] There are occasional references in earlier sources to the throne of glory ascending through the heavens, in fashion similar to the crown. See A. M. Habermann's edition of *Sefer Qerovah* in *Yediʿot ha-Makhon le-Ḥeqer ha-Shirah ha-ʿIvrit*, vol. 3 (Berlin, 1936), p. 126 and the sources cited there.

crown. As he brings forth or emanates a lower divine rung, he allows that one also to partake of his royal symbols, to be "lesser king" as he is greater. One is tempted to see here a latter-day descendent of the ancient Meṭaṭron/Yehoel/Yah Qatan traditions, but now integrated into a new symbolic context.

Israel are the crown of God, but they seem here also to be His throne. That is perhaps not so surprising as it first seems. God "is enthroned in the praises of Israel" (Ps. 22:4). He dwelt in the tabernacle they made for Him, seated upon the cherubim. In fact the tabernacle itself is once depicted as God's crown, possibly providing a source for the strange imagery here.[24]

The point is that this crown/throne/Israel has varied positions. Sometimes they are on His head, sometimes on His arm, sometimes given over to a lesser figure. Is there some coordination between these varied states and the actual historical situation of Israel? Are they "the crown upon His head" while the Temple is standing, but given over to the rule of a lesser being when they wander in exile? Such a connection is not made explicit in the passage, but the images here would certainly seem to serve well as a way of accounting for the vissicitudes of Israel's fate. Though the *Bahir* seems mostly to be discussing events in an upper symbolic universe that is rather detached from the realm of history, the earthly fate of Israel appears clearly to be present in the background of a number of its teachings. That is most likely the case also in the following passage, commenting on a verse in the Book of Lamentations, recalling the destruction of the earthly Temple:

TEXT #42

They said to him: Is it not written: "He has cast from heaven to earth the glory of Israel" (Lam. 2:1)? If so, they have fallen. He replied: if they have read [once] but not repeated, if they have read it a second time but not a third.[25] To what may this be compared? To a king who had a beautiful crown upon his head and a beautiful woolen cloak upon his shoulders. He received bad news and he cast the crown off his head and the cloak from before him.[26]

The crown (*ᶜaṭarah*) is now cast down to earth. This too seems to be Israel, cast off into exile as God hears the "bad news" of her sin that led to the Temple's destruction. Here we see the upper and lower worlds of Gnostic/Jewish symbolism, the pleromatic and historic realms, thoroughly intermingled. Israel, God's crown, is cast down within history, because of sin. But this exiled lower crown is surely also the pearl, the daughter, the bride, or the

[24] *Pesiqta DRK* 1: 3 (ed. Mandelbaum 7) and parallels, as discussed above in Chapter 9, n. 5.

[25] This formula, which is taken from b. *Berakhot* 18a, end, seems to be a way of saying, "You do not yet understand." At least that is its function in the Talmudic source. Indeed, the ensuing passage indicates that the interlocutor did not properly understand Israel's situation. They are not simply "fallen," but intentionally cast off.

[26] *Bahir* #23; based on *Echah Rabbah* 2:1 (ed. Buber, p. 96). See also the discussion by E. Wolfson in *Along the Path: Studies in Kabbalistic Myth, Symbolism, and Hermeneutics* (Albany: SUNY, 1995), p. 117nn.39–40.

lower *sophia*, seen in other passages of the *Bahir* as a figure exiled from the pleromatic realm and seeking to return to favor. This is the *Bahir*'s mythic rendition of "Wherever Israel were exiled, Shekhinah was exiled with them."

The next passage we shall examine is another difficult one, since it could easily bear at least two quite different interpretations:

TEXT #43

Said Rabbi Reḥumai: Light preceded the world that "is surrounded by cloud and fog" (Ps. 97:2), as it says, "'Let there be light,' and there was light." (Gen. 1:3) They said to him, Before your son was formed, would you make a crown for him? He replied, Yes. This may be compared to a king who longed for a son. He found a beautiful and praiseworthy crown (*ᶜaṭarah*). He rejoiced greatly and said: This will be for my son, for his head, because it is fitting for him. They said to him, Does he know that his son is [will be?] worthy? He replied, Silence! Thus it has arisen in thought! And it is known what is said, "He thinks thoughts [so that the banished not be banished from Him]" (2 Sam. 14:14).[27]

The reply: "Silence! Thus it has arisen it thought!" is taken from the famous Talmudic tale in which Moses seeks an explanation for the suffering of R. Akiva.[28] Here it is entirely removed from that context and is chosen because of the presence in it of the phrase *ᶜalah ba-maḥashavah* (arose in thought). The word *maḥashavah*, appearing with some frequency in the *Bahir*,[29] seems to be another term used for the first or highest element in the pleromatic universe; this is to say, it is symbolically identifiable with *keter ᶜelyon*. The phrase is being read with an interesting double entendre: "Thus it has arisen in thought" means that the crown being given to the king's son originates in the highest realm. But the same phrase also means, "Thus he ascends in[to] thought." The son is being given this crown that will allow him to rise to the highest level, to reach the rung of primal divine thought. The crown is made of, or identified with, the light of the first day in the creation tale. If we allow for a permeability between *maḥashavah* and *keter ᶜelyon*, even though the latter term is not used here, we would be saying once again that the "lower" crown is made of or derived from the upper one and is the means by which the "banished" one will be restored to it.

But who is the son in this parable? Here we seem to have two different plausible readings. The son may again be a lesser divine principality, a "lower king" within the pleromatic world. This king, crowned with the crown that his higher maker has given him, will be able to rise to the rung of "thought." He will be able to do so because that crown itself comes from the world of primal light, that which existed before the lower divine realm (of which it is said, "He is surrounded by cloud and fog; righteousness and judgment are the founda-

[27] *Bahir* #12; see possible continuation of this teaching in #60.

[28] b. *Menahot* 29a.

[29] See Scholem, *Origins*, index s. v. "*maḥshabah*."

tion of His throne" [Ps. 97:2]) came into being. The lower king, the "son," crowned with his *ʿaṭarah* of light, will ascend to the highest realm of thought, and the pleromatic universe will thus be unified.[30]

Another quite plausible reading is that this son is the people Israel.[31] They are given a crown by God, fashioned of the primal light. That light would be Torah, often likened to light and present with God before the creation of the world. It is they who, with the gift of this crown, can ascend to the very highest place within divinity. Of course that is precisely the myth of coronation that we have traced all along: Israel, through their words (here perhaps Torah has become *tefillah*), rise to become God's highest crown. This reading would best explain the concluding verse and its reference to banishment. God prepares for Israel, even before he is created, a crown of words that will allow him to overcome the banishment that is to be a part of his fate. Or, perhaps to state it even more boldly: that God "thinks thoughts" is to say that the single realm of thought enters into multiplicity of realms in the first place for the sake of banished Israel (or humanity), as a way of reaching out toward them. As we shall see shortly, I believe that the most "correct" reading of the Bahir's mythical puzzle is precisely one that combines both of these readings.

These are the key references to the crown as a symbol in *Sefer ha-Bahir*. Crowns are mentioned in a number of other places, including two references that seem to indicate that the *Bahir*'s editors also knew of bridal crowns as a living tradition.[32] These references will not add significantly to our understanding of this complex of symbols. But now that we have seen the texts in which the *Bahir* deals with the crown motif, we are in a position to summarize and to compare this treament with parallel development in the German Hasidic world, particularly with the *Sefer ha-Hokhmah* passage. We have seen

[30] I am aware of E. Wolfson's phallic reading of *ʿaṭarah* references in the Kabbalistic corpus and I have tried to imagine such a reading of this text as well. The king's son would be the *ṣaddiq*/phallus figure, associated in the *Bahir* with the sixth/seventh and in later sources with the ninth *sefirah*. But the reading makes no sense here. The king would hardly create the corona of his son's phallus before the son is born. But he *would* fashion a crown for him, perhaps a royal office, a principality (remember the petty "realms" that typified the medieval German lands) that he is setting aside for him to rule. It is then a crown for his head that the father is fashioning, not a corona for his penis.

[31] The printed Margaliot text of the *Bahir* adds the word *Israel* after "your son," resolving the issue quite simply. But this is obviously a gloss that has crept into the text. It is neither in Ms. Munich nor in the quotation from the *Bahir* in Bahya ben Asher to Ex. 34:7. Bahya does, however, connect the passage with Israel, and in fact with metempsychosis, rather than with an internal sefirotic development.

[32] In *Bahir* #36 the king's comely daughter is crowned as she is wed to a prince; in #137 Torah as God's bride is crowned. See also the interesting *Bahir* fragment quoted by Scholem (*Origins*, p. 103f.) from the writings of Ephraim ben Shimshon, a thirteenth-century German mystic, but differing from the parallel in our *Bahir*. There a king buys a crown for each of his sons when the son is born. I wonder whether there is some reflection of actual royal or noble custom in this that might help us determine where this stratum of the *Bahir* materials originated.

two crowns in the *Bahir*: one called only by the name *keter ʿelyon*, standing in a fixed place at the head of the pleroma, and the other, called *keter*, *taga*, *ʿaṭarah*, or by some other related symbol-term (precious stone, pearl, throne), coming from below. This lower crown, identical at times either with Israel themselves or with their prayers, seeks to ascend and reunite with the higher crown, which was her place of origin, and from which she fell or was separated in some other unspecified fashion.

I have generally avoided using the term *sefirot* with regard to the *Bahir*, as the association of that term with the symbol-clusters that the *Bahir* develops is not yet a commonplace.[33] Similarly, I have tried to avoid referring to the lower crown as either the "last" or the "tenth" of these symbolic groupings. This too is alien to the *Bahir*, in which the descriptions and ordering of the lower parts of the pleroma are quite fragmentary and inconsistent. Symbols of the feminine seem to be associated with the sixth, seventh, and eighth groups. While it is probably best not to be any more specific than the text actually warrants, the lower crown would belong somewhere among these. The *Bahir*'s account of the ninth and tenth realms is also, however, of significant interest to us here:

Text #44

What is the ninth? He said to him: The ninth and the tenth are together, parallel to one another, but one is taller than his companion by five hundred years. They are like two *ofanim*, one tending toward the northern side and one tending toward the west. . . .[34]

The figures who lie behind this description will be strikingly familiar to the reader of this book. They are none other than the two angels on either side of the merkavah, at a much earlier date named Sandalphon and Meṭaṭron. Now they have been assimilated from the world of named and specifically designated angelic persons into the transpersonal realm of Kabbalistic symbols. Once again we see how the personified angelic realm of the merkavah is giving way to a new spiritual/intellectual Gestalt.

But these two *ofanim* are familiar to us not only because of their ancient associations. We have met them more recently as well, when *Sefer*

[33] The term *sefirot* does appear in Bahir #87, but its meaning there is somewhat ambiguous. First it is used in the same sense as in *Sefer Yeṣirah*, which was clearly an important influence on the *Bahir*. Then the word *sefirah* is associated with *sapir* (sapphire), an interpretation to be widely quoted throughout later sources. This identification probably already does show a rudimentary "Kabbalistic" understanding of *sefirah*.

[34] *Bahir* #115. See also continuation in ibid., #119 and #123. See the parallel to this in the *Raza Rabba* fragments published by Scholem in his *Reshit ha-Qabbalah*, p. 218, as well as the discusson of this text, and of the next portion of it, by Wolfson in *Feet*, p. 160f. For a later stage in the history of these symbolic entities, see the passages in R. Jacob ben Jacob's *Commentary on the Chariot of Ezekiel* discussed by Wolfson and to be treated briefly in Chapter 14.

ha-Ḥokhmah mentioned that Shekhinah/*keter*/*bat melekh* had "two thrones, two crowns, and two ofanim [wheels], one above and one below. Each of them is five hundred parasangs higher than creation." The two ofanim we meet here at the end of the *Bahir*'s pleroma[35] certainly seem to be "the same" as these. They are the emissaries or lower manifestations of this Shekhinah figure (or sometimes of her male counterpart, *ṣaddiq*); in the *Bahir* they turn out, once hierarchy and numbering have begun, to also be just slightly below the Shekhinah/daughter/*ʿaṭarah* configuration.

What has happened between the *Sefer ha-Ḥokhmah* material (that is, the pseudo-Hai Gaon stratum within it, according to Dan) and *Sefer ha-Bahir* is the emergence of *multiplicity* and *hierarchy* within the divine realm. The *Bahir* is much concerned with the question of numbering, of trying to place the various potencies in their proper order. As H. Pedaya has pointed out,[36] a concern for hierarchy is also to be seen in some sections,[37] where such questions as whether one ascends or descends, what is up and what is down, and the like, take on great importance. Pedaya suggests that this hierarchical ordering may reflect a late stage in the *Bahir*'s editorial process. This concern around the issues of order and hierarchy, which makes particular sense in a text where the ordering is quite an innovation, cannot be taken for granted as it is in later Kabbalistic texts. In this connection, there is one other *Bahir* text I would like to consider. Though it does not refer specifically to the crown, I think it will be significant in helping us to understand the tensions that must have existed as this new hierarchical ordering of divine potencies was being promulgated:

Text #45

He was seated and taught them, "Shekhinah is below just as Shekhinah is above."[38] Say that this is the light emanated from the first light, which is wisdom. It also turns everything around [or "surrounds everything"], as it says: "The whole earth is filled with His glory" (Is. 6:3). What does this mean? (Lit.: "What is it doing here?") This may be compared to a king who had seven sons, and he assigned each one to a place. He said to them, Stand one above the other. The lowest one said, I will not dwell below! I will not be so far from you! He said to them, I will turn [everything] around [or "surround everything"] and I will see you all day long. This

35 They surround a figure called "end of the Shekhinah" in the ensuing passage.

36 *JSJT* 9 (1990): 150, 154f.

37 Cf. *Bahir* #60, #132.

38 Quoted from *Seder Rabbaʾ de-Bereshit*; published in Wertheimer, *Battey Midrashot* 1:30. A reference to Shekhinot in the plural is found in the responsum of R. Hai Gaon printed in *Oṣar ha-Geʾonim, Ḥagigah, teshuvot*, p. 21. This surprising reference almost sounds like the usage familiar from the Mandaean sources. This source has to be added to the single reference to Shekhinot, also from Gaonic literature, noted by Scholem in *On the Mystical Shape of the Godhead* (New York: Schocken, 1991), p. 294n.19. These texts are also discussed by E. Wolfson in *Speculum*, p. 157.

is "the whole earth is filled with His glory." Why is he in their midst? To make them firm and steady.[39]

Here we see a fascinating vignette of rebellion against hierarchy in the upper world. The tale is reminiscent of much earlier mythic motifs, some of which surely underlie it. On the second day of creation, according to an old midrash, once God had divided the upper from the lower waters, the lower waters wept and complained that they did not want to be so far from their Creator.[40] That aggadah is in turn a reflex of old pre-Israelite myths of the battle of sky gods and primal waters, a mythic complex that has left many imprints within biblical texts.[41] It may be related to various Gnostic motifs as well. Here it is the lower light, emanated from the first light, who complains about his distance from the source. While the passage depicts a rebellion against hierarchy from within the symbolic constructs, I wonder whether it does not also indicate some objection to this new hierarchical ordering on the part of the editors of the Bahir themselves. God seems rather readily open to compromise the hierarchy, presumably by taking a place inside [or surrounding?] the seven, so that He may continually turn them around (like the planets going about the earth!) and all will be equidistant from Him.

But the passage began with something quite unusual in Jewish literature: the mention of two Shekhinot. While this is a quotation from an older source, its usage here is striking and quite different from that of its late midrashic source. The first light, *ḥokhmah*, is also called Shekhinah here. In this passage, in other words, we have the same duality with regard to the Shekhinah symbol that we have seen elsewhere regarding the crown. At one point[42] there was a single crown, which in the *Bahir* is divided into two, the lower seeking to return to the upper. In *Sefer ha-Ḥokhmah* there was a single Shekhinah, and here we have a lower Shekhinah, or an emanated light, longing to be reunited with its upper source. The dividing of originally single symbols, making for

[39] *Bahir* #116. The God who "surrounds all" (if this is indeed the way *mesovev* should be read) is familiar to us as the one of whom the rabbis say, "He is the place of the world and the world is not His place." (*Bereshit Rabbah* 68:10) Compare that rabbinic dictum with the description found in the "Gnostic" Gospel of Truth 2:25–26: "the depth of the one who encircles all places while there is none that encircles him." See discussion by W. R. Schoedel in "Monism and the Gospel of Truth," in *The Rediscovery of Gnosticism*, vol. 1, *The School of Valentinus* (Leiden: E. J. Brill, 1980), pp. 379–90. Put into Hebrew, this formula sounds remarkably parallel to language such as one might find in *Sefer Yeṣirah*.

[40] The clearest statement is in *Tiqquney Zohar* #5, f. 19b. See also Zohar 1:17b and *Pirqey Rabbi Eliezer* 18. The demonization of the lower waters is something that Kabbalah has in common with ancient Gnosticism. Cf. *Midrash ha-Neʿelam* in *Zohar Ḥadash* 9b, where they are called "evil waters," and the *Book of Baruch*, attributed to the Gnostic Justin, quoted in Hippolytos V: 27:3. The history of this parallel calls for further study.

[41] See the work of John Day to which I have referred above in Chapter 1, n. 6, and various parallel studies.

[42] Reflected in the *Sefer ha-Ḥokhmah* materials.

the Kabbalistic universe of multiplicity and hierarchy, has here become transparent.[43] The fact that the *Bahir* seems especially attracted to biblical passages where the same word is found twice in a particular verse, so that it can be interpreted in one way or the other, reflecting on the double nature of that particular quality, probably reflects this same process.[44] Most interesting among these, in addition to the double crown and double Shekhinah, is the double notion of *maḥashavah,* as divine thought and human contemplation, that Scholem has discussed in his treatment of the *Bahir.*[45] The lower *maḥashavah* represents *both* the seventh *sefirah*—the feminine—and human contemplation.

What has taken place in the Bahir is the opening up of a single symbol cluster to allow for a much more complex symbolic universe. The symbolic-associative patterns we have seen in our Ashkenazic sources, most clearly in *Sefer ha-Ḥokhmah,* have been joined to several strands derived from various aspects of the tradition, some esoteric and some not previously seen in that way, all of which point to a certain *nonpersonified multiplicity* attached to divinity: among these are the three "holies" of the *qedushah,* the seven *middot* serving before the divine throne,[46] the ten utterances by which the world was created, the ten *sefirot* that structure the cosmos, the thirteen attributes of mercy, and others. This multiplicity, especially in the decad form that it took almost[47] universally in the later sources, becomes a grid or a symbolic "tree," on whose branches the various symbol-terms for the divine realm can now be stretched out. This "stretching" immediately allows for much more complex and nuanced interaction among the symbols, creating the "pleroma" or "universe" that is the field of action in the *Bahir* and throughout the later Kabbalah.

But as powerfully as the thinkers around the *Bahir* may have been at-

[43] A more primitive stage in the grouping and ranking of such symbol terms may be glimpsed in the passage from Ms. Paris 772, Eleazar's Commentary on the Liturgy, that Elliot Wolfson brings in "*Demut Yaʿaqov,*" p. 182n.225. A careful reading of that text seems to show two distinct symbol-clusters: an upper one, including head/crown/Israel, and a lower one, *demut Yaʿaqov/ qedosh Yaʿaqov*/God's back. The lower configuration can be seen; the upper only admired. Here of course we return to the Saʿadyan source, the double-*kavod* theory that underlies a great deal of this development. As more of the extensive manuscript material is uncovered, the stages in this complex development will undoubedly emerge more clearly.

[44] See the treatment of *kavod . . . kavod* (Prov. 25:2) and the double *kavod* in *Bahir* #33, where the higher *kavod* may be identifiable with *keter ʿelyon*; *ṣedeq ṣedeq* (Deut. 16:20) in #50; YHWH YHWH in #94. These discussions are based on the doubling of the relevant nouns in Scripture, but that is surely an excuse to get to an issue that concerns the *Bahir.*

[45] Scholem, *Origins,* p. 127.

[46] *Avot de-Rabbi Nathan* A, Chapter 37 (ed. Schechter p. 110). See the varia in Schechter's notes as well as the list (also on p. 110) of the "seven things with which God created His world." Scholem discusses the place of this material in the background of Kabbalah in *Origins,* pp. 81ff.

[47] The inexplicable phrase "tenth kingdom" in the *Sefer ha-Ḥokhmah* passage may indicate that this process had begun, though not fully emerged, before that passage was written.

tracted to this broadening and deepening of their own capability for spiritual/intellectual expression, there must have been concern aroused as well. Here it would be hard to deny that a new multiplicity had entered the way Jews were thinking and talking about God. The attacks of Meir ben Simeon[48] and so many others over the centuries to come must have been at least in part anticipated by these thinkers. Though their work was done with great symbolic subtlety, partly to hide its dangerous implications, the makers of these symbols were aware of what they were doing. They were no longer just talking about ten utterances spoken *by* the one God, or about seven *middot* that served *before* the throne of glory. For them, God lay within and elusively among these symbols, not transcendently surpassing them. That in itself would bring them close enough to possible charges of *ribbui*, "theoretical polytheism."

But there was also something about this new symbolic articulation that seemed to underscore humanity's distance and alienation from God. There is no number-ordering without hierarchy, and hierarchy has to make for distancing and alienation. If there are numbers that proceed from the One, somebody—and most often the human soul (and/or the symbolic female!)—will be at the far end of the line. Though the *Bahir* is not yet Neoplatonic in any formal sense, the introduction of number-ordering among the potencies that together constitute this divine world will make room for the rereading of this myth in precisely ordered Neoplatonic terms. That development will take place in the Kabbalah of the early thirteenth century.

Concern with this emerging hierarchy and its misleading quality is found in an interesting parable offered by Moses ben Eleazar ha-Darshan, a late-thirteenth-century German mystic and author of *Perush Sefer ha-Qomah*, a text that both knows the *Bahir* and preserves fragments of *Raza Rabba*, an early pre-*Bahir* source. There we find the following:

Text #46

It is like a king of flesh and blood who had various kingdoms. It was the rule in one kingdom that whoever ruled over it would be called a count (*peḥah*). But the king was really ruler over all. While there were those called duke of one realm or count of another, "king" was the supreme title (*shem ha-ʿelyon*). So it is with the Holy One. All is His; He emanated ten *sefirot* even though the tetragrammaton is over all.[49]

[48] G. Scholem, "*Teʿudah Ḥadashah le-Toledot Reshit ha-Qabbalah.*" In *Sefer Bialik*, ed. Y. Fichman (Tel Aviv: Waʿad ha-Yovel, 1934), pp. 141–62. Cf. *Origins*, p. 42f., 54f.

[49] *Reshit ha-Kabbalah*, p. 222. The Gnostic universes are filled within kingdoms and principalities, and hierarchy is very much the point there. See the close parallel to this *Sefer ha-Qomah* text in a Valentinian fragment quoted by F. Fallon, *The Enthronement of Sabaoth* (Leiden: E. J. Brill, 1978), p. 78. I am not claiming more than coincidence here, but the resemblance is striking nonetheless.

Of course this text is a bit later, and it reflects a notion of a God beyond the *sefirot* who is their source. But it shows an understanding that the ordering of divine principalities was very much like the ordering of their earthly counterparts. The duke or margrave of a particular territory may have his title, but really the king is ruler over all. The rule of the locals is in any case at royal whim.

Creators of the *Bahir*'s hierarchy of symbols knew that this was true in the heavenly kingdom as well. They surely did not want multiplicity, division, or hierarchy within the divine to be the ultimate meaning of their myth. On the contrary they insisted that the hierarchy also be seen as a closed circle. The lowest is rooted in the very highest, with which it finds union. The second Shekhinah, the far-flung crown, the distant son, or the "lower" thought all ascend to the very highest, making their way back to their source in the uppermost crown, "head," or the primal light.

The Kabbalists are aided in asserting this circularity by the fact that the *sefirot* are already said by *Sefer Yeşirah* to be in circular or uroboric form: "Their beginning is set into their end, and their end into their beginning."[50] Early in the emergence of Spanish Kabbalah this circularity will also be attached to the older philosophic saying, "The last in deed is the first in thought."[51] The ordering of the symbols in this grid will be used as a way to assert their ultimate unity, played out through the mythic tales that their tentative multiplicity permits. *The very heart of Kabbalah will be the ascent of the tenth sefirah to reunion with the first, or the assertion that the two crowns on either end of the Kabbalistic pleroma are in fact one, made so once again by the merits of human prayer and deed.*[52]

But there is another point to this as well, and this makes the *Bahir*'s myth a

[50] *Sefer Yeşirah* 1:7. This fact may have contributed to the ultimate choice of *sefirot* (rather than *ma'amarot*, *ketarim*, or *middot*, for example) as the key term for these symbol-clusters. See the commentary of Sabbatai Donnolo ad loc. (ed. D. Castelli, Firenze, 1880, p. 38): "Their beginning is God and their end is God." This is not said anywhere of *middot* or *ma'amarot*. Such a statement could have had great influence on the *Bahir* circles. Elliot Wolfson has made the claim that Donnolo is already proposing a theosophic reading of the sefirot. See his "The Theosophy of Sabbatai Donnolo, with Special Emphasis on the Doctrine of *Sefirot* in *Sefer Hakhmoni*," *Jewish History* 6 (1992): 298 as well as the summarization of this article in chapter four of his *Speculum*.

[51] On this saying see S. M. Stern, " 'The First in Thought Is the Last in Action': The History of a Saying Attributed to Aristotle," *Journal of Semitic Studies* 7 (1962): 234–52. See the most interesting comment by an anonymous fourteenth-century Kabbalist, connected with this saying, quoted by M. Idel in *Kabbalah*, p. 197.

[52] To the sources collected in Idel, *Kabbalah*, p. 196, there should be added that quoted by Wolfson, *Speculum*, p. 301, previously referred to by Idel in his doctoral dissertation on Abraham Abulafia [unpublished dissertation: Hebrew university, 1976], p. 261). I quote that text in Wolfson's translation: "The first name refers to the supernal crown (*Keter ʿElyon*), the first gradation, and the second name is the tenth gradation, which is the Diadem (ʿAtarah), and afterwards it will ascend a bit, that is, the tenth gradation [will ascend] to the Supernal Crown, which is the first gradation."

truly *mystical* one. The distanced, banished, or alienated figure throughout these parables is an element within the sacred domain of the pleroma. In a great many passages, most of which we have not had occasion to examine here, that figure is a female one, often either the King's bride or daughter.[53] The most essential mythic motif of the *Bahir* is that of her return and reunion with a higher and male divine realm. But that same female figure can always in one way or another be identified, as we have seen in several cases, with God's people Israel. The return of that alienated element within divinity is also the return of Israel or of the one who offers prayers. God's inner redemption or restored wholeness is also the restoration to God of His most beloved self, that manifest in the human soul or in the people Israel. It is the community of Israel "below" that is placed on God's head, restored to her proper place as the most high crown. Israel are the crown restored to God's head; the union of the *sefirot* is in this symbolic way a cosmic/collective act of *unio mystica*, a reincorporation of Israel to the body of God.

It may be said that the development of a spiritualized *hieros gamos* has reached a delicate and critical point in the emergence of the *Bahir*. The division of symbols associated with the sacred realm into multiple clusters and the narrative descriptions of the interaction among them have allowed for the reemergence of myth in its fullest sense. Within this myth there flourish symbols of male and female, both belonging to the divine pleroma. The restoration of the pleroma will come about as the result of their union. Here we have possible that which was not possible since religion before the Bible: a sexually defined union of the male deity with a heavenly partner, with someone other than His earthly consort Israel. For this reason the texts insist, through a subtle enrichment and complication of symbols, that every such symbolic union of the blessed Holy One with Shekhinah, *kavod*, pearl, or lower crown *also* be seen as His union with the community of Israel, a symbol in no way separable from the Jewish people here on earth. Though male and female as categories are now being readmitted to the realm of divine hypostases, the essential and distinctive affirmation of the classical *Jewish* version of *hieros gamos*, the claim that *Israel* is God's only true bride, is by no means to be set aside. [54] Nor can the religious life of the individual be set aside; the lost and precious one who takes the journey home has to, after all, also include you, the reader who meditates on this symbol. Only in the complex and subtle mind of myth can all of these be true at once.

[53] See the discussion by Scholem in *Origins*, p. 164ff. as well as Wolfson's "Female Imaging of the Torah," in *From Ancient Israel to Modern Judaism: Essays in Honor of Marvin Fox*, ed. J. Neusner et al. (Atlanta: Scholars' Press, 1989), to which I have referred above.

[54] It may also be interesting in this connection to examine the relationship between "Gnostics" and "Aeons" in their alienation and longing to return to the pleroma, the presence of the Father, etc. in Gnostic sources. See the brief comments by W. Schoedel, "Monism and the Gospel of Truth," p. 386f.

CHAPTER FOURTEEN

The Early Kabbalah

Sefer ha-Bahir stands at an important transition point in the history of the coronation motif in Judaism. It may be considered both a beginning and an end. The document that marks the birth of what can be clearly designated as Kabbalah, itself a font for much of the later symbolic development, is also the end of the free flow of crown symbolism. The Bahiric symbols are joined to the developing traditions of Provençal and early Catalonian Kabbalah, and in these the crown ceases to function as an independent symbolic entity. As I have already indicated, *keter ʿelyon* becomes fixed as the key pictorial element in the first symbol-cluster, and *ʿaṭarah* is one of the very many terms to be associated with what will become the tenth. Once these clusters are firmly fixed, however, to say "the *ʿaṭarah* ascends" is meant to be quite synonymous with "Shekhinah ascends," "the kingdom ascends," "Jerusalem ascends," "the bride ascends," "the moon rises," and many others. The individual symbol-term loses a good deal of its identity by belonging to the cluster. The fixed pattern of symbolic associations that lies at the very heart of Kabbalistic speech has in a sense harnessed all these once-independent symbols for its own purpose, that of providing a language through which the complex inner life of God might be articulated and oneness and harmony restored to the pleroma of divine life.

The most essential symbol of this oneness is that of the relationship between the beginning and the end of the sefirotic world. The fact that this ascent motif is often "triggered" by the prominence of *keter* and *ʿaṭarah* in their respective associative clusters is already true in the earliest Kabbalistic sources[1] and does not change as Kabbalah develops and enriches its language. In the rising of Shekhinah/*malkhut*/*ʿaṭarah* to the highest level, where she completes the journey by ascending to the "head" of the divine *anthropos* or becoming one with *keter*, it is clear that we have not departed from the ancient symbolic rite of coronation. The intermediary stage, where the tenth is united with the sixth *sefirah*, is also partly a coronation rite: she is revealed as *ʿaṭeret tifʾeret* (following Is. 62:3 etc.) or the crown on the head of the male deity, a figure

[1] *ʿAṭarah* is found as the name of a *sefirah*, quite distinct from *keter*, in the writings of R. Isaac the Blind. See his *Commentary to Sefer Yeṣirah*, published as an appendix to Scholem's *Ha-Qabbalah be-Provence* (Jerusalem: Mifʿal ha-Shikhpul, 1963), lines 38, 90, 92, etc. *Keter* as a term appears only rarely in that text; see lines 49 and 302 ("*ha-maḥashavah ha-makhtirah*"). On this text see the doctoral dissertation of M. Sendor, *The Emergence of Provençal Kabbalah: Rabbi Isaac the Blind's Commentary on Sefer Yezirah* (Harvard University, 1994), containing an annotated English translation.

familiar to us from *Shir ha-Kavod*. The pattern of associations here is complicated, however, by another aspect of "crown" symbolism. *ʿAṭarah* also develops a sexual meaning in Kabbalistic literature,[2] articulated most fully in the Zohar. Because the term *ʿaṭarah* is used (primarily in halakhic literature) to denote the corona of the male organ, revealed by circumcision, the Kabbalists used it in a sexually symbolic way.[3] The ninth *sefirah*[4] represents the phallus when the divine is depicted in anthropic imagery. It is often designated by symbol terms like *covenant* or *pillar* that imply this meaning even when sexuality is not invoked directly. More generally, this element is called *ṣaddiq*, representing the figure of the righteous male, proper "guardian of the covenant" (i.e., sexual purity, chastity) in its divine manifestation. The Kabbalist in turn ideally sees himself as an earthly *ṣaddiq*, identifying most directly with this element in the divine self. The attempt at *imitatio Dei* thus combines a self-image of potency and chastity; the *ṣaddiq* is the font of divine grace in the

2 This symbolic association seems to begin with the so-called Gnostic circle of Castilian Kabbalists in the generation before the Zohar. A significant example is found in R. Jacob ha-Kohen's *Commentary to the Chariot of Ezekiel*. In the course of quoting a passage of R. Eleazar of Worms concerning the image of Jacob on the divine throne (the original is discussed by E. Wolfson in *Along the Path: Studies in Kabbalistic Myth, Symbolism, and Hermeneutics* [Albany: SUNY, 1995], pp. 32–33), R. Jacob introduces the statement that "the crown of glory *Yisraʿel ʿami li* for she is composed of the prayers of Israel . . . rises up to unite with the throne of glory, for she is *ʿaṭeret tifʾeret* and *ʿaṭeret berit* [the crown of the covenant]." Here the ancient coronation tradition is tied to a phrase that seems to have a sexual overtone ("Crown" and "covenant" are not linked in any way other than by association with circumcision, the covenant that reveals the corona.) *Perush Merkevet Yeḥezkeʾel*, ed. A. Farber (Jerusalem: Hebrew University, 1978), p. 27. Other examples are undoubtedly scattered through the writings of this circle. See the passages by R. Moshe of Burgos quoted by Wolfson in *Speculum*, p. 368n.149. In Todros Abulafia's *Shaʿar ha-Razim* (ed. M. Kushnir-Oron; Jerusalem: Bialik Institute, 1989), p. 84, l. 796ff. we find the *ʿaṭarah* mentioned in a passage immediately following rather obviously sexual references on the relationship of *yesod* and *malkhut*, but the connection is not made directly. See also his comment to b. *Berakhot* 17a in *Oṣar ha-Kavod* (Jerusalem: Makor, 1970), 6b, as well as my disagreement with Wolfson on the reading of this passage in my review of his *Speculum* in *History of Religions*, n. 11. Contrast these with R. Ezra of Gerona's comment to Canticles 3:11 (*Kitvey RaMBaN*, ed. C. Chavel, vol. 2, p. 495): "He fashions of them a crown for the blessed Holy One, as it says: 'Blessing for the head of the Righteous' (Prov. 10:6), Life of the Worlds." Though there is an association here with *yesod*, sexual symbolism is lacking. Nahmanides (Ex. 16:6) associates the *ʿaṭarah* with the divine light (of which the manna is an incarnation) and the crowns of light to be given to the righteous in the world to come. But here there is no hint that "light" and "seed" are synonymous. Cf. also Nahmanides to Gen. 24:1. I admit that the distinction among these sources is sometimes subtle, and it is thus difficult to say just where the first assumed, if muted or unstated, association of these symbols is to be located.

3 See the extensive discussions by E. Wolfson in his various writings, many of which have been quoted above. See also my critique of what I believe to be his overemphasis of this symbol as the essential key to Kabbalistic myth and symbolism in my review of his *Speculum* (above, n. 2).

4 We are referring here to the symbols as developed in Spanish Kabbalah. In the *Bahir* this cluster is sixth or seventh.

lower world, but one who takes constant care lest any of the powerful energies he controls be siphoned off to support the forces of evil. Because of its halakhic use in this context, it is always the term *ʿaṭarah* that serves as a symbol for the corona of the divine phallus, while *keter* remains the crown on the divine head. The ascent of *ʿaṭarah* at its first stage represents sexual union within divinity, the attachment of *malkhut* to *yesod*, graphically portrayed by this reading of the term *ʿaṭarah*. She becomes one with him to the point of indistinction; the feminine/receptive tenth *sefirah*, when in the mode of ascent, reveals herself to be a part of her male counterpart. This union of the two lowest *sefirot*[5] becomes a necesary prelude to further stages in the Kabbalistic journey.

The union with *tifʾeret* is also complicated by this sexual usage of *ʿaṭarah* symbolism. This stage in the ascent is at once the mating or sexual union of male and female, the re-uniting of divine "son" and "daughter," either as twins or as two parts of the single dual-gendered divine self, the proclamation of God's kingship (the coming of *malkhut* to the *melekh*) and thus His coronation—all in ways that are symbolically interchangeable and thus inseparable from one another. This too, however, is but a stage in the ultimate ascent of all the *sefirot* and their union with *keter ʿelyon*, the highest and ultimately the singular crown of God.

Keter ʿelyon is much discussed, to be sure, by Kabbalists throughout the later twelfth and thirteenth centuries. There is a great debate in early Kabbalah as to the status of *keter*.[6] Is it one with *Eyn Sof* and therefore not to be counted as one of the ten *sefirot*? This debate is partly a Kabbalistic reflection of the debate concerning the will of God in medieval Neoplatonism. Indeed it has been suggested that the philosophical poetry of Ibn Gabirol has had a direct influence on shaping this discussion among the early Kabbalists.[7] Questions are raised throughout early Kabbalistic literature concerning the origins of the

[5] The revelation that the two lowest *sefirot* are in fact one or differentiated aspects of the same self does not depend wholly on the phallic imagery. They are linked, for example, in the symbolism of *Shabbat*, beginning in the *Bahir*. Later they are Sabbath eve, the feminine, and Sabbath day, the masculine. They are also frequently designated as *ṣaddiq* and *ṣedeq*, "righteousness," related seemingly as doer and deed. It will be recalled that the ninth and tenth *sefirot* in the *Bahir* were derivative of the "two wheels" in *Sefer ha-Ḥokhmah* and ultimately may be traced back to Sandalphon and Meṭaṭron on either side of the throne. Thus it is not surprising that the final two are seen, even after much further symbolic development (in which sixth and seventh of the *Bahir* combine with ninth and tenth), as a pair that have a single origin.

[6] For a short history of this debate and a brief outline of the various positions, see Tishby, *Wisdom of the Zohar*, vol. 1, pp. 242ff. There is much material to supplement and enrich this discussion in Scholem's *Origins* (see index s.v. "crown" and "kether") and in Verman's edititton of *The Books of Contemplation* (Albany: SUNY, 1992).

[7] See G. Scholem, "*ʿIqvotaw shel Gabirol ba-Qabbalah*," in *Maʾassef Sofrey Ereṣ Yisraʾel* (Tel Aviv, 1940), pp. 171–74 and Y. Liebes, "R. Solomon Ibn Gabirol's Use of the Sefer Yeṣira and a Commentary on the Poem 'I Love Thee,'" *Jerusalem Studies in Jewish Thought* 6: 3–4 (1987): 73–123.

first *sefirah*, its possible threefold nature (thus mediating between the ten *sefirot* and the thirteen divine attributes)[8] its relationship to *Eyn Sof*, and so forth. The first *sefirah* is said to contain ten *sefirot* within itself, a hidden upper version of the entire divine self-manifesting process.[9] But these questions have nothing in particular to do with its being a *crown*; they could as well be (and often are) asked concerning *rum maʿalah, afisat ha-maḥashavah,* or any other term associated with that primal cluster. The use of the term *keter* within this first[10] symbol cluster is mostly taken for granted. It is already found, without questioning, in the earliest Kabbalistic writings we have, those of R. Isaac the Blind.[11] He offers no hint, however, as to any special meaning attached to this name for the highest *sefirah*, sometimes also called *rum* or zenith. Early Kabbalistic writings also identify *keter* and *ayin*, primal Nothingness.[12] It is clear that for the Kabbalists of Gerona, Catalonian receivers of the Provençal traditions of R. Isaac and R. Asher, the cluster of associations in which *keter* plays a key part was already quite fixed.

The fact that the highest and lowest clusters were both commonly designated as "crowns," however, does not entirely lose significance for the developing Kabbalistic imagination. There are hints that the use of *keter* to designate the first *sefirah* refers to its completeness or self-sufficiency; this *sefirah* "is called *ayin*, for it is a *keter* (circle?), known to itself but grasped by no one outside it."[13] Where the *sefirot* are depicted as a series of concentric circles, each succeeding circle within the one preceding it, *keter* is so named because "it encircles and surrounds all the *sefirot*."[14] All of the *sefirot* are quite frequently designated as *ketarim* in this early literature, and the term should here be thought of, given the growing level of abstraction, as meaning both "crown" and "circle." *Keter ʿelyon* thus comes to be seen as the uppermost of

[8] See especially Verman, *The Books of Contemplation*, pp. 142ff. and index s.v. "*Sefirah: keter*."

[9] See discussion by Idel in "Kabbalistic Material from the school of R. David ben Yehudah he-Ḥasid," *Jerusalem Studies in Jewish Thought* 2 (1983): 175n.19 and in "The Image of Man Above the Sefirot," *Daʿat* 4 (1980): 41–55.

[10] Though also, but rarely, described as second. See the *Commentary on the Ten Sefirot from the Circle of Sefer ha-ʿIyyun* (Ms. Jer. 1/488) published by Scholem in his *Kitvey Yad ba-Qabbalah* (Jerusalem: Hebrew University, 1930), p. 204: "These are the ten sefirot *beli mah*. The first is named Light of Primal Intellect; it is the First Glory. The second is the Fixed Intellect (*sekhel qavuʿa*) because it is *keter*, surrounded (*nikhtar*) by the Primal that preceded it (?)."

[11] See n. 1 above.

[12] Cf. Y. Dan's selection of sources, *Qabbalat Rabbi Asher ben David* (M. A. Seminar Materials, 1980. Hebrew University, Jerusalem), pp. 17 and 58. On *ayin* in early Kabbalah, see D. Matt, "Ayin: The Concept of Nothingness in Jewish Mysticism," in *The Problem of Pure Consciousness: Mysticism and Philosophy*, ed. R. Forman (New York: Oxford University Press, 1990).

[13] Joseph Gikatilla, *Shaʿarey Ṣedeq* (Riva di Trento, 1561), f. 21c.

[14] Joseph Gikatilla, *Sod Ṣiṣit*, in Jehiel Luria's *Hekhal ha-Shem* (Venice, n.d. [1605]), f. 38b. See also Luria's own accounting for *keter* on f. 6a.

these ten *ketarim,* whether or not that is the origin of this usage.[15] The author of *Maʿarekhet ha-ʾElohut,* comments thus on the opening section of *Sefer Yeṣirah*:

TEXT #47

It says "ten and not nine" in order not to separate the first in emanation from the nine [others], because of its supreme status, nor the last in emanation from the one above it, on account of its lowly status, for the aspect of unity (*ṣad ha-yiḥud*) is equal in them all. Thus they said in *Sefer Yeṣirah*: "Their end is linked to their beginning [and their beginning to their end]." For from the end of a thing its beginning may be known (*nimṣaʾ*) and from its beginning one may know its end. There is no end without a beginning nor any beginning without an end. Similarly, the beginning and end of a thing are equal in existence and oneness, since neither exists without the other. This conforms to the saying of those whose memory is blessed: "The beginning of thought is the end of deed."[16]

R. Judah Ḥayyaṭ, the early-sixteenth-century commentator on the *Maʿarekhet,* offers a lion (rather than a snake!) to illustrate this picture of the *sefirot* as an endless circle:

TEXT #48

Among the lower creatures, the lion points to this, curling his tail onto his head. And the blessed Holy One is called a lion. For this reason too is *malkhut* called *ʿaṭarah,* because she curls up to be a crown on the king's head. Of this the sages said, "Be a tail to lions."[17]

This nonvertical ordering of the *sefirot* is also found in the writings of R. Isaac ha-Kohen, founder of the Kabbalistic group designated by Scholem as the "Gnostic circle" and an important link in the rising mythic consciousness that leads to the Zohar. In an epistle that supposedly traces the history of Kabbalistic symbols, he says:

TEXT #49

All the crowns (i.e., all the *sefirot*) exist in triads, [standing] in relation to one another. But *keter ʿelyon* is a world hidden unto itself; all the others receive of its flow. It alone is hidden and joined to the root of all roots, which no thought can grasp. It is constantly and in utter silence receiving from that root. It causes its fullness to be poured out and emptied as blessing upon the other crowns, which remain ever close to its flow. It is ever drawing forth and pouring out; from the Holy

[15] Another term for "circle," *galgal,* was already widely used in medieval Jewish philosophical literature to refer to the "spheres" that lay in an intermediate position between the divine and sublunar worlds. Both terms contain the implication of circular completeness and pefection.

[16] *Maʿarekhet ha-ʾElohut* (Mantua, 1558), f. 36a. On the saying "The beginning of thought" etc. see above, Chapter 13, n. 50. See also f. 72a for the author's remarks on *Peleʾ* as a name for Shekhinah and the reversibility of the word *aleph.*

[17] R. Judah Hayyat, *Commentary on Maʿarekhet ha-ʾElohut,* 366; M. *Avot* 4:15.

Spirit, which is at the center, receiving [its flow], along with all the crowns, each to and from one another. It is not a constant flow, however, but only in accord with the will, the root of all roots. Each triad receives in unison (?), three giving and three receiving, until [the flow] reaches the "treasure-house of mysteries," *keter malkhut*, the creator in the beginning (*yoṣer bereshit*), the one distinguished among all the hosts above and below.[18] This is the reason we say that "the upper hosts praise Him threefold, saying 'Holy, holy, holy is the Lord of Hosts.'" He further explained to his humble students in the academy, saying: "Know, O holy seed, that the worlds are entirely internal, *triads that are encompassed by one another and encompass one another. [Each] surrounds the other but is also surrounded by it. Each is above the other, yet the other is also above it, each beneath the other yet the other is beneath it. All of them draw from one another. The first is the middle and the middle the first; the first is the last and the last is the first; the middle is the last and the last is the middle, all following the supernal will, to show that they are all His creatures and were created following His intent and His will."*[19]

These and other passages depict the sefirotic "crowns" standing in a complicated pattern of relationship to one another, though all derivative from the uppermost among them, which is therefore called *keter ʿelyon*. The final crown, *ʿaṭarah* or *malkhut*, also stands in a particular relationship to the crown at the upper end of the sefirotic world. Elsewhere R. Jacob makes it clear that the union of crown with crown, the lowest with the highest, is the ultimate goal of prayer. In an extended comment on the Sandalphon passage from the Talmud, he say that "this crown, which is called the Praise of Israel and Crown of Holiness . . . goes of its own accord [after being adjured by Sandalphon] and becomes one with the crown above."[20]

These texts should be taken into consideration as standing against any uni-

[18] The terminology of this sentence causes me to support Scholem's early dating of this text and its attribution to R. Isaac, over the view of J. Dan, as discussed in the following note.

[19] Emphasis mine. This text is quoted in Shem Tov Ibn Gaon, *Baddey ʾAron*, f. 62a (122). A portion of a somewhat different version is translated and its authorship is discussed by Scholem in *Origins*, p. 357 and by Verman, *The Books of Contemplation*, p. 170ff. Joseph Dan has raised the possibility that this epistle was authored by R. Shem Tov Ibn Gaon himself. See his remarks in "The Kabbalistic Book *Baddei ha-ʾAron* and Kabbalistic Pseudepigraphy in the Thirteenth Century," *JSJT* 3:1–2 (1983–84) 111–38 and especially p. 132.

[20] *Commentary of the Chariot of Ezekiel* (ed. A. Farber; Jerusalem: Hebrew University, 1978), p. 35. See also his *Commentary on the Letters* published by G. Scholem in his "*Qabbalot R. Ya'aqov we-R. Yiṣḥak Beney R. Yaʿaqov ha-Kohen*," p. 50. Reprint from *Madaʿey ha-Yahadut* 2 (1927): 165–293: "When they sanctify the name of the blessed Holy One in heaven and earth and those above and below proclaim Him King, they [the two crowns] become as one single crown, brilliantly shining and radiant. This goes and is seated *ʿal rosh keter malkhuto* (atop His already crowned royal self?)." Here, as frequently in the writings of this "Gnostic" circle, the picture is exceedingly complex and somewhat confusing. The union of *keter* and *ʿaṭarah* as the ultimate goal of prayer is also clear in the manuscript passage to which I have referred in chapter 13, n. 52 above.

dimensional reading of either the symbolic "meaning" of the *sefirot* or their hierarchical ordering. It is true that in Castilian Kabbalah,[21] and especially in the Zohar, the fascination with sexual symbolism is so great that all other constructions of sefirotic union seem to recede to the sidelines. For Moshe De Leon and the circle around him, almost every one of the *miṣwot* serves as yet another symbol for the union of *tif'eret* and *malkhut* or *yesod* and *malkhut*, divine male and female. This stands in contrast to the rather more varied field of interpretations found in the writings of his Catalonian counterparts. But it may also be said that the primary mystical concern of this circle is that of the flow of primal energy through the sefirotic channels, into humans, primarily the Kabbalists themselves, and thence back into the sefirotic world. This flow of energy is depicted by means of three cardinal symbols: light, water, and semen. The three of these flowing substances, entirely interchangeable in the Kabbalists' imagination, all represent the divine life-force with which all existence is charged.

Crowns and accounts of coronation are used by the Zohar with astounding frequency and in a great variety of ways. The verb stem *ʿṬR*, used in the Aramaic *afʿel* and *itpaʿel* constructions is a great favorite of the author and it is a term that needs to be translated in a great variety of ways. The *sefirot* are all crowned with light (or water or seed) that flows from that which lies "above" or beyond them, as they are with light or energy flowing from Israel's devotion below. Among the individual *sefirot* it is particularly *tif'eret*, the male deity or "King" who is crowned, both by His mother *binah* above (cf. the frequent references to Cant. 3:11) and by *malkhut* or *ʿaṭarah* from below. *Yesod*, or the ninth *sefirah*, is crowned, and *malkhut* herself is crowned by *tif'eret*, by all the *sefirot*, and by Israel below. There are literally hundreds of passages in the Zohar that could be adduced to illustrate this usage; we shall limit ourselves to but a few of the very richest in the employment of this symbol. We begin with a description of the upper crowns that is unrivaled for "visual" detail:

TEXT #50

It has been taught about the Mother:[22] At the time of her coronation, there emerge within her crowns one thousand five hundred surfaces with graven ornamentation. When She desires to unite with the King, she is crowned with a diadem of four colors that flash in all four directions, each one three times, making twelve graven

[21] *ʿAṭarah* is glaringly missing from the list of symbols for the tenth *sefirah* in Joseph Gikatilla's Kabbalistic lexicon *Shaʿarey Orah*. This can hardly be an oversight in this rather thorough work, especially because he did include it in the briefer version that appeared as *Shaʿarey Ṣedeq* (Riva di Trento, 1561, 5c). Could it be that Gikatilla was disturbed by the blatant sexuality found in this symbol by some of his colleagues in the Zohar circle and therefore chose to omit it?

[22] This refers to *malkhut*, as will become clear. Cf. A. Azulai, *Or ha-Ḥamah* (Beney Beraq: Yahadut, 1973) as well as Scholem's notes in *Sefer ha-Zohar shel Gershom Scholem* (Jerusalem: Magnes Press, 1992) *ad loc.*

areas[23] that then enter into and are joined to twelve others. On the top of the crown, there are four walls facing the four directions, each topped with a tower, as Scripture says, "towers of spices (Cant. 5:13)."[24] What are these spices? Those referred to in "of all the merchant's powders (Cant. 3:6)." Each tower has three openings, fixed with precious stones on each side. This crown shines with golden gourds[25] for the glory of the King. Under the crown are bells of gold, a bell on this side and a bell on that, and a single pomegranate. In the pomegranate are a thousand bells, each one flashing white and red. This pomegranate is divided into four quarters and is open so that the bells can be seen. There are three hundred twenty-five bells on each side, and all four directions are illumined with the radiance of each quarter. These are called the "pomegranate split open" of which Scripture says, "Your brow [gleams] like a pomegranate split open from behind your veil (Cant. 4:4)." There are four wheels on the four corners to bear the crown. As they carry it, they are turned straight upward until they reach the wheel of the highest quarter, which makes a cooing sound day and night. The four quarters are all joined and they take the crown and raise it up. The sound of those wheels is heard through all the firmaments, and all the hosts of heaven are excited by their sweet music and inquire of one another until they all say: "Blessed is the glory of God from His place (Ezek. 3:12)."

When the King joins the Matrona, this crown ascends and settles on the head of the Matrona. Then there comes down a supernal crown studded with all kinds of precious stones and with garlands of lilies around it. It comes with six wheels in the six directions, borne by six wings of eagles. In its quarter are fifty grapes round about traced by the supreme Mother, set with precious stones white and red and blue and black and green and purple, six hundred and thirteen pairs to each side. There are a thousand and six hundred turrets on each side. Each tower has molded columns that fly upward to draw from the beaker[26] of the supernal Mother, with her oil of anointing. Then the Mother silently sends down noble gifts and fixes them in that crown.

Finally there fall streams of oil of holy anointing on the head of the King, whence it flows down onto His precious beard and from there onto the garments of the King, as Scripture says: "Like the goodly oil upon the head that runs down upon the beard, the beard of Aaron (Ps. 133:2)." Then the crown returns[27] and the supernal Mother

23 This passage may be seen as a highly pictorial elaboration of the rather dry text on directions in *Sefer Yeṣirah* 5:1.

24 It is this verse that lent itself to the artistic form of the spice tower used in the *havdalah* service. While no such Jewish objects survive from medieval Spain, there are monstrances (jeweled containers for the host, open so that the host may be seen) used in the church that could well fit the elaborate description here, and that may have been the prototype for the spice tower.

25 I can find no meaning for *dilugin de-ʾofir* and am suggesting a reading of *deluʿin*, from *delaʿat*, meaning gourd-shaped gold ornaments hanging from the sides of the crown. That would be an appropriate shape for such pendants.

26 *Kitonaʾ*, though spelled with a *kaf*, must be an attempt at *qitonaʾ*, a well-known Talmudic term.

27 It has apparently been set aside so that the Mother can first anoint his head.

crowns Him with that crown and spreads over Him and the Matrona precious garments. Then a voice is heard throughout the worlds, proclaiming: "Go forth and see, O daughters of Jerusalem, King Solomon, and the crown with which his mother has crowned him. . . ." (Cant. 3:11) Then there is joy among all the sons of the King. Who are they? Those who come from the sides of Israel, since they (the King and Matrona) are not coupled with and do not stand with anyone save Israel, who are of their household and serve them. The blessings which then issue from them are for Israel. Israel take all and send a portion thereof to the other peoples, who thence derive their sustenance.[28]

We should not seek precise meaning in each element of the rich picture presented here. Rather we should bear in mind that the Zohar is a work of fantastic imagination, but not allegory. The elaborate crowns of this and other passages are objects of visionary experience or fantasy, the lines between which are by no means clear in this sort of imaginative creativity. The speaker (R. Abba) "sees" *malkhut* or Shekhinah adorned with the elaborate turreted crown as she seeks to unite with the King. Then the still more elaborate crown is prepared by Binah, the supernal Mother, to be placed on the King's head after she has anointed him. Here the twin symbols of kingship, the older biblical rite of anointing and the well-known contemporary medieval rite of coronation by elaborately wrought crowns of precious metal, are joined together in the mystic's imagination. The Zohar, truly a compendium of all of the ancient esoteric traditions of Israel, also manages to combine the *qedushah* motif (the use of Ezek. 3:12 witnesses this) with the marital crowns, now given to male and female within God rather than exchanged by God and Israel. Binah, the supernal Mother within the sefirotic realm, is now the giver of the crown, following Canticles 3:11. In this passage Israel have no active role in the making or the giving of the crowns; they are merely the beneficiaries of the flow of blessing that pours down upon them in this hour of divine grace. But elsewhere in the Zohar, their role is indeed depicted as a much more active one, especially in the coronation of the Matrona:

Text #51

For this reason the pious of old did not sleep on that night [Shavuʿot] but studied Torah, saying, "Come let us inherit our holy legacy, for us and our children, in both worlds." On that night the Community of Israel is crowned over them and comes to be united with the King. Both of them are crowned over those who so merit. Rabbi Simeon said thus in the hour when the companions assembled with him on that night: "Come let us adorn the Bride with her jewels, so that tomorrow she will be properly bedecked before the King. Happy is the lot of the companions when the King asks the Matrona who it was who set out her jewels, caused her crown to shine, and arrayed her. No one in the world but the companions knows

[28] Zohar 3:209a.

how to arrange the Bride's adornments. Happy is their lot in this world and the world-to-come!

Come and see: On this night the companions set out the adornments of the Bride and crown her with her crown before the King. But who prepares the King on this night so that He can be present to His Bride and unite with the Matrona? The holy river, deepest of all rivers, the supernal Mother, as Scripture says: "Go forth and see, O daughters of Jerusalem . . . (Cant. 3:11)." After She has prepared the King and crowned Him, She goes to purify the Matrona and those who are found with Her.

This is like a king who had an only son and was about to wed him to an elegant lady. What does his mother do all that night? She goes into the treasure house and brings forth a sublime crown surrounded by seventy precious stones with which to crown him. She brings forth garments of fine wool in which to clothe him, to deck him out in royal attire. Then she goes to the bride's house. She beholds her maidens who are fashioning the crown, the garments, and the jewels for her adornment. She says to them: "I have set up a place for immersion, a place of flowing waters surrounded by fragrances and aromatic spices, for my daughter-in-law's bath. Let her come, my daughter-in-law and my son's queen, along with her maidens, and let them bathe in that immersion-place of flowing waters that I have. Afterward they will set her jewels in place, dress her, and crown her. Then, when my son comes to wed his bride,[29] he will set up a palace for one and all; he will dwell together with all of you."[30]

Here we have the more typical Zohar presentation of human and divine participation in preparation for the cosmic wedding, the new *hieros gamos* of the Kabbalist. Israel, in this case the Kabbalists/"companions" themselves, prepare and crown the bride while Binah, the supernal Mother, adorns and crowns her son. What is particularly of interest here is the use of parabolic form, even though the *mashal* is essentially nothing but a retelling of the symbolic events already described on the "upper" plane. There is something that seems quite realistic in this parable, perhaps reflecting wedding-practices of the day. The mother-in-law would be responsible for hosting the bathing party for the bride, doing so in most elegant fashion. The bride's maidens accompany her in going to dwell in the new palace of the prince. These details from real life are used to enhance and enliven the otherwise standard symbolic treatment.[31] The role of the companions as attendants at the wedding is quite clear and unambiguous in the Zohar. Sometimes we are not sure whether a passage concerning the "maidens of the bride," or, for that matter, the "war-

[29] *le-ʾizdaggewa.* In this context it clearly refers to the wedding and not to the moment of sexual union. We should note this and realize that it often may have this meaning. There is a tendency today to translate the Zohar in overly sexual ways, a natural reaction against the rather puritanical translations of earlier generations.

[30] Zohar 3:98a-b.

[31] But is the king's mother's role in fashioning his crown a part of these realia? I suspect not; here the shaping hand of Scripture shows itself to be greater than that of real life!

riors" who protect her, refers to the Kabbalists or the angels. In this passage it is clearly the "companions" who directly attend the bride, but elsewhere it is the angelic hosts who adorn and crown her, while the Kabbalist is the *shushbin*, the agent, arranger, or even officiant at the marriage.[32] But nowhere in the Zohar corpus are the Kabbalists to be confused with the bride herself. The rich ambiguity of *Sefer ha-Bahir* on the question of who it was that united with the King, returned to the source, or was reconstituted into the highest crown, has now been resolved. The *Bahir*, representing a fresh outbreak of mythic creativity, had the borders between the upper and lower worlds quite fluid, in accord with the indeterminate meaning of true myth. Myth is the tale of the "upper" realm, the most ancient world, and the soul of the reader/hearer all at once; that is its unique power. In true myth one can never quite say whether the "real" meaning is theosophical, cosmogonic, or personal/pneumatic. But by the time of the *Zohar*, the myth has been refined and that indeterminacy is no longer present. The clear border between the divine and human realms has been reasserted. It is the Bride/Queen/Matrona who ascends, couples/unites with the King, and ultimately becomes His crown as *ʿaṭarah* and *keter ʿelyon* are reconstituted as one. She may take her people with her; the "handmaidens" will come along to dwell in the palace of the King. In other passages they too will be crowned with light from above.[33] It is somewhat unclear exactly how far they go on her journey, but essentially the ultimate blessing, as far as they are concerned, is that of dwelling in the presence of the King.[34] The *kenesset Yisraʾel* who ascends to the highest rung within the Godhead is yet another name for the female hypostasis; she is the Bride, Matrona, Queen, Moon, or Sea; she is clearly the *ʿaṭarah* who rises. But "Community of Israel" is no longer the community of Jews gathered here on earth. This strange division between the cosmic *Ecclesia* and the earthly, historic Jewish people is the price the Kabbalist has to pay for promulgating a vision of mythic reunion that still draws a clear border between the divine and human realms.[35]

[32] Zohar 2:144b-145a. There the Kabbalist is embodied in the person of (the earthly) King Solomon. I have translated this passage in "The Song of Songs in Early Jewish Mysticism," *Orim: A Jewish Journal at Yale* 2(1987): 61–62.

[33] Or with the flowing seed-fluid of *shefaʿ*, pouring through *malkhut* as she unites with her Spouse, and from her into the lower worlds. See the passages quoted by Wolfson in *Speculum*, p. 365.

[34] In that sense the Zohar is strangely faithful to the Bible. The ultimate reward is being present in the Temple, where one basks in the King's presence. I am thinking of the writings of J. Levenson, *Sinai and Zion* (Minneapolis: Winston, 1985) and especially his essay "The Jerusalem Temple in Devotional and Visionary Experience," in *Jewish Spirituality*, vol. 1, ed. A. Green (New York: Crossroad, 1986), 32–61. Here of course the palace is not located in the physical dimension.

[35] The separation of the hypostatic Community of Israel from the earthly community of Jews is a key part of the Kabbalistic promulgation of a feminine divinity who is both the spouse of the

The Zohar thus revives all the old symbols of kingship and coronation. The throne, the anointing oil, the scepter, and other trappings of royalty are all adapted to the new myth and take on an esoteric (and often erotic) meaning. The ascent of the crown is one of these, to be sure: the coronation of the King is one of the Zohar's ways of proclaiming the majesty of God's rule throughout the universe. But it also has a more basic role than any of those others. The ancient myth of the ascent of prayer and its formation into the divine crown has now *become* the myth of the ascent of Shekhinah, *malkhut*, or *kenesset Yisraʾel. The very structure of Kabbalah's central myth is a restatement of the flight of the* ʿaṭarah *to unknown and unknowable heights.*

We are now ready for some final comments on the historic evolution of crown symbolism as we have surveyed it in these pages. We began with ancient kingship and the parallel between earthly kingdoms and that of heaven. Noting that earthly kingship at an early date became vestigial in Israel, we saw ongoing and even increased attention to symbols of royalty within the upper realm. Having no part in the world of earthly kings and their splendor, the Jews concentrated their fascination with kingship and its trappings on the heavenly halls of splendor. A relative newcomer among the symbols of divine majesty in the first centuries of the common era was the crown, woven by an angel of the prayers of Israel, and placed on God's head amid the singing of the *qedushah* chorus, the great prayer of the hosts of heaven. Though new to Israel, the crowned deity was a figure of great antiquity in Babylonia, and it was probably by means of renewed contact with the late Babylonian religious world that this figure entered postbiblical Judaism.

Speculations abounded concerning that crown, including its relation to angels, divine names, magic seals, heavenly amulets, and the various other crowns of heaven. These speculations are found widely within both the rabbinic homilies and the esoteric texts written by Jews in late antiquity. Sometimes those discussions took more aggadic form, asking, for example, which biblical verses were to be found in God's *tefillin*. But the very same symbol was used in magical/theurgical contexts as well. In the coronation rite and the crown, we encounter a myth and a set of symbols that transcend the supposed borders between the aggadic and merkavah traditions. In reading these groups of sources in tandem with one another, I have attempted to demonstrate a continuum of mythic/religious/magical thought among Jews in the early centuries of the Common Era, an approach that I would carry well beyond the domain of this particular symbolic constellation. Such key symbols as Torah

male deity and the object of the Kabbalists' own devotions. I hope to show in a future paper the relationship between this important development and the changes in interpretation of the Song of Songs in the twelfth century in both Jewish and Christian circles. Once the Canticle was read as referring to the individual soul's love of God rather than that of the historical community, the erotic (and potentially homoerotic) pressures were too great for the Jewish reader to bear, forcing the interposition of a new feminine divine self.

and its giving at Sinai, as well as such crucial religious activities as prayer and Torah study, as others have shown, existed across the same spectrum. Those who partook of the merkaval traditions, both in study and in actual religious praxis, were sufficiently "rabbinic" to be participants in the very same mythic universe as those who composed and studied the aggadah.

From the divine crown and those of angels, we turned to the midrashim in which Israel too are wearers of divine crowns, showing that the act of coronation stands in relation to Israel's sacred marriage myth, mutatis mutandis, as it did to that of pagan societies many centuries earlier. I have suggested both here and elsewhere that this image of Israel as the beloved/bride of God is critical to the religious self-understanding of the rabbis, and that the language of love and espousal vies with king/servant and father/son as a key metaphor of rabbinic religion. This image, too, straddled the supposed distinction between rabbinic and esoteric Judaism.

Tracing reflections of this body of tradition among poets and mystical teachers in the early Middle Ages, we saw increased interest in the crown itself as a dynamic, ascending entity, and a tendency to detach contemplation of the crown from its setting in the liturgy of the angels. We saw the crown identified with the community of Israel, itself God's chosen treasure whom He wears with pride upon His head. This combination of symbols, developed from the older sources by intense speculation in early Ashkenaz, became the legacy of the *Bahir*, where a double (or divided) crown symbolism played a key role in a text that would help to shape the emerging traditions of Kabbalah.

In a nearly essay-length note to which I have referred several times in the course of this study, Asi Farber has suggested[36] that the ascent of the mystic or visionary to the merkavah is metathesized in the writings of *Ḥasidey Ashkenaz* into the ascent of prayer, symbolized by the flight of the crown. That transformation plays a key role, she suggests, in the development of Kabbalistic prayer symbolism, with its combination of mystical, theurgic, and magical elements.

My own understanding of this tradition and its evolution overlaps with Farber's in some places but is essentially different. I do not see the ascent of the individual to the merkavah as central to the history of prayer or crown symbolism. I believe that the ascent of prayer, depicted quite literally in the sources we have seen, is itself a transference of the ascent of sacrificial offering, rising to heaven and giving pleasure to the ancient gods, and then to the God of Israel.[37] Sacrifice is a gift to God, as biblical terminology clearly

[36] In *Concept*, n. 40, to which we have referred several times above, p. 237 and passim.

[37] Scholars who study the history of religions have developed a considerable literature on sacrifice as a devotional form. The starting place of this literature is M. Mauss's *Essai sur le Don* (The Gift), 1926. For recent bibliography, see the *Encyclopedia of Religion*, s.v. "sacrifice." The biblical Book of Leviticus is notable for its lack of explanation of sacrifice as gift, but this intentional omission is amply compensated for by references elsewhere. Cf. Jeremiah 7, Ps. 50, etc.

indicates. Ancient Israel maintained a vertical understanding of the relationship between the divine and human worlds; the heavenly Temple was located directly above that on earth.[38] It was to there that sacrifice rose, offered to God by the priests and the people gathered directly below. Already in biblical times prayer, and especially prayer recited in or directed to that holy place, also had the power to reach God in heaven. It was only later, however, and mostly after the destruction of the Second Temple, that prayer took on the form of a verbal offering, a gift to be prepared and cherished with all the attention to detail, including proper timing, ordering, and phrasing that had once been lavished on the cultic gifts. Now prayer, and the *ʿamidah* in particular, was "established parallel to the sacrifices." It was only natural that it, like the sacrifice, should quite literally rise to heaven. In this period of transition, and possibly as a way of enhancing the status of liturgical prayer, it came to be described as the wreath or crown that was to rise up and be placed on God's head.

The magical and theurgic associations with the crown of prayer were part of the common legacy of Jews and others in the late Roman world and are not in themselves surprising. The persistence of these esoteric traditions, only partially committed to writing, from antiquity into the Middle Ages, and their ability to survive the wanderings of their bearers from the Near East to Western Europe, is considerably more remarkable. In the course of exile, the aggadah had a great need to underscore the love of God for Israel, and especially the ongoing love and election that were so vigorously denied by Israel's Christian rival and oppressor. The notion that Israel themselves are God's crown, developed out of an old biblical metaphor, came to be homologized with the image of prayer as crown. God's beloved offered themselves to Him in prayer, through which they both gave and became the crown of God.

The ascent of prayer to heaven here is joined to the return of God's exiled children, who also come home to Him and ascend to become His crown. Redemption is viewed in the Bahiric myth as restoration to God, reintegration within the world of divine fullness, and finally the reunion of the alienated one—a figure who is at once both divine and human—with the highest divine realm. At this point the truly mystical element in these traditions comes most fully to the fore. The ascent of the verbal gift and the striving of Israel to return to the Eden of primal harmony within the divine world are joined together as one.

The Kabbalist is heir to this entire complex of literary and devotional motifs. As his mythic imagination spins forth the complex web of symbol-clusters that will undergird a new sacred language, the myth of the ascending crown takes hold as the most formative mental construct of all. Even in Castile, where symbols of bride and groom and sexual union overcame all the

[38] Cf. the treatments by V. Aptowitzer, "The Heavenly Temple in the Agada," *Tarbiẓ* 2 (1931): 137–53, 257–87 (Hebrew) and R. Patai, *Man and Temple* (London: Thomas Nelson, 1947).

rest, the reunion of male and female was symbolized by the ascent of the (now sexually charged) *ʿaṭarah*. As the Zohar receives this myth, transmitted through the various Kabbalistic schools of the thirteenth century, it takes the descriptions of crown, of flight, and of ascent to new heights, far, far above the power of angels, let alone us mere mortals, to describe.

APPENDIX

Original Texts of Principal Primary Source Citations

Text #1

אמר ר' אלעזר מלאך אחד שהוא עומד בארץ
וארא החיות והנה אופן אחד בארץ אצל החיות.
וראשו מגיע אצל החיות.
במתניתא תנא סנדלפון שמו הגבוה מחברו
מהלך חמש מאות שנה ועומד אחורי
המרכבה וקושר כתרים לקונו איני והכתיב
ברוך כבוד ה' ממקומו מכלל דמקומו ליכא
דידע ליה דאמר שם אתגא ואזל ויתיב ברישיה

b. *Ḥagigah* 13b

Text #2

דאמר רבי אלעזר אדם הראשון מן הארץ עד לרקיע
שנאמר למן היום אשר ברא אלהים אדם על הארץ
וכיון שסרח הניח הקב"ה ידיו עליו ומיעטו שנאמר
אחור וקדם צרתני ותשת עלי כפך אמר רב יהודה
אמר רב אדם הראשון מסוף העולם ועד סופו היה

b. *Ḥagigah* 12a

Text #3

אמרו עליו על סנדלפון שהוא גבוה מחביריו מהלך חמש מאות שנה ומשתמש
אחר המרכבה וקושר כתרים לקונו וכי תעלה על דעתך שיודעים מלאכי
השרת היכן הוא והלא כבר נאמר (יחזראל ג' יב') ברוך כבוד ה' ממקומו ואילו
מקומו לא ראו אלא משביע את הכתר ועולה ויושב בראש אדונו ובשעה שיגיע
בתר כל חיילי מעלה מזדעזעים וחיות דוממות ונהמות כארי באותה שעה עונין
כולם ואומרים קדוש קדוש ה' צבאות בשעה שמגיע לכסאו
מתגלגלים גלגלי כסאו ומתרעשים אדני שרפרף וכל הרקיע כולם אוחזם חלחלה בשעה
שהוא עובר על כל חיילי מרום וכתר שלו פותחים פיהם ואומרי' ברוך
כבוד ה' ממקומו. בא וראה שבחו וגדולתו של הקב"ה בשעה שמגיע כתר לראשו מחזיק
עצמו לקבל כתר מעבדיו וכל חיות ושרפים ואופנים וגלגלי המרכבה וכסא הכבוד בפה
אחד אומרים ימלוך ה' לעולם אלהיך ציון לדור ודור הללויה.

Pesiqta Rabbati 20 (97a)

Text #4

אמרו על סנד"לפון שהוא גבוה מחבירו מהלך ת"ק שנה ועליו כתיב
והנה אופן א' בארץ אצל החיות זה סנד"לפון שעומד אחר המרכבה
וקושר כתרים לקונו.וכי תעלה על דעתך שמלאכי השרת יודעין
היכן הב"ה שרוי והלא כתי' ברוך כבוד ה' ממקומו במקומו לא נאמר
אלא ממקומו מלמד שאין מכירין מקומו של הב"ה. אלא משביע
סנדלפון את הכתר שמכתירין מקומו של הב"ה בקדושות ועולה הכתר
מעצמו ויושב בראש אדוניו. מיד כל חיילי מרום חלים וזעים וחיות
הקדש דוממותושרפי הקדש נוהמי' כאריה ועונים השרפים ואומרים
קדוש קדוש קדוש ה' צבאות מלא כל הארץ כבודו (וזה פירושו קדוש בעליונים
קדוש בתחתונים קדוש בכל עולמים ה' הנקדש בסוד צבאות
ישראל). ובשעה שמגיע הכתר לכסא הכבוד מיד גלגלי המרכבה
מתגלגלין ומתרעשין אדני שרפרף וכל רקיעי' כולם אוחזת חלחלה.
ובשעה שהכתר עובר על כסא הכבוד לישב במקומו כל חיילי מקום
פוצחי' פיהם ואומרי' ברוך כבוד ה' ממקומו. בא וראה שבחו של
הב"ה שבשעה שמגיע הכתר בראשו מחזיק ה' ראשו לקבל הכתר
מעבדיו וכל חיו' ושרפי' וגלגלי מרכבה וכסא הכבוד וחיילי מעלה
וחשמלי' וכרובים מתגדלים ומתחברים ומתגאים ונותנין הוד והדר
וממליכים אותו כולם ואומרים בפה אחד ה' מלך ה' מלך ה'
ימלוך לעולם ועד (וזהו פי' ה' מלך קודם שנברא העולם ה' מלך
משנברא העולם ה' ימלוך לעולם ועד לעולם הבא) ואף הקב"ה
ישתבח שמו מסכים עמהם ואומר ימלוך ה' לעולם אלהיך ציון לדור
ודור הללויה.

Maʿayan Ḥokhmah

Text #5

'שמע תפלה עדיך כל בשר יבאו', מהו: 'שמע תפלה', אמר ר' פינחס
בשם ר' מאיר ור' ירמיה בשם ר' חיא בר אבא: בשעה שישראל מתפללין אין
אתה מוצא שכלן מתפללין באחד אלא כל כנסיה וכנסיה מתפללת בפני עצמה,
הכנסת הזו תחלה ואחר כך הכנסת האחרת, ומאחר שכל הכנסיות גומרות כל
התפלות, המלאך הממנה על התפלות נוטל כל התפלות, שהתפללו בכל
הכנסיות כלן, ועושה אותן עטרות ונותנן בראשו של הקדוש ברוך הוא, שנאמר:
'עדיך כל בשר יבאו', ואין 'עדיך' אלא עטרה, שנאמר: 'כי כלם כעדי תלבשי',
וכן הוא אומר: 'ישראל אשר בך אתפאר', שהקדוש ברוך הוא מתעטר בתפלתן
של ישראל, שנאמר: 'ועטרת תפארת בראשך'.

Shemot Rabbah 21:4

Text #6

כך כל יום ויום העליונים מכתירים לפני הקב"ה
שלש קדושות וא' קדוש קדוש קדוש, מה הק' עושה, נותן בראשו אחת ושתים בראשן
של ישראל. הה"ד דבר אל כל עדת בני ישראל וגו' והתקדשתם והייתם קדושים.

Wa-Yiqra' Rabbah 24:9

Text #7

וברא אופן אחד בארץ וראשו כנגד חיות הקודש והוא מתורגמן בין
ישראל ובין אביהם שבשמים שנא' והנה אופן אחד בארץ אצל החיות
וסנדלפון שמו וקושר כתרים לבעל הכבוד מקדוש ומבורך הוא ומאמן
יהא שמי' רבא ששונים בני ישראל בבית הכנסת ומשביע את הכתר
בשם המפורש והולך ועולה לו בראש האדון. מכאן אמרו חכמים כל
המבטל קדוש וברוך ואי"שר גורם למעט העטרה וחייב נידוי עד
שישוב ויביא קרבן לפני הצדיקים לעתיד לבוא:

Midrash Konen

Text #8

וכיון שראוני שרי המרכבה ושרפי להבה נתנו עיניהם בי מיד נרתעתי
וגזדעזעתי ונפלתי מעומדי ונרדמתי מפני זוהר דמות עיניהם וזיו
מראה פניהם עד שגער בהם ה'ב'ה' ואמר להם משרתי שרפיי כרוביי
ואופניי כסו עיניכם מלפני ישמעאל בני אחובי חביבי וכבודי והציגני
על רגלי ועדיין לא היה בי כח לומר שירה לפני כסא כבודו של מלך
הכבוד אדיר כל המלכים זוהר כל הרוזנים עד שכלתה שעה. לאחר שעה
פתח לי ה'ב'ה' שערי שכינה ש' שלום. ש' חכמה. שערי כח. שערי גבורה.
שערי דיבור. שערי שירה. שערי קדושה. שערי נעימה. והאיר את עיני
ואת לבי באמרי תהלה ושבח ורנה ותודה וזמרה פאר ונאוה הלול עז. וכשפתח
את פי ושבחתי שירה לפני כסא הכבוד. חיות הקדש מתחת כסא של מלך הכבוד
ולמעלה מן הכסא עונים אחרי ואומרים קדוש וברוך כבוד ה' ממקומו.

3 Enoch 1

Text #9

ומנין שאין מלאכי השרת מזכירים שמו של הקדוש ברוך הוא מלמעלה עד
שיזכירו ישראל מלמטה שנאמר שמע ישראל ה' אלהינו ה' אחד ואומר ברן יחד
כוכבי בוקר והדר ויריעו כל בני אלקים. כוכבי בוקר, אלו ישראל
שמשולים בכוכבים שנאמר והרבה ארבה את זרעך ככוכבי השמים.
ויריעו כל בני אלהים, אלו מלאכי השרת וכן הוא אומר ויבואו בני האלהים
להתיצב על ה'.

Sifre Devarim 306

Text #10

עגול ראשו ש' רבבות וג' אלפי' ול'ג' פרסאות. גובה עטרה יאדוריה שמו. כתר שבראשו
ישר' שמו. שיעורו ש' אלפי על ש' אלפי רבבו' פרסאו'.

Shiʿur Qomah

Text #11

כתר שבראשו חמש מאות אלף על חמש מאות ישראל שמו. ואבן יקרה שבין
קרניו ישראל עמי לי חקוק עליה דודי צח ואדום וגו'. ראשו כתם פז קווצותיו
תלתלים וגו'. עיניו כיונים על אפיקי מים.

Sefer ha-Qomah

Text #12

א"ר אבין בר רב אדא א"ר יצחק מנין שהקב"ה מניח תפילין שנאמר
נשבע ה' בימינו ובזרוע עוזו. בימינו זו תורה שנאמר מימינו אש דת למו
ובזרוע עוזו אלו תפילין שנאמר ה' עוז לעמו יתן. ומנין שהתפילין עוז הם
לישראל דכתי' וראו כל עמי הארץ כי שם ה' נקרא עליך ויראו ממך ותניא
ר' אליעזר הגדול אומר אלו תפילין שבראש. אמר רב נחמן בר יצחק לרב חייא בר אבין הני
תפילין דמרי עלמא מה כתיב בהו א"ל ומי כעמך ישראל גוי אחד בארץ.

b. *Berakhot* 6a

Text #13

א'ר ישמעאל אני ראיתי מלכו של עולם יושב
על כסא רם ונשא וגדוד אחד היה עומד מן
הארץ ועד הרקיע וסנדלפון שמו ובשע' שהוא
מבקש רוזיי יה"וה אלהי ישראל להשבע בתפילין
ולהשליך שבועה בידו הוא נוטל תפילין
מראשו ומבטל גזירות מן הארץ.

Merkavah Rabbah

Text #14

אמר ר' ישמעאל אמר לי מטטרון מלאך שר הפנים חדר מרום כל בתחלה
הייתי יושב על כסא גדול בפתח היכל שביעי ודנתי את כל בני
מרומים פמיליא של מקום מרשות ה'ב'ה' החלקתי גדולה ומלכות רבות
ושלטון הדר ושבח ועטרה וכתר וכבוד לכל שרי מלכיות כשאני יושב
בישיבה של מעלה ושרי מלכיות עומדים עלי מימיני ומשמאלי מרשות ה'ב'ה'
וכיון שבא אחד להסתכל בצפיית המרכבה ונתן עיניו בי והוא מתיירא
ומזדעזע מלפני ונפשו מבוהלת לצאת ממנו מפני פחדי ואימתי ומוראי
כשראה אותי שאני יושב על כסא כמלך ומלאכי השרת היו עומדים עלי
כעבדים וכל שרי מלכיות קשורים כתרים סובבים אצלי באותה שעה פתח
את פיו ואמר ודאי שתי רשויות בשמים. מיד יצאתה בת קול מלפני השכינה
אומרת שובו בנים שובבים חוץ מאחר דלא. באותה שעה בא ענפיאל יוי השר
נכבד נהדר נחמד נפלא נורא נערץ משליחות של ה'ב'ה' והכני ששים פולסאות
של אור והעמידני על רגלי.

3 Enoch 16

Text #15

ה'ב'ה'... עשה לי לבוש של גאה שכל מיני מאורות
קבועין בו והלבישני ועשה לי מעיל כבוד שכל מיני תאר זיו זוהר הדר קבועין
בו והעטני ועשה לי כתר מלכות שקבועין בו ארבעים ותשע אבני תאר כאור
גלגל חחמה שזיוו הולך בארבע רוחות ערבות רקיע ובשבעה רקיעים
ובארבע רוחות העולם וקשרו על ראשי וקראני יוי הקטן בפני כל פמיליאה
שלו שבמרו' שנאמ' כי שמי בקרבו.

3 Enoch 12

Text #16

למעלה מהן יש שר אחד
אדיר ומופלא אמיץ ומשובח בכל מיני שבח כרוביאל יוי שמו שר גבור מלא
בח גבורות שר גאה וגאה שמו שר צדיק ועמו צדקה שר קדוש ועמו
קדושה. שר מפואר באלפי צבאות שר מסתלסל בריבי חיילות. מקצפו תרעש
תבל ומרגזו ירעדון מחנות ומאימתו יחילו יסודות. ומגערתו ירעשו ערבות.
קומתו מליאה גחלים רום קומתו כרום שבעה רקיעים ורחב קומתו כרחב
שבעה רקיעים ועובי קומתו כעובי שבעה רקיעים מפתח פיו דולק כלפיד
ולשונו אוכלת אש ועפעפיו כזוהר ברק. ועיניו בזיקוקי זוהר ומראה פניו באש
יוקדת וכתר קדושה על ראשו ששם המפורש חקוק בו ושממנו ברקים יוצאים
וקשת שכינה בין כתיפיו וחרבו כברק על מתניו וחצו כברק על חגוריו ותרים
אש אכלה על צוארו וגחלי רתמים על סביבותיו וזיו שכינה על פניו. וקרני
ההוד על אופניו וצניף מלוכה על קדקדו

3 Enoch 22

Text #17

וכתר שעל ראשו כזיו כסא הכבוד. שיעור של כתר מהלך
חמש מאות ושתי שנים ואין מיני זיו ואין מיני זוהר ואין
מיני נוגה ואין מיני מאור בעולם שאין קבועין באותו הכתר
ואותו השר שרפיאל יוי שמו. וכתר שבראשו שר שלום שמו.

3 Enoch 26

Text #18

תניא א"ר ישמעאל בן אלישע פעם אחת נכנסתי
להקטיר קטורת לפניו ולפנים וראיתי אכתריאל
יה ה' צבאות שהוא יושב על כסא רם ונשא ואמר
לי ישמעאל בני ברכני אמרתי לו יה"ר מלפניך
שיכבשו רחמיך את כעסך ויגולו רחמיך על
מדותיך ותתנהג עם בניך במדת הרחמים ותכנס
להם לפנים שורת הדין ונענע לי בראשו.

b. *Berakhot* 7a

Text #19

אמ' אלישע בן אבויה כשהייתי עלה בפרדס ראיתי את
אכתריאל יה' ה' צבאות שהוא יושב על פתח פרדס וק'כ' ריבוא של מלאכי
השרת מקיפין לו. שנ' אלף אלפין ישמשוניה וריבוא ריבון וג'. כיון שראיתי
אותם נבהלתי ונרתעתי ודחקתי את עצמי ונכנסתי לפני הק'ב'ה' אמרתי לפניו
רב' של עו' כתבתה בתורתך הן ליוי אלהיך השמים ושמי | השמים וג'. וכת'
מעשה ידיו מגיד הרקיע אחד בלבד. אמ' לי אלישע בני כלום באתה אלא
לחרהר על מידותי לא שמעת משל שמושלין בני אדם

Razo shel Sandalphon

Text #20

וכשעלה משה למרום ...
ובקש ... רחמים תחלה על ישראל ואחרי כך על עצמו. ופתח היושב
על המרכבה את החלונות אשר על ראשי הכרובים...
וקבלו התפילות של ישראל ונתנו אותן לכתר
בראשו של הקב"ה ואמר שמע ישראל יוי אלהינו ה' אחד...
באותה שעה נענה אכתריאל
יה' יהוד צבאות ואמר למטטרון ש"ח. כל מה שמבקש מלפני אל תחזירהו ריקם

3 Enoch 15b

Text #21

הכניסיני לגנזי ישועות ולגינזי נחמו׳ וראיתי כתות של מלאכי השרת שהן יושבין ואורגין בגדי ישועו׳ ועושין כתרי חיים טובים ואבנים טובות של מרגיליות קבועין בה ומרקחין ובכל מיני בשמים ויינות ממותקים לצדיקים. וראיתי כתר אחד משונה מכל כתרים וחמה ולבנה ושנים עשר מזלות קבועות בו. אמרתי הדר זיוי כתרים הללו למי או׳ לי לדוד מלך ישראל. אמר׳ לו הדר זיוי הראני כבודו של (דוד). או׳ לי ידידי המתן לי שלש שעות עד שיבא דוד לכאן ותראה בגדולתו.

הושיבני בחיקו או׳ לי מה אתה רואה. אמר׳ לו אני רואה שבעה ברקים שהם רצין כאחד. או׳ לי כבוש עיניך שלא תזדעזע מהללו שיצאו לקראת דודי מיד נעשו כל אופנים ושרפים ואוצרות שלג ואוצרות ברד ועננֵי כבוד ומזלות וכוכבים ומלאכי חשרת ולחוטי זבול. ואומ׳ למנצח מזמור לדוד השמים מספרים ושמעתי קול רעש גדול שבא מגוזך ואו׳ ימלוך ה׳ לעולם. והנה דוד מלך ישראל בא בראש וראיתי כל מלאכי בית דוד אחריו וכל אחד ואחד כתרו בראשו וכתרו של דוד מובהק ומשונה מכל הכתרים וזיוו הולך מסוף העולם ועד סופו כיון שעלה דוד מלך ישראל לבית המדר׳ גדול שברקיע מוכן לו כסא של אש שהוא ארבעים פרסאות גובה וכפליים אורכו וכפליים רחבו.

וכיון שבא דוד וישב לו על הכסא שלו. מוכן נגד כסא של קונו. וכל מלכי בית דוד יושבין לפניו ומלכי בית ישראל אחריו.מיד או׳ דוד שירות ותושבחות שלא שמעתן אוזן מעולם וכיון שפתח דוד ואמר ימלוך ה׳ אלקיך ציון לדור ודור הללויה. פתח מטטרון וכל המזלות ואמרו׳ ק׳ק׳ק׳ ה׳ צבאות מלא כל הארץ כבודו. וחיות הקדש משבחות ואומרו׳ ברוך כבוד ה׳ ממקומו. והרקיעים או׳ ימלוך ה׳ וגו׳. והארץ אומר׳ ה׳ מלך ה׳ מלך (ה׳) ימלוך לעולם ועד. וכל מלכי בית דוד אומ׳ והיה ה׳ למלך על כל הארץ.

Hekhalot Rabbati

Text #22

דרש ר' סימאי בשעה שהקדימו ישראל נעשה
לנשמע באו ששים ריבוא של מלאכי השרת
לכל אחד ואחד מישראל קשרו לו שני
כתרים אחד כנגד נעשה ואחד כנגד נשמע
וכיון שחטאו ישראל ירדו מאה ועשרים
ריבוא מלאכי חבלה ופירקום שנאמר
ויתנצלו בני ישראל את עדים מהר חורב
א"ר חמא בר' חנינא בחורב טענו בחורב
פרקו דכתיב ויתנצלו בני ישראל וגו' א"ר יוחנן
וכולן זכה משה ונטלן דסמיך ליה ומשה
יקח את האהל

b. *Shabbat* 88a

Text #23

כשעמדו בסיני ואמרו נ ע ש ה ו נ ש מ ע ניתן להם עטרת בראשם. א"ר אבא בר כהנא
בשם ר' לוי כיון שקיבלו ישראל עשרת הדברות ירדו מאה ועשרים ריבוא מלאכי השרת
וזוניאות ועטרות בידיהם. והיו שנים מהן נזקקים לכל אחד ואחד. אחד נותן עטרות ואחד
חוגרו בזוניאות.

Pesiqta Rabbati 10 (37a)

Text #24

רבי אלעזר בן ערך אומר, כשירד הקדוש ברוך הוא לתן
תורתו לישראל, ירדו עמו ששים רבוא של מלאכי השרת
כנגד ששים רבוא של גבורי ישראל ובידם זינות ועטרות,
ועטרו את ישראל בכתר שם המפרש. כל אותן הימים, עד
שלא עשו אותו המעשה, היו טובים לפני הקדוש-ברוך-הוא
כמלאכי השרת, ולא משל בהם מלאך המות, ולא היו יוצאין
לנקביהם כבני אדם. כיון שעשו אותו המעשה, כעס עליהם
הקדוש ברוך הוא ואמר להם, סבור הייתי שתהיו לפני
כמלאכי השרת, שנאמר, אני אמרתי אלהים אתם ובני עליון
כלכם. ועכשיו, אכן כאדם תמותון

Pirqey Rabbi Eliezer 47

Text #25

מיד כל אחד ואחד נעשה לו אוהב ומסר
לו דבר שנאמר עלית למרום שבית שבי
לקחת מתנות באדם בשכר שקראוך אדם
לקחת מתנות אף מלאך המות מסר לו דבר
שנאמר ויתן את הקטורת ויכפר על העם
ואומר ויעמוד בין המתים ובין החיים וגו'

b. *Shabbat* 88b–89a

Text #26

מיד קרא הב"ה ליפיפי"ה שר התורה ומסר לו את התורה ערוכה בכל
ושמור' וכל מלאכי השרת נעשו אוהביו וכל אחד ואחד מסר לו דבר
רפואה וסוד שמות שהן יוצאין מכל פרשה ופרשה כל שמושיהן
שכן הוא אומר עלית למרום שבית שבי לקחת מתנו' באדם. ואף
מלאך המות מסר לו דבר שכן כתיב ויתן את הקטרת ויכפר על
העם. וזהו השמוש הנכבד שמסרו לו המלאכים על ידי יפיפ"יה
שר התורה ועל ידי מטטרון שר הפנים ומסרה משה לאלעזר ואלעזר
לפנחס בנו שהוא אליהו כהנא רבה ויקירא זכור לטוב אמן:

Maʿayan Ḥokhmah

Text #27

'בעטרה שעטרה לו אמו'. זה המשכן. למה קראו עטרה אלא מה העטרה מצויירת כך המשכן
היה מצוייר שנאמר ורוקם בתכלת ובארגמן וכו'. אמר ר' יצחק חזרתי בכל המקרא ולא
מצאתי שעשתה בת שבע עטרה לשלמה - ר' שמעון בן יוחאי שאל את ר' אלעזר
ברבי יוסי: אפשר ששמעת מאביך מהו: 'בעטרה שעטרה לו אמו'? אמר לו:
הן' משל למלך שהיתה לו בת יחידה, והיה מחבבה יותר מדאי והיה קורא אותה
בתי, לא זז מחבבה עד שקראה אחותי ועד שקראה אמי, כך הקדוש ברוך הוא
בתחלה קרא לישראל בת, שנאמר: 'שמעי בת וראי והטי אזנך ושכחי עמך ובית
אביך', לא זז מחבבן עד שקראן אחותי, שנאמר: 'פתחי לי אחתי רעיתי יונתי תמתי
שראשי נמלא טל קוצתי רסיסי לילה', לא זז מחבבן עד שקראן אמי, שנאמר:
'הקשיבו אלי עמי ולאומי אלי האזינו כי תורה מאתי תצא ומשפטי לאור עמים ארגיע',
עמד ר' שמעון בן יוחאי ונשקו על ראשו.

Shemot Rabbah 52:5

Text #28

בעטרה שעיטרה לו אמו על חים כמה שנ'
ה' ימלוך לעולם ועד אמ' להם הקב"ה כביכול אתם קשרתם קשר
מלכות בראשי ביום חתונתו זו עמידת הר סיני שמחת לבו ימי
המלואים: ד"א צאינה וראינה כל האומות ניסי פלאים שהוא עושה
לבניו והכבוד והעטרה שהוא מתעטר ביום בינוס גליות שנ' ימלוך ה'
עליהם בהר ציון מעתה ועד עולם והלא שלו היא המלכות שנ' ה'
ימלוך לעולם ועד ה' מלך עולם ועד אבדו גוים מארצו אלא שאמ'
לישר' כביכול אין לי מלכות ולא חיילות עד שהעמדתם והמלכתם אותי

Aggadat Shir ha-Shirim, line 1000

Text #29

וחכת"ר בגימ' ש"ל א"ש ובגימטריא וחרוחו"ת, כי חרוחו' מוליכים חכתר
למטטרון, ומטטרון משביע אותה שחולכת על ראשם (!) של הקב"ה, לכך: הכתר
גנ"ז אלפים רבבות פרסאות, שהוא גנוז ונגנז. במסכת בבא קמא פר' מרוב'

ובמסכת סוטה בפרק הח' וביבמות פרק הבא על יבימתו: אין חשכינה שורה
על פחות מב' אלפים רבבות ישראל, שנאמר: "ובנוחה יאמר שובה ה' רבבות אלפי
ישראל". והעטרת ששמה ישראל, בגימטרי' "ותפילה", סלא בי'.
במסכת סוטה בפקמ"א ובמסכת סנהדרין פרק חלק: יש אם למקרא יש אם
למסורת כמו בסכת בסכת בסוכות להכתר קושרים תפילות של ישראל. וכן יסד
חקליר ז"ל ובסילוק של ראש חשנה: "ויקבלו תפילות מלכות באות ויתנו'
לראש אלחי חצבאות". והכתר משבח לחקב"ה ואומר: "ימלוך ה' לעולם אלהיך ציון
לדור ודור חללויה".
ובספר היכלי קודש ובמדרש אבא גוריון: בעליית חכתר
רצים ומשתחוים ומניחים את בתריחן על הערבות ונותני' לו המלוכה.
ועליו אמר שלמה חמלך: "ראשו כתם פז קווצותיו תלתלים שחורות כעורב".
כבו"ד האותיות יש,כח מלאכי השרת נותנים לחקב"ח כבוד, ואנו
ישראל מעטרים בכל יום ויום בבקר בפ"ז תיבות שיש ב"ברוך שאמר". "ראשו
כתם פז קווצותיו תלתלים שחורות כעורב" בגימטרי': וכת"ר ח' סנדלפון וז"ח הו"א קוש"ר
להצו"ר בע"ל רחמי"ם לחנ"ון ורחו"ם ה' והו"א יחי"ד שד"י.
ומטטרון וסנדלפון חם הממוני' על הכתר. וחמשה שמות יש לסנדלפון: יגידיאל,
חביביאל, עיר וקדיש, וי"א חדרניאל, וחוא משבח את קונו. וכן יסד רבינו
שמעון הגדול בר' יצחק באופן של שבועות: 'בריקמי שיר מעוטר
ומעוסף ומפואר". בריקמי - כמו לשון "מעשה רוקם". והכתר
פוצה פיה ומשבחת את חקב"ח ואומר: "ימלוך ה' לעולם וכו'...
ועשרה מלאכים חקוקים בכתר במרגליות
של אבנים טובים, אילו חן: אכתריאל, אהביאל, חניאל, חסדיאל, רחמיאל, שמועאל,
יחודהיאל, נבבדיאל, שריאל, שושניאל עומד על כתר למעלה לפניו,
שנאמר: "ואחיה כטל לישראל ויפרח כשושנה ויך שרשיו כלבנון",
ועומד כמו שקורין בלשון לעז בוסון שעומד כליל על ראשי הכלות
שקורין בלשון אשכנז קוצא. וי' מלאכים שחקוקים בכתר כנגד י' מקומות
שנדמו ישראל לכלה,בדאית' במדרש פסיקת' בפרשת שוש אשיש: בי' מקומות
נקראו ישראל כלה, שנאמר: "ליבבתיני אחותי כלה", "גן נעול אחותי כלה", "איתי מלבנון
כלה", "כמשוש חתן על כלה", "שוש אשיש" וגומר עד "וככלה תעדי כליה" , "קול ששון וקו
שמחה קול חתן וקול כלה"
וכל העונה אמן אחר ברכת התפילה הוא עושה קשר לעטרה של הקב"ה, ואם
אין קשר כל אות ואות וכל תיבה ותיבה שלתפילה יפול מן העטרה.

Sefer ha-Navon

Text #30

חוח גי' בים וכן גי' אהיה לפי שהוא שם השכינה שנ' ואהיה אצלו אמון והיא צלותא,
וקול התפילה העולה למעלה כמו שפרש"י ויהי' קול מעל הרקיע אשר על ראשם בעמדם
תרפינה כנפיהם פי' ויהי קול תפילתם של ישראל כי התפילה הולכת למעלה על הרקיע
אשר על ראשם והולכת ויושבת בראשו של הקב"ה ונעשית לו עטרה... כי התפילה
יושבת כעטרה... כי כשהצלותא והתפילה עולה למעלה אז מתלחשים ומלחשים
החשמל כנגד התפילה שלנו... והעטרה של הקב"ה ס' רבבות אלף פרסאות כנגד ס'
ריבאות של ישראל ושמה של העטרה שריאל והוא גימ' תפילה אב
אחד. לפי שאב אחד מסדר מן התפילות עטרה ובעלית הכתר רצים משתחווים וממהרים
להניח כתריהם בערבות, ונותני' לו המלוכה. וממעל לרקיע אשר על ראשו במראה
אבן ספיר דמות כסא ועל דמות כסא מראה דמות אדם. וכן התפילות העטרות והעולות
על הכסא, דומות לכסא והכסא מתוקן מאבן ספיר.

Eleazar of Worms,
Ms. New York 1786
Ms. Oxford 1812

Text #31

וכשהתפלל משה על ישראל ועל עצמו, פתח היושב על המרכבה
את החלונות אשר על ראשי הכרובים ויצאו אלף ות"ת סניגורין
ומטטרון שר הפנים עמהם וקבלו התפילות ונתנום בראש אכתריאל

Sodey Razaya'

Text #32

על שר הפנים קאמר ששמו כשם רבו או שמא יש אחד למעלה
הימנו נאצל מן הסיבה העליונה ויש בו כח עליון והוא שנראה
לו למשה והוא שנראה ליחזקאל במראה אדם מלמעלה והוא
שנראה לנביאים, אבל עילת העילות לא נראה לשום אדם לא
בימין ולא בשמאל לא בפנים ולא באחור, וזה הסוד במעשה
בראשית: כל היודע שיעורו של יוצר בראשית מובטח לו וכו',
ועל זה נאמר 'נעשה אדם בצלמנו

Abraham ben David

Text #33

כשישראל מתפללים בכוונת לבם סנדלפון בורר תיבות הבאות מן חלב ומתקן הכתר והכתר חי כי הבל הדיבור סל רוח ואש, תדע שהרי כל האדם מוציא רוח והדיבור מלוכלך כאשר תראה בימות החורף לפני פיך על עודה שלך, וגם הדיבור חם כן הדיבור עולה למעלה והוא חבר כל השמים וחביב מהבל מלאכי השרת שמוציאים מפיהם לפידי אש, ונקרא סנדלפון סנדלפון הם אבנים טובות כן דברים טובים שבתפילה, פו"ן על שם פנה אל תפילת הערער וממשלתו בשחקים במקום שאומרים שירה לומר אין שיר ישר לאל כשיר ישראל, אותיות ישראל הם שיר א"ל לפי שה' אחד וישראל גוי אחד וסנדלפון נקרא אופן אחד בארץ ראוי לאחד לקבל תפילת אחד לאל אחד.
שחקים רקיע נכבד וסנדלפו"ן ממונה עליו והנה אמרו סנדלפון עומד אחורי המרכבה וקושר כתרים למה עומד אחורי המרכבה לפי שאם יתפלל אדם שלא בכוונה שמועיא"ל השוער ושא שומרי השער אין מניחין לעלות אותה התפילה למעלה, אבל תפילה שהיא בכוונת הלב באה לפניו שנאמר ושועתי לפניו תבא באזניו, נמצא שהתפילה לפני הכבוד וכיון שהיא ראויה בא דרך אחורי הכבוד אליו וסנדלפון בורר התפילה כאדם שבורר כסף וזהב ואבנים טובות לתקן לו עטרה כך הוא בורר איזה יכשר, זהו פנה אל תפילת הערער, ואם רואים השוערים והמלאכים את התפילה שהיא ראוי פותחין השער התפילה והיא עולה לפני הכבוד ומעבירה מלפניו ומלבישה אורה מחדר אחר חדר עד שפוגעת בסנדלפו"ן ומקבלה ויודע לאיזה צד בעטרה יש לקבוע אם כנגד הפנים כמו שכתוב שפכי כמים לבך נוכח פני ה' או לאחורי כבוד כמו שכתוב ושועתי לפניו תבא באזניו הרי אצל האזנים, וכשרוצה הקב"ה באותו התפילה מוסיף עליה אור וזוהר והוד ומלאך מקבלה ומוליכה לסנדלפון ולפי שמעוטרת הוד וזוהר קובעה בעטרה לנוכח פני הכבוד ומבחין סנדלפון איזה של זה או של זה זו בינה הגיגי זהו מוצא שפתי נוכח פניך היה.

וכששולח הקב"ה אור וזיו על התפילה לקול הצדיק מזה האור ישמח קול האדם למעלה וכנגד לב האדם למטה שמח באהבת הקב"ה זהו על אלו"ה נורא הוד, הכתר, זהו אור צדיקים ישמח כשיש התפילה באור אז ישמח לב מבקשי ה' וכתיב באור פניך יהלכון לכך בשמך יגילון כל היום כי תפארת עוזמתו אתה, שאור זוהר הכתר שלו על ראש צדיקים שנאמר יהיה ה' צבאות לעטרת צבי ולצפירת תפארה לשאר עמו למי שמשים עצמו שירים לשאר העולם שהוא אחרו וזנב לכל, יפאר ענוים בישועה בעטרת אורה.

ולמה עושה שריון בצדקה ועטרת בשבחות כי כתיב צדק לבשתי וילבשני והיה צדק אזור מתניו והאמונה אזור חלציו ובשבחות עושה עטרות כי האומר שבח בקול רם ראש של אדם אומר וראש הכבוד מתכבד וכתיב וכובע ישועה בראש, ועל ישועה אומרי' הודאה, ובתפילין של מעלה כתיב עם נושע בה' וכן ולתתך עליון על כל הגוים אשר עשה לתהלה ולשם ולתפארת, ולתתך עליון איזה דבר עליון הוי אומר עטרה של עליון וכתיב לתהלה וכתיב ולשם שעל ידי השבעת השם ולתפארת תפילין של עליון, וכובע ישועה בראשו למה נקרא כ לפי שמדבר בתפילין שכתוב בהם עם נושע בה'

כך הראה לנביא במלבושיו ועטרת תהלה בראש וכתיב הסר מעלי המון שיריך הרי שחשבה עליו דכתיב ישראל אשר בך אתפאר פאר של שבחות, זהו ראשו כתם פז קווצותיו תלתלים תל תפלה אחת תלים הרי ב' תפלות וכל עטרה נדחית מפני חבירתה, ועתיד להראות לכל צדיק עטרה שתיקן בתפילותיו ותהלותיו ששיבח בכוונות לבו ולשמה ובשמחת לבב, כשהאדם מברך בכוונות הלב בברכות שטבעו חכמים הכבוד מוסיף זיו וזוהר ולעתיד לבא יזכה לאותה אורה ועליך יזרח ה' כי הכבוד והזוהר מתרבה בברכה דכתיב וחסדיך יברכוך כבוד מלכותך יאמרו, וכבוד והדר מלכותו, וכשמתפלל הצדיק בכוונה יוצאים י"ח מאות מלאכים ומקבלים אותה כמו שפיים ר' אליעזר הקליר זצ"ל ויצאו אלף שמונה מאות ויקבלו תפילות מלבות באות, ויתנם בראש אלקי הצבאות כי המלאך מתקן ומחבר כל שבח התפילה שמלב באה ומכין לעטרה בהוד והדר, והולכת על ראש הכבוד, וכל שיר שהוא בכוונה באהבת שמים שבלבו, עושה המלאך טס אחד מתפילת צדיק זה ומתפילת צדיק אחר טס אחר, ושם הצדיק עליו, כל הכתוב לחיים, ומחבר ביחד ברתיקות הוד והדר, והיא עולה לראש הכבוד עד זמן תפילה, ומעביר הראשונה מפני האחרונה, ומקבל בכל יום חדשה דכתיב חדשים לבקרים, והראשונה מצניע לצדיק זהו יהי' ה' צבאות לעטרת צבי ולצפירת תפארה לשאר עמו.

Text #34

כך הקב"ה מתאוות לחזכיר את ישראל בכל שעה. אמר רבי יהודה בר סימון משל לאחד שחיה
עושה עטרה עבר אחד ראה אותה. א"ל כל מה שאתה יכול לקשט בה אבנים טובות ומרגליות
קשט ותקן בה שהיא עתידה להנתן בראשו של מלך. כך אמר הקב"ה למשה כל מה שאתה
יכול לשבח את ישראל לפני ולפארן עשה שבהם אני מתפאר שנאמר ויאמר לי
עבדי אתה ישראל אשר בך אתפאר:

*Tanḥuma Tissa*ʾ 8

Text #35

כתר הנעשה מתפילות ישר' עליו וכשעולה אז מלאך שברקיע הראשון
מקבלו ומפארו והוא מתרחב ומתפאר וכן מלאך שיני מקבלו ומפארו וחוא מתרחב
יותר וכן בכל רקיע ורקיע, שהכת' מתפאר ומתרחב יותר ויותר עד שמגיע לדמות
יעקב החקוק בכסא הכבוד, אז מתרחב לפי הכבוד מתפאר לגמרי ועל זה אומ'
ישר' אשר בך אתפאר, על זה אומר ולתתך עליון, כלומ' כשהכתר על הקב"ה,
אז ישר' עליון (על) כל הגוים, למה יהיה זה הכתר, כי כל הגוים לתהילה, היינו
לשבח שיהיו ישר' משובחין על כל הגוים ולתפארת, כלומ' בשביל הכתר המתפאר
בזכות תפילתו של ישר' וכשהכתר מתפאר לגמרי, אז הקב"ה מכניס בו אורה
ומאירו בזוהר שאין לו דוגמא, זהו שאמר אור פני המלך חיים, וכשמאיר הכתר
מיד הולך ויושב בראש הכבוד.

ʿArugat ha-Bosem

Text #36

'ה' פניו אליך', נוקד על אותיות יופיא"ל בה"ן, וכן יש"א ה' פני"ו אלי"ך ויש"ם ל"ך, ר"ת יופיא"ל. הרי למדת, שכהן הזה אומר בתחילת עליה ברכת כהנים, ומקבלת מי"ח מאות מלאכים המקבלים שירת ישראל; ברקי"אל, והוא מקריבה על המזבח למעלה, ועליו אמר משה: יקר"ב א"ל המזב"ח,

נקוד על אותיות ברקיא"ל ואותו מלאך יש לו שג"ם מיני אורות בגלגל החמה, כמניין ברקי"אל, והוא ממונה על הגשם. ואותו (מלאך) נותן אותה לסנדלפון, והוא גבוה מאלף מחנות, מהלך ת"ק שנה, והוא נקרא בשם ה', והוא (התגלה) למשה מאוהל מועד, שנאמר: 'ויקרא אל משה', ולך א' ד' ויקרא' קטנה, כי אל"ף הקטנה גימטריא סנדלפון ויופיא"ל, ולפי שאותו אלף קטנה גבוה מהלך ת"ק מכולם.
ומושב העטרה בראש הבורא בשם מ"ב, ועליו אמר יחזקאל: 'הנה אופן אחד בארץ', אופן גימטריא יופיא"ל. ומיד כשהוא משים העטרה אז באים מיד פניאל ואוריאל לפנים מז' מחנות, ולפנים מד' חיות, והם מתעלפים וכורעים מחמת שעליו. ועליו אמר משה: 'פני לא יראו'- אותיות אוריא"ל, וכן יהפך-פניא"ל.
וכשהעטרה בראש הבורא, אז נקראת העטרה אכתריאל, ואז (היא) הכתר, היא נסתרת מכל המלאכים הקדושים, ונסתר בת"ק אלפים רבבות פרסאות. ואז שואלים זה לזה: 'איה מקום כבודו', ועליו אמר דוד : 'יושב בסתר עליון בצל שדי יתלונן'- בצלות שדי נלון. וכן אותיות 'צלות' דנן יש לו, לפי שהתפילה היא צלותא לקב"ה, והיא יושבת בשמאל הקב"ה ככלה אצל חתן, ונקראת בת מלך, ולפעמים על שם השליחות נקראת בת קול. ועליו אמר שלמה: 'ואהיה שכונה אצלו', ושם של שכינה - אחי"ה, ותרגום של אצלו ÷ תרביה, אותיות מברתי"ה, לפי שנקראה בת מלך, על שם ששכינה אצלו, והיא מלכות עשירית, והיא סוד כל הסודות.

ותדע כי נעלם של סוד - סמ"ך ו"ו דל"ת. ולכל צד חשכינה יש כתרי מלכות, וזה עצמו גדול רל"ו, אלפים רבבות פרסאות, ועליו אמר דוד: 'גדול אדונינו ור"ב כ"ח' בגימטריא רל"ו, 'ולבינתו אין מספר'. וירמיה אמר עליו: 'וה' אלהים אמת הוא אלוהים חיים ומלך עולם' וגו'. רל"ו והיא מנהגת את העולם על פיה, ונקראת מלאך השם, על שם השליחות; אבל אין בה פירוד.
וזה שאמר הכתוב: 'הנה אנכי שולח מלאך לפניך', זה היה השכינה, כי 'מלאכי' - מ"ם למ"ד אל"ף כ"ף יו"ד - בגי' שכינה. וזה מה שאמר(ו) חכמים: 'ויפול משה על פניו' - מלמד שהיה השכינה נשתטח לפני הקב"ה. ולפיכך היו רואים הנביאים את השכינה, לפי שהיא נאלצת, כמו שיש ב'ספר היכלות', שהשכינה היתה שורה תחת הכרוב והיו רואים אותה המלאכים והאנשים, וכיון שחוטאו(!) דור אנוש אז עלתה השכינה למעלה. אבל הבורא ורב לשכינה הוא נעלם מכל, ואין לו שיעור ולא דמיון ועין לא ראתה אותו. ומה שאמר 'פה אל פה', וראה אותו - בכל פעם דרך אספקלריא מצוחצחת, שנאמר : ' ולכל מורא הגדול' - גי' שכינה.
וכן ראה כתר הגדול מאחוריו, כמו שנאמר: 'וראית את אחורי' , מלמד שהראה לו קשר של תפילין, וכן הכתר הראה לו, שנאמר: 'ושמתיך בנקרת הצור', סופי תיבות 'כתר'. ופיו אש ולשונו אש והוא עצמו שלולית אש, והוא מנהגת העולם (!) והיא מנהגת העולם, אלא לפי שהיא מלכו"ת עשיריו"ת, אותיות עול"ם שת"י כתר"י, כי לשכינה יש שתי כסאות ושני כתרים, שני אופנים, אחד מלמטה ואחד מלמעלה, וכל אחד גבוה ממעשה בראשית ת"ק, ועל זה אמר שלמה: 'משכיל על', גימ' ת"ם...

וזהו סוד הכתר וסוד השכינה, וכל היודעין יש לו חלק לעולם הבא ונוחל ב' עולמות וניצל מדינה של גיהנם ואהוב למעלה ונחמד למטה'.

Sefer ha-Ḥokhmah

Text #37

מאי ניהו עשרה מאמרות, ראשון כתר עליון ברוך
ומבורך שמו ועמו, ומי עמו, ישראל, דכתיב דעו
כי ה' אלהים הוא עשנו ולא אנחנו עמו, ולאל"ף אנחנו,
להכיר ולידע אחד האחדים המיוחד בכל שמותיו.

Bahir #96

Text #38

ומאי הוי קדוש קדוש ואחר
כך ייי' צבאות, אלא קדוש כתר עליון, קדוש שרש האילן, קדוש נדבק ומיוחד בכלן י' צבאות
מלא כל הצבא בבודו. ומאי ניהו קדוש שהוא מיוחד, אלא מלה"ד, למלך שהיה לו בנים ולבנים
בנים, בזמן שבניהם עושים רצונו נכנס ביניהם ומעמיד הכל ומשביע הכל ומשפיע להם טובה
כדי שישבעו האבות והבנים, אין הבנים עושים רצונו משפיע להם לאבות כדי צרכם.

Bahir #89

Text #39

ישב רבי אמוראי ודרש מאי
דכתיב סגול, אלא סגולה שמה
כדאיתא לעיל, בתר זרקא, מ"ט
זרקא, כשמו בן הוא דהוא נזרק
כגון דבר הנזרק ובתריה אתיא
סגולת מלכים והמדינות.
ומ"ט זרקא, דכתיב ברוך כבוד ה'
ממקומו, מכלל דליבא דידע את
מקומו, ואמרינן שם אתגא ואתיא
לראש קונה, דכתיב קונה שמים
וארץ, וכד אזלא הוי כזרקא וסגולה
אבתריה והוי בראש כל אותיות.
ומאי טעמא היא בסוף התיבה ואינה
בראשה, ללמדך שאותה תגא עולה
עד למעלה למעלה, ומאי משמע
שהאי תגא אבן יקרה היא מכוללת
ומעוטרת דכתיב אבן מאסו הבונים
היתה לראש פנה, ועולה עד המקום
אשר נחצבה ממנו דכתיב משם רועה
אבן ישראל.

Bahir #61

Text #40

ד"א פעלך בקרב שנים חייהו משל
למה"ד למלך שהיה לו מרגלית טובה
והיא חמדת מלכותו ובעת שמחתו מחבקה
ומנשקה ושמה על ראשו ואוהב אותה,
אמר חבקוק אע"פ שהמלאכים עמך, אותה
המרגלית חמדה היא בעולמך, על כן בקרב
שנים חייהו

Bahir #49

Text #41

... למלך שהיה לו כסא. לפעמים לקח אותו בזרועו ולפעמים על ראשו. אמרו לו למה שהוא
נאה וחס לישב עליו. אמרו לו ואנה שמו. על ראשו...

אמרת כסאו, והא אמרינן דהו כתרו
של הקב"ה, דאמרינן בשלשה
כתרים נכתרו ישראל כתר כהונה וכתר
מלכות וכתר תורה עולה על גביהן. משל
למה"ד למלך שהיה לו כלי נאה ומבושם
ואוהבו המלך מאד. לפעמים שמו בראשו והיינו
תפלין שבראש, לפעמים נוטלו בזרועו בקשר של תפלין
לפעמים משאילו לבנו לשבת עמו. פעמים נקרא כסאו כי בזרועו נוטלו
בקמיע בעין כסא.

Bahir #25, 101

Text #42

אמרו לו הכתיב השליך
משמים ארץ תפארת ישראל וא"כ
נפלו אמר להם אם קרו לא שנו ואם שנו
לא שלשו, מלה"ד למלך שהיה לו עטרה
נאה על ראשו מלת נאה בכתפיו ובא לו
שמועה רעה השליך העטרה מעל ראשו
וחמלת מלפניו

Bahir #23

Text #43

אמר ר' רחומאי האורה קדמה
לעולם שענן וערפל סביביו שנאמר
ויאמר אלהים יהי אור ויהי
אור, אמרו לו קודם יצירת (ישראל) בנך
תעשה לו עטרה, א"ל הן, משל למה"ד
למלך שהתאוה לבן ומצא עטרה נאה קלוסה
ומשובחת שמח שמחה ואמר זה לבני
לראשו כי לו נאה, א"ל ויודע הוא שבנו
ראוי, אמר שתוק כך עלה במחשבה ונודע
שנאמר וחשב מחשבות וגו'

Bahir #12

Text #44

תשיעי מאי הוי, א"ל תשיעי ועשירי
הם יחד זה כנגד זה, והאחד גבוה
מחבירו ת"ק שנה, והם כעין שני אופנים,
האחד נוטה לצד צפון והאחד נוטה לצד מערב

Bahir #115

Text #45

ישב ודרש להם שכינה למטה כשם ששכינה למעלה. ומאי שכינה זו הוי
אומר זה האור הנאצל מן האור הראשון שהוא חכמה, גם הוא מסובב הכל
שנאמר מלא כל הארץ כבודו, מאי עבידתיה הכא, משל למה"ד למלך
שהיו לו שבעה בנים ושם לכל אחד ואחד מקומו, אמר להם שבו זה ע"ג
זה, אמר התחתון אני לא אשב למטה ולא אתרחק ממך, אמר להם הריני
מסובב ורואה אתכם כל היום והיינו מלא כל הארץ כבודו, ולמה הוא
ביניהם, כדי להעמידם ולקיימם.

Bahir #116

Text #46

למלך בשר ודם שיש לו כמה מלכיות
ויש מלכות שדינו שמי שר עליו נקרא פחה והמלך שר על
הכל מ"מ נקרא דוכוס מאותו מלכות ופחה מאותו מלכות ומלך
הוא שם העליון. כן הק' הכל שלו ועשר ספירות האציל מאתו
אעפ"י ששם בן ד' אותיות על הכל

Perush Sefer ha-Qomah

Text #47

ואמ' עשר ולא ט' שלא להפריד הראשונ'
באצילות מהתשע לגדל מעלתה ולא
האחרונה באצילות מאותה שלפניה
למעוט מעלת' כי צד היחוד שוה בכולם
וכמו שאמרו בספר יצירה נעוץ סופן
בתחלתן כי מסוף דבר נמצא ראשו
ומראשו נמצא סופו ואין סוף בלתי
ראש ולא ראש זולתי סוף. כיוצא בזה
כי ראש דבר וסופו שוים במציאותו
ובאחדותו כי לא ימצא זה זולתי זה דומ'
למה שאמרו רז'ל תחלת המחשבה הוא סוף המעש'

Maʿarekhet ha-ʾElohut 36a

Text #48

והאריה רמז לזה
בבריות השפלות
שמגלגל זנבו על
ראשו והקב"ה נקר'
אריה וגם לזה נקראת
המלכות עטרה כי היא
מתגלגלת להיות
עטר' בראש המלך
ועל זה אמרו חז"ל
הוי זנב לאריו' וכו'

R. Judah Ḥayyat on *Maʿarekhet ha-ʾElohut* 36b

Text #49

כל הכתרים עולם עולם משולש ועולם זה קשור בעולם זה וכתר עליון עולם גנוז בפני עצמו וכולם מקבלים מאצילותו. והוא לבדו גנוז וקשור בשרש כל השרשים שאין המחשבה תופסת בו. והוא מקבל תמיד מן השרש בלי שום הפסק בדממה דקה והוא מאציל ומריק בכתרו על שאר הכתרים הקרובים לאצילותו תמיד. תמיד שואב ומריק ומשם מקבל רוח הקדש האמצעי עם כל הכתרים זה מזה וזה מזה לא קבלה תמידית רק כפי הרצון שהוא שרש כל השרשים. וכל שלש שלש מקבלות ייחוד. שלש מריקות ושלש שואבות עד אוצר חרזים והוא כתר מלכות. יוצר בראשית. אות בכל צבאות מעלה ומטה. זהו טעם שאנו אומרים וצבאות מעלה משלשים ואומרים ק' ק' ק' יי' צבאות. ועוד הוסיף ביאור ז"ל לתלמידי ישיבה הצנועים דעו זרע קדש כי בעולמים כולם פנימיים שלש שלש מוקף ומקיף. סבוב ומסבב. זה בתוך זה וזה בתוך זה. זה על גב זה וזה על גב זה. זה מתחת זה וזה מתחת זה. זה שואב מזה וזה שואב מזה. ראשון אמצעי ואמצעי ראשון. ראשון אחרון ואחרון ראשון. אמצעי אחרון ואחרון אמצעי. הכל לפי הרצון להראות כי הכל מעשיו וכולם נבראו לחפצו ורצונו.

R. Isaac ha-Kohen

Text #50

תאנא מסטרא דאמא כד איהי מתעטרא נפקין בעטרהא אלף וחמש מאה סטרי גליפין בתכשיטהא וכד בעאת לחזדווגא במלכא מתעטרא בחד עטרא דארבע גוונין. אינון גוונין מתלהטן בארבע סטרי עלמא כל גוונא וגוונא מתלהטא תלת זמנין בההוא סטרא דאינון תריסר תחומי גליפין ועאלין ואתכלילו בתריסר אחרנין. ברישא דעטרא אית ד' שורין לד'סטרין ואינון מגדלות כד"א מגדלות מרקחים מחו מרקחים כמה דאת אמר מכל אבקת רוכל ועל כל מגדלא ומגדלא ג' פתחין קביעין באבנין טבן מכל סטרא וסטרא. האי עטרא נהירא בדלוגין דאופיר בגין יקרא דמלכא כמה דכתיב אוקיר אנוש מפז וגו'. תחות עטרא תליין זגי דדהבא בסחרנהא זגא דדהבא מסטרא דא וזגא דדהבא מסטרא דא וחד רמונא בגוון ההוא רמונא אית בה אלף זגין וכל זגא מנייהו מתלהטא בסומקא בחוורא ההוא רמונא אתפלג בפלוגין ארבע וקיימא פתיחא לאתחזאה זגהא תלת מאה ועשרין וחמש זגין לסטרא דא וכן לכל סטרא וסטרא עד דמתלהטן ארבע סטרי עלמא מחיזו דכל פלכא ופלכא ואינון אקרון פלח הרמון כמה דכתיב כפלח הרמון רקתך מבעד לצמתך ארבע גלגלין בפלכי ארבע זווין נטלין בגלגולא לההוא עטרא וכד נטלי לה אזדקפן לעילא עד דמטו לגלגולא דפלכא עלאה דנהים יממא וליליא מתחברן כל אינון פלכין ונטלין לעטרא וזקפן לה. וקלא דאינון גלגלין אשתמע בכלהו רקיעין לקל נעימותא מתרעשין כל חילי שמיא וכלהו שאלין דא לדא עד דכלהו אמרי ברוך כבוד ה' ממקומו כד מזדווג מלכא במטרוניתא סלקא עטרא דא ואתישבת ברישא דמטרוניתא כדין נחית חד עטרא עלאה קביעא דכל אבן טבא וחיזור ושושן בסחרנהא בשית גלגלין אתיא לשית סטרין דעלמא שית גדפין דנשר נטלין לה בפלבוי חמשין ענבין סחרנהא דגליף בה אימא עלאה קביעאן באבן טבא חוור וסומק ירוק ואוכם תכלא וארגוונא שית מאה ותלת עשר זוויין לכל סטרא וסטרא. אלף ושית מאה מגדלין לכל סטרא וסטרא .וכל מגדלא ומגדלא טורין קביעין פרחין לעילא אשתאבן בביתונא דאימא עלאה במשח רבות דילה. בדין אימא בלחישו נגיד מתנן עלאין ושדר וקבע לון בההוא עטרא לבתר אנגיד נחלי דמשח רבות קדישא על רישא למלכא ומרישיה נחית ההוא משחא טבא עלאה על דיקניה יקירא ומתמן נגיד על אינון לבושי מלכא הה"ד כשמן הטוב על הראש יורד על הזקן וגו' לבתר אתחדד עטרא ומעטרא ליה אימא עילאה בההוא עטרא ופרישא עליה ועל מטרוניתא לבושי יקר בההוא עטרא כדין קלא אשתמע בכלהו עלמין צאינה וראינה וגו'. כדין חדוותא הוא בכל אינון בני מלכא ומאן אינון כל אינון דאתו מסטרייהו דישראל דהא לא מזדווגי בהו ולא קיימין עמהון בר אינון ישראל דאינון בני ביתא ומשמשי להו בדין ברכאן דנפיקי מנייהו דישראל הוא. וישראל נטלין כלא ומשדרי חולקא מניה לשאר עמין. ומההוא חולקא אתזנו כל אינון שאר עמין.

Zohar 3:209a

Text #51

על דא חסידי קדמאי לא חווי ניימי בהאי ליליא
והוו לעאן באורייתא ואמרי ניתי לאחסנא ירותא
קדישא לן ולבנן בתרין עלמין וההוא ליא
כנסת ישראל אתרעטרא עלייהו ואתיא לאזדווגא
ביה למלכא ותרווייהו מתעטרי על רישיהו
דאינון דזכאן להכי. ר"ש הכי אמר בשעתא
דמתכנשי חברייא בהאי ליליא לגביה ניתי
לתקנא תכשיטי כלה בגין דתשתכח למחר
בתכשיטהא ותקונהא לגבי מלכא כדקא
יאות. זכאה חולקהון דחבריא כד יתבע מלכא
למטרוניתא מאן תקין תכשיטהא ואנהיר עטרהא
ושוי תקונהא. ולית לך בעלמא מאן דידע לתקנא
תכשיטי כלה אלא חברייא זכאה חולקהון בעלמא
דין ובעלמא דאתי. תא חזי חברייא מתקני בהאי
ליליא תכשיטהא לכלה ומעטרי לה בעטרהא לגבי
מלכא ומאן מתקין ליה למלכא בהאי ליליא
לאשתכחא בה בכלה לאזדווגא בה במטרוניתא
נהרא קדישא עמיקא דכל נהרין. אימא עלאה
הה"ד צאינה וראינה בנות ציון במלך שלמה
וגו'. לבתר דאתקינת ליה למלכא ואעטרת ליה
אתיית לדכאה לה למטרוניתא ולאינון דמשתכחי
גבה. למלכא דהוה ליה בר יחידאי אתא לזוגא ליה
במטרוניתא עלאה מאי עבדת אמיה כל ההוא ליליא
עלאת לבי גניזהא אפיקת עטרא עלאה בשבעין
אבני יקר סחרנהא ואעטרת ליה אפיקת לבושין
דמילת ואלבישת ליה ואתקנת ליה בתקוני
דמלכין. לבתר עאלת לבי כלה חמאת עולימתהא
דקא מתקני עטרהא ולבושהא ותכשיטהא לתקנא
לה. אמרה לון הא אתקינת בי טבילה אתר דמיין
נבעין וכל ריחין ובוסמין סוחרני אינון מיין לדכאה
לכלתי ליתי כלתי מטרוניתא דברי ועולימתהא
ויתדכון בההוא אתר דאתקינת בההוא בי טבילה
דמיין נבעין דעמי לבתר תקינו לה בתכשיטהא אלבישו לה לבושהא אעטרו לה בעטרהא.
לבתר כד ייתי ברי לאזדווגא במטרוניתא. יתקין היכלא לכלהו וישתכח מדוריה בכו בחדא.

Zohar 3:98a–b

Bibliography

Note: Premodern Jewish and cognate sources have been referenced in accord with accepted practice, using standard paginations and/or critical editions where available. Editions cited are those used in the preparation of this work, sometimes as dictated by convenience or availability. Anonymous/collective works are listed by title. Such standard reference works as dictionaries, encyclopedias, and the like have not been listed.

Premodern Sources

Abraham ben Azriel. *ʿArugat ha-Bosem*. Ed. E. Urbach. 4 vols. Jerusalem: Mekize Nirdamim, 1939–63.

Abraham ben Nathan of Lunel. *Sefer ha-Manhig*. Jerusalem: Mossad Ha-Rav Kook, 1978.

Abudarham, David ben Joseph. *Abudarham ha-Shalem*. Jerusalem: Usha, 1963.

Abulafia, Todros ben Joseph. *Oṣar ha-Kavod*. Warsaw, 1879. Reprint Jerusalem: Makor, 1970.

———. *Shaʿar ha-Razim*. Ed. M. Kushnir-Oron. Jerusalem: Bialik Institute, 1989.

Aggadat Shemaʿ Yisraʾel. Ed. A. Jellinek. In *Bet ha-Midrasch* 5, 165–66.

Aggadat Shir ha-Shirim. Ed. S. Schechter. Cambridge: Deighton, Bell, 1896.

Arzey Levanon. Venice: Juan De Gara, 1601.

Asher ben David. *Perush Shem ha-Meforash* [and Other Writings]. Ed. M. Hasidah. In *Ha-Segullah* 1–2 (1934–35): 2–27

Avot de-Rabbi Natan. Ed. S. Schechter. Vienna, 1887; rpt. New York: P. Feldheim, 1945.

Azriel of Gerona. *Perush ha-ʾAggadot*. Ed. Y. Tishby. Jerusalem: Mekize Nirdamim, 1945.

———. *Perush le-Sefer Yeṣirah*. In Kitvey *RaMBaN*. Ed. C. Chavel. Jerusalem: Mossad Ha-Rav Kook, 1963, vol. 2, pp. 449–61.

Azulai, Abraham. *Or ha-Ḥamah*. Przemysl, 1896–97; rpt. Beney Beraq, Israel: Yahadut, 1973.

Bacharach, Naftali. *ʿEmeq ha-Melekh*. Amsterdam: E. Benveniste, 1648.

[*Sefer ha-*] *Bahir*. {German translation] *Das Buch Bahir, ein Schriftdenkmal aus der Frühzeit der Kabbala*. Ed. and tr. G. Scholem. Leipzig: W. Drugulin, 1923.

———. Ed. R. Margaliot. Jerusalem: Mossad Ha-Rav Kook, 1951.

———. Ed. D. Abrams. Los Angeles: Cherub Press, 1994.

Bahya Ben Asher. *Kitvey Rabbenu Baḥya*. Ed. C. Chavel. Jerusalem: Mossad Ha-Rav Kook, 1969.

———. *Beʾur ʿal ha-Torah*. Ed. C. Chavel. 3 vols. Jerusalem: Mossad Ha-Rav Kook, 1971–72.

Battey Midrashot [=*Batei Midrashot*], *Twenty-Five Midrashim Published for the First Time from Manuscripts Discovered in the Genizoth of Jerusalem and Egypt with Introductions and Annotations*. Ed. A. Wertheimer. 2 vols. Jerusalem: Mossad Ha-Rav Kook, 1953–54.

Bet ʿEqed ha-ʾAggadot. Ed. H. M. Horovitz. Vol. 1, no. 1 (all published). Frankfurt-am-Main: E. Slobotski, 1881.

Bet ha-Midrasch, Sammlung kleiner Midraschim und vermischter Abhandlungen aus der ältern jüdischen Literatur. Ed. A. Jellinek. 6 vols. in 2. Leipzig, 1873–78; rpt. Jerusalem: Bamberger and Wahrmann, 1938.

A Coptic Gnostic Treatise Contained in the Codex Brucianus. Ed. Charlotte A. Baynes. Cambridge: Cambridge University Press, 1933.

Donollo, Sabbatai. *Perush Sefer Yeṣirah*. Ed. D. Castelli. Firenze, 1880.

Eleazar of Worms. *Sefer ha-Ḥokhmah*. Ms. Oxford 1568.

———. *Sodey Razayaʾ*. Ed. Y. Camelhar. Bilgoray, 1936.

———. *Shaʿarey ha-Sod ha-Yiḥud weha-Emunah*. Ed. Y. Dan. In *Ṭemirin* I (1972): 141–56.

———. *Perush Shir ha-Shirim*. Jerusalem, 1982.

———. *Sodey Razayaʾ*. Ed. S. Weiss. Jerusalem: Shaarey Ziv Institute, 1991.

1 Enoch. Tr. E. Isaac. In *Old Testament Pseudepigrapha*. Ed. J. Charlesworth. Garden City, New York: Doubleday, 1983.

2 Enoch. Tr. F. I. Andersen. In *Old Testament Pseudepigrapha*. Ed. J. Charlesworth. Gerden City, New York: Doubleday, 1983.

3 Enoch. (=*Sefer Hekhalot)*. Ed. H. Odeberg. Cambridge: Cambridge University Press, 1928.

3 Enoch. Tr. P. Alexander. In *Old Testament Pseudepigrapha*, Ed. J. Charlesworth. Garden City, New York: Doubleday, 1983.

Ezra ben Solomon of Gerona. *Perush Shir ha-Shirim*. Ed. C. Chavel. In *Kitvey RaMBaN*, vol. 2, pp. 471–518. Jerusalem, Mossad Ha-Rav Kook, 1963.

Geonica. Ed. L. Ginzberg. 2 vols. New York, 1909, rpt. New York: Hermon, 1968.

Gikatilla, Joseph ben Abraham. *Shaʿarey Ṣedeq*. Riva di Trento, 1561.

———. *Shaʿarey Orah*. Ed. J. Ben Shlomo. 2d corrected printing. Jerusalem: Bialik Institute, 1981.

Hananel ben Hushiel. Commentary to the Talmud. Published in standard editions.

Ḥarba de-Moshe. Ed. M. Gaster. London: D. Nutt, 1896.

Havdalah de-Rabbi ʿAqivaʾ. Ed. G. Scholem. In *Tarbiz* 50 (1981): 243–281.

[*Hekhalot*.] *Synopse zur Hekhalot-Literatur*. Ed. P. Schaefer. Tübingen: J.C.B. Mohr, 1981.

Hekhalot Rabbati. In Schaefer, *Synopse*.

Hekhalot Zuṭarti. Ed. R. Elior. Jerusalem: Jerusalem Studies in Jewish Thought, 1982, Supplement I.

[*Sefer ha-*] *Ḥesheq*. Ed. J. M. Epstein. Lvov: 1865.

Ibn Adret, Solomon *Teshuvot ha-RaSHBAʾ ha-Meyuḥasot la-RaMBaN*. Tel Aviv: Eshel 1958.

Ibn Gaʾon, Shem Tov ben Shem Tov. *Baddey ha-ʾAron*. Ms. Paris 840. Facsimile Edition by S. Loewinger. Jerusalem: Orient and Occident, 1977.

Ibn Habib, Yaʿaqov, Ed. *ʿEyn Yaʿaqov*. Vilna, 1883–84; rpt. Jerusalem: Qeren Sifrey Rabbaney Bavel, 1965.

Isaac the Blind. *Perush Sefer Yeṣirah*. In G. Scholem, *Ha-Qabbalah be-Provence*. Ed. R. Schatz. Jerusalem: Mifʿal ha-Shikhpul, 1963.

[*Sefer ha-*]*ʿIyyun*. Ed. M. Verman. Albany, State University of New York Press, 1992.

Jacob ben Asher. *Arbaʿah Ṭurim*. 7 vols. Jerusalem: Makhon Ḥatam Sofer, 1965.
Jacob ben Jacob ha-Kohen *Perush Merkevet Yeḥezkeʾel*. Ed. A. Farber. Jerusalem: Hebrew University, 1978.
Jacob ben Meir Tam (attr.). *Sefer ha-Yashar*. Ed. S. Schlesinger. Jerusalem: Kirjath Sefer, 1959.
Judah ben Barzilai of Barcelona. *Perush Sefer Yeṣirah*. Ed. S. Halberstamm. Berlin: Mekize Nirdamim, 1885.
Judah ben Yaqar. *Perush ha-Tefillot weha-Berakhot*. 2 vols. Ed. S. Yerushalmi. Jerusalem: Meʾorey Yisraʾel, 1968–69.
Judah Ha-Levi. *Kitab al-Hujja waʾal-Dalil fi Nasr al-Din al-Dhalil* [=*Sefer ha-Kuzari*]. Tr. Y. Ibn Tibbon, Ed. A. Zifroni. Tel Aviv [?]: Maḥberot le-Sifrut, n.d.
Luria, Jehiel. *Hekhal ha-Shem*. 1605; reprint Venice, n.d.
Maʿarekhet ha-ʾElohut. Mantua, 1558; reprint Jerusalem: Meqor Hayyim, 1963.
Maʿaseh Merkavah. In Schaefer, *Synopse* and in G. Scholem, *Jewish Gnosticism*, pp. 103–17.
Maʿayan Ḥokhmah. Ed. A. Jellinek. In *Bet ha-Midrasch*, vol. 1, pp. 58–61.
[*Sefer*] *Maḥkim*. Ed. J. Freimann. Krakow, 1909.
Maḥzor Kol ha-Shanah, Ke-fi Minhag Qehilot Qodesh Italiane. Ed. S. D. Luzzatto. 2 vols. Leghorn: S. Belporte, 1866.
Maḥzor le-Yamim Noraʾim. Ed. D. Goldschmidt. Jerusalem: Koren, 1970.
Maphteaḥ Shelomo. Ed. S. Gollancz. Oxford: Oxford University Press, 1914.
Mekhilta de-Rabbi Ishmael. Ed. H. S. Horovitz and I. A. Rabin. Jerusalem: Bamberger and Wahrmann, 1960.
Mekhilta de-Rabbi Shimʿon ben Yoḥai. Ed. J. N. Epstein. Jerusalem: Mekize Nirdamim, 1955.
Memar Marqah: The Teachings of Marqah. Ed. and tr. J. Macdonald. Berlin: A. Topelmann, 1963.
Merkavah Shelemah. Ed. S. Mussaiouf. Jerusalem: S. Mussaiouf, 1921.
Midrash Abba Gurion. Ed. S. Buber. Vilna: Romm, 1886.
Midrash Be-Midbar Rabbah. In *Midrash Rabbah*, Ed. M. A. Mirkin, vol. 9–10. 3d printing. Tel Aviv: Yavneh, 1981–82.
Midrash Bereshit Rabbah. Ed. J. Theodor and H. Albeck. Berlin: 1903.
Midrash Devarim Rabbah. Ed. S. Lieberman. Jerusalem: Bamberger and Wahrmann, 1940.
Midrash Ekhah Rabbah. Ed. S. Buber. Vilna: Romm, 1899.
Midrash Konen. Ed. A. Jellinek. In *Bet ha-Midrasch*, vol. 2, pp. 23–39.
Midrash Mishle. Ed. B. Visotzky. New York: Jewish Theological Seminary, 1990.
Midrash Shemot Rabbah. In *Midrash Rabbah*. Ed. M. A. Mirkin, vols. 5–6. 3d printing. Tel Aviv: Yavneh, 1980–81.
Midrash Shir ha-Shirim. Ed. E. Gruenhuet. Jerusalem: W. Gross, 1897.
Midrash Shir ha-Shirim Rabbah. Ed. S. Donski. Jerusalem: Dvir, 1980.
Midrash Shir ha-Shirim Zuṭa. Ed. S. Buber. Berlin: Mekize Nirdamim, 1894, reprint Tel Aviv, n. d.
Midrash Tanḥuma. Ed. S. Buber. Vilna: Romm, 1885.
Midrash Tanḥuma. Jerusalem: Levin-Epstein, 1953.
Midrash Tehilim. Ed. S. Buber. Vilna: Romm, 1891; reprint New York: Om, 1947.

Midrash Wa-Yiqra' Rabbah. Ed. M. Margulies. 5 vols. Jerusalem: Ministry of Education and Culture, 1953–60.

Midreshey Ge'ulah. Ed. Y. Ibn Shmuel. Jerusalem: Bialik Institute, 1954.

Montgomery, James A., Ed. *Aramaic Incantation Texts from Nippur*. Philadelphia: University Museum, 1913.

Moses ben Maimon. *Commentary on the Mishnah Tractate Sanhedrin*. Ed. M. Gottlieb. Hannover, 1906.

———. *Teshuvot ha-RaMBaM*. Ed. A. H. Fraiman. Jerusalem: Mekize Nirdamim, 1934.

———. *Mishneh Torah*. Jerusalem: Pardes; Vilna: Romm, 1959.

Moses ben Nahman. *Torat ha-Adam*. Ed. C. Chavel. In *Kitvey RaMBaN*. Jerusalem: Mossad Ha-Rav Kook, 1963, vol. 2, pp. 9–311.

———. *Perush ha-Torah*. Ed. C. Chavel. 2 vols. Jerusalem: Mossad ha-Rav Kook, 1969.

Naftali Herz [Drifzan] of Treves. *Diqduq Tefillah*. Printed in the prayerbook *Male'ah Ha-Areṣ De'ah*. Thuengen, 1560); reprint Israel: Grand Rabbi Ch. Morgenshtein, 1971.

Nathan bem Judah. *Sefer Maḥkim*. Ed. Jacob Freimann. Krakow, 1909.

[*Sefer ha-*] *Navon*. Ed. Y. Dan. In *'Iyyunim*, pp. 112–33.

Oṣar ha-Ge'onim. Ed. B. M. Lewin. 12 vols. Jerusalem: Mossad Ha-Rav Kook, 1928–62.

Otiyyot de-Rabbi 'Akiva'. Ed. A. Wertheimer. In *Battey Midrashot*, vol. 2, pp. 333–418.

Pereq Shirah. In *Siddur Oṣar ha-Tefillot*. Vilna: Roman, 1915; reprint New York: Sefer, 1946, vol. 1, pp. 68–73.

Perush Sefer ha-Qomah. Mss. Angelica 27 and JTS 844, as quoted by G. Scholem in *Reshit ha-Qabbalah*, pp. 212–37.

Pesiqta de-Rav Kahana. Ed. B. Mandelbaum. 2 vols. New York: Jewish Theological Seminary, 1987.

Pesiqta Rabbati. Ed. M. Friedmann. Vienna, 1880.

Pirqey Rabbi Eliezer. Edited with commentary by R. David Luria. Warsaw, 1852; reprint Jerusalem, 1963.

Sa'adya ben Joseph Gaon. *Kitāb al-Amānāt wa'l-'Itiqadat*. (=*Sefer ha-Emunot weha-De'ot*) Ed. S. Landauer. Leiden: E. J. Brill, 1880.

———. *Pitron Sefer Emunot*. Ed. R. Kiener. Ph.D. dissertation, University of Pennsylvania, 1984.

———. *Sefer ha-'Emunot weha-De'ot*. Leipzig: Y. Fischel, 1859; reprint New York: Om, 1947.

———. *The Book of Beliefs and Opinions*. Tr. S. Rosenthal. New Haven: Yale University Press, 1948.

[*Sefer ha-*] *Razim*. Ed. M. Margulies. Jerusalem: American Academy for Jewish Research, 1966.

Seder 'Avodat Yisra'el. Ed. S. Baer. Roedelheim, 1868; reprint Berlin: Schocken, 1937.

Seder Rabba' de-Bereshit. Ed. A. Wertheimer. In *Battey Midrashot*, vol. 1, pp. 3–48.

Seder Rav 'Amram Ga'on. Ed. D. Goldschmidt. Jerusalem: Mossad Ha-Rav Kook, 1971.

Sha'arey Teshuvah, Teshuvot ha-Ge'onim. Leipzig, 1858.

Shirey ha-Yiḥud weha-Kavod. Ed. A. M. Habermann. Jerusalem: Mossad ha-Rav Kook, 1949.

Shiʿur Qomah: Texts and Recensions. Ed. M. Cohen. Tübingen: Mohr, 1985.

Siddur Oṣar ha-Tefillot. Vilna, 1915; reprint New York: Sefer, 1946.

Siddur Rav Saʿadia Gaʾon. Ed. I. Davidson et al. Jerusalem: Mekize Nirdamim, 1941.

Sifra. Ed. Isaak Hirsch Weiss. Vienna, 1862.

Sifre ʿal Sefer Be-Midbar. Ed. H. S. Horovitz. 2d corrected printing. Leipzig, 1917; reprint Jerusalem: Wahrmann, 1966.

Sifre Devarim. Ed. L. Finkelstein. 2d edition. New York: Jewish Theological Seminary, 1969.

Sifre Zuṭa. Ed. H. S. Horovitz. Leipzig, 1917; reprint 2nd corrected printing. Jerusalem: Wahrmann, 1966.

Simḥah ben Samuel of Vitry. *Maḥzor Vitry*. Nuremberg: Mekize Nirdamim, 1923.

Sirkis, Joel. *Hagahot ha-BaḤ*. Printed in standard editions of the Babylonian Talmud.

Songs of the Sabbath Sacrifice. Ed. C. Newson. Atlanta: Scholars Press, 1985.

Taku, Moshe. *Ketav Tamim*. Ed. Y. Dan. Jerusalem: B. Dinur Centre, 1984.

Talmud Bavli. 20 vols. Vilna, 1880–86; reprint New York: E. Grossman, 1957.

Talmud Yerushalmi. Krotoschin, 1866; reprint Jerusalem: Torah La-ʿAm, 1960.

Tiqquney Zohar. Ed. R. Margaliot. Tel Aviv: Mossad Ha-Rav Kook, 1948.

Tosafot [Notes of the Franco-German rabbis to the Babylonian Talmud] Published in standard editions of Talmud text.

Tosefta. Ed. S. Lieberman with commentary *Tosefta ki-Feshuṭah*. New York: Jewish Theological Seminary, 1955–73.

Yalqut Reʾuveni. Amsterdam: Etias, 1700.

Yalqut Shimʿoni. 2 vols. Warsaw: Y. Goldman, 1876.

Yannai (7th century). *The Liturgical Poems of Rabbi Yannai*. Ed. Z. M. Rabinovitz. 2 vols. Jerusalem: Bialik Institute, 1985–87.

[*Sefer*] *Yeṣirah*. Warsaw, 1884; reprint Jerusalem: M. Ettiah, 1962.

Yosi ben Yosi. *Poems*. 2d edition. Edited with an Introduction, Commentary, and Notes by A. Mirsky. Jerusalem: Bialik Institute, 1991.

Zacuto, Abraham. *Sefer Yuḥasin*. Ed. A. H. Fraymann [Fraiman]. Frankfurt: A. Vohrmann, 1925.

Zohar. Ed. R. Margaliot. 3 vols. Jerusalem: Mossad Ha-Rav Kook, 1960.

Zohar Ḥadash. 2d edition. Ed. R. Margaliot. Jerusalem: Mossad Ha-Rav Kook, 1978.

MODERN WORKS

Works in Hebrew that are listed by English title are marked (h.).

Alexander, Philip. "Comparing Merkavah Mysticism and Gnosticism: An Essay in Method." *JJS* 35 (1984): 1–18.

———. "Prayer in the Heikhalot Literature." In *Prière, Mystique et Judaisme*, Ed. R. Goetschel. Paris: Presses Universitaires de France, 1984. pp. 43–64.

Alon, Gedalya. "בשם." *Tarbiz* 21 (1950): 30–39.

Aloni, Nehemia. "Ha-Shiṭṭah ha-ʾAnagramit shel ha-Millonut ha-ʿIvrit be-Sefer Yeṣirah." *Ṭemirin* 1 (1972): 63–99.

———. "Zeman Ḥibburo shel Sefer Yeṣirah." *Ṭemirin* 2 (1981): 41–50.

Altmann, Alexander "The Gnostic Background of the Rabbinic Adam Legends." *JQR* n.s. 35:4 (1945): 371–91.

———. "Saadya's Theory of Revelation: Its Origin and Background." In *Saadya Studies: In Commemoration of the One Thousandth Anniversary of the Death of R. Saadya Gaon*. Manchester: University Press, 1943, pp. 4–25.

Aptowitzer, Viktor. "בשכמל״ו" Geschichte einer liturgische Formel." *MGWJ* 73 (1929): 93–118.

———. "The Heavenly Temple in the Agada." *Tarbiz* 2 (1931): 137–53; 257–87. (h.)

Avenary, H. "Der Einfluss der jüdischen Mystik auf der Synagogengesang." *Kairos* 16 (1974): 79–87.

Badger, G. P. *The Nestorians and Their Rituals*. London: J. Master, 1852.

Baer, Seligmann, Ed. *Seder ʿAvodat Yisraʾel*. Roedelheim, 1868.

Bar-Ilan, Meir. "The Idea of Crowning God in Hekhalot Mysticism and the Karaite Polemic." *EJM*, pp. 221–33. (h.)

———. *The Mysteries of Jewish Prayer and Hekhalot*. Ramat Gan: Bar Ilan University, 1987. (h.)

Baumgarten, J. M. "The Duodecimal Courts of Qumran, Revelation, and the Sanhedrin." *JBL* 95 (1976): 59–78.

Baus, K. *Der Kranz in Antike und Christentum*. Bonn: P. Hanstein, 1940.

Beit-Arie, Malachi. *Pereq Shirah: Mevoʾot; Mahadurah Biqqoretit*. Unpublished doctoral dissertation, Jerusalem: Hebrew University, 1967.

Ben Barak, Z. "The Coronation Ceremonies of Joash and Nebopolassar in Comparison." (h.) *History of the Jewish People and the Land of Israel* (Haifa) 5 (1980): 43–56.

Blau, Ludwig. "Origine et Histoire de la Lectur du Schema." *REJ* 31 (1895): 179–201.

———. "La Recitation du Schema et de la Haftara." *REJ* 55 (1908): 209–20.

Blech, M. *Studien zum Kranz bei den Griechen*. Berlin: De Gruyter, 1982.

Bloch, Philip. "Die Yorede Merkabah, die Mystiker der Gaonenzeit, und ihr Einfluss auf die Liturgie." *MGWJ* 37 (1893): 18–25; 69–74; 257–66; 305–11.

Boyarin, Daniel. "Two Introductions to the Midrash on Song of Songs." *Tarbiz* 56 (1987): 479–500. (h.)

———. *Intertextuality and the Reading of Midrash*. Bloomington: Indiana University Press, 1990.

Brettler, Marc Z. *God Is King: Understanding an Israelite Metaphor*. *JSOT* Supplement Series #76. Sheffield: JSOT, 1989.

Buber, Martin *Kinghip of God*. New York: Harper and Row, 1967.

Buccellati, G. "The Enthronement of the King and the Capital City" *Studies Presented to A. Leo Oppenheim*. Chicago: Oriental Institute, 1964.

Büchler, Adolph. *Types of Jewish-Palestinian Piety*. London: Jews' College, 1922.

Chernus, Ira. *Mysticism in Rabbinic Judaism*. Berlin: de Gruyter, 1982.

———. "Visions of God in Merkavah Mysticism." *Journal for the Study of Judaism* 13 (1982): 123–46.

Cohen, Gerson D. "The Song of Songs and the Jewish Religious Mentality." In *The Samuel Friedland Lectures, 1960–1966*. New York: Jewish Theological Seminary of America, 1966, pp. 1–21.

Cohen, Martin. *The Shiʿur Qomah: Liturgy and Theurgy in Pre-Kabbalistic Jewish Mysticism*. Lanham: University Press, 1983.

Cohen, Stuart. *The Three Crowns: Structures of Communal Politics in Early Rabbinic Jewry*. Cambridge: Cambridge University Press, 1990.

Daiches, S. *Babylonian Oil Magic in the Talmud and in the Later Jewish Literature*. London: Jews' College, 1913.

Dan, Joseph. "The 'Exceptional Cherub' Sect in the Literature of Medieval German Hasidism." *Tarbiẓ* 35 (1966): 349–72. (h.)

———. *Ḥuggey ha-Mequbbalim ha-Rishonim*. Jerusalem: Akademon, 1966.

———. "'Sepher Harazim' edited by M. Margalioth." *Tarbiẓ* 37 (1968): 208–14. (h.)

———. "Shaʿarey ha-Sod ha-Yiḥud weha-Emunah le-Rabbi Eleazar mi-Worms." *Ṭemirin* 1(1972): 141–56.

———. *Studies in Ashkenazi-Hasidic Literature*. Ramat Gan: Massada, 1975. (h.) [abbreviated in notes as *ʿIyyunim*]

———. "Ashkenazi Hasidic Commentaries on the Hymn *Ha-Aderet weha-Emunah*." *Tarbiẓ* 50 (1981): 396–404. (h.)

———. *The Esoteric Theology of Ashkenazi Hasidism*. Jerusalem: Bialik Institute, 1968. (h.) [abbreviated in the notes as *Torat ha-Sod*]

———. "The Emergence of Mystical Prayer." In *Studies in Jewish Mysticism*, Ed. J. Dan and F. Talmage. Cambridge, MA: Association for Jewish Studies, 1982, pp. 112–15.

———. "The Seventy Names of Meṭaṭron." *Proceedings of the Eighth World Congress of Jewish Studies*. Jerusalem: World Congress of Jewish Studies, 1982, vol. 3, pp. 19–23. (h.)

———. "ʿAnfiel, Metatron, and the Creator." *Tarbiẓ* 52 (1983): 447–57. (h.)

———. "The Kabbalistic Book Baddei ha-Aron and Kabbalistic Pseudepigraphy in the Thirteenth Century." *JSJT* 3: 1–2 (1983–84): 111–38. (h.)

———. "The Religious Experience of the Merkavah." In *Jewish Spirituality* I, Ed. A. Green. New York: Crossroad, 1988, pp. 289–307.

Day, J. *God's Conflict with the Dragon and the Sea: Echoes of a Canaanite Myth in the Old Testament*. Cambridge: Cambridge University Press, 1985.

Deubner, L. "Die Bedeutung des Kranzes im klassischen Altertum." *ARW* 30 (1933): 70–104.

Deutsch, Nathaniel. *The Gnostic Imagination: Gnosticism, Mandaeism, and Merkabah Mysticism*. Leiden: E. J. Brill, 1995.

Elbogen, Ismar. "La Recitation du Schema et de la Haftara" [Response to article of same title by L. Blau]. *REJ* 56 (1908): 222–27.

———. *Ha-Tefillah be-Yisraʾel*. Translation of *Der jüdische Gottesdient in seiner geschichtlichen Entwicklung*. Leipzig, 1913. Translated, augmented, and updated by J. Heinemann, Tel Aviv: Dvir, 1972.

Elior, Rachel. "The Concept of God in Hekhalot Mysticism." *EJM*, pp. 13–64. (h.)

———. "Merkabah Mysticism." *Numen* 37:2 (1990) 223–49.

———. "Mysticism, Magic, Angelology: The Perception of Angels in Merkavah Mysticism." *JSQ* 1: 1 (1993–94): 3–53).

Engnell, Ivan. *Studies in Divine Kingship in the Ancient Near East*. Uppsala: Almquist and Wiksells, 1943.

Epstein, J. N. "Gloses Babylo-Araméennes." *REJ* 73 (1921): 27–58.

Falk, Z. W. "Forms of Testimony." *Vetus Testamentum* 11 (1961): 88–91.

Fallon, F. T. *The Enthronement of Sabaoth: Jewish Elements in Gnostic Creation Myths*. Leiden: E. J. Brill, 1978.

Farber, Asi. *The Concept of the Merkabah in Thirteenth Century Jewish Esotericism—"Sod ha-Egoz" and Its Development.* Doctoral dissertation. Jerusalem: Hebrew University, 1986. (h.)

Feuchtwanger, Naomi. "The Coronation of the Virgin and the Bride." *Jewish Art* 12–13 (1987).

Feuillet, Andre. "Les Vingt-Quatre Vieillards de l'Apocalypse." *Revue Biblique* 65 (1958): 5–32.

Fishbane, Michael. "Some Forms of Divine Appearance in Ancient Jewish Thought." In *From Ancient Israel to Modern Judaism . . . Essays in Honor of Marvin Fox*, ed. J. Neusner et al. Atlanta, Scholars Press, 1989.

Flusser, David. "Sanktus und Gloria." In *Abraham unser Vater: . . . Festschrift für Otto Michel*. Leiden: Brill, 1963, pp. 129–52.

Frankfort, Henri. *Kingship and the Gods*. Chicago: University of Chicago Press, 1978.

Frazer, James and Gaster, Theodore. *The New Golden Bough*. New York: New American Library, 1959.

Friedländer, Moritz. *Der vorchristliche judische Gnostizismus*. Göttingen, 1898.

Frymer-Kensky, Tikva. *In the Wake of the Goddess*. New York: Free Press, 1992.

Gaster, Theodore. *Festivals of the Jewish Year*. New York: William Sloane, 1955.

———. *Thespis*. New York: Anchor, 1961.

———. *Myth, Legend, and Custom in the Old Testament*. Gloucester, MA: Peter Smith, 1981.

Ginzberg, Louis. *Legends of the Jews*. 7 vols. Philadelphia: Jewish Publication Society, 1909–38.

Gollancz, H. , ed. *Sepher Maphteah Shelomo*. Oxford: Oxford University Press, 1914.

Goodenough, E. R. *Jewish Symbols in the Greco-Roman World*. 13 vols. New York: Pantheon, 1953–68.

Gordon, Cyrus H. "Aramaic Incantation Bowls." *Orientalia* 10 (1941): 272–84.

Gottlieb, H. "Myth in the Psalms." In *Myth in the Old Testament*, ed. B. Otzen et al. Londom: SCM, 1980.

Grätz, Heinrich. *Gnostizismus und Judenthum*. Krotoschin, 1846.

Gray, J. *I and II Kings*. Philadelphia: Old Testament Library, 1975.

Green, Arthur. "The Children in Egypt and the Theophany at the Sea." *Judaism* 24 (1975): 446–56.

———. "The Zaddik as Axis Mundi in Later Judaism." *JAAR* 45 (1977): 327–47.

———. *Tormented Master: A Life of Rabbi Nahman of Bratslav*. Tuscaloosa, AL: University of Alabama Press, 1979.

———. "Bride, Spouse, Daughter: Images of the Feminine in Classical Jewish Sources." In *On Being a Jewish Feminist: A Reader*, ed. S. Heschel. New York: Schocken, 1983, pp. 248–60.

———. "Religion and Mysticism: The Case of Judaism." In *Take Judaism for Example*, ed. J. Neusner. Chicago: University of Chicago Press, 1983, pp. 67–91.

———, ed. *Jewish Spirituality*. 2 vols. New York: Crossroad, 1986–87.

———. "The Song of Songs in Early Jewish Mysticism." *Orim: A Jewish Journal at Yale* 2 (1987): 49–63.

Greenfield, Jonas. "Lexicographical Notes II." *HUCA* 30 (1959): 141–51.

Grözinger, Karl. *Ich bin der Herr, Dein Gott! Eine rabbinische Homilie zum ersten Gebot (PesR 20).* Frankfurt: Lang, 1976.

Gruenwald, Itamar. "Preliminary Critical Edition of Sefer Yezira." *Israel Oriental Studies* 1 (1971): 154ff. (h.)

———. "Jewish Sources for the Gnostic Texts from Nag Hammadi?" *WCJS* 6 (1973) 3: 45–56.

———. "Knowledge and Vision: Towards a Clarification of Two Gnostic 'Concepts' in the Light of Their Alleged Origins." *Israel Oriental Studies* 3 (1973): 63–107.

———. *Apocalyptic and Merkavah Mysticism.* Leiden: Brill, 1980.

———. "Aspects of the Jewish-Gnostic Controversy." In *The Rediscovery of Gnosticism*, ed. B. Layton. Leiden: Brill, 1981, pp. 713–23.

———. "Shirat ha-Mal'akhim, ha-Qedushah, u-Ve'ayat Ḥibburah shel Sifrut ha-Hekhalot." In *Peraqim be-Toledot Yerushalayim bi-Yemey Bayyit Sheni: Sefer Zikaron le-Avraham Shalit.* Jerusalem: Ben Zvi Institute, 1981, pp. 459–81.

———. "Jewish Merkavah Mysticism and Gnosticism." In *Studies in Jewish Mysticism*, ed. J. Dan and F. Talmage. Cambridge, MA: Association for Jewish Studies, 1982, pp. 41–55.

———. "The Impact of Priestly Traditions on the Creation of Merkavah Mysticism and the Shiur Komah." In *EJM*, pp. 65–120. (h.)

———. "Jewish Mysticism's Transition from Sefer Yesira to the Bahir." *JSJT* 6 (1987): 15–54. (h.)

———. Ha-Ketav, ha-Mikhtav, weha-Shem ha-Meforash—Magiah, Ruḥaniyyut, u-Mistiqah." In *Massu'ot: Studies in Kabbalistic Literature and Jewish Philosophy in Memory of Prof. Ephraim Gottlieb*, ed. M. Oron and A. Goldreich. Jerusalem: Bialik Institute, 1994, pp. 75–98.

Habermann, A. M., ed. *Shirey ha-Yiḥud weha-Kavod.* Jerusalem: Mossad Harav Kook, 1949.

Hallo, William. "Cult, Statue, and Divine Image: A Preliminary Study." In *Scripture in Context II*, ed. W. Hallo et al. Winona Lake, IN: Eisenbrauns, 1983.

———. "Texts, Statues, and the Cult of the Divine King." In *Congress Volume* (*Vetus Testamentum* Supplements #40) Leiden: E. J. Brill, 1988.

Halperin, David. *The Merkabah in Rabbinic Literature.* Leiden: E. J. Brill, 1980.

———. *The Faces of the Chariot.* Tübingen: J.C.B. Mohr, 1988.

Halpern, Baruch. *The Constitution of the Monarchy in Israel.* Chico, CA: Scholars Press, 1981.

Haran, Menahem. "The Shining of Moses' Face: A Case Study of Biblical and Ancient Near Eastern Iconography." In *In the Shelter of Elyon: Essays . . . in Honor of G. W. Ahlstrom*, ed. W. B. Barrick. Sheffield: JSOT, 1984.

Hayman, A. P. "Sefer Yesira and the Hekhalot Literature." In *EJM*, pp. 71–86.

Heinemann, Joseph. *Prayer in the Period of the Tanna'im and the Amora'im.* Jerusalem: Magnes, 1966. (h.)

———. *'Iyyuney Tefillah.* Jerusalem: Magnes, 1983.

Heschel, Abraham J. *Torah min ha-Shamayim.* Vol. 2. London: Soncino, 1965; New York: JTSA, 1990.

Himmelfarb, Martha. *Ascent to Heaven in Jewish and Christian Apocalypses*. New York: Oxford University Press, 1993.

Hirschman, Marc. *Mikra and Midrash: A Comparison of Rabbinics and Patristics*. [Israel]: Ha-kibbutz ha-Meuchad, 1992. (h.)

Hocart, A. M. *Kings and Councillors*. Cairo: Egyptian University, 1936.

Hoffer, A. "Perush ʾal shem ben 12 u-ven 42 u-ven 72 otiyyot." *Ha-Ṣofeh me-Ereṣ Hagar* 2 (1912): 127–32.

Horowitz, Carmi. "Aggadic Interpretation in the Derashot of Rabbi Joshua Ibn Shuʿeib." *JSJT* 5 (1986): 113–39. (h.)

Horowitz, C. M., ed. *Bet ʿEqed ha-ʾAggadot*. Frankfurt-am-Main: E. Slovottski, 1881.

Ibn Shmuel, J. *Midreshey Geʾulah*. Jerusalem: Mossad Bialik, 1954.

Idel, Moshe. *The Writings of Abraham Abulafia and His Teaching*. Doctoral dissertation, Hebrew University, 1976. (h.)

———. "Demut ha-Adam she-meʿal la-Sefirot." *Daʿat* 4 (1980): 41–56.

———. "The Image of Man above the Sefirot." *Daʿat* 4 (1980): 41–55. (h.)

———. "The Concept of the Torah in Heikhalot Literature and in the Kabbalah." *JSJT* 1 (1981): 23–84. (h.)

———. "Kabbalistic Material from the School of R. David ben Yehudah he-Hasid." *Jerusalem Studies in Jewish Thought* 2 (1983): 170–93. (h.)

———. "Enoch Is Metatron." In *EJM*, pp. 151–70. (h.)

———. "The Problem of the Sources of the Bahir." *JSJT* 6 (1987): 55–72 (h.).

———. *Kabbalah: New Perspectives*. New Haven: Yale University Press, 1988.

———. "Jewish Magic from the Renaissance to Early Hasidism." In *Religion, Science, and Magic, in Concert and in Conflict*, ed. J. Neusner et al. New York: Oxford, 1989, pp. 82–117.

———. *Golem: Jewish Magical and Mystical Traditions on the Artificial Anthropoid*. Albany, State University of New York, 1990.

———. "Defining Kabbalah: The Kabbalah of the Divine Names." In *Mystics of the Book: Themes, Topics, and Typology*, ed. R. A. Herrera. New York: P. Lang, 1993, pp. 97–122.

———. *Hasidism: Between Ecstasy and Magic*. Albany: State University of New York, 1995.

Idelsohn, Abraham Z. *Jewish Liturgy and Its Development*. New York: Holt, 1932.

International Congress for the History of Religions VIII. *The Sacral Kingship*. Leiden: E. J. Brill, 1959.

James, E. O. *Myth and Ritual in the Ancient Near East*. London: Thames and Hudson, 1958.

Johnson, Aubrey R. *Sacred Kingship in Ancient Israel*. Cardiff: University of Wales Press, 1967.

Jonas, Hans. *The Gnostic Religion*. Boston: Beacon, 1958.

Kapah, Joseph. *Yahadut Teman: Pirqey Meḥqar we-ʿIyyun*. Jerusalem: Ben Zvi Institute, 1976.

Kiener, Ronald. "The Hebrew Paraphrase of Saadia Gaon's Kitāb al-Amānāt waʾl-Itiqādāt. *AJS* Review 11 (1986): 1–25.

Knohl, Yisrael. *Tefisat ha-Elohut weha-Pulḥan be-Torat Kehunah uva-Askolat ha-Qedushah*. Unpublished doctoral dissertation, Hebrew University, 1988.

Kohler, Kaufmann. "The Origin and Composition of the Eighteen Benedictions." *HUCA* 1 (1924): 387–425.

Kraeling, C. H. *Anthropos and the Son of Man: A Study in the Religious Syncretism of the Hellenistic Orient*. New York: Columbia University Press, 1927.

Kraus, Samuel. *Talmudische Archäologie*. Leipzig: G. Fock, 1911.

———. *Paras we-Romi ba-Talmud uva-Midrashim*. Jerusalem: Mossad Harav Kook, 1948.

Lamm, Norman. *Halakhot we-Halikhot*. Jerusalem: Mossad Ha-Rav Kook, 1990.

Layton, Bentley, ed. *The Rediscovery of Gnosticism*. Vol. 2, *Sethian Gnosticism*. Leiden: E. J. Brill, 1981.

Levenson, Jon. *Sinai and Zion*. Minneapolis: Winston, 1985.

———. "The Jerusalem Temple in Devotional and Visionary Experience." In *Jewish Spirituality*, Vol 1, ed. A. Green, pp. 32–61.

Liber, M. "La Récitation du schema et des Bénédictions." *REJ* 58 (1909): 1–22.

Lieberman, Saul. *Sheqiʿin*. Jerusalem: Bamberger and Wahrmann, 1939.

———. *Hellenism in Jewish Palestine*. New York: Jewish Theological Seminary, 1950.

———. *Tosefta Ki-Feshuṭah*. New York: Jewish Theological Seminary, 1955–73.

Liebes, Yehuda. *Sections of the Zohar Lexicon*. Unpublished doctoral dissertation. Jerusalem: Hebrew University, 1976. (h.)

———. "R. Solomon Ibn Gabirol's Use of the Sefer Yeṣira and a Commentary on the Poem 'I Love Thee.'" *Jerusalem Studies in Jewish Thought* 6: 3–4 (1987): 73–123. (h.)

———. *Ḥeteʾo shel Elisha*. Jerusalem: Academon, 1990.

———. *Studies in Jewish Myth and Jewish Messianism*. Albany: State University of New York, 1993.

Lys, D. "L'Onction dans la Bible." *Etudes Theologiques et Religieuses* 29 (1954): 3ff.

Mach, Michael. *Entwicklungsstadien des jüdischen Engelglaubens in vorrabbinischer Zeit*. Tübingen: Mohr, 1992.

Mach, Rudolf. *Der Zaddik in Talmud und Midrasch*. Leiden: E.J. Brill, 1957.

Maier, J. *Vom Kultus zur Gnosis*. Salzburg: Müller, 1964.

Marcus, Ivan. *Piety and Society: The Jewish Pietists of Medieval Germany*. Leiden: E. J. Brill, 1981.

Marmorstein, Arthur "Binden und Lösen im Zauber." *Jahrbuch für jüdische Volkskunde* 1 (1923): 291ff.

Matt, Daniel. "Ayin: The Concept of Nothingness in Jewish Mysticism." In *The Problem of Pure Consciousness: Mysticism and Philosophy*, ed. R. Forman. New York: Oxford University Press, 1990.

Matter, E. Ann. *The Voice of My Beloved: The Song of Songs in Western Medieval Christianity*. Philadelphia: University of Pennsylvania Press, 1990.

Mauss, Marcel. *The Gift: Forms and Functions of Exchange in Archaic Societies*, tr. Ian Cunnison. Glencoe: Free Press, 1954. Originally published as *Essai sur le don*. Année sociologique, Novelle série I, 1924.

Meeks, Wayne. *The Prophet-King: Moses Traditions and the Johanine Christology*. Leiden: E. J. Brill, 1967.

Merhavya, Ch. "Sepher ha-Razim, Ed. . . . by M. Margalioth." *Kirjath Sefer* 42 (1967): 297–303. (h.)

Milgrom, Jacob. *The JPS Torah Commentary: Numbers*. Philadelphia: Jewish Publication Society, 1989.

Mirsky, Aharon. "*Yesod Qerovah*." *Sinai* 57 (1965): 127–32.

———. *Ha'Piyuṭ: The Development of Post-Biblical Poetry in Eretz Israel and the Diaspora*. Jerusalem: Magnes, 1990. (h.)

Montgomery, James A. *Aramaic Incantation Texts*. Philadelphia: University Museum, 1913.

———, ed. *The Samaritans, the Earliest Jewish Sect: Their History, Theology, and Literature*. Philadelphia, 1907; rpt. New York: Ktav, 1968.

Morgenstern, J. "Moses with the Shining Face." *HUCA* 2 (1925): 1–27.

Mowinckel, S. *Psalmenstudien*. Kristiana: Jacob Dybwad, 1921.

Muffs, Yochanan. *Love and Joy: Law, Language, and Religion in Ancient Israel*. New York: Jewish Theological Seminary, 1992.

Myers, C., and E. Myers. *Haggai, Zechariah 1–8*. Garden City, NY: Doubleday, 1987.

Naveh, J., and S. Shaked. *Amulets and Magic Bowls: Aramaic Incantations of Late Antiquity*. Jerusalem: Magnes, 1985.

Nemoy, L. "Al-Qirqasani's Account of the Jewish Sects and Christianity." *HUCA* 7 (1930): 350ff.

Niditsch, Susan. "The Cosmic Adam: Man as Mediator in Rabbinic Literature." *JJS* 34 (1983): 137–46.

Obermann, Julian. "Two Magic Bowls: New Incantation Texts from Babylonia." *American Journal of Semitic Languages and Literatures* 57 (1940): 1–31.

Pallis, S. *The Babylonian Akitu Festival*. Copenhagen: Bianco Lunos, 1926.

Patai, Raphael. *Man and Temple*. London: Thomas Nelson, 1947.

Paul, Shalom M. "Jerusalem—A City of Gold." *Israel Exploration Journal* 17 (1967): 259–63.

Pearson, B. A. "Biblical Exegesis in Gnostic Literature." *Armenian and Biblical Studies*, ed. Michael E. Stone. Jerusalem: St. James Press, 1976.

Pedaya, Haviva. " 'Flaw' and 'Correction' in the Concept of the Godhead in the Teachings of Rabbi Isaac the Blind." *JSJT* 6 (1987): 157–286. (h.)

———. "The Provençal Stratum in the Redaction of Sefer ha-Bahir." *JSJT* 9 (=Pines Jubilee Volume, 1990): 139–64. (h.)

Pines, Shlomo. "Points of Similarity between the Doctrine of the Sefirot in the Sefer Yezirah and a Text from the Pseudo-Clementine Homilies: The Implications of This Resemblance." *Israel Academy of Sciences and Humanities* 7: 3 (1989): 63–142.

Prigent, P. "Ce que l'oeil n'a pas vu; I Cor. II: 9." *Theologische Zeitschrift* 14 (1958): 416–29.

Quispel, G. "Der Gnostische Anthropos und die jüdische Tradition." *Eranos Jahrbuch* 22 (1953): 195–234.

Rosenau, W. "Some Notes on Akteriel." *Paul Haupt Festschrift*. Leipzig: Hinrichs, 1926, pp. 103–5.

Saldarini, Anthony. "Apocalypses and 'Apocalyptic' in Rabbinic Literature and Mysticism." *Semeia* 4 (1979): 187–205.

Sarna, Nahum. *The JPS Torah: Exodus*. Philadephia: Jewish Publication Society, 1989.

Schaefer, Peter. *Rivalität zwischen Englen und Menschen*. Berlin: de Gruyter, 1975.

———. "Die Beschwörung des Sar ha-Panim." *Frankfurter Judaistische Beiträge* 6 (1978): 107–45.

———. *Synopse zur Hekhalot-Literatur*. Tübingen: J.C.B. Mohr, 1981. [abbreviated in notes as Schaefer, *Synopse*]

———. "Gershom Scholem Reconsidered: The Aim and Purpose of Early Jewish Mysticism." The Twelfth Sacks Lecture. Oxford, 1986.

———. *Konkordanz zur Hekhalot-Literatur*. Tübingen: J.C.B. Mohr, 1986–88.

———. *The Hidden and Manifest God: Some Major Themes in Early Jewish Mysticism*. Albany: SUNY, 1992.

Scheindlin, Raymond. *The Gazelle: Medieval Hebrew Poems on God, Israel, and the Soul*. Philadelphia: Jewish Publication Society, 1991.

Schiffman, Lawrence. "A Forty-Two Letter Divine Name in the Aramaic Magic Bowls." *Bulletin of the Institute of Jewish Studies* 1 (1973): 97–102.

———. "*Merkavah* Speculations at Qumran: The 4Q Serekh Shirot 'Olat ha-Shabbat." *Mystics, Philosophers, and Politicians: Essays in Jewish Intellectual History in Honor of Alexander Altmann*, ed. J. Reinharz and D. Swetchinski. Durham: Duke University Press, 1982, pp. 35–45.

———. "Hekhalot Mysticism and the Qumran Literature." *EJM* 121–38.

Schoedel, W. R. "Monism and the Gospel of Truth." *The Rediscovery of Gnosticism*. Vol. 1, *The School of Valentinius*. Leiden: E. J. Brill, 1980, pp. 379–90.

Scholem, Gershom. "*Qabbalot R. Yaʿaqov we-R. Yiṣḥaq Beney R. Yaʿaqov ha-Kohen*." *Madaʿey ha-Yadahut* 2 (1927): 165–293.

———. *Kitvey Yad ba-Qabbalah*. Jerusalem: Hebrew University, 1930.

———. "*Teʿudah Ḥadashah le-Toledot Reshit ha-Qabbalah*." In *Sefer Bialik*, ed. Y. Fishman. Tel Aviv: Waʿad Yovel, 1934, pp. 141–62.

———. "ʿIqvotaw shel Gabirol ba-Qabbalah." *Maʾasef Sofrey Ereṣ Yisraʾel*. Tel Aviv: Aggudat ha-Sofrim, 1940. pp. 160–78.

———. *Major Trends in Jewish Mysticism*. New York: Schocken, 1954.

———. *Reshit ha-Qabbalah*. Jerusalem: Schocken, 1948.

———. "The Paradisic Garb of Souls and the Origin of the Concept of Ḥaluka de-Rabbanan." *Tarbiz* 24 (1955): 290–306. (h.)

———, ed. *Jewish Gnosticism, Merkabah Mysticism, and Talmudic Tradition*. New York: Jewish Theological Seminary, 1960. [abbreviated in notes as Scholem, *Jewish Gnosticism*]

———. *Ursprung und Anfänge der Kabbala*. Berlin, de Gruyter, 1962.

———. *On the Kabbalah and Its Symbolism*. New York: Schocken, 1969.

———. "Havdalah de-Rabbi ʿAkivaʾ." *Tarbiẓ* 50 (1981): 243–81.

———. *Origins of the Kabbalah*. Phladelphia: Jewish Publication Society, 1987. [abbreviated in notes as Scholem, *Origins*]

———. *On the Mystical Shape of the Godhead*. New York: Schocken, 1991.

———. *Sefer ha-Zohar shel Gershom Scholem*. Handwritten notes to the Zohar text. 5 vols. Jerusalem: Magnes Press, 1992.

Schultz, Joseph. "Angelic Opposition to the Ascension of Moses and the Revelation of the Law." *JQR* n. s. 61 (1970–71): 282–307.

Segal, Alan F. *Two Powers in Heaven: Early Rabbinic Reports about Christianity and Gnosticism*. Leiden: E. J. Brill, 1977.

Sendor, Mark. *The Emergence of Provençal Kabbalah*. Doctoral dissertation, Harvard University, 1994.

Shahar, S. "Catharism and the Beginnings of the Kabbalah in Languedoc." *Tarbiẓ* 40 (1971): 483–507. (h.)

Simonsen, David. "Unechte Verse in שיר הכבוד." *MGWJ* 37 (1893): 463–67.

Smith, Morton. "Some Observations on Hekhalot Rabbati." *Biblical and Other Studies*, ed. A. Altmann. Cambridge: Harvard University Press, 1963, pp. 142–60.

Snaith, Norman Henry. *The Jewish New Year Festival: Its Origin and Development*. London: SPCK, 1947.

Stern. S. M. "'The First in Thought Is the Last in Action': The History of a Saying Attributed to Aristotle." *Journal of Semitic Studies* 7 (1962): 234–52.

Stroumza, G. "Aher: A Gnostic." In *The Rediscovery of Gnosticism*, ed. B. Layton. Leiden: E. J. Brill, 1981, vol. 2, pp. 808–18.

Strugnell, John. *The Angelic Liturgy. Vetus Testamentum*, Supplement #7 (1959–60).

Swartz, Michael. *Mystical Prayer in Ancient Judaism: An Analysis of Maʿaseh Merkavah*. Tübingen: J.C.B. Mohr, 1992.

Tal, Shelomo. "*Ana be-khoah*." *Sinai* 92 (1982–83): 287–88.

Thompson, R. Campbell. *Semitic Magic*. London: Luzac, 1908.

Thorndike, Lynn. *A History of Magic and Experimental Science*. London: Macmillan, 1923.

Tishby, Isaiah, ed. *Wisdom of the Zohar*. 3 vols. Oxford: Oxford University Press, 1989.

Trachtenberg, Joshua. *Jewish Magic and Superstition*. New York: Behrman's Jewish Book House, 1939.

Twersky, Isadore. *Rabad of Posquieres*. Cambridge: Harvard University Press, 1962.

Urbach, Yaʿakov. "Be-sod qeriʾat shemaʾ." *Sinai* 92 (1982–83): 86–90.

Vaux, Roland de. *Ancient Israel*. New York: McGraw-Hill, 1961.

———. *The Bible and the Ancient Near East*. Garden City, NY: Doubleday, 1971.

Verman, Mark, ed. *The Books of Contemplation: Medieval Jewish Mystical Sources*. Albany: State University of New York, 1992.

Vermes, Geza. *Jesus the Jew: A Historian's Reading of the Gospels*. New York: Macmillan, 1974.

Von Rad, G. "Das jüdische Königsritual." *Theologische Literaturzeitung* 62 (1947): 211–16.

———. *The Problem of the Hexateuch*. Edinburgh: Oliver and Boyd, 1966.

Weinfeld, Moshe. "*Ha-Sifrut ha-Shumerit we-Sefer Tehillim: Mavoʾ le-Meḥqar Hashwaʾati*." *Bet Miqra* 19: 2 (57) (1974): 136–60.

———. "The Traces of Kedushat Yozer and Pesukey de-Zimra in the Qumran Literature and in Ben Sira." *Tarbiz* 45 (1976): 15–26. (h.)

Weinstock, Israel. "Le-Verur ha-Nosaḥ shel Sefer Yeṣirah" *Ṭemirin* 1 (1972): 9–61.

Werner, Eric. *The Sacred Bridge*. New York: Ktav, 1984.

———. "Hebraisms in Prima Clementis." In *Harry Austryn Wolfson Jubilee Volume*. Jerusalem: American Academy for Jewish Research, 1985, pp. 793–818.

Wheatley, M. *The Hieros Gamos in the Ancient Near East and in Israel*. Unpublished doctoral dissertation, University of Iowa, 1966.

Widengren, Geo. *The Ascension of the Apostle and the Heavenly Book*. Uppsala: Lundequist, 1950.

———. *The King and the Tree of Life in Ancient Near Eastern Religion*. Uppsala: Lundequist, 1951.

———. *Sakrales Königtum in Alten Testament*. Stuttgart: W. Kohlhammer, 1955.

Wieder, Naphtali. "The Controversy about the Liturgical Composition ʿYismaḥ Moshe': Opposition and Defence." In *Studies in Aggadah, Targum, and Jewish Liturgy in Memory of Joseph Heinemann*, ed. J. Petuchowski and E. Fleischer. Jerusalem: Magnes, 1981, pp. 75–89. (h.)

Wolfson, Eliot. "Circumcision, Vision of God, and Textual Interpretation: From Midrashic Trope to Mystical Symbol." *History of Religion* 27:2 (1987): 189–215.

———. "Mystical-Theurgical Dimensions of Prayer in Sefer ha-Rimmon." In *Approaches to Judaism in Medieval Times*, ed. D. Blumenthal. 3 vols. Atlanta: Scholars Press, 1988.

———. "Biblical Accentuation in a Mystical Key: Kabbalistic Interpretation of the Teʿamim." *Journal of Jewish Music and Liturgy* 11 (1988–89): 1–16; 12 (1989/90): 1–13.

———. "Female Imaging of the Torah: From Literary Metaphor to Religious Symbol." In *From Ancient Israel to Modern Judaism—Intellect in Quest of Understanding: Essays in Honor of Marvin Fox*, ed. J. Neusner et al. Atlanta: Scholars Press, 1989, vol. 2, pp. 271–307.

———. "Merkavah Traditions in Philosophical Garb: Judah Halevi Reconsidered." *PAAJR* 57 (1991): 179–242.

———. "Images of God's Feet: Some Observations on the Divine Body in Judaism." In *People of the Body*. Ed. H. Eilberg-Schwartz. Albany: State University of New York Press, 1992, pp. 143–81. [abbreviated in the notes as Wolfson, "Feet"]

———. "*Yeridah la-Merkavah*: Typology of Ecstasy and Enthronement in Ancient Jewish Mysticism." In *Mystics of the Book: Themes, Topics, and Typologies*, ed. R. A. Herrera. New York: Lang, 1993, pp. 13–44.

———. "*Demut Yaʿaqov Ḥaquqah be-Kisse' ha-Kavod*." In *Massu'ot: Studies in Kabbalistic Literature and Jewish Philosophy in Memory of Prof. Ephraim Gottlieb*, ed. M. Oron and A. Goldreich. Jerusalem: Bialik Institute, 1994, 131–85.

———. *Through a Speculum That Shines: Vision and Imagination in Medieval Jewish Mysticism*. Princeton : Princeton University Press, 1994. [abbreviated in the notes as Wolfson, *Speculum*]

———. *Along the Path: Studies in Kabbalistic Myth, Symbolism, and Hermeneutics*. Albany: State University of New York Press, 1995.

———. *Circle in the Square: Studies in the Use of Gender in Kabbalistic Symbolism*. Albany: State University of New York Press, 1995.

Wolfson, H. A. "Maimonides on Negative Attributes." In *Louis Ginzberg Jubilee Volume*. New York: Jewish Theological Seminary, 1945, pp. 411–46.

Yaʿari, A. *Toledot Ḥag Simḥat Torah*. Jerusalem: Mossad Ha-Rav Kook, 1964.

Yeivin, S. "King and Covenant." *Journal of Semitic Studies* 2 (1957): 6ff.

Zulay, M. *ʿIyyuney Lashon be-Fiyyuṭey Yannai*. In *Studies of the Research Institute for Hebrew Poetry in Jerusalem*. Vol. 6. Jerusalem: Schocken, 1945, pp. 161–248.

Selective Index of Texts

Note: The citations in the left column are from the primary sources; those in the right column locate the chapter and note numbers in this book where these passages are discussed and may be quoted (sometimes in the corresponding text). Parenthetical references next to the citations in the left column are to specific editions of relevant primary sources. Appendix citations are not indexed.

BIBLE

Genesis

28:12 Chap. 4, n.24

Exodus

15:18 Chap. 3, n.28
33:18 Chap. 11, n.13
33:20 Chap. 11, n.13
34:7 Chap. 13, n.31

Numbers

6:27 Chap. 5, n.17
11:17 Chap. 12, n.21
11:25 Chap. 12, n.21
12:8 Chap. 11, n.13
16:4 Chap. 12, n.23

Deuteronomy

16:20 Chap. 13, n.44
26:19 Chap. 12, n.35

Judges

20:43 Chap. 1, n.14

I Samuel

15:30 Chap. 1, n.3
10:17–24 Chap. 1, n.16

II Samuel

3:18 Chap. 1, n.3
5:2 Chap. 1, n.3
5:3 Chap. 1, n.16
7:7–8,11 Chap. 1, n.3
15:10 Chap. 1, n.16

I Kings

1:32–39 Chap. 1, n.16

II Kings

1:4–20 Chap. 1, n.16
11:4–12 Chap. 1, n.16

Isaiah

6:3 Chap. 2, n.25; Chap. 10, n.16
28:5 Chap. 11, n.22
33:17 Chap. 11, n.17
49:3 Chap. 12, n.35
59:17 Chap. 10, n.53
61:10 Chap. 9, n.10

Jeremiah

7 Chap. 14, n.37

Ezekiel

3:12 Chap. 2, n.21; Chap. 2, n.25
16:12 Chap. 9, n.10

Zechariah

6:11–15 Chap. 1, n.21

Malachi

1:11 Chap. 4, n.23

Psalms

19:9 Chap. 8, n.13
50 Chap. 14, n.4
68:18 Chap. 8, n.23
68:26 Chap. 9, n.3
139:5 Chap. 3, n.9
146:10 Chap. 3, n.28

Proverbs

10:6 Chap. 11, n.15
13:9 Chap. 8, n.13

Song of Songs

1:1 Chap. 9, n.3
5:11 Chap. 12, n.35

Nehemiah

9:5 Chap. 5, n.18

I Chronicles

28:5 Chap. 12, n.5

II Chronicles

23 Chap. 1, n.16
23:20 Chap. 12, n.5

APOCRYPHA AND PSEUDEPIGRAPHA

1 Enoch

39:12 Chap. 2, n.20

2 Enoch

21 Chap. 2, n.20
22:8–10 Chap. 7, n.4

MISHNAH

Bikkurim

3 Chap. 9, n.21

Shabbat

5:1 Chap. 9, n.17

Pesaḥim

4:8 Chap. 5, n.18

*Yoma*ʾ

3:8 Chap. 5, n.18
4:1 Chap. 5, n.18

Megillah

4:8 Chap. 6, n.20

Soṭah

9:14 Chap. 9, n.15

Avot

4:13 Chap. 13, n.21
5:1 Chap. 13, n.3

Yadayim

3:5 Chap. 9, n.2

Tosefta

Berakhot

1:9 Chap. 2, n.22

Soṭah

3 Chap. 3, n.6
13 Chap. 1, n.21
13:8 Chap. 5, n.11
15:8 Chap. 9, n.15

Yadayim

2:5 Chap. 5, n.11

Palestinian Talmud

Pesaḥim

31b Chap. 5, n.18

Ḥagigah

2 Chap. 13, n.22

Soṭah

24b Chap. 9, n.17

Babylonian Talmud

Berakhot

3a Chap. 7, n.15
6a Chap. 6, n.14; Chap. 9, n.22
7a Chap. 7, n.15
11a Chap. 11, n.11
12a Chap. 2, n.1
18a Chap. 13, n.25
21b Chap. 2, n.22
28a Chap. 9, n.19
34b Chap. 7, n.24
55a Chap. 6, n.3

Shabbat

88a Chap. 8, n.1
88b Chap. 8, n.23; Chap. 11, n.10
88b-89a Chap. 8, n.17
89a Chap. 9, n.30

ʿEruvin

13a Chap. 6, n.1

Pesaḥim

56a Chap. 5, n.18

Yoma'

21b Chap. 9, n.25
37a Chap. 5, n.18
54a Chap. 9, n.25

Rosh Ha-Shanah

16b Chap. 1, n.10
32a Chap. 13, n.3

Ta'anit

16b Chap. 5, n.18
26b Chap. 9, n.1

Megillah

12b Chap. 4, n.3
15b Chap. 8, n.10; Chap. 10, n.51

Mo'ed Qaṭan

16b Chap. 6, n.24

Ḥagigah

12b Chap. 4, n.12
13b Chap. 3, nn.7, 25; Chap. 10, n.48 Chap. 13, n.13; Chap. 13, n.14
14b Chap. 9, n.5
15a Chap. 7, n.1
15b Chap. 9, n.28

Yevamot

64a Chap. 4, n.7

Ketubot

6b Chap. 11, n.11

Soṭah

38a Chap. 5, n.11
49a–b Chap. 9, n.17

Qiddushin

71a Chap. 5, nn.5; n.11; n.17

Sanhedrin

111b Chap. 8, n.10; Chap. 10, n.61

Shevu'ot

35b	Chap. 9, n.4
38b	Chap. 6, n.23

Menaḥot

29a	Chap. 13, n.28
35a	Chap. 6, n.20

Ḥullin

91b	Chap. 2, n.22; Chap. 4, n.15

MIDRASH

Mekhilta

PISḤA

16 (ed. Horovitz/Rabin p. 61)	Chap. 5, n.19

BA-ḤODESH

5	Chap. 11, n.7

SHIRTA

4	Chap. 11, n.7

Mekhilta de-Rabbi Shim'on ben Yoḥai

BE-SHALAḤ

15	Chap. 11, n.7

Sifra

SHEMINI

15	Chap. 9, n.5

Sifre Be-Midbar

#119 (ed. Horovitz p. 143)	Chap. 4, n.24

Sifre Zuṭa

NASO'

27	Chap. 5, n.11

Sifre Devarim

#62	Chap. 5, n.11
#306	Chap. 5, nn.14, 19
#356	Chap. 8, n.10

Bereshit Rabbah

27:1	Chap. 11, n.5
65:21	Chap. 5, n.14
68:10	Chap. 13, n.39

Shemot Rabbah

21:4 Chap. 4, n.2
45:2 Chap. 8, n.2
51:8 Chap. 8, n.2
52:5 Chap. 9, n.5

Wa-Yiqra' Rabbah

2:5 Chap. 11, n.23
24:9 Chap. 4, n.4

Be-Midbar Rabbah

2:3 Chap. 6, n.1
3:2 Chap. 11, n.17
12:3 Chap. 12, n.18
19:4 Chap. 9, n.29

Devarim Rabbah

2:36 Chap. 3, n.23; Chap. 5, n.19

Shir ha-Shirim Rabbah

4:4 Chap. 6, n.12; Chap. 8, n.4
5:4 Chap. 8, n.7

Echah Rabbah

2:1 (ed. Buber p. 96) Chap. 13, n.26

Tanḥuma

TEṢAWWEH
11 Chap. 8, n.2

TISSA'
8 Chap. 11, n.23

SHELAḤ
13 Chap. 8, n.2

PEQUDEY
3 Chap. 8, n.10

Tanhuma Buber

WA-'ERA'
9 Chap. 8, n.2

YITRO
14 Chap. 7, n.14

TEṢAWWEH
7 Chap. 8, n.2

SHELAḤ
addendum 1: Chap. 8, n.2

ḤUQQAT
4 Chap. 9, n.29

Yelammedenu (ed. Jellinek, *Bet ha-Midrasch*)
6:89 Chap. 13, n.13

Midrash Tehillim (ed. Buber)
8:7(78) Chap. 8, n.11
19:7(166f.) Chap. 4, n.2; Chap. 11, n.15
88:2(380) Chap. 4, n.2
91:2(397) Chap. 8, n.5
103:8(435) Chap. 8, n.4; Chap. 8, n.5

Midrash Mishle
47a Chap. 12, n.23

Aggadat Shir ha-Shirim (ed. Schecter)
ln. 1000 Chap. 9, n.8
ln. 220 Chap. 5, n.19

Midrash Shir ha-Shirim (ed. Gruenhuet)
5:2(38a) Chap. 11, n.10
5:11(39b) Chap. 12, n.35

Pesiqta de-Rav Kahana (ed. Mandelbaum)
1:1(2f.) Chap. 12, n.30
1:3(7) Chap. 9, n.5; Chap. 13, n.24
2:7(29) Chap. 11, n.23
4:4(67) Chap. 8, n.12
9:1(147) Chap. 10, n.20

Pesiqta Rabbati (ed. Friedmann)
10(37a) Chap. 8, n.4
10(38b) Chap. 11, n.23
14(62b) Chap. 8, n.12
20(97a) Chap. 9, n.27
20(97a) Chap. 3, n.17
20(98b) Chap. 8, n.23
21(100b) Chap. 11, n.7
21(102a) Chap. 8, n.11
21(103b) Chap. 8, n.4
33(154a) Chap. 8, n.5

Pirqey Rabbi Eliezer
3 Chap. 4, n.8
4 Chap. 5, n.4
11 Chap. 12, n.32
18 Chap. 13, n.40

41 Chap. 8, n.11
47 Chap. 8, n.8

Avot de-Rabbi Nathan (ed. Schechter)

37(110) Chap. 13, n.45
12(56) Chap. 5, n.2

Targum Yerushalmi

BERESHIT
49:22 Chap. 13, n.13

HEKHALOT

Passages are listed according to the number in Schaefer, *Synopse*

#15 Chap. 7, n.2
#15–17 Chap. 4, n.14
#16 Chap. 6, n.1
#18 Chap. 7, n.3
#20 Chap. 7, n.1
#28 Chap. 1, n.10
#29 Chap. 3, n.6
#33 Chap. 7, n.6
#34 Chap. 7, n.7
#41–42 Chap. 7, n.8
#46 Chap. 5, n.7; Chap. 12, n.35
#59 Chap. 6, n.3
#71 Chap. 5, n.1; Chap. 5, n.2
#73 Chap. 8, n.14
#79 Chap. 3, n.22
#115 Chap. 3, n.6
#122–26 Chap. 7, n.23
#168 Chap. 5, n.10
#170–71 Chap. 7, n.9
#243ff. Chap. 7, n.10
#244 Chap. 7, n.11; Chap. 10, n.17
#298 Chap. 6, n.9
#376 Chap. 6, n.12
#390 Chap. 5, n.10
#487 Chap. 6, n.11
#490 Chap. 8, n.14
#501 Chap. 7, n.22
#550 Chap. 6, n.22; Chap. 9, n.28
#552 Chap. 5, n.2
#560 Chap. 12, n.7
#562 Chap. 6, n.7
#582 Chap. 6, n.16
#590 Chap. 5, n.10
#597 Chap. 7, n.1; Chap. 7, n.17
#655 Chap. 6, n.22

#667 Chap. 7, n.20
#679 Chap. 6, n.10
#697 Chap. 5, n.4
#698 Chap. 5, n.6
#727 Chap. 13, n.22
#784 Chap. 13, n.22
#840 Chap. 13, n.22
#841 Chap. 5, n.1
#949 Chap. 5, n.6; Chap. 5, n.8
#951 Chap. 6, n.11
#952 Chap. 10, n.31
#961 Chap. 5, n.10

NEW TESTAMENT

Matthew

12:46–50 Chap. 3, n.16
28:10 Chap. 3, n.16

Mark

3:31–35 Chap. 3, n.16
10:30 Chap. 3, n.16

Luke

2:14 Chap. 2, n.22

I Corinthians

8:11 Chap. 3, n.16

Hebrews

2:11 Chap. 3, n.16

Revelation

4 Chap. 2, n.22; Chap. 3, n.35

EARLY CHRISTIAN WRITINGS

Apostolic Constitutions 7:33 Chap. 4, n.23
Eusebius, *Praeparatio Evangelica* 3:1 Chap. 8, n.15
Gospel of Truth 2:25–26 Chap. 13, n.39
Hippolytos V:27:3 Chap. 13, n.40
Origen, *De Principiis* 1:8:1 Chap. 4, n.12
Tertullian, *De Corona* ch. 13 Chap. 9, n.12

CLASSICAL WRITINGS

Ammianus Marcellinus 20:4:17 Chap. 1, n.19
Ammianus Marcellinus 21:1:4 Chap. 1, n.19

Philo, *2 Moses* 114	Chap. 5, n.11
Pliny, *Natural History* 21:19, 25:21, 55, 94	Chap. 6, n.7

MISCELLANEOUS JEWISH SOURCES

R. Abraham ben David (cited in Scholem, *Reshit ha-Kabbalah*) 75f.	Chap. 10, n.42
[*Sefer*] *Abudarham* (ed. Jerusalem, 1963), 361f.	Chap. 9, n.21
Arbaʿah Ṭurim Even ha-ʿEzer 65	Chap. 9, n.21
ʿArugat ha-Bosem 1:215	Chap. 2, n.5
ʿArugat ha-Bosem 2:184	Chap. 3, n.28
ʿArugat ha-Bosem 2:184f.	Chap. 3, n.23
ʿArugat ha-Bosem 3:80f.	Chap. 12, n.3
ʿArugat ha-Bosem 3:81	Chap. 10, n.49
ʿArugat ha-Bosem 3:481	Chap. 3, n.7; Chap. 12, n.4; Chap. 12, n.35
ʿArugat ha-Bosem 3:535	Chap. 3, n.17
Sefer ha-Bahir 12, 60	Chap. 13, n.27
Sefer ha-Bahir 17	Chap. 11, n.3
Sefer ha-Bahir 23	Chap. 13, n.20
Sefer ha-Bahir 25	Chap. 13, n.26
Sefer ha-Bahir 33	Chap. 13, n.44
Sefer ha-Bahir 36	Chap. 13, n.32
Sefer ha-Bahir 49	Chap. 12, nn.18, 32
Sefer ha-Bahir 50	Chap. 13, n.44
Sefer ha-Bahir 60	Chap. 13, n.37
Sefer ha-Bahir 61	Chap. 13, n.16
Sefer ha-Bahir 63	Chap. 9, n.7
Sefer ha-Bahir 75	Chap. 13, n.44
Sefer ha-Bahir 79	Chap. 11, n.3
Sefer ha-Bahir 87	Chap. 13, n.33
Sefer ha-Bahir 88	Chap. 13, n.11
Sefer ha-Bahir 89	Chap. 13, n.9
Sefer ha-Bahir 90	Chap. 11, n.3
Sefer ha-Bahir 94	Chap. 13, n.44
Sefer ha-Bahir 96	Chap. 13, n.4
Sefer ha-Bahir 101	Chap. 13, n.22
Sefer ha-Bahir 115	Chap. 13, n.34
Sefer ha-Bahir 116	Chap. 13, n.39
Sefer ha-Bahir 117	Chap. 12, n.40
Sefer ha-Bahir 119	Chap. 13, n.34
Sefer ha-Bahir 123	Chap. 13, n.34
Sefer ha-Bahir 132	Chap. 13, n.37
Sefer ha-Bahir 137	Chap. 13, n.32
Sefer ha-Bahir 141	Chap. 11, n.3
Derishot be-ʿInyeney Malʾakhim (Cordovero) 4:7	Chap. 3, n.12
ʿEmeq ha-Melekh (ed. Bacharach) 178c	Chap. 3, n.12
3 Enoch (ed. Odeberg) 15b	Chap. 7, n.21; Chap. 8, n.22

Haggadat Shema' Yisra'el (ed. Jellinek) *Bet ha-Midrasch* 5:165	Chap. 3, n.23
Ḥarba de-Moshe (ed. Gaster) 3	Chap. 6, n.1
Ḥarba de-Moshe (ed. Gaster) 22	Chap. 5, n.2; Chap. 8, n.6
Havdalah de-Rabbi 'Akiva' (ed. Scholem, *Tarbiz* 50) 262	Chap. 6, n.8
Hekhalot Zuṭarti (ed. Elior) 22, ln. 28	Chap. 5, n.1
Hekhalot Zuṭarti (ed. Elior) 30, ln. 274	Chap. 5, n.3
Hekhalot Zuṭarti (ed. Elior) 28, ln. 223ff.	Chap. 6, n.8
[*Sefer ha*]-*Ḥesheq* 14	Chap. 8, n.10
[*Sefer ha*]-*Ḥesheq* 22	Chap. 4, n.12
[*Sefer ha*]-*Ḥesheq* 39	Chap. 10, n.30
[*Sefer ha*]-*Ḥesheq* 43	Chap. 4, n.12
[*Sefer ha*]-*Ḥesheq* 46	Chap. 10, n.30; Chap. 11, n.13
[*Sefer ha*]-*Ḥesheq* 67	Chap. 4, n.11; Chap. 10, n.7
[*Sefer ha*]-*Ḥokhmah* (R. Eleazar of Worms; ed. Dan, in *Torat ha-Sod*) pp. 119ff.	Chap. 12, n.24
Ketav Tamim (R. Moshe Taku; ed. Dan) 4	Chap. 3, n.7
Kitvey Rabbenu Baḥya (ed. Chavel) 379	Chap. 4, n.8
Kuzari 4:3	Chap. 12, n.33
Ma'ayan Ḥokhmah (ed. Jellinek, *Bet ha-Midrasch*) 1:61	Chap. 8, n.19
Maḥzor Vitry (491; p. 599)	Chap. 9, n.21
[*Sefer ha*]-*Manhig*, laws of prayer, 52	Chap. 2, n.5
Midrash Konen (ed. Jellinek, *Bet ha-Midrasch*) 2:26	Chap. 4, n.9
Midreshey Ge'ulah (ed. Ibn-Shmuel) 7	Chap. 7, n.19
Midreshey Ge'ulah (ed. Ibn-Shmuel) 144–52	Chap. 7, n.25
Mishneh Torah, Laws of Oaths, 11:11–12	Chap. 6, n.23
Sefer ha-Navon (ed. Dan, *'Iyyunim*) 128ff.	Chap. 10, n.21
Oṣar ha-Ge'onim Berakhot (*teshuvot*) 16	Chap. 10, n.25; Chap. 10, n.36; chap. 10, n.38
Oṣar ha-Ge'onim Berakhot (*teshuvot*) 17	Chap. 10, n.27
Oṣar ha-Ge'onim Ḥagigah (*perushim*) 57	Chap. 4, n.10
Otiyyot de-Rabbi 'Akiva' version 2 (ed. Wertheimer) 2:396	Chap. 6, n.1
Otiyyot de-Rabbi 'Akiva' version 2 (ed. Wertheimer) 378f	Chap. 10, n.11
Perush ha-'Aggadot (R. Azriel of Gerona; ed. Tishby) 134	Chap. 12, n.37
Perush Sefer Yeṣirah (R. Judah ben Barzilai) 21	Chap. 10, n.27
Perush Shir ha-Shirim (R. Eleazar of Worms) 3:11	Chap. 12, n.27
Perush Shir ha-Shirim (R. Ezra) (ed. Chavel, *Kitvey RaMBaN*) 2:494f.	Chap. 4, n.2
Perush ha-Torah (Moses ben Nachman) Genesis 46:1	Chap. 12, n.34
Piyyuṭey Rabbi Yannai (ed. Rabinovitz) 2:199f.	Chap. 13, n.13

Piyyuṭey Rabbi Yannai (ed. Rabinovitz) 2:267–87 — Chap. 11, n.20
Piyyuṭey Rabbi Yannai (ed. Rabinovitz) 2:286 — Chap. 11, n.21
Piyyuṭey Yosi ben Yosi (ed. Jerusalem, 1991), 94 — Chap. 13, n.13
Seder Rabbaʾ de-Bereshit (ed. Wertheimer, *Battey Midrashot*) 1:30 — Chap. 13, n.38
Seder Rabbaʾ de-Bereshit (ed. Wertheimer, *Battey Midrashot*) 1:45 — Chap. 4, n.15
Shaʿarey ha-Sod ha-Yiḥud weha-ʾEmunah (R. Eleazar of Worms; ed. Dan, *Temirin* 1) 144f. — Chap. 11, n.3
Shaʿarey ha-Sod ha-Yiḥud weha-ʾEmunah (R. Eleazar of Worms; ed. Dan, *Temirin* 1) 150 — Chap. 4, n.10
Shaʿarey ha-Sod ha-Yiḥud weha-ʾEmunah (R. Eleazar of Worms; ed. Dan, *Temirin* 1) 151 — Chap. 11, n.8
Shaʿarey Orah (Gikatilla; ed. Ben Shlomo) 1:172 — Chap. 12, n.41
Shaʿarey Orah (Gikatilla; ed. Ben Shlomo) 2:107ff. — Chap. 12, n.37
Shaʿarey Teshuvah (Responsa) 287 — Chap. 9, n.18
Sodey Razayaʾ (R. Eleazar of Worms; ed. Weiss) 88 — Chap. 12, n.6
Sodey Razayaʾ (R. Eleazar of Worms; ed. Weiss) 89ff. — Chap. 10, n.47
Sodey Razayaʾ (R. Eleazar of Worms; ed. Weiss) 109 — Chap. 10, n.29
Sodey Razayaʾ (R. Eleazar of Worms; ed. Weiss) 147f. — Chap. 11, n.3
Sodey Razayaʾ (R. Eleazar of Worms; ed. Jerusalem) 167 — Chap. 11, n.11
Teshuvot ha-RaMBaM (ed. Friemann) #373:343 — Chap. 10, n.1
Tiqquney Zohar #5, 19b — Chap. 13, n.40
Torat ha-ʾAdam (ed. Chavel, *Kitvey RaMBaN*) 1:262 — Chap. 9, n.20
Tosafot Shabbat 59a — Chap. 9, n.20
Tosafot Pesaḥim 36a — Chap. 9, n.21
Sefer ha-Yashar (attr. R. Tam; ed. Schlesinger) 204 — Chap. 9, n.20
Sefer Yeṣirah 1:7 — Chap. 13, n.50
Zohar 1:17b — Chap. 13, n.40
Zohar 3:243a — Chap. 8, n.11
Zohar Ḥadash 9b — Chap. 13, n.40

General Index

Abraham ben David of Posquieres, Rabbi, 99
Abrams, D., 134n
Adam, as giant, 23, 24, 31
adi, definition of, 34–35
adjuration, of God's name, 25–26, 27, 36, 55–56, 102, 123, 124. *See also* names, divine
Aḥer, 58, 63–64
aggadah, 20, 20–21n, 23, 27, 36–37, 39, 53–54, 56, 58, 75, 81, 85, 86, 89, 95–96, 99, 105, 111, 137n, 146, 162, 163; literal truth of, 88–89
Akhtariel, 59n, 99, 116, 129; ambiguous status of, 62–65
Akiva, Rabbi, 78 and n, 85, 86–87
Alexander, P., 17n, 39n, 48n
Aloni, N., 49n
alphabet (Hebrew), and the crown, *49–57*, 87n, 111. *See also* inscription, on the crown; names, divine; tetragrammaton
Alter, J. L., 71
Altmann, A., 23n, 98n
'Amidah, 12, 13n, 18n, 37
angels, 7 and n, 12–13, 16, 17, 22, 23, 24, 33, 92–93, 139, 162; as brothers of humans, 23–25; as collectors of human prayers, 33–34, 38–39, 43–44, 76, 122, 127–28; as crowning Israel, 69–77; equated with God, 62–65; equated with humans, 65–68; as glorifiers of the crown, 122; and Israel, 19; liturgy of, 47, 163; and the name of God, 45; nature of, 71, 129–30; as priests, 43–44, 127–28; as recipients of crowns, 58–68; as recipients of human prayers, 76; as rivals to humans, 73 and n; songs of, 28, 30; as worshipers, 12–19. *See also* Cherubim; *ḥayyot*; *individual names*
anointment: of kings, 8–9, 10–11, 59, 162; of priests, 8–9; replaced by coronation, 11
anthropomorphism, 37, 42–43n, 53–54, 63n, 89, 96–97, 103, 106, 122, 132. *See also* dualism; head, of God; heresy; marriage, sacred; polytheism; sexuality, and the divine
anthropos myths, 23 and n, 30–31
apocalyptic traditions, 59, 64, 67–68, 70–71
Arzey Levanon, 27–28
ascent: of the crown, 26, 27, 29–30, 36, 122, 124, 138, 151, 153, 162, 163, 164–65; imagery of, x, 13; of kings, 3; of prayers, 95–96, 163; of voyagers, 60
'aṭarah, 8, 95, 141, 142, 143, 144, 151, 162; and circumcision, 112n, 143n, 152; definition of, 43; as distinguished from *keter*, 131–32, 140, 153; as feminine, 161; in the Kabbalah, 156; sexual connotations of, 152n, 165

Babylon, and Jewish tradition, 6, 7n, 9n. *See also* Near East
Bacharach, Naphtali, 24n
Baer, S., 106n
Bahir, 80, 84n, *90*, *121*, *131*, *134–50*, *151*
Bahya ben Asher, 36n
Baraqi'el, 125
Bar-Ilan, M., 18n, 20n, 29n, 54n19
barukh shem, 46–47n
Barzilai, Judah ben, 97n, 98, 114n
Baus, K., 82n
beauty, of God and angels, 115, 116–17
Beit-Arie, M., 39n
Ben Barak, Z., 5n, 9n
Bezalel, 50
Binah, 157, 159, 160
binding, of crowns, 22–23, 27–28, 36–37, 51–52, 101; and magic, 51–52; of *tefillin*, 54. *See also* weaving
Blau, L., 47n
blessings: from God, 116, 135, 159; of Israel, 36, 44, 71–74; in liturgy, 46–47n. *See also* exchange; reward
body, of God, 132. *See also* anthropomorphism; beauty; head, of God; sexuality, and the divine
Boyarin, D., 53n, 78–79n
Brettler, M. Z., 4–5n, 117n
brotherhood: of Jesus, 24–25; of Sandalphon, 23–24; of Sandalphon and humans, 25; of Sandalphon and Meṭaṭron, 38
Büchler, A., 47n

Chernus, I., 16n, 42n, 70n, 86n
cherubim, 60
Christianity: and crowns, 82–83; and Jewish tradition, ix-x, 10, 14, 18n, 24, 69n, 72n, 164
Cohen, G. D., 85n
Cohen, M., 53n, 117n
Cordovero, Moses, 24n
coronation: development of, 3–11; distinguished from the crown, 105; historical development of, 3–11; of Israel, 69–77; in the Kabbalah, 151–52; of Torah, 110
Creation, 4, 31, 146
crown, 8 and n, 34–35, 43, 73, 82–83, 105; and marriage, 82–83, 94; of Meṭaṭron, 58–59; and prayers, 28, 31–32, 33–41, 55, 57; Talmud and, 83–84; Torah as, 139; weaving of, 25, 33, 43. See also *ʿaṭarah*; binding, of crowns; *keter*; *taga*

Dan, J., 37–38n, 59n, 62, 90n, 91, 100n, 122, 136n, 145, 156n
David, enthronement of, 66–67
David Abudarham, Rabbi, 84
Day, J., 146n
De Leon, Moshe, 157
divine: femininity and the, 80–81, 130, 144, 150, 153, 161–62; hierarchy, 61–64, 145–46, 148–49; kingship, 3–11, 28–30, 31–32n, 67, 81, 153, 162; masculinity and the, 116–17; pleroma, 94, 128, 135, 138, 140–41, 142–43, 145, 150, 151; sexuality and the, 5–6, 81, 85, 110, 112–13, 114, 116–20, 150, 152–53, 157, 162. *See also* names, divine
Donnolo, S., 149n
dualism, 32, 58–64, 89, 111, 130, 131, 146. *See also* anthropomorphism; heresy; polytheism

Eden, Garden of, 71 and n, 164
Elbogen, I., 12–13n
Eleazar of Worms, Rabbi, 37, 54, 90, 91, 94, 96, 104, 106n, 122, 124, 129, 152n
Elior, A., xi
Elior, M., xi
Elior, R., xi, 14n, 16 and n, 19n, 42n, 62, 75n, 140n
Elisha ben Abuyah. *See* Aḥer
Enoch, 72n. *See also* Meṭaṭron
Epstein, J. N., 51n
esoteric traditions, 7, 14, 27, 30, 43, 44, 53, 74, 85–87, 88, 162, 163, 164; and divine names, 87; of *Ḥasidey Ashkenaz*, 89–105. *See also* merkavah traditions
exchange, between God and humans, 35–36, 40, 104–5, 113, 122–23, 124. *See also* blessings; prayers; reward
exile, of Israel, 142, 143, 164. *See also* sin, of Israel
Ezekiel, wheel of, 22, 23, 29, 125

Falk, Z. W., 8n
Farber, A., 20n, 36n, 127n, 163
femininity, and the divine, 80–81, 130, 144, 150, 153, 161–62
Feuchtwanger, N., 94n
Finkelstein, L., 44
Fishbane, M., xi, 98n
Flusser, D., 17n, 18n, 47n
Frymer-Kensky, T., 6n, 85n

Gaster, T. H., 3n, 7n
giants, and angels, 22–23, 24
gifts. *See* blessings
Gikatilla, J., 157n
glory, of God, 25–26, 28, 34, 36, 43, 96–97, 98, 100–103, 108, 109, 110, 113, 114, 119, 136. *See also* homilies; praise; prayers; *qedushah*
Gnosticism, 14, 15 and n, 18n, 23, 30–31, 42n, 59n, 61, 88, 97, 135n, 139, 141–42, 146, 148n, 152n, 155
Gollancz, H., 51n
God: and angels, 62–65; beauty of, 115, 116–17; blessings from, 116, 135, 159; body of, 132; exchange with humans, 35–36, 40, 104–5, 113, 122–23, 124; glory of, 25–26, 28, 34, 36, 43, 96–97, 98, 100–103, 108, 109, 110, 113, 114, 119, 136; head of, 92, 102n, 105, 106 and n, 107, 108–9, 115, 116, 123, 124, 132, 153, 158; Israel and, 4 and n, 78–87, 94, 120, 124, 150; Meṭaṭron and, 37–38; mother of, 80, 81, 157–60; name of, 25–26, 27, 36, 45, 55–56, 102, 123, 124; praise of, 39, 67, 108, 115, 119; prayers and, 128; reward from, 104, 105; *tefillin* of, 53–57, 76–77, 92, 99, 102, 114, 119, 124, 139–40, 162
Goodenough, E. R., 82n
Gray, J., 8n

Greece, influence of on Jewish tradition, 9–10
Groezinger, K., 25, 26n, 49n
Gross, Avi, 36n
Gruenwald, I., 13n, 15n, 16n, 18n, 19n, 35n, 48n, 49n, 52n

Hai Gaon, Rabbi, 37, 48, 88
halakhic traditions, 20–21n, 75, 114
Hallo, W., 3
Halperin, D., 14n, 24n, 26n, 27, 37n, 68, 75n
Halpern, B., 8n
Haran, M., 72n
Ḥasidey Ashkenaz, 121–33
Hasidism, esoteric traditions of, 89–105
Hayman, A. P., 49–50n
ḥayyot, 29
head, of God, 92, 102n, 105, 106 and n, 107, 108–9, 115, 116, 123, 124, 132, 153, 158. *See also* anthropomorphism; body, of God; sexuality, and the divine
Hekhalot Sefer, 58
hekhalot traditions, 45, 46n, 92, 105. *See also* merkavah traditions
heresy, 32, 55 and n, 58, 63–64. *See also* anthropomorphism; dualism
Heschel, A. J., 69n
Hesheq, Sefer ha, 37–38
hierarchy: divine, 61–64, 145–46; divine and human, 148–49; in the Kabbalah, 132–33, 135, 140–41, 142–43, 144, 145–47, 153, 154–56; of *sefirot* 154–57
hieros gamos. *See* marriage, sacred
Hillel, 42, 50
Himmelfarb, M., 60
Hirshman, M., 79n
Hirz, Naftali, 31n
Hocart, A. M., 3n
homilies, x, 34–35, 75. *See also* hymns; praise
Horowitz, C., 47n
hymns, 7, 16, 40, 67, 108, 109. *See also* homilies; liturgy; songs

Ibn Gabirol, 153
Ibn Shmuel, Y., 66n, 67
Idel, M., xi, 20n, 23n, 30, 36n, 42n, 50n, 55n, 75, 86n, 95n, 149n
inscription, on the crown, 42–48, 49–57, 93, 94, 124. *See also* alphabet (Hebrew)
Isaac ha-Kohen, Rabbi, 155
Isaac the Blind, Rabbi, 151n, 154
Ishmael, Rabbi, 39, 63–64
Ish Shalom (Friedmann), M., 70n
Israel: and angels, 19; as bride of God, 94, 120, 150; coronation of, 69–77; as crown of God, 124; exile of, 142, 143, 164; as God's people, 4 and n; inscribed on the crown, 52–55; in the Kabbalah, 159–60, 161; prayers of, 33–41, 92; sin of, 70, 71, 141–42

Jacob ben Jacob, Rabbi, 100n, 132n, 144n, 152–53
Jellinek, A., 27
Johnston, G., 25n
Jonas, H., 139n
Josiah, Rabbi, 44
Judah ben Yaqar, Rabbi, 35n
Judah Ḥayyaṭ, Rabbi, 155
Judah the Ḥasid, 90, 91

Kabbalah: coronation in, 151–52; origins of, x, 36, 90, 95–96, 99, 118, 119–20, 121–33, 163; Israel in, 159–60, 161; Meṭaṭron in, 144; Sandalphon in, 144, 156; and sacred marriage, 85. *See also* hierarchy; Zohar
kalil, definition of, 73
Kapah, J., 97n
Karaites, 88
kavod, 97, 100, 101–3, 104–5, 106, 110, 111, 117, 122, 124, 147n. *See also* glory
kawwanah, 123
Keruviel, 60–61
keter, 70n, 127; called *keter ʿelyon*, 115n, 130 and n, 134–35, 136–37, 138, 142, 144, 147n, 151, 153, 154–56; as a circle, 154; definition of, 22, 43, 49n; distinguished from *ʿaṭarah*, 131–32, 140, 153; early uses of, 8; magical associations of, 52
Kiener, R., 96n
kingship: conceptions of, 3–4; divine, 3–11, 28–30, 31–32n, 67, 81, 153; divine and human, 3, 162; history of, 8–9, 122–23n; and kingship, 12–19; as metaphor, 4; sources of, 36. *See also* anointment
Knohl, Y., 8n
Kraus, S., 10n

Lamm, N., 46n

Levenson, J., 161n
Lieberman, S., 44n, 53, 78, 78–79n, 89n
Liebes, Y., xi, 49n, 59n, 63n, 86n, 87n, 135n
light, 101–2, 104, 108, 112, 124, 142, 146; symbolism of, 97, 117, 152n, 157; and the Torah, 143
liturgy, 7, 10–11, 35, 48, 57, 72–73, 75, 94, 106; among angels, 47, 163; blessings in, 46–47n; and kingship, 12–19; and merkavah traditions, 12–19; and the name of God, 45; and the Song of Songs, 118 and n; for Yom Kippur, 38n, 46, 57. *See also* prayers; *qedushah*; ritual
Liver, J., 8n
Luria, Jehiel, 132n

Mach, M., 9n, 17n
magic, 9, 13, 22n, 48, 57, 70n, 119, 140n, 162; and merkavah traditions, 50–52; and mysticism, 104n; and names, 55, 74–75, 123, 138; and prayer, 52n, 164; and ritual, 51–52; and sacred marriage, 86
Maier, J., 18n
Maimonides, 88–89, 111
Marcus, I., 90n
Margaliot, M., 104n
Margaliot, R., 134n
Marmorstein, A., 51n
marriage: and crowns, 82–83, 94; of God and Israel, 78–87, 120; and magic, 86; metaphors of, 78–87; sacred, 84–85, 93, 94, 120, 124, 128, 129, 150, 159–61, 163, 164–65. *See also* anthropomorphism; dualism; monotheism; polytheism; sexuality
masculinity, and the divine, 116–17
Mauss, M., 163n
Meeks, W., 72n
merkavah traditions, x, 7n, 13, 14, 20–32, 38–40, 43, 45–46, 48n, 49–50n, 57, 58–62, 91, 98, 100, 107, 116–17, 123, 163; and beauty, 117n; history of, 14–15; and liturgy, 12–19; and magic, 50–52. *See also* merkavah, mysticism; voyagers
Messiah, 11, 116
Meṭaṭron, 7n, 24, 37–38, 40, 58, 61, 64, 67, 71, 74, 89, 92–93, 99, 114n, 141; coronation of, 58–59; and coronation of God, 37–38; Moses and, 99; as symbol in the Kabbalah, 144
midrash, 31
midrashic traditions, 20, 20–21n, 26, 31, 35n, 38, 46n, 53, 69–71, 73, 79n, 80, 81, 85, 90, 91, 119, 137n, 163
Milgrom, J., 43–44n, 117n
Mirsky, A., 72n, 73n, 118n
Mishnah, 42, 46, 83–84
monotheism: and divine sexuality, 5–6, 85; and myth, 6. *See also* anthropomorphism; dualism; polytheism
Morgan, M., 103n
Morgenstern, J., 72n
Moses, 69–77; and Meṭaṭron, 99; as paradigm, 86–87
mother, of God, 80, 81, 157–60
Mowinckel, S., 4n
Muffs, Y., 76–77
mysticism, x, 15–19, 26, 30, 40, 48, 89, 97, 98, 150, 163, 164; and the Hebrew alphabet, 50; history of, 13, 105; and magic, 104n. *See also* merkavah traditions; voyagers, merkavah
myth, ix-xi, 4–6, 21n, 70–71; development of, xi; and history, ix; and monotheism, 6; nature of, ix, 150, 161; and rabbinic traditions, 6–7, 34

Nahmanides, 89, 130n, 152n
names, divine, 12, 16, 25, 33, 36–37, 42–48, 104, 108, 113, 123, 162; and esoteric traditions, 87; and magic, 55, 74–75, 123, 138; recitation of, 44–45, 47–48, 49n. *See also* adjuration, of God's name; alphabet (Hebrew); inscription, on the crown; tetragrammaton
Naveh, J., 51n
Navon, Sefer ha, 84n, 91–94
Near East, influence of on Jewish tradition, 4–6, 7n, 9n, 85. *See also* Babylon
Neoplatonism, 97–98, 104, 133, 135n, 148, 153
Neusner, J., 86
New Year festivals, 4n, 5–7. *See also* Rosh Ha-Shanah
nezer, definition of, 8 and n
Niditsch, S., 23n
numbers, symbolism of, 92, 94, 95, 126, 129 and n, 134–35, 145, 147–48, 155, 158

payyeṭanim, 94
Pearson, B. A., 32n
Pedaya, H., 145

Pesiqta Rabbati, 25–26, 27
phenomenology, and religious experience, x, 15–16n
phylacteries. See *tefillin*
Pines, S., 117
Pirqey Rabbi Eliezer, 70–71
piyyuṭim, 7, 118, 122
pleroma, divine, 94, 128, 135, 138, 140–41, 142–43, 145, 150, 151
polytheism, 80, 147–48. *See also* anthropomorphism; dualism; monotheism
praise, of God, 39, 67, 108, 115, 119. *See also* glory
prayers, x, 12, 15–16, 22, 31–32, 90, 95, 104, 105, 109, 119, 125–26, 127n, 143; ascent of, 95–96, 163; as bride of God, 128; collected by angels, 33–34, 38–39, 43–44, 76, 122, 127–28; and the crown, 28, 31–32; of Israel, 33–41, 92; and magic, 52n, 164; as material for the crown, 33–41, 55, 57; and the name of God, 45; and sacrifice, 37, 41, 57, 115–16, 163–64; and theurgy, 65. *See also* exchange; liturgy; ritual
priests, 10, 74; and angels, 43–44, 127–28; anointment of, 8–9; traditions of, 15

qedushah, 12–19, 26, 28–30, 31–32, 33, 37, 39, 40, 44, 46, 47, 48 and n, 57, 67, 68, 75, 105, 136, 159, 162; origins of, 18n. *See also* liturgy; ritual
Qirqisani, Jacob, 54
Qumran sources, 13–14, 19n

rabbinic traditions, x, xi, 3, 11, 14, 20–21, 23, 31, 44, 53–54, 56, 88–89, 96, 163; and myth, 6–7, 34
rationalism, and Jewish traditions, 88–89, 98, 103
Razim, Sefer ha, 50n
rebellion, against the divine order, 146
revelation, 97
reward, from God, 104, 105. *See also* blessings; exchange
righteous [people], the, 36, 52n
ritual: in heaven, 23–32; and magic, 51–52. *See also* liturgy; prayers; *qedushah*
Rome, and Jewish tradition, 9–10
Rosh Ha-Shanah, 7. *See also* New Year

Saʿadya Gaon, 37, 96–98
sacrifice, 9, 37–38, 125, 128; and prayers, 37, 41, 57, 115–16, 163–64
Salmon ben Yeruham, 54
sanctus. See *qedushah*
Sandalphon, 22, 23–32, 35, 36, 38, 51, 54, 56, 93, 100–101, 123, 125, 128; absent from *Sefer ha-Bahir*, 138; etymology of, 23, 100, 103; in the Kabbalah, 144, 156
Sarafiel, 60–61
Schaefer, P., 14n, 24n, 42n, 117
Scheindlin, R., 118n
Schiffman, L., 17n, 35n, 43n
Schoedel, W. R., 146n
Scholem, G., 13n, 15n, 30, 40 and n, 49n, 54, 64, 65, 95n, 121, 126n, 130n, 132n, 134n, 136, 139, 147, 155
Schultz, J., 24n
sefirah, 130
sefirot, 81, 129, 130, 131, 132, 149–50, 153–54; hierarchy of, 154–57
Segal, A. F., 32n, 111n
Sendon, M., 151n
seraphim, 29, 39, 60
sexuality: and the divine, 5–6, 81, 85, 110, 112–13, 114, 116–20, 150, 152–53, 157, 162; symbolism of, 143n. *See also* anthropomorphism; body, of God; dualism; head, of God; marriage, sacred; polytheism
Shaked, S., 51n
Shekhinah, 40, 58, 97–98, 126–27, 128, 129, 131, 142, 145, 146–47, 149, 151, 159, 162; meaning of, 95–96
shemaʿ, 46–47
Shir ha-Kavod, 106–20, 139
Shiʿur Qomah, 52–54, 60, 79n, 88–89, 97–98, 133
Shoshaniel, 93
Simeon ben Yoḥai, Rabbi, 70
Simonsen, D., 115n
sin, of Israel, 70, 71, 141–42. *See also* exile
Sinai, as site of Israel's coronation, 69–77
Sirkis, Rabbi Joel, 22n
ṣiṣ, definition of, 8, 43
Ṣiyyuni, Menahem, 28n
Snaith, N. H., 7n
Sodey Razayaʾ, 122, 123
Solomon, 78–80
Song of Songs (Canticles), 53, 78–80, 85, 93–94, 107, 112, 113, 161–62n; and liturgy, 118 and n

songs, 101, 108, 115; of angels, 28, 30. *See also* hymns; liturgy; praise
Stern, S. M., 149
Stroumza, G. G., 59n
Strugnell, J., 17n
symbolism: of the divine, 143n; evolution of, x, 118, 128–29, 147–48, 151; in the Kabbalah, 90, 164–65; of light, 97, 117, 152n, 157; of sexuality, 143n; of Torah, 162–63

tabernacle, 80, 141
taga, 70n, 138, 144; definition of, 42–43
Taku, Moshe, 22n
Talmud, 20, 21–22, 26, 27, 38, 45, 53, 54, 56, 62–63, 72, 92, 99, 122–23; and the wearing of crowns, 83–84
tefillin, of God, 53–57, 76–77, 92, 99, 102, 114, 119, 124, 139–40, 162
Temple, destruction of the, 10, 141–42
tetragrammaton, 43, 45–46, 48n, 62, 64–65, 148. *See also* alphabet (Hebrew); names, divine
theurgy, 49–50, 57, 65, 86, 104, 119, 138, 162; and prayers, 65
Thompson, R. C., 51n
Thorndike, L., 51n
thrones, 4, 10, 24, 25–26, 28, 38, 40, 58, 60–61, 65, 99, 101, 122 and n, 139–40, 140–41. *See also* merkavah traditions
Tishby, I., 153n
Torah: as crown, 139; coronation of, 10; as gift, 73–75, 78; legends concerning, 73–75; and light, 143; and metaphoric marriage, 78; symbolism of, 162–63
Trachtenberg, J., 43n, 51n
traditions. *See individual entries*
Twersky, I., 100n

Urbach, Y., 47n

vengeance, 112, 114
Vermes, G., 51n
Von Rad, G., 8n
voyagers, merkavah, 7n, 16, 39–40, 58–62, 66, 86. See also merkavah traditions; mysticism

weaving, of crowns, 25, 33, 43. *See also* binding
Weinfeld, M., 12n, 17n, 19n
Weinstock, I., 49n
Weiss, S., 100n
Werblowsky, R.J.Z., 121n
Werner, E., 18n
Wheatley, I., 85n
Wheatley, M., 5n
Widengren, G., 7n, 19n
Wieder, N., 72n
Wolfson, E., xi, 13n, 16n, 20n, 40n, 55n, 94n, 98n, 106n, 112n, 114–15n, 122, 130n, 147, 149, 152n

Yehudah ben Pazi, Rabbi, 140n
Yeivin, S., 8n
Yeṣirah, Sefer, 49
Yofiel, 127–28
Yom Kippur, liturgy on, 38n, 46, 57

Zangwill, I., 107
zarqa', 137–38
Zerachiah ha-Levi, Rabbi, 100n
Zohar, 79n, 90, 112n, 152, 156, 157–62
Zulay, M., 137n

GPSR Authorized Representative: Easy Access System Europe - Mustamäe tee 50, 10621 Tallinn, Estonia, gpsr.requests@easproject.com

www.ingramcontent.com/pod-product-compliance
Lightning Source LLC
Chambersburg PA
CBHW061441300426
44114CB00014B/1786